Justice in Social Relations

CRITICAL ISSUES IN SOCIAL JUSTICE

Series Editor: **MELVIN J. LERNER**
University of Waterloo
Waterloo, Ontario, Canada

A Continuation Order Plan is available for this series. A continuation order will bring
delivery of each new volume immediately upon publication. Volumes are billed only
upon actual shipment. For further information please contact the publisher.

Justice in
Social Relations

Edited by

HANS WERNER BIERHOFF

University of Marburg
Marburg, West Germany

RONALD L. COHEN

Bennington College
Bennington, Vermont

and

JERALD GREENBERG

The Ohio State University
Columbus, Ohio

Plenum Press • *New York and London*

Library of Congress Cataloging in Publication Data

Justice in social relations.

(Critical issues in social justice)
Bibliography: p.
Includes indexes.
1. Social justice—Congresses. 2. Social interaction—Congresses. 3. Distributive
justice—Congresses. I. Bierhoff, Hans Werner, 1948–   . II. Cohen, Ronald L. III.
Greenberg, Jerald. IV. Series.
HM216.J876   1986   302   86-15089
ISBN 0-306-42181-X

© 1986 Plenum Press, New York
A Division of Plenum Publishing Corporation
233 Spring Street, New York, N.Y. 10013

Printed in the United States of America

Contributors

HANS WERNER BIERHOFF, Fachbereich Psychologie der Philipps-Universität Marburg, Marburg/Lahn, West Germany

ERNST BUCK, Fachbereich Psychologie der Philipps-Universität Marburg, Marburg/Lahn, West Germany

LAURA BURRIS, Department of Psychology, Georgetown University, Washington, DC

CATHERINE CENSOR, The Dalton School, New York, New York

RONALD L. COHEN, Social Science Division, Bennington College, Bennington, Vermont

KAREN S. COOK, Department of Sociology, University of Washington, Seattle, Washington

FAYE CROSBY, Department of Psychology, Smith College, Northampton, Massachusetts

CLAUDIA DALBERT, Fachbereich I—Psychologie, Universität Trier, Trier, West Germany

MORTON DEUTSCH, Department of Psychology, Teachers College, Columbia University, New York, New York

ROBERT FOLGER, A. B. Freeman School of Business, Tulane University, New Orleans, Louisiana

JERALD GREENBERG, Faculty of Management and Human Resources, Ohio State University, Columbus, Ohio

KAREN A. HEGTVEDT, Department of Sociology, Emory University, Atlanta, Georgia

ROBERT W. HYMES, Department of Psychology, University of Michigan at Dearborn, Dearborn, Michigan

RENATE KLEIN, Fachbereich Psychologie der Philipps-Universität Marburg, Marburg/Lahn, West Germany

HELMUT LAMM, Institut für Psychologie, Universität zu Köln, Köln, West Germany

ROBERT J. MacCOUN, Department of Psychology, Northwestern University, Evanston, Illinois

E. R. MacKETHAN, Department of Psychology, Yale University, New Haven, Connecticut

JOANNE MARTIN, Graduate School of Business, Stanford University, Stanford, California

LAWRENCE A. MESSÉ, Department of Psychology, Michigan State University, East Lansing, Michigan

GEROLD MIKULA, Karl-Franzens-Universität Graz, Institut für Psychologie, Graz, Austria

LEO MONTADA, Fachbereich I—Psychologie, Universität Trier, Trier, West Germany

HARRY T. REIS, Department of Psychology, University of Rochester, Rochester, New York

EDWARD E. SAMPSON, The Wright Institute, Berkeley, California

MANFRED SCHMITT, Fachbereich I—Psychologie, Universität Trier, Trier, West Germany

THOMAS SCHWINGER, Psychologisches Institut IV, Universität Münster, Münster, West Germany

SIEGFRIED SPORER, Erziehungswissenschaftliche Fakultät der Universität, Nürnberg, West Germany

TOM R. TYLER, Department of Psychology, Northwestern University, Evanston, Illinois

INGEBORG WENDER, Seminar für Psychologie, Fachbereich 9 der Technischen Universität Braunschweig, Braunschweig, West Germany

Preface

From July 16 through July 21, 1984 a group of American and West German scholars met in Marburg, West Germany to discuss their common work on the topic of justice in social relations. For over 30 hours they presented papers, raised questions about each other's work, and in so doing plotted a course for future research and theory building on this topic. The participants were asked to present work that represented their most recent state-of-the-science contributions in the area. The contributions to this volume represent refined versions of those presentations—papers that have been improved by the authors' consideration of the comments and reactions of their colleagues. The result, we believe, is a work that represents the cutting edge of scholarly inquiry into the important matter of justice in social relations.

To give the participants the freedom to present their ideas in the most appropriate way, we, the conference organizers and the editors of this volume, gave them complete control over the form and substance of their presentations. The resulting diversity is reflected in this book, where the reader will find critical integrative reviews of the literature, reports of research investigations, and statements of theoretical positions. The chapters are organized with respect to the common themes that emerged in the way the authors addressed the issues of justice in social relations. Each of these themes—conflict and power, theoretical perspectives, norms, and applications—is represented by a part of this book.

The reader may find a number of similarities among the various papers, not only within but between the different sections of the book. Because this state of affairs allows us to identify important recurring issues in the field, we made no attempt to reduce any such apparent redundancies. Indeed, we believe that readers' interests would be best served by noting the similarities among the chapters as well as the differences.

The present undertaking, involving as it does the simultaneous coordination of activities across the Atlantic Ocean, is a herculean task. Clearly, its success reflects the efforts of many individuals and institutions who deserve our sincerest acknowledgment. First, we wish to thank the National Science Foundation and the Deutsche Forschungsgemeinschaft for their financial support, which made this conference possible. We also wish to acknowledge the support of our home institutions, particularly those individuals who facilitated our efforts in securing and administering the grant, running the conference, and preparing this book. These include Michael Herner and Mathias Blanz at the Philipps-Universität Marburg, Joanne Schultz at Bennington College, and Dick Hill and Mary Lauber at Ohio State University.

Eliot Werner, our editor at Plenum, and Mel Lerner, the editor of the Critical Issues in Social Justice Series, have been very helpful and supportive at all stages of preparing this volume. Finally, on a more personal note, we wish to thank our families, without whose encouragement and support none of this would have been possible.

HANS WERNER BIERHOFF

RONALD L. COHEN

JERALD GREENBERG

Contents

PART IV   APPLICATIONS OF JUSTICE RESEARCH

Part I

CONFLICT, POWER, AND JUSTICE

Chapter 1

Cooperation, Conflict, and Justice

MORTON DEUTSCH

Recently I completed a book, *Distributive Justice: A Social Psychological Perspective* (Deutsch, 1985), which could have been entitled "Cooperation, Conflict, and Justice." These are three of the themes that run throughout the book and that have been the foci of my career as a social psychologist. Here, I would like to present an overview of the work my co-workers and I have done on these themes and to consider the relationship among them.

COOPERATION–COMPETITION: INITIAL STUDIES OF DISTRIBUTIVE JUSTICE

Although I was unaware of it as I conducted my dissertation experiment on the effects of cooperation and competition on group process (Deutsch, 1949b), this study has direct relevance to basic issues in the psychology of distributive justice. As originally formulated, the experiment was meant to test my theory of cooperation and competition, which focused on the social psychological effects of different types of

This chapter is based upon material more fully presented in M. Deutsch *Distributive justice: A social psychological perspective*. New Haven: Yale University Press. For more details, it should be consulted.

MORTON DEUTSCH • Department of Psychology, Teachers College, Columbia University, New York, NY 10027.

goal interdependence in combination with different types of instrumental actions (Deutsch, 1949a). Only much later, as my attention centered on distributive justice, did I realize that this early experiment was a study of the effects of two different distributive principles: a competitive form of equity and equality.

This early experiment involved five-person groups of M.I.T. students who were in an introductory psychology course I was teaching. During each of five sessions, the groups were constituted as a board of human relations advisors and asked to discuss and formulate a written response to a letter asking their advice about a personal problem. Half of the groups (the competitive-meritocratic groups) were told that their discussions of the human relations problem would be graded in the following manner: each individual's contribution to the group's discussion and group product would be compared with the contributions of each of the other group members, and the best contributor would get an A, the next best a B, and so on. The other half of the groups (the cooperative-egalitarian groups) were told that they would be graded so that every person in the group would get the same grade, the grade being determined by how well the group's discussion and product compared with those of four other similar groups; all the members in the best group would get A's, those in the next best group would get B's, and so on.

The results of the experiment showed striking differences between the cooperative-egalitarian and competitive-meritocratic groups. As compared with the competitively graded groups, the cooperative ones showed the following characteristics.

1. More effective intermember communication. More ideas were verbalized, and members were more attentive to one another and more accepting of and influenced by one another's ideas. They had fewer difficulties in communicating with or understanding others.

2. More friendliness, more helpfulness, and less obstructiveness was expressed in discussions. Members were also more satisfied with the group and its solutions and more favorably impressed by the contributions of the other group members. In addition, members of the cooperative groups rated themselves higher in desire to win the respect of their colleagues and in obligation to other members.

3. More coordination of effort, more division of labor, more orientation to task achievement, more orderliness in discussion, and higher productivity were manifested in the cooperative groups (the group tasks required effective communication, coordination of effort, division of labor, and the sharing of resources.)

4. More feeling of agreement and similarity in ideas and more

confidence in one's own ideas and in the value that other members attached to those ideas were obtained in the cooperative groups.

It is evident that the two distributive principles had profoundly different consequences. The students in the groups that operated under the equality principle (i.e., the cooperative groups) were not only more productive, they also developed friendlier interpersonal relations, and felt more esteemed and more self-confident as compared to those in the groups that functioned under the competitive meritocratic principle.

It should be noted that the meritocratic principle is not always competitive; it is so only when a fixed amount (a constant sum) is being allocated; hence, the more one person gets, the less is available for another. An individualistic form of this principle occurs whenever the amount to be allocated is variable and dependent on the level of the total contributions—here, the allocations the individuals receive are independent of one another. Thus, the results of this early experiment had no direct relevance to the individualistic form of meritocracy.

Since my 1949 study of cooperation and competition, many hundreds of related studies have been conducted. They have investigated individualistic as well as cooperative and competitive groups; they have studied cooperative and competitive relations between groups as well as within groups; they have conducted research in classrooms, in work settings, and in the laboratory; they have studied groups whose compositions were homogeneous and groups that were composed of individuals of diverse ability, or of diverse racial and ethnic background, or of people who were physically disabled and not disabled. David Johnson, a former student of mine, and his colleagues have been the leading researchers in this area and have presented integrative summaries of the research that has been conducted during the past 35 years (see Johnson & Johnson, 1983, for such a summary and for references to their research).

The results of this large body of research are very consistent with my theory of cooperation–competition and with my early study of the effects of cooperation and competition on group process. I do not believe it is overstating things to say that the findings in this area, and the conclusions to be drawn from these findings, are among the most solidly grounded and socially significant in all of social psychology. The findings are unequivocal in demonstrating substantial differences in the social psychological effects of the two distributive justice principles, the cooperative-egalitarian and the competitive-meritocratic, on interpersonal relations, self-attitudes, attitude toward work, and group performance.

CONFLICT AND BARGAINING STUDIES: CONDITIONS FOR
ESTABLISHING A SYSTEM OF JUSTICE

Following our research on cooperation–competition, we started a
program of research on conditions affecting the initiation of cooperation
(see Deutsch, 1973). The research took the form of experimental studies
of bargaining and conflict. I did not at the time realize that these studies
had direct relevance to a central question in the social psychology of
justice: namely, what are the conditions for establishing a system of
justice?

The experimental study of the bargaining process and of bargaining
outcomes provides a means for laboratory study of the development of
social norms of distributive justice. It is well to recognize, however, that
bargaining situations have certain distinctive features that, unlike those
involved in many other types of social situations, make it relevant to
consider the conditions that determine both whether or not a social norm
will develop and its nature if it does develop. Bargaining situations
highlight for the investigator the need to be sensitive to the possibility
that, even where cooperation would be mutually advantageous, shared
purposes may not develop, agreement may not be reached, and interaction may be regulated antagonistically rather than for mutual gain.

In terms of our prior conceptualization of cooperation and competition, it is evident that bargaining is a situation in which the participants have mixed motives toward one another. On the one hand, each
has an interest in cooperating so that they can reach an agreement; on
the other hand, they have competitive interests with regard to the nature
of the agreement that they reach. In effect, to reach agreement the
cooperative interests of the bargainers must be strong enough to overcome their competitive interests. However, agreement is not only contingent on the motivational balance of cooperative and competitive
interests but also on the situational and cognitive factors that would
facilitate or hinder the recognition or invention of a bargaining agreement that would reduce the opposition of interest and enhance the
mutuality of interest.

Over a number of years, we conducted a series of experiments that
focused on the important question: Under what conditions are people
with conflicting interests able to work out an agreement (i.e., a system
of justice defining what each shall give and receive in the transaction
between them) that is stable and mutually satisfying? In these experiments we have used several different research formats, among them
were the Prisoner's Dilemma (PD), the Acme-Bolt Trucking, and the
Behavioral Strategy games (see Deutsch, 1973). In answering this question, I have proposed a summarizing and integrating principle that I

have termed Deutsch's crude law of social relations: the typical effects of a given social relation tend to induce that social relation.

The typical effects of a cooperative system of interaction that is experienced as fair by its participants provide the basic conditions for the development of such a system of interaction, whereas the typical consequences of a competitive system of interaction have the opposite influence: they inhibit the development of such a system. Thus, the ability to work out a fair agreement is enhanced when the conflicting parties have a positive interest in each other's welfare; they see themselves as having similar values, they perceive the differences between them to be small, their communication indicates a positive responsiveness to each other's needs, they view themselves as equal, they have positive attitudes toward one another, and so forth. In contrast, the ability to work out such an agreement is inhibited by the use of threats and coercive tactics, the perception that opposed values and large differences exist between self and other, exploitative behavior, minimal communication, attempts to gain superiority over the other, and so forth. Thus, to the extent that the social and psychological conditions favor cooperative interaction, they increase the likelihood of fair agreements that are stable and mutually satisfying.

DISTRIBUTIVE JUSTICE

Although I now recognize that my studies of cooperation–competition and of bargaining and conflict are directly related to the social psychology of justice, I consciously entered this area only after Mel Lerner, in 1972, asked me to write a paper for a conference he was organizing on injustice in North America. Soon thereafter he invited me to contribute to the volume of the *Journal of Social Issues* that he was editing on the justice motive. The two papers I wrote as a result of his urgings were "Awakening the Sense of Injustice" (Deutsch, 1974) and "Equity, Equality, and Need: What Determines Which Value Will Be Used as the Basis of Distributive Justice?" (Deutsch, 1975). In preparing these papers, I reviewed the then existing work on the social psychology of justice and became quite dissatisfied with the dominant approach to this area: equity theory. My dissatisfaction led me to write an extensive critique of equity theory (Deutsch, 1977) and to embark on a program of research in this area.

The program of research has had three main components: (a) experimental studies of the effects of different systems of distributive justice; (b) research into the determinants of the choice of distributive systems; and (c) investigations of the sense of injustice. The results, so far, are briefly described below.

EXPERIMENTAL STUDIES OF THE EFFECTS OF DIFFERENT SYSTEMS OF DISTRIBUTIVE JUSTICE

Our research into the effects of different systems of distributive justice was, in part, stimulated by the assumption implicit in equity theory that people will be more productive if they are rewarded in proportion to their contribution. Our research, and the research of many other investigators on cooperation–competition had clearly demonstrated that this assumption is not correct when the individuals are working on tasks where it is helpful for them to cooperate, to share information and resources, or to coordinate their activities. Perhaps the assumption has validity only when the individuals are involved in non-interdependent tasks, in work that is not facilitated by effective cooperation.

In fact, careful thought about the circumstances under which rewarding members in proportion to their contribution to a group (or rewarding individuals in proportion to their performance) would most likely induce relatively high productivity suggests that there are a number of basic requisites. These include the following: (a) the task to be accomplished must be clearly defined and specified; (b) the individuals involved must believe that their performance can be measured reliably, validly, and with sufficient precision; (c) achievement must be readily susceptible to continued improvement by increased effort and this is believed to be so by the individuals involved; (d) the type of reward offered for performance must be desired by the individual and its value to the individual must increase with the amount of reward received; (e) the dependence of an individual's reward on his or her accomplishment must be known to the individual and subjectively salient during the individual's work; and (f) neither individual nor group task performance should depend on effective social cooperation.

A number of experiments that contrasted different principles of distributive justice were conducted. Some of these studies were designed to create the six task and situational characteristics just listed in order to maximize the chance of finding support for the assumption of the equity theorists that performance will be enhanced by the expectation of being rewarded in proportion to one's contributions. The first two were fashioned with this purpose in mind. In them, the subjects worked in separate cubicles, on identical tasks that were neither interesting nor difficult (Mei, 1978; Wenck, 1979; Ziviani, 1978). Both experiments systematically varied the type of distributive system, using the same task;

the second also varied the magnitude of the rewards available to the subjects and used female as well as male subjects. In the third experiment (Ziviani, 1981), the subjects worked face-to-face on several different types of very brief tasks under different distributive systems. In contrast to the first three where the subjects worked in three-person groups, in the fourth study (Medvene, 1981), the subjects worked alone under one or another reward system similar in character to the different distributive justice systems. In a fifth (Wenck, 1981), the subjects worked face-to-face on a highly interdependent, extended task. In a sixth (Tuchman, 1982), the "good" being distributed within the group was grades rather than money; the grades were distributed either according to the equality or proportionality principle and were based on either the amount of effort or the level of performance.

Each of the experiments had unique attributes. However, in most measures were taken of the subjects' initial attitudes toward the different distributive systems; their expectations regarding their effort, motivation to work, and their performance under the different systems; their attitudes toward themselves, the other group members (in the group experiments), and the task; their actual performances; their reported effort and motivation while they worked; and their attitudes toward the distributive systems at the end of the experiment.

The subjects in the various studies were undergraduates and graduate students at Columbia University. They ranged in age from 17 to over 40 but were mostly in their early 20s. The vast majority indicated that they were participating in the research because of the money they could earn. Although there was a sprinkling of students from other countries, most were born in the United States. All students were paid a fee for participating in the experiment and they knew they could get additional bonus money of a significant amount: in the group experiments, how much bonus money a subject was paid was a function of how much money his group earned and how that money was distributed within his group. Four different principles of allocating the group's earnings to its members were used in a number of the studies. These were described as follows:

- *Winner-takes-all*: Under this system, whoever performs the task best in the group wins all the money the group is paid.
- *Proportionality*: Under this system, each person is rewarded in proportion to his contribution to the group score. In other words, the person who contributes 50% of the group's total output will get 50% of the money to be distributed within the group; a person who contributes 10% of the group's total output would get 10% of the money to be distributed within the group, and so on.

- *Equality*: Under this system, each person in the group will get an equal share of the money to be distributed within the group. In other words, each person will get one third of the group's total earnings.
- *Need*: Under the need distribution system, each group member will be rewarded according to the need expressed on the biographical data sheet. In other words, the person who needs the money most would get proportionately more money; the person who needs the money least would get the least amount of money.

The overall results of the six experiments will be presented in terms of a number of key questions asked of all the data.

1. Did the different distributive systems have differential effects on performance? There is clear and consistent evidence in all of the relevant experiments that there are *no* reliable effects of the distribution system on individual or group productivity when neither individual nor group task performance depends on effective social cooperation. This result is obtained when the individual is working in a group context and also when working alone. That is, there is no evidence to indicate that people work more productively when they are expecting to be rewarded in proportion to their performance than when they are expecting to be rewarded "equally" or on the basis of "need."

2. Were there initial differences in attitudes toward the different distributive systems? The subjects initially strongly preferred the proportionality over the other distributive systems. The second most favored was equality; need was disfavored; and they had the most negative reaction to the winner-takes-all system. Similar results were obtained for the subjects' ratings of the fairness of the systems and also for how much they expected to enjoy working under the systems, except that the differences between proportionality and equality largely disappeared. However, on scales relating to performance expectations under the different systems, the winner-takes-all and proportionality systems were both rated quite high and significantly higher than the equality and need options.

3. What is the relationship between the subjects' attitudes toward the distributive system under which they worked and their performance? Although the subjects expected that their judgment of the fairness of the distributive system would be positively related to their own performance and to their group's total output, the data show no relationships between how fair they considered a distributive principle to be and their actual performance under that principle. There was also no relationship between whether the subjects worked under a preferred system or not and their performance. Similarly, the subjects' expectation that they would exert more effort under the proportionality and

winner-takes-all system than under the equality and need systems was not confirmed by their ratings of how hard they worked on the task made immediately after finishing the task; in all conditions, they reported working very hard. There was a low but significant correlation ($r = .33$, $p. < .01$) between the subjects' reported effort and their performance; in contrast, the correlation between the subjects' anticipated effort and their performance was insignificant.

4. Were attitudes toward other group members affected by the different distributive principles? Even when the groups were nominal rather than interacting groups (as in the first two experiments), there were some significant effects of the distributive system on attitudes toward other group members. The subjects in the equality and need conditions reported having cooperative feelings toward one another; those in the winner-takes-all and proportionality conditions reported having competitive feelings toward one another; and those in the two control or choice conditions felt more personal involvement with the other group members than did subjects in the other conditions.

5. How were attitudes toward the tasks and work affected by the different distributive systems? Under the equality system, the subjects found the tasks more interesting and more pleasant than in the other systems. They also reported (when rating the importance of various of the components of the motivation to perform well on the task) the highest intrinsic motivation to perform well, the highest motivation to perform because of task enjoyment, a high desire to increase the group's performance, and the lowest desire to outperform the other group members. Subjects in all conditions indicated very high intrinsic motivation to perform well, and this was universally rated as the strongest component of their motivation to perform well.

6. How were attitudes toward the different distributive systems affected by participating in the experiment? In the two experiments that utilized nominal groups rather than interacting ones, there was little change in attitudes toward the different distributive systems from the beginning to the end of the experiment. In contrast, there were marked changes in the attitudes of the subjects in the interacting, face-to-face groups of the third experiment. Associated with the development of friendly, cooperative group atmospheres in the latter groups was the emergence of an increased favorableness toward equality as a distributive principle so that it came to be viewed as not only the most enjoyable but also as the fairest and most preferred principle in all but the proportionality condition.

7. What effects, if any, resulted from giving the groups the opportunity to choose the distributive system under which they would work rather than assigning them to a given distributive system? When the subjects knew that they had a choice about the distributive system, their

individual and collective preference for equality became stronger and the strong favoring of the proportionality system was reduced or disappeared. We speculate that the voting led the subjects in the two choice conditions to have a greater sense of personal involvement with one another than did the subjects in the more impersonal, nominal groups. This greater personal involvement is apt to increase the attractiveness of the equality principle.

8. Does it make a difference if effort rather than achievement is the basis of evaluating individual and group performance? One study addressed this question. The results indicate that in the groups where rewards were to be distributed on the basis of achievement, significantly more problems were solved per unit of time; in the groups that were rewarded on the basis of effort, the groups worked for significantly longer periods of time. In terms of attitudes toward their grading system, their groups, and their performance, more favorable attitudes occurred when achievement was linked with the proportionality rather than with the equality distributive system; also, more favorable attitudes occurred when effort was linked with an equality rather than proportionality distributive system.

9. Were there any consistent differences in the reactions of the male and female subjects in our experiments? In general, the differences that emerged were small rather than large. The women's initial self-ratings as compared to the men indicated that they were less self-confident, less tough, and more pleasure oriented. The women also tended to have more negative attitudes toward the winner-takes-all system than the men, but had more positive attitudes toward equality and need. There was a surprising interaction between gender and distributive system on two of the tasks: the women performed better than the men under the proportionality system but worse than the men under an equality or "flat rate" system.

10. Did the amount of money to be distributed have significant effects? The magnitude of reward had few simple effects. It had no effect on the level of performance by itself, nor in interaction with the distributive systems. There was a tendency, however, to consider whatever distribution they had been assigned to as being less fair and less enjoyable, the higher the reward condition in which the subjects were.

11. Did the high, medium, and low performers in the various conditions differ from one another in their preferences and attitudes? Even before task performance had occurred, those who were to have different performance ranks in their groups had different preferences regarding the distribution principles: the better one's future performance, the more one preferred the winner-takes-all principle and the less one preferred the need and equality principles; the medium performers

(those whose performance was neither best nor worst) preferred the proportionality principle more than either the low or high performers. In the nominal groups, the relationship between task performance and preference for distributive principle remained essentially the same from the pretask to posttask measurement. Parallel results were obtained for the ratings of the fairness of the distributive principles.

However, in the face-to-face interacting groups, the relationship between task performance and preferences for the different distributive systems changed during the course of the experiment. After performing the various tasks, the proportionality, equality, and need systems were in each case just as likely to be chosen by high and low performers. Only the choice of the winner-takes-all system appeared to reflect self-interest: it was chosen by winners only.

12. What were the correlates of individual productivity? There were a number of measures taken prior to the performance, and before the subjects knew which distribution system they would be working under, which showed low but significant correlations with a measure of overall individual productivity. The more the male subjects felt they were "powerful," "a winner," or "unemotional," the higher was their performance score; the more the female subjects considered themselves to be "intuitive," "logical," or "lucky," the higher their performance scores.

When we partial out the effects of the differences in the initial self-rating scales, it is interesting to note that it was only the high performing women and not the men who consistently felt better about themselves (more "daring," "self-confident," and "like a winner") and their groupmates (more "cooperative," "sociable," "friendly," etc.) as a result of their good performances.

13. What were the preexperimental correlates of initial attitudes toward the different distributive systems? Preferences for winner-takes-all and, to a lesser extent for proportionality were associated with a sense of power, toughness, self-confidence, a more conservative political orientation, a feeling of competitiveness, and a tendency to downplay one's groupmates. In contrast, preferences for the equality and need principles were correlated with more favorable attitudes toward one's fellow group members and less favorable views of one's own chances and capabilities. The greater the tendency to be Machiavellian, the higher the subject's preference for winner-takes-all and the lower their preference for equality.

Our results provide little support for the equity theory assumption that productivity would be higher when earnings are closely tied to performance. Despite the fact that the tasks were neither particularly interesting nor demanding, and despite participating in the experiment primarily to earn money, the subjects seemed more motivated to perform well by their own needs to do as well as they could rather than by the greater amount of pay they might earn from higher performance in the proportionality and winner-takes-all conditions. Their motivation to perform was determined more by self-standards than by external reward.

These results are not surprising if one takes into account that the subjects were college students who were not alienated from themselves, their colleagues, or the experimenters. They had no reason not to do as well as they could whether or not they would earn more money by so doing. If they had felt alienated from themselves and their capabilities and had little pride in their own effectiveness, then their performances might have been more influenced by the external reward. It is possible that the assumption that people will be more productive if they are rewarded in proportion to their contribution is valid only when people are alienated from their work.

Our results also indicate that the distributive system under which a group functions can significantly affect the social attitudes and social relations that develop within the group. This effect is likely to be enhanced if the task or social context of the group has characteristics that enable the incipient social relations induced by the distributive system to be nurtured and expressed in interactions among the group members; it is likely to be reduced if the task or social context of the group has demand characteristics that are incongruent with the social relations induced by the distributive system.

The Choice of Distribution System

Here, I briefly summarize four studies in which the psychological orientations of the subjects were systematically varied through our experimental procedures so as to create either solidarity-oriented or non-solidarity-oriented subjects. In the first experiment (Seiler & Deutsch, 1973), this was done by assigning the subjects, who were working together, different objectives that were either oriented to friendship formation or to task accomplishment. In the second (Curtis, 1973, 1979) and third experiments (Lansberg, 1983), this was achieved by creating positive or negative attitudes between the noninteracting subjects. And, in our fourth experiment (Horowitz, 1983), we employed professional actresses who were asked to play characters who had clearly different personalities: one of whom had a personality associated with a solidarity psychological orientation and the other with an economic orientation.

No matter how induced, the solidarity psychological orientation led to a tendency to employ generous or egalitarian distributive principles whereas the economic, task-oriented, or impersonal nonsolidarity psychological orientation led to a tendency to prefer some sort of relative contribution or self-serving distributive principle. In other words, the politeness ritual and the desire to make a good impression operated among people who were well-disposed toward one another so that they allocated less to themselves and more to others than self-interest would have dictated. In contrast, among people lacking positive bonds to one another, self-interest led to deviations from the merit principle in the direction favoring self: a pseudoegalitarianism in low performers, and a winner-takes-all attitude in high performers.

Behind the Rawlsian veil of ignorance, where uncertainty existed with respect to one's relative performance, the politeness ritual was inappropriate and self-serving behavior was muted: here, ignorance of how to be generous or how to advantage oneself resulted in a clear favoring of equal sharing.

The Sense of Injustice

Four studies relating to the sense of injustice were conducted. The first study (Steil, Tuchman, & Deutsch, 1978) revealed that an experienced injustice, whether to oneself or another, involves one as a member of a moral community whose norms are being violated and it evokes an obligation to restore justice. Because it implicates one socially as a member of a community, it leads to more intense emotional responsiveness when another experiences an injustice as compared to frustration; it also leads to the expectation that others will respond more intensely when one experiences an injustice rather than a frustration.

However, our second (Steil, 1980, 1983) and third studies (Fine, 1981) found that not all will experience an injustice, whether inflicted upon oneself or another, as unjust. The evidence from these two studies is that the sensitivity to an injustice is greater among those who are disadvantaged than among those who are advantaged by it. The findings of these studies also suggest that the sensitivity to injustice can be increased by providing social support for its acknowledgment and viable options for its remedy.

The fourth study (Weinglass & Steil, 1981a,b) highlights the importance of ideological factors in affecting whether or not one will perceive inequalities as unfair and, also, their importance in influencing one's readiness to support social change to eliminate the inequalities. The religious inequalities between Orthodox Jewish men and women are not considered unfair by Orthodox women who support religious fundamentalism and believe that the religious needs of men and women differ basically. The same inequalities are viewed as rather unfair for self and other Orthodox Jewish women by women who have been exposed to and endorse a feminist ideology.

SOME CONCLUSIONS

Below, I list a few of the important conclusions that can be drawn from the research in our laboratory.

1. Cooperative, as compared to competitive, systems of distributing rewards—when they differ—have more favorable effects on individual and group productivity, social relations, self-esteem, task attitudes, and a sense of responsibility to other group members.

2. In a situation of conflict, the ability of the conflicting parties to work out a just agreement that is stable and mutually satisfying is enhanced by the conditions that typically foster cooperation and reduced by the conditions that typically foster competition.

3. There is no reliable or consistent evidence to indicate that people work more productively as individuals or as group members when they are expecting to be rewarded in proportion to their performance than when they are expecting to be rewarded equally or on the basis of need.[1]

4. The preference for sociocentric principles of distributive justice (such as "egalitarianism" and "generosity") is associated with positive, social-emotional solidarity-oriented social relations whereas the preference for individual-centered principles (such as proportionality or equity) is associated with impersonal, task-directed, economic-oriented social relations.

5. The sensitivity to injustice can be increased by providing social support for its acknowledgment and viable options for its remedy.

REFERENCES

Curtis, R. C. (1973). *Effects of knowledge regarding potential advantages and social relationship upon perceptions of justice*. Unpublished doctoral dissertation, Teachers College, Columbia University.

Curtis, R. C. (1979). Effects of knowledge of self-interest and social relationship upon the use of equity, utilitarianism and Rawlsian principles of allocation. *European Journal of Social Psychology, 9*, 165–175.

---

[1]This is, perhaps, our most controversial finding. It flouts the common belief that tangible incentives, such as money rewards or bonuses, stimulate better performance. It is not our contention that this common belief is completely wrong but rather that it is true only under special circumstances. Our research has not identified these circumstances. However, this common belief seems clearly wrong when people have intrinsic motivation to perform well or when they are not alienated from work or from the social context in which they are working.

Deutsch, M. (1949a). A theory of cooperation and competition. *Human Relations, 2*, 129–151.

Deutsch, M. (1949b). An experimental study of the effects of cooperation and competition upon group processes. *Human Relations, 2*, 199–232.

Deutsch, M. (1973). *The resolution of conflict: Constructive and destructive processes.* New Haven, CT: Yale University Press.

Deutsch, M. (1974). Awakening the sense of injustice. In M. Ross & M. Lerner (Eds.), *The quest for justice* (pp. 19–42). Toronto: Holt, Rinehart & Winston.

Deutsch, M. (1975). Equity, equality and need: What determines which value will be used as the basis of distributive justice? *Journal of Social Issues, 31*, 137–149.

Deutsch, M. (1977). *The social psychology of distributive justice.* Unpublished manuscript, Teachers College, Columbia University.

Deutsch, M. (1985). *Distributive justice: A social psychological perspective.* New Haven, CT: Yale University Press.

Fine, M. M. (1981). *Options to injustice: Seeing other lights.* Unpublished doctoral dissertation, Teachers College, Columbia University.

Horowitz, S. V. (1983). *Social character and choice: The influence of psychological orientations and social relations on distributive justice situation.* Unpublished manuscript, Teachers College, Columbia University.

Johnson, D. W., & Johnson, R. T. (1983). The socialization and achievement crises: Are cooperative learning experiences the solution? In L. Bickman (Ed.), *Applied social psychology annual*, Vol. III. Beverly Hills, CA: Sage.

Lansberg, I. (1983). *The boundaries of justice: An experimental study.* Unpublished doctoral dissertation, Teachers College, Columbia University.

Medvene, L. J. (1981). *Distributive justice: Individual study.* Unpublished manuscript, Teachers College, Columbia University.

Mei, D. M. (1978). *The effects of far different principles of distributing earnings within a group on task attitudes, performance, and preference for principles.* Unpublished manuscript, Teachers College, Columbia University.

Seiler, M., & Deutsch, M. (1973). *Goal orientation, mode of payment and the distribution of outcomes in cooperative groups.* Unpublished manuscript. Social Psychology Laboratory, Teachers College, Columbia University.

Steil, J. M. (1980). *Efficacy and the response to injustice by relatively advantaged and disadvantaged persons.* Unpublished doctoral dissertation, Teachers College, Columbia University.

Steil, J. M. (1983). The response to injustice: Effects of varying levels of social support and position of advantage or disadvantage. *Journal of Experimental Social Psychology, 19*, 239–253.

Steil, J. M., Tuchman, B., & Deutsch, M. (1978). An exploratory study of the meanings of injustice and frustration. *Personality and Social Psychology Bulletin, 4*, 393–398.

Tuchman, B. (1982). *The effects of four grading systems on task performance, learning, group interaction and attitudes.* Unpublished doctoral dissertation, Teachers College, Columbia University.

Weinglass, J., & Steil, J. (1981a, August). *When is unequal unfair: The role of ideology.* Paper presented at the meeting of the American Psychological Association, Los Angeles, CA.

Weinglass, J., & Steil, J. (1981b, May). *The experience of injustice: An empirical examination of its preconditions.* Paper presented at the meeting of the American Psychological Association, Los Angeles, CA.

Wenck, W. A. (1979). *Attitudes as a function of potential earnings, type of distribution system and sex.* Unpublished manuscript. Teachers College, Columbia University.

Wenck, W. A. (1981). *The effect of distribution systems on psychological orientation.* Unpublished doctoral dissertation, Teachers College, Columbia University.

Ziviani, C. (1978). *Productivity as a function of potential earnings, type of distribution system and sex.* Unpublished manuscript. Teachers College, Columbia University.

Ziviani, C. (1981). *The effects of pay, distributive justice and social interdependence on task group performance, process, and attitudes.* Unpublished doctoral dissertation, Teachers College, Columbia University.

Chapter 2

Justice and Power

AN EXCHANGE ANALYSIS

KAREN S. COOK and KAREN A. HEGTVEDT

INTRODUCTION

There is a curious omission of the topic "power" in much of the research on equity and distributive justice. Homans (1976), in his commentary on the 1976 Berkowitz and Walster volume, *Equity Theory: Toward a General Theory of Social Interaction*, writes: "the authors of these papers have little to say about the relationship between equity and power" (p. 242). More recently, Greenberg and Cohen (1982) make the same judgment concerning a different set of articles, concluding "the structure of power among individuals in the situation has received less explicit attention" (p. 449). They further argue that an analysis of power "seems crucial for an understanding of how normative constraints are expressed in overt action" (p. 449). If an investigation of the structure of power is essential for understanding justice behavior on the part of individuals, it is even more critical when the level of analysis shifts from interpersonal relations to intergroup relations.

Whereas discussions of power are somewhat rare in the literature on equity theory, power is a prominent theme in exchange theory. Blau (1964), for example, includes that topic in the title of his major treatise

KAREN S. COOK • Department of Sociology, University of Washington, Seattle, WA 98185. KAREN A. HEGTVEDT • Department of Sociology, Emory University, Atlanta, GA 30322.

on exchange. He argues that "exchange processes give rise to differentiation in power" (1964, p. 22). Other exchange formulations (e.g., Coleman, 1972; Emerson, 1972; Homans, 1974) similarly focus primary attention on the analysis of power. Even though the dominant theoretical perspective on equity is the exchange formulation (cf. Cook & Parcel, 1977), there have been few theoretical treatments of the link between equity and power. Exceptions include Austin and Hatfield (1980), Cook and Emerson (1978), and Greenberg (1978).[1]

Drawing on recent research on power and equity in exchange networks, we begin to analyze the link between power and justice processes in one class of interpersonal relations, those characterized by Greenberg and Cohen (1982) as "bargaining" relations. It is our hope that this work will eventually inform the analysis of justice and power in intergroup relations. Toward this end, we conclude our paper with some comments concerning the implications of our work for the analysis of intergroup phenomena. Before narrowing our discussion, we describe briefly some of the diverse lines of research bearing on the relationship between power and justice.

POWER AS A DETERMINANT OF REWARD DISTRIBUTIONS

Various authors indicate that power ultimately determines the distribution of rewards in a group or social system (e.g., Homans, 1976; Lenski, 1966; Marx, 1875; Parkin, 1972; Walster & Walster, 1975). Social stratification research tends to substantiate this general claim. Mills (1956) and Domhoff (1967), for example, note that the concentration of power in America parallels the concentration of wealth and income. Cross-cultural research also indicates a high degree of correspondence between the distribution of power and income in the world economy (e.g., Bornschier & Ballmer-Cao, 1979).

At the micro level of analysis, experimental studies demonstrate that power imbalances in exchange networks result in the unequal distribution of profit (or benefit) across actors. Over a series of exchange transactions, actors in power-advantaged network positions accrue more profit than actors in power-disadvantaged positions (Cook & Emerson, 1978; Stolte, 1983). In addition, the distribution of power is likely to

---

[1]Some authors explicitly exclude power from their discussions of justice. For example, Miller (1976) as cited in Austin and Hatfield (1980) states, "I exclude power from among the benefits to be considered under social justice, since . . . other concepts (explain) the distribution of power in society." Miller (1976) thus treats the two processes as distinct arguing that the distribution of power is "causally" and not "conceptually" relevant to social justice.

determine the bases of allocation. Although power is rarely manipulated in experimental studies, actors commonly express self-interested perferences in many allocation situations. As is evident in a variety of studies, actors tend to emphasize their strengths and de-emphasize their weaknesses as bases for allocation (see a review of this research in Cook and Hegtvedt, 1983).

Findings from allocation studies imply that when power differences exist, powerful (as well as powerless) actors are likely to promote the distribution that maximizes their own outcomes. The resources that powerful actors have at their disposal enable them to affect the attitudes and behaviors of others, most importantly to extract their compliance (see Collins & Guetzkow, 1964). If those in power can influence others to accede to the basic fairness of the distribution of benefits, legitimating its inequality (Austin & Hatfield, 1980; Kipnis, 1976; Lenski, 1966; McClintock & Keil, 1982), then the "just" distribution of the outcomes is merely a reflection of the distribution of power. As Berger and Luckman (1967) put it, "he who carries the bigger stick has a better chance of imposing his definition of reality" (p. 109). Or as Homans (1976) concludes, "I believe power to be the more primitive phenomenon that lies behind distributive justice" (p. 243).

Legitimation makes it easier for the powerful to obtain compliance (Dornbusch & Scott, 1975; French & Raven, 1959; Weber, 1922/1978). The bases for legitimation may be either *internal* (e.g., a result of actor's self-evaluations) or *external* (e.g., structurally determined). Della Fave (1980), focusing on internal bases, argues that actors are likely to infer that wealthy or powerful individuals possess other positive characteristics, and are thereby legitimately entitled to a greater share of the resources.

Stolte (1983), drawing on Della Fave's argument, suggests that if levels of self-efficacy (based upon actors' structural positions in a network) and expected outcomes are positively related, then power differences among the actors in the network would not affect the perceptions of the fairness of inequality in exchange ratios. In effect, individuals would simply accept the status quo as fair. Findings from his experimental study failed to confirm this hypothesis; less powerful actors defined the inequalities as more unfair than did the powerful actors. Results from another study (Steil, 1983) also indicate that fairness perceptions vary across advantaged and disadvantaged positions. Findings from these studies cast doubt on the hypothesized internal mechanism of legitimation.

Other studies focus on the legitimation of power rather than the distribution of rewards. Recent experimental work by Zelditch, Walker, and their colleagues (e.g., Zelditch & Walker, 1984; Zelditch, Harris,

Thomas, & Walker, 1983) examines factors external to the individual that promote compliance to more powerful actors. Their findings indicate that actors are more compliant when their peers endorse the existing system or when variation in actors' abilities justify reward differentials. In essence, these are conditions under which actors perceive a system to be legitimate in the absence of coercion. But even "legitimate" systems are subject to scrutiny. Sell and Martin (1983) demonstrate that actors will attempt to reject a legitimate distribution rule when it is in their self-interest and in the collective interest of their group to do so. Interestingly, they also find that such rejection is more likely to occur if those in authority (in this case, the experimenter) promote an equal rather than a proportional distribution.

POWER AS A DETERMINANT OF REACTIONS TO INJUSTICE

Power is related not only to the distribution of rewards in a group or social system, but also to individual and collective reactions to injustice. Powerful actors, as indicated previously, may determine the nature of the distribution rule and extract compliance from others when reward inequalities are legitimized. In addition, they may control resources that limit the range of individual and collective reactions to injustice. Yet, from the perspective of the less powerful members of the social system, justice may become the basis for opposition to the status quo.

Perceptions of injustice arise when the actual distribution of outcomes does not correspond to what is accepted as the just distribution (Berger, Zelditch, Anderson, & Cohen, 1972; Homans, 1974). Injustice, in other words, is the violation of a normative standard. Less powerful actors may recognize this violation when the legitimized distribution is disrupted in a way that serves the interest of the powerful, or when they realize the bias inherent in the existing system.

Regardless of the source of injustice, responses may occur at the individual or the group level. Specifying the nature of these responses, however, is a complex theoretical problem involving a series of assessments about the situation. First, actors in the situation must evaluate whether or not they are being treated "unjustly"; given the existence of multiple conceptions of justice (Deutsch, 1975; Lerner, 1975, 1977; Leventhal, 1976), this also requires a complicated assessment process. Second, the actors must then (a) determine the availability of the means to redress the injustice, and (b) assess the probability that any given action will effectively restore equity (or a state of distributive justice).

Adams (1965) and Walster, Berscheid, and Walster (1973) attempt to specify the possible range of individual reactions to inequity. These theorists assume that actors will choose the least costly and most adequate means to restore equity (i.e., the equivalence of outcome/input ratios). Whether actors perceive the existing ratios as inequivalent depends on what they define as the relevant outcomes and inputs, and with whom they choose to compare their ratios.

The theoretical formulations, however, deal only superficially with these two issues. The significance of the relevance problem is clearly indicated in recent research that demonstrates that actors weight inputs differentially (Cook & Yamagishi, 1983; Kayser & Lamm, 1980; Lamm & Kayser, 1978). Work by Berger *et al.* (1972) and Berger, Fisek, Norman, and Wagner (1983) explicates the theoretical importance of the comparison process. Berger and his colleagues argue convincingly that individuals compare themselves to reference groups (or standards) as well as to single individuals, yet the selection of a specific set of comparison others remains an issue of some discussion (see Austin, 1977; Tornblom, 1977; and in the relative deprivation tradition, Crosby, 1976; and Martin, 1981).

Though there is a vast amount of evidence relating to individual reactions to inequity (e.g., changes in levels of productivity, tendencies to reallocate more equitably), these results are not without alternative interpretations (Goodman & Friedman, 1971; Lawler, 1968; Pritchard, 1969). In addition, this literature tells us little about the relationship between justice and power. Typically, the individuals involved in the study are co-workers, team members, or partners who differ in terms of their inputs (e.g., contributions, performance levels, effort). Power differences, if they exist at all among actors in these studies, are not directly examined.

Power is analyzed more often in the investigation of collective reactions to injustice.[2] Although people who participate in rebellions, revolutions, or other forms of collective protest sometimes express concerns over injustice (cf. Gurr, 1970; Moore, 1978), collective reactions require more than a simple aggregation of individual sentiments of injustice (as Jasso, 1983, seems to imply). The analysis of forms of collective reactions to injustice requires treatment not only of the determinants of individual level assessments of injustice, but also of the correlates of group formation and successful collective action.

Shared perceptions of injustice among individuals in a particular group or class of actors legitimize opposition to the powerful and provide an ideological basis for solidarity (Blau, 1964; Eckhoff, 1974). The development of solidarity within a group, however, requires more than a

---

[2]Theories of revolution more often focus on power differences and structural factors (e.g., Skocpol, 1979) than on ideology.

common ideology.[3] Obstacles to group formation include multiple membership groups, mobility across groups, lack of contact among similarly situated actors, failure to realize differences with other (dominant) groups or the similarity of subjective and objective interests within a group, and the lack of unifying symbols (e.g., Balbus, 1971; Parkin, 1972; Rosenberg, 1953). Miller, Gurin, Gurin, and Malanchuk (1981) argue that group consciousness develops when individuals feel as if they belong to a group, preferring it to other groups and expressing dissatisfaction with the group's current (low) status vis-à-vis power or resources that they jointly believe are due to "system" inequalities rather than individual failings.

If individuals achieve such group consciousness, they are likely to shift from acceptance of their current status to an expression of grievance as common victims of injustice. Costly forms of collective reactions, such as rebellion or revolution, however, are likely to be affected by other factors in addition to group consciousness.

Gurr (1970) and, to some extent, Moore (1978), built their theories of revolution based on notions of the psychological processes of the participants, most notably their sense of relative deprivation. Three critical elements are omitted from these formulations. The first, clearly identified by current relative deprivation theorists (e.g., Crosby, 1976; Martin, 1981), is the omission of the sense of fraternal deprivation (Runciman, 1966) that epitomizes the group's low standing in relation to other comparison groups. The second is the structural characteristics of the society, such as the relationship between the government and elites (Goldstone, 1982). Finally, these formulations omit explicit treatment of the logistics of successful collective action, such as the existence of selective incentives, the ease of resource mobilization, the difficulties of organization, and the role of leadership (see Hardin, 1982; Marwell & Oliver, 1984; Olson, 1965; Parkin, 1972; Tilly, 1978; Turner & Killian, 1972).

The complex issues surrounding collective action are often more obscured in experimental studies of collective reactions to injustice than in the historical analyses of revolutions. Results from several experimental studies (e.g., Lawler, 1975; Lawler & Thompson, 1979; Overstreet, 1972; Webster & Smith, 1978) indicate that coalitions between two "weak" members in three person groups are likely to form when leaders allocate rewards inequitably. However, as argued above, perceived injustice on the part of the less powerful group members is often not enough to overcome certain structural or situational factors that mitigate against the occurrence of collective reactions. For example, Lawler (1975)

---

[3]The development of group consciousness may be considered to be a more general case of class consciousness (Marx, 1875).

demonstrated that status differences among subordinates undermine common interests and hence reduce the potential for coalition activity among the subordinates; power differences among subordinates may have a similar inhibiting effect.

Although the reactions of less powerful actors are most often studied, powerful actors may react when injustices arise due to changes in the distribution they promote. Any deviation from a formerly legitimized distribution may engender collective reactions that threaten powerful actors' advantageous positions (e.g., Michener & Burt, 1974). The threat of excessive loss due to the institutionalization of an alternative distribution encourages powerful actors to maintain the status quo.

This review of some of the relevant literature illustrates the complexity of the link between justice and power. No existing theoretical formulation encompasses both with much ease. Various aspects of the problem are addressed in a fairly diverse literature. Integration of the insights provided by these sources must be achieved, but that is a large undertaking. Our analysis begins this process by narrowing the scope of the endeavor and addressing the problem from within the framework of a well-developed theoretical orientation—the exchange perspective. Both power and justice processes have been examined from this perspective, albeit not often in the same piece of research.

AN EXCHANGE ANALYSIS AND SOME PRELIMINARY EVIDENCE

Social exchange is typically conceptualized as the transfer of valued resources from one party to another, often as the result of implicit or explicit bargaining or negotiation (cf. Cook & Emerson, 1978; Molm, 1981). The give-and-take nature of exchange distinguishes it from pure allocation or distribution situations (see Blalock & Wilken, 1979; Eckhoff, 1974, on this distinction). Furthermore, exchange processes are best understood in terms of the relationship between the actors involved (Emerson, 1976). Of major interest is the nature of the conditions under which exchange relations develop and are maintained or terminated.

In simple terms, an exchange relation consists of two actors, A and B, each possessing at least one resource (x for A and y for B) that the other actor values. The relation is a longitudinal series of transactions between the two parties that results in the exchange of valued resources. The exchange rate is either implicitly determined by the value of the units of resource given up and received over time, or explictly negotiated in the terms of trade.

Although much of the existing research focuses on dyadic exchange, Emerson's work (1972, 1976) extends exchange theory to apply to networks of connected exchange relations among three or more actors who are either "natural persons" (cf. Coleman, 1972) or corporate groups (which often act through designated agents). In this theory, exchange relations can be connected in two fundamental ways: (a) negatively— in which case exchange in one relation precludes or hinders exchange in the other exchange relation (e.g., the situation in which two males are competing for the affection of one woman), or; (b) positively—in which case the two exchange relations are not mutually exclusive, but foster exchange in each relation (see Emerson, 1972).

Power in an exchange network is determined by an actor's location in the network of connected relations. For negatively connected networks, such as those we will discuss below, dyadic power-dependence notions (Emerson, 1962, 1972) provide the basis for determining the power structure. Specifying the power structure in positively connected networks is more complex (see Cook, Emerson, Gillmore, & Yamagishi, 1983). Emerson (1962) defines the power of actor A over B as a function of the degree of dependence of B on A for valued resources (i.e., $Power_{AB} = Dependence_{BA}$). Dependence is defined in terms of two factors: (a) the value of the resources B can provide A (in a two-party exchange relation); and (b) the availability of that valued resource from alternative sources (e.g., from other actors in the network). More specifically, dependence is assumed to be a direct function of the value of the resource A can get from B, and an inverse function of its availability from other sources.

These notions have been explored in the analysis of exchange networks by Cook and Emerson (1978) and Cook et al. (1983). In these studies, network structures are established in a computerized laboratory. Power differences in these networks are structurally determined by the access occupants of each position have to alternative sources of the resources they value. Furthermore, actors have knowledge only of their local access to other exchange partners, not of the structure of the entire network. Thus, positions that might appear similar to the occupants of those positions may be quite different in terms of positional power as a result of the structure of the more remote network connections. Of interest is the subjects' use of the power provided by their network positions in bargaining. We note an important distinction between positional power as a *potential* and the actual *use* of power, because these may be guided by very different principles.

In previous research, we have investigated the structural determinants of power and factors, such as normative constraints (e.g., justice concerns and commitment between actors), which affect power use in exchange networks. Cook and Emerson (1978) report the findings of an experiment on four-person exchange networks that demonstrate the impact of network structure on power and power use. In addition, the results indicate that normative constraints operate to influence actual power use. Here we extend our research into the specific role of equity as a constraint on the exercise of power in exchange networks. First, we examine some evidence from several experiments concerning perceptions of fairness in power-balanced and power-imbalanced exchange networks (see Emerson, 1972). Then we present the major results from an experiment designed to examine equity constraints on power use in power-imbalanced networks.[4]

PERCEPTIONS OF FAIRNESS IN EXCHANGE NETWORKS

The networks presented in Figure 1 represent exchange structures operationalized in our computerized laboratory (see Cook & Emerson, 1978, for details concerning the laboratory and operationalizations). The data discussed here focus on the actors' perceptions of the fairness of the distribution of exchange outcomes. Data from two separate studies are included in the analysis. One study involved the four-party networks diagrammed in Figures 1d and 1e, which are described in Cook and Emerson (1978). The other study examined three-party networks, varying in degree of power imbalance (Figures 1a–1c). In these networks, power-disadvantaged actors were allowed to form coalitions in order to attempt to improve their exchange outcomes (for more details see Cook & Gillmore, 1984). Figures 1a and 1d represent power-balanced networks in which all actors have equal potential power because none occupies a structurally determined power-advantaged position. In the other networks, the exchange structures are power imbalanced; actors who occupy position C_i have a structural power advantage resulting from the greater availability of the resources they value.

These networks are negatively connected; thus, exchange in one relation during any single episode precludes a transaction in any other relation. In the figures, the nodes represent positions actors occupy, and the lines indicate exchange opportunities, differentially valued. The numbers (somewhat arbitrarily set) refer to a fixed sum available as profit or benefit in any single transaction between two actors sharing an exchange opportunity.[5]

---

[4]Both Eckhoff (1974) and Greenberg and Cohen (1982) discuss the dual role of justice considerations: normative and strategic.

[5]Although the transaction table each actor used to make exchanges included a fairly wide

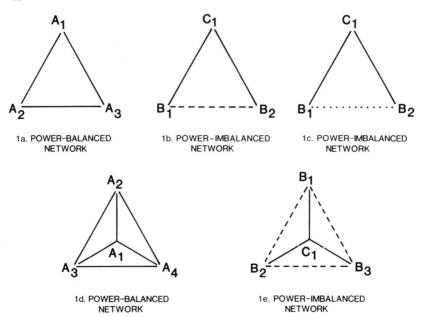

FIGURE 1.   Exchange networks studied in laboratory experiments. Letters identify net-work positions (A_1 = power equals, B_1 = power-disadvantaged actors). Numerical sub-scripts identify the position of occupants. Lines represent exchange opportunities that vary in potential benefit (solid lines represent the negotiated exchange of 24 points, dashed lines = 8 points, dotted lines = 0 points).

In the power-balanced networks, no actor has a structural power advantage; thus it is unlikely that over time any single actor (A_i) will obtain significantly more profit than others in the network. In contrast, in the power-imbalanced networks, the structural advantage available to the occupants of position C_i should lead to a marked inequality in the distribution of profits in the network over time if the actors in these positions use their power. In this case, power determines the distribution of rewards, as discussed earlier in the literature review.

In order to investigate the link between the exercise of power and fairness evaluations, we begin by analyzing the perceptions of fairness of the actors engaged in exchange processes in different types of power-balanced and imbalanced network structures. We assume that actors in these networks bring with them certain conceptions of distributive jus-tice, most typically, equity, which they apply to their evaluations of the

---

range of potential trades, only a certain range of the transactions was mutually beneficial to both actors. Subjects did not know the extent of this range, nor did they know the actual value of the available fixed sum in each potential exchange relation.

distribution of exchange outcomes. In order for justice norms to operate in exchange situations, actors must have information concerning the actors' outcomes and inputs (i.e., their exchange ratios) or, at a minimum, information regarding the distribution of exchange profits, which allows inferences about exchange ratios.[6] Prior research (Steil, 1983; Stolte, 1983) suggests that actors who benefit from the inequality of outcomes are more likely to judge the distribution as fair than actors who do not benefit. In Figures 2 through 4, we present evidence regarding the differential fairness perceptions of actors occupying power-advantaged and power-disadvantaged positions.

Questionnaire responses from the subjects who participated in the two experiments briefly described earlier provide data for our analysis. These data were obtained at the conclusion of the exchange negotiation phase in each study. Actors in the four-person networks were presented with the final distribution of exchange outcomes for the occupants of each position. The subjects rated the fairness of each actor's profits on a 7-point scale where 1 represented extreme unfairness and 7, extreme fairness. In the analysis of data from the power-balanced networks, one actor was randomly selected to represent the power-advantaged actor in order to make the data comparable to that obtained from the actual power-advantaged actor in the power-imbalanced networks. For both types of networks, responses of the remaining actors were averaged to represent their perceptions of fairness as disadvantaged actors.

The results from this experiment indicate that the perceived fairness of the distribution of exchange profits received by the power-advantaged and the disadvantaged actors varies as a function of both network structure (power balanced vs. power imbalanced) and network position (advantaged vs. disadvantaged). Figure 2 illustrates the significant interaction effect of these factors, $F(1,48) = 4.791$, $p < .03$, in the analysis of the profits that accrued to the power-advantaged actors. A main effect for network structure also obtains, $F(1,48) = 4.776$, $p < .03$. In power-balanced networks, as anticipated, there is little variation in the extent to which actors in different structural positions perceive the powerful actor's profits as fair. In power-imbalanced networks, in contrast, actors in power-disadvantaged positions perceive the distribution of profits to be more unfair than do the occupants of the power-advantaged positions.

As depicted in Figure 3, network structure and position produce a similar significant interaction effect in the analysis of perceptions of fairness concerning the distribution of profits to the power-disadvantaged

---

[6]Although we acknowledge the existence of differing justice norms, we were interested in examining the nature of the subjects' perceptions of fairness regardless of the specific norm of justice they applied to the exchange situation.

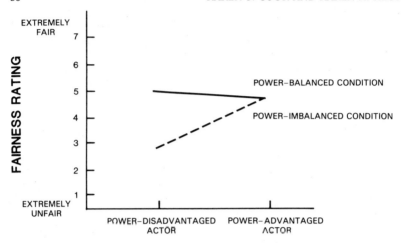

FIGURE 2.   Fairness of the distribution of exchange profits to the power-advantaged actor (network position × power-balance interaction effect).

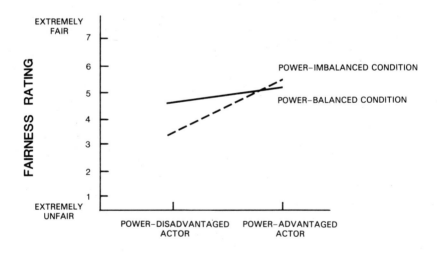

FIGURE 3.   Fairness of the distribution of exchange profits to the power-disadvantaged actor (network position × power-balance interaction effect).

actors, $F(1,48) = 6.160$, $p < .02$. Again, as predicted, perceptions of fairness vary little across the actors in the power-balanced networks; but in the power-imbalanced networks, power-advantaged actors judge the distribution of profits to the power-disadvantaged as more fair than do the power-disadvantaged actors.

In the study of three-actor networks, (Figures 1a–1c), in which actors occupying power-disadvantaged positions could form coalitions, the actors in the power-advantaged positions were still able to obtain more profit over the long haul (see Cook & Gillmore, 1984). The degree of power imbalance is greater in the network presented in Figure 1c than in the network in Figure 1b due to the variation in the range of exchange profits available to the disadvantaged actors in each network. In the extreme power-imbalanced condition (Figure 1c), the power-disadvantaged actors have no profitable alternative to exchange with the powerful actor. In the more moderate power-imbalanced condition, the power-disadvantaged actors can engage in profitable exchange with each other, although exchange with the powerful actor remains the most valued exchange opportunity. Again, for the purposes of comparison, we randomly selected an actor in the power-balanced network (Figure 1a) to compare to the power-advantaged actor in the other two networks.

Following the procedure described for the first experiment, the subjects in this experiment rated the fairness of the profits obtained by the power-advantaged actor. As expected, a main effect for position (advantaged vs. disadvantaged) emerged, $F(1,72) = 21.400$, $p < .001$. The mean fairness rating for actors in the power-advantaged position was 5.43; for those in the power-disadvantaged position, the mean was 4.04. These findings indicate that subjects occupying disadvantaged positions judged the powerful actor's profits as more unfair than the powerful actors judged their own profits.

Taken as a whole, these data support the thesis that those who benefit from positions of advantage are more likely to judge the distribution of outcomes that result from their position as fair than those who do not benefit. These differences in fairness perceptions may result in part from differing perceptions concerning the origin of the inequality of outcomes.

THE PERCEIVED ORIGINS OF INEQUALITY AND REACTIONS TO INJUSTICE

Actors involved in negotiation or bargaining relations are in a situation of high interdependence and low intimacy (Greenberg & Cohen, 1982; Lerner, 1975, 1977). Typically, exchange partners' knowledge of each other is limited to their immediate interaction in the course of the negotiations. The impersonal nature of this setting, in conjunction with the self-interested goals that shape bargaining strategies, attenuate actors' concerns for justice. If justice concerns emerge under these conditions, they are sure to emerge in situations involving higher degrees of interpersonal contact and intimacy. Thus, we asked: What factors enhance concern for justice in bargaining situations, especially those characterized by power imbalances?

As previously discussed, few studies address the link between power and justice. The omission of power differences is particularly critical given the effect of position on actors' perceptions of fairness. Furthermore, power differences are likely to shape individuals' reactions to injustice. From our previous study (Cook & Emerson, 1978) we learned that knowledge of the distribution of outcomes in the four-person exchange network affected individual bargaining behavior, resulting in a temporary increase in the profits accruing to the power-disadvantaged actor. Although it appeared that justice concerns influenced these negotiations, it remained unclear whether the power-advantaged actors attempted to restore justice by constraining their power use, or power-disadvantaged actors reacted to the injustice by driving harder bargains. In a second study, we attempt to investigate these reactions further by exploring the impact of information concerning the perceived origins of the inequalities in exchange benefits.

In a study of three-person exchange networks illustrated in Figure 1c, we varied the nature of the knowledge actors were given about their situation. Specifically, we examined the influence of three levels of knowledge on the exchange process. In the control condition (Condition 1), subjects lacked knowledge about the full network structure and about the distribution of exchange profits over time. In Condition 2, the actors remained uninformed about the network structure, but received information concerning the distribution of exchange profits. In Condition 3, the full knowledge condition, actors were given information about the distribution of exchange profits and about the full network structure, specifying positions of structural advantage and disadvantage.

The control condition provides a baseline of "unrestrained" power use against which one can measure the effect of information on the salience of justice concerns and their constraints on power use. In this condition, justice concerns cannot operate because subjects have no way of assessing how their profits compare to those of other members of their exchange network.

In Condition 2, knowledge about the distribution of accumulated profits over time should activate justice concerns, but actors are likely to attribute the origins of inequality in this situation to person-related factors, not to structural factors about which they have no information. But, the attributed origins of the inequality in exchange profits are likely to bear on the nature of actors' perceptions of fairness and their subsequent behavior. Based on the concepts of internal and external attributions (see Kelley, 1973; Weiner, et al., 1972) and previous examinations of bargaining behavior (e.g., Bacharach & Lawler, 1980), we predict that in the absence of information concerning the full network structure, actors are more likely to attribute their exchange outcomes to internal or personal factors like bargaining skill, talent, individual aggressiveness— or lack of skill, talent, and aggressiveness. Outcomes, as Della Fave's (1980) research and experiments by Cook (1975) and Harrod (1980) suggested, are often linked by actors to positive or negative traits or characteristics of the actors (e.g., skill, sex, self-evaluation, prestige). That is, a correspondence between outcomes and inputs is assumed to exist in the absence of evidence to the contrary (Cook, 1975). Thus, actors in power-advantaged positions are perceived as deserving of their superior outcomes and, similarly, power-disadvantaged actors are perceived as deserving lesser outcomes. To counter the negative image created by lower outcomes, power-disadvantaged actors are likely to be motivated to bargain harder.

In contrast to the implications of the information available in Condition 2, knowledge of the network structure provided in Condition 3 clarifies the structural determinants of any emergent inequalities in outcomes, and eliminates the necessity for an internal attribution. In this case, the perceived origin of the inequality will be located in the structure and not in any inherent traits or characteristics of the individual actors. The external attribution attenuates personal responsibility for the outcomes, thus decreasing the power-disadvantaged actors' motivation to bargain harder. In addition, if inequalities are structurally determined, only those occupying power-advantaged positions can effectively alter the distribution. Any action to change the distribution, however, may be qualified by the general tendency for powerful actors to view their exchange outcomes as more fair than less powerful actors do.

In sum, the perceived origins of inequality are expected to influence the extent to which justice concerns constrain power use in exchange networks. Furthermore, power-advantaged and -disadvantaged actors will be differentially influenced by the nature of the perceived origins of the inequality in outcomes. In line with this reasoning, an interaction effect was predicted: power-disadvantaged actors are more likely to constrain the exercise of power in the network (e.g., by driving harder bargains) when the perceived origin of the inequality is internally attributed, whereas the power-advantaged actors are more likely to constrain their own power use (e.g., by not driving hard bargains) when the perceived origin of the inequality is external. In these power-imbalanced networks, the inequality in outcomes is assumed to activate a justice process in all but Condition 1, in which no information concerning comparative profits is provided to the subjects.

The experimental design was a factorial type, containing three balanced, between-subjects variables (network position, knowledge condition, and sex), and one within-subjects variable (transaction periods, broken into 6 blocks of 12 trials each for analysis purposes). Within the all-male and all-female networks, subjects were randomly assigned to a power-advantaged or power-disadvantaged position. Networks were randomly assigned to one of the three knowledge conditions.

To enhance standardization of the bargaining process across networks in each condition, simulated actors were used in each network to represent the other actors. Thus, if a subject was randomly assigned to the power-advantaged position, he or she would face two simulated power-disadvantaged actors. If a subject was assigned to a power-disadvantaged position, then the power-advantaged actor was simulated.[7] Subjects were not informed of the simulation until the experiment was completed.

As in the experiments previously described, structural power advantage and disadvantage were operationalized in terms of the availability of highly valued resources. Knowledge was manipulated by providing two different types of information. In Condition 2, subjects were given information about the accumulated exchange profits for all network members on every five consecutive trials, as well as information concerning the average profit obtained on each set of five transaction periods. In addition to the profit information, subjects in Condition 3 received a diagram illustrating the network structure, emphasizing the variation in profit potential across positions.

---

[7]The simulated actors (SIMNET PROGRAM) were programmed to act "rationally." This means simply that these actors attempt to maximize their profits. More specifically, during bargaining the simulated actor is programmed according to the following criteria: (a) it accepts the better of any two offers received from others, (b) it raises its demand for profit the next time when its offer has been accepted on the prior trial, and (c) it lowers its demand for profit when its offers go unaccepted. To decrease suspicion, the simulated actors were also programmed to send messages to their trading partners occasionally. This program has been used in other studies in our laboratory with success. Because justice concerns do not enter into the simulated actor's bargaining strategy, we are able to isolate the impact of the justice concerns of the real actors on the bargaining process and the distribution of exchange outcomes. It is assumed that subjects reactions to the simulated actor will depend on their position in the network relative to the simulated actor, because the behavior of the simulated actor is the same regardless of network position.

The entire network formed the basic unit of analysis. Data presented here are aggregated over trial blocks to give some idea of time trends.[8] There were five groups of networks included in each cell of the $2 \times 2 \times 3$ design. The measure of power use was the profit that accrued to the subjects placed in the power-advantaged positions. In the case of the conditions in which the real subjects were assigned to power-disadvantaged positions, the data reflect the amount of profit the simulated actor was able to obtain in negotiation with the disadvantaged subjects over time. For ease of interpretation, however, the graph in Figure 4 presents the data for the real subjects only. That is, it shows

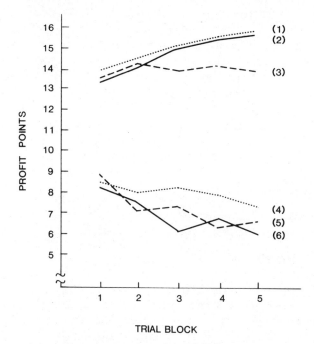

FIGURE 4. Graph of the distribution of profits over time by network position and knowledge condition (trial block × knowledge × network position interaction). (1) Knowledge of profits, power-advantaged; (2) no knowledge, power-advantaged; (3) full knowledge, power-advantaged; (4) knowledge of profits, power-disadvantaged; (5) no knowledge, power-disadvantaged; (6) full knowledge, power-disadvantaged.

---

[8]When two actors bargain, the behavior of each actor is partially dependent upon the other actor's behavior. The more one actor receives from an exchange, the less the other actor obtains (e.g., C's profit = 24-B's profit). Furthermore, exchanges in different relations in the network are nonindependent events. In three-person networks, when one dyad completes an exchange in a negatively connected network, the third actor is left out. Because of these dependencies, the entire network was used as the unit of analysis.

the amount the real power-advantaged actors were able to obtain from simulated power-disadvantaged actors (lines 1–3), and the amount the real disadvantaged actors were able to obtain from the simulated power-advantaged actors (lines 4–6).[9]

The significant trial block × knowledge × network position interaction effect supports our basic prediction, $F(8,72) = 2.279; p = .02$. As illustrated in Figure 4, power-advantaged actors who have knowledge of profits and of the structure have the lowest level of power use. In contrast, power-advantaged actors in the other conditions increase their profits over time. Power-disadvantaged actors who received knowledge concerning the network structure, as well as information about the profit inequalities, appeared resigned to their fate as illustrated by the decrease in their profits. When power-disadvantaged actors have knowledge only of the inequality in profit distributions and no information about the opportunity structure, the power-advantaged actor fails to accrue such high profits, indicating less resignation to their fate. As a consequence, such actors press for harder bargains, thereby limiting the profit gain of those in the advantaged position.

The results of this experiment confirm the important role of the perceived origins of outcome inequalities in justice and exchange processes. Ultimately, power differences among actors in these exchange networks determine not only the actors' perceptions of fairness, but also their reactions to injustice.

CONCLUDING COMMENTS: FROM INTERPERSONAL TO INTERGROUP RELATIONS

Our research indicates that theory concerning the interrelationship between power and justice must be developed further. Power imbalances in exchange networks create inequalities in the distribution of profits over time. These outcome inequalities are more likely to be defined as unfair by those in power-disadvantaged positions than by those in power-advantaged positions, as equity theory would suggest (Adams, 1965; Homans, 1974). In addition, the perceived origin of the inequality

[9]Due to the perfect rationality of the simulated actors, their profits were expected to be higher than those of the real subjects occupying the same position. The profits of the simulated power-advantaged actors are significantly higher than those of the real actors, $F(1,60) = 28.47$, $p = .001$. There is also a main effect for trial block as anticipated because power use is expected to increase over time in power-imbalanced networks, $F(4,240) = 15.99$, $p = .001$. In order to compare the average profits of the power-advantaged actors and the power-disadvantaged actors we computed a mean overall profit. These values are 14.46 for the power-advantaged and 7.31 for the power-disadvantaged actors.

(internal vs. external) affects the extent to which actors attempt to alter the distribution of outcomes through their bargaining behavior. These results suggest interesting directions for future research.

First, the structure of the power relations among actors must be incorporated into theories of distributive justice. Current typologies of important relationship dimensions (e.g., Greenberg & Cohen, 1982; Lerner, 1977) focus primarily on interdependence and intimacy but do not explicitly consider power differentials. As Homans (1976) suggests, power may indeed be the more "primitive phenomenon" underlying distributive justice. The task is to specify how it relates to justice behavior in the broadest sense. To accomplish this task, we will have to move beyond more narrow conceptions of "retaliation distress" and power as simply one type of input to be included in the "equity equation."

Second, in order to move to the level of intergroup relations, we must develop theory which can apply across levels of analysis. Austin and Hatfield (1980) state that, "The equity theorist . . . finds himself looking at social justice from the ground floor of 'micro level' social relations up to the 'macro level' of intergroup dynamics and social justice" (p. 32). Exchange theory can help bridge the gap between micro and macro levels of analysis, but to do so it must begin to deal with the more complex problems of collective action (Coleman, 1972).

Third, it is important to begin to investigate more fully the impact of structural and cultural factors on justice behavior (at the interpersonal as well as the intergroup level). The articles in the recent Lerner and Lerner (1981) volume provide some examples of this type of inquiry. In this context, we should carefully examine the difference between normative and strategic conceptions of justice, and attempt to relate these notions to the broader problem of inequality in society (Coleman, 1972; Rawls, 1971).

REFERENCES

Adams, J. S. (1965). Inequity in social exchange. In L. Berkowitz (Ed.), *Advances in experimental social psychology* (Vol. 2, pp. 267–299). New York: Academic Press.

Austin, W. (1977). Equity theory and social comparison processes. In J. Suls & R. Miller (Eds.), *Social comparison theory: Theoretical and empirical perspectives* (pp. 279–305). New York: Hemisphere.

Austin, W., & Hatfield, E. (1980). Equity theory, power and social justice. In G. Mikula (Ed.), *Justice and social interaction* (pp. 25–62). New York: Springer-Verlag.

Bacharach, S. B., & Lawler, E. J. (1981). *Bargaining: Power, tactics and outcomes.* San Francisco: Jossey-Bass.

Balbus, I. D. (1971). The concept of interest in pluralist and Marxist analysis. *Politics and Society, 1*, 151–177.

Berger, P. L., & Luckman, T. (1967). *The social construction of reality*. Garden City, NJ: Anchor Books.

Berger, J., Zelditch, M., Anderson,B., & Cohen, B. P. (1972). Structural aspects of distributive justice: A status value formulation. In J. Berger, M. Zelditch, & B. Anderson (Eds.), *Sociological theories in progress* (Vol. 2, pp. 119–146). Boston, MA: Houghton Mifflin.

Berger, J., Fisek, H., Norman, R. Z., & Wagner, D. G. (1983). The formation of reward expectations in status situations. In D. M. Messick & K. S. Cook (Eds.), *Equity theory: Psychological and sociological perspectives* (pp. 127–68). New York: Praeger.

Blalock, H. M., Jr., & Wilken, P. H. (1979). *Intergroup processes: A micro-macro perspective*. New York: Free Press.

Blau, P. (1964). Justice in social exchange. *Sociological Inquiry, 34*, 193–246.

Bornschier, V., & Ballmer-Cao, T. H. (1979). Income inequality: A cross national study of the relationship between MNC-penetration, dimensions of the power structure, and income distribution. *American Sociological Review, 44*, 487–506.

Coleman, J. (1972). Systems of social exchange. *Journal of Mathematical Sociology, 2*, 145–163.

Collins, B. E., & Guetzkow, H. A. (1964). *A social psychology of group processes for decision-making*. New York: Wiley.

Cook, K. S. (1975). Expectations, evaluations and equity. *American Sociological Review, 40*, 372–377.

Cook, K. S., & Emerson, R. M. (1978). Power, equity and commitment in exchange networks. *American Sociological Review, 43*, 721–739.

Cook, K. S., & Gillmore, M. R. (1984). Power, dependence and coalition formation in exchange networks. In E. J. Lawler (Ed.), *Advances in group processes: Theory and research* (Vol. 1, pp. 27–58). Greenwich, CT: JAI Press.

Cook, K. S., & Hegtvedt, K. A. (1983). Distributive justice, equity and equality. *Annual Review of Sociology, 9*, 217–241.

Cook, K. S., & Parcel, T. L. (1977). Equity theory: Directions for future research. *Sociological Inquiry, 47*, 75–88.

Cook, K. S., & Yamagishi, T. (1983). Social determinants of equity judgments: The problem of multidimensional input. In D. M. Messick & K. S. Cook (Eds.), *Equity theory: Psychological and sociological perspectives* (pp. 95–126). New York: Praeger.

Cook, K. S., Emerson, R. M., Gillmore, M. R., & Yamagishi, T. (1983). The distribution of power in exchange networks: Theory and experimental results. *American Journal of Sociology, 89*, 275–305.

Crosby, F. (1976). A model of egoistic relative deprivation. *Psychological Review, 83*, 85–113.

Della Fave, L. R. (1980). The meek shall not inherit the earth. *American Sociological Review, 45*, 955–971.

Deutsch, M. (1975). Equity, equality and need: What determines which value will be used as the basis of distributive justice? *Journal of Social Issues, 31*, 137–149.

Domhoff, G. W. (1967). *Who rules America?* Englewood Cliffs, NJ: Prentice-Hall.

Dornbusch, S. M., & Scott, W. R. (1975). *Evaluation and the exercise of authority*. San Francisco: Jossey-Bass.

Eckhoff, T. (1974). *Justice: Its determinants in social interaction*. Rotterdam: Rotterdam University Press.

Emerson, R. M. (1962). Power-dependence relations. *American Sociological Review, 27*, 31–40.

Emerson, R. M. (1972). Exchange theory, part II: Exchange relations and networks. In J. Berger, M. Zelditch, & B. Anderson (Eds.), *Sociological theories in progress* (Vol. 2, pp. 58–87). Boston, MA: Houghton Mifflin.

Emerson, R. M. (1976). Social exchange theory. *Annual Review of Sociology, 2*, 335–362.

French, J. R. P., & Raven, B. (1959). The bases of power. In D. Cartwright (Ed.), *Studies in social power* (pp. 150–167). Ann Arbor, MI: University of Michigan Press.

Goldstone, J. A. (1982). The comparative and historical study of revolutions. *Annual Review of Sociology, 8,* 187–207.

Goodman, P. S., & Friedman, A. (1971). An examination of Adam's theory of inequity. *Administrative Science Quarterly, 16,* 271–88.

Greenberg, J. (1978). Effects of reward value and retaliative power on allocation decisions: Justice, generosity or greed? *Journal of Personality and Social Psychology, 36,* 367–379.

Greenberg, J., & Cohen, R. L. (1982). Why justice? Normative and instrumental interpretations. In J. Greenberg & R. L. Cohen (Eds.), *Equity and justice in social behavior* (pp. 437–470). New York: Academic Press.

Gurr, T. R. (1970). *Why men rebel.* Princeton, NJ: Princeton University Press.

Hardin, R. (1982). *Collective action.* Baltimore, MD: John Hopkins University Press.

Harrod, W. J. (1980). Expectations from unequal rewards. *Social Psychology Quarterly, 43,* 126–130.

Homans, G. C. (1974). *Social behavior: Its elementary forms.* New York: Harcourt, Brace & World.

Homans, G. C. (1976). Commentary. In L. Berkowitz & E. Walster (Eds.), *Advances in experimental social psychology* (Vol. 9, pp. 231–44). New York: Academic Press.

Jasso, G. (1983). Social consequences of the sense of distributive justice: Small-group applications. In D. M. Messick & K. S. Cook (Eds.), *Equity theory: Psychological and sociological perspectives* (pp. 243–294). New York: Praeger.

Kayser, E., & Lamm, H. (1980). Input integration and input weighting in decisions on allocations of gains and losses. *European Journal of Social Psychology, 10,* 1–15.

Kelley, H. H. (1973). The processes of causal attribution. *American Psychologist, 28,* 107–128.

Kipnis, D. (1976). *The powerholders.* Chicago, IL: The University of Chicago Press.

Lamm, H., & Kayser, E. (1978). The allocation of monetary gain and loss following dyadic performance: The weight given to effort and ability under conditions of low and high intra-dyadic attraction. *European Journal of Social Psychology, 8,* 275–278.

Lawler, E. E. (1968). Equity theory: A predictor of productivity and work quality. *Psychological Bulletin, 70,* 596–610.

Lawler, E. J. (1975). An experimental study of factors affecting the mobilization of revolutionary coalitions. *Sociometry, 88,* 163–179.

Lawler, E. J., & Thompson, M. E. (1979). Subordinate responses to a leader's cooperative strategy as a function of the type of coalition power. *Representative Research in Social Psychology, 9,* 69–80.

Lenski, G. (1966). *Power and privilege.* New York: McGraw-Hill.

Lerner, M. J. (1975). The justice motive in social behavior: An introduction. *Journal of Social Issues, 31,* 1–19.

Lerner, M. J. (1977). The justice motive: Some hypotheses as to its origins and forms. *Journal of Personality, 45,* 1–52.

Lerner, M. J., & Lerner, S. C. (Eds.) (1981). *The justice motive in social behavior.* New York: Plenum Press.

Leventhal, G. S. (1976). The distribution of rewards and resources in groups and organizations. In L. Berkowitz & E. Walster (Eds.), *Advances in experimental social psychology* (Vol. 9, pp. 91–131). New York: Academic Press.

Martin, J. (1981). Relative deprivation: A theory of distributive injustice for an era of shrinking resources. In L. Cummings & B. Staw (Eds.), *Research in organizational behavior* (Vol. 3, pp. 53–107). Greenwich, CT: JAI Press.

Marwell, G., & Oliver, P. (1984, April). *The critical mass in collective action.* Paper presented at the West Coast Conference on Small Groups Research, Seattle, WA.

Marx, K. (1978). Critique of the Gotha Program, 1875. In R. C. Tucker (Ed.), *The Marx-Engels reader*. New York: W. W. Norton.

McClintock, C. G., & Keil, L. (1982). Equity and social exchange. In J. Greenberg & R. L. Cohen (Eds.), *Equity and justice in social behavior* (pp. 337–387). New York: Academic Press.

Michener, H. A., & Burt, M. R. (1974). Legitimacy as a base of social influence. In J. T. Tedeschi (Ed.), *Perspectives on social power*, (pp. 310–348). Hawthorne, NY: Aldine.

Miller, A.H., Gurin, P., Gurin, G., & Malanchuk, O. (1981). Group consciousness and political participation. *American Journal of Political Science, 25*, 494–511.

Miller, D. (1976). *Social justice*. London: Oxford University Press.

Mills, C. W. (1956). *The power elite*. New York: Oxford University Press.

Molm, L. D. (1981). The conversion of power imbalance to power use. *Social Psychology Quarterly, 44*, 151–163.

Moore, B. (1978). *Injustice: The social bases of obedience and social revolt*. White Plains, NY: M. E. Sharpe.

Olson, M. (1965). *The logic of collective action*. Cambridge, MA: Harvard University Press.

Overstreet, R. E. (1972). Social exchange in a 3-person game. *Journal of Conflict Resolution, 16*, 109–23.

Parkin, F. (1972). *Class inequality and political order: Social stratification in capitalist and communist societies*. London: Paladin Books.

Pritchard, R. D. (1969). Equity theory: A review and critique. *Organizational Behavior and Human Performance, 4*, 176–211.

Rawls, J. (1971). *A theory of justice*. Cambridge, MA: Harvard University Press.

Rosenberg, M. (1953). Perceptual obstacles to class consciousness. *Social Forces, 32*, 22–27.

Runciman, W. (1966). *Relative deprivation and social justice*. London: Routledge & Kegan Paul.

Sell, J., & Martin, M. (1983). The effects of benefit and type of distribution rule on non-compliance to legitimate authority. *Social Forces, 61*, 1168–1185.

Skocpol, T. (1979). *States and social revolutions*. Cambridge, MA: Harvard University Press.

Steil, J. M. (1983). The response to injustice: Effects of varying levels of social support and position of advantage or disadvantage. *Journal of Experimental Social Psychology, 19*, 239–253.

Stolte, J. F. (1983). The legitimation of structural inequality: The reformulation and test of the self-evaluation argument. *American Sociological Review, 48*, 331–42.

Tilly, C. (1978). *From mobilization to revolution*. Reading, MA: Addison-Wesley.

Tornblom, K. J. (1977). Distributive justice: Typology and propositions. *Human Relations, 31*, 1–24.

Turner, R., & Killian, L. (1972). *Collective behavior*. Englewood Cliffs, NJ: Prentice-Hall.

Walster, E., & Walster, G. W. (1975). Equity and social justice. *Journal of Social Issues, 31*, 21–43.

Walster, E., Berscheid, E., & Walster, G. W. (1973). New directions in equity research. *Journal of Personality and Social Psychology, 25*, 151–176.

Weber, M. (1978). *Economy and society*. G. Roth & C. Wittich (Eds.). Berkeley, CA: University of California Press. (Original work published 1922).

Webster, M., & Smith, L. R. (1978). Justice and revolutionary coalitions: A test of two theories. *American Journal of Sociology, 84*, 267–92.

Weiner, B., Frieze, I., Kukla, A., Reed, L., Rest, S., & Rosenbaum, R. M. (1972). Perceiving the causes of success and failure. In E. E. Jones, D. E. Kanouse, H. H. Kelley, R. E. Nisbett, S. Valins, & B. Weiner (Eds.), *Attribution: Perceiving the causes of behavior* (pp. 95–120). Morristown, NJ: General Learning Press.

Zelditch, M., Jr., & Walker, H. A. (1984). *Legitimacy and the stability of authority* (Working paper no. 84-1). Stanford, CA: Center for Sociological Research, Stanford University.
Zelditch, M., Jr., Harris, W., Thomas, G. M., & Walker, H. A. (1983). Decisions, non-decisions, and metadecisions. *Research in Social Movements, Conflicts and Change, 5,* 1–32.

Chapter 3

Justice Considerations in Interpersonal Conflict

HELMUT LAMM

INTRODUCTION

A GLANCE AT THE LITERATURE

What role do justice considerations play in interpersonal conflict? Several authors have noted that justice considerations may help conflict resolution. Pruitt (1972), under the heading of "norm following," delineates how "equity norms" may be used as a "method for resolving differences of interest," and he also gives attention to the problems with equity norms in the context of conflict resolution. Writing on negotiation as one particular kind of conflict process, Pruitt (1982, pp. 58–64) shows how the availability of a "prominent" solution (that is, one that appears as just to both parties) may facilitate agreement.[1]

Deutsch (1973) mentions "fairness, justice, equality" among the social norms by which "conflict can be limited and controlled" (p. 377).

---

[1]As the later discussion implies, a particular solution alternative qualifies as a prominent one by virtue of its justness only if *both parties* consider that solution as just (in other words, when there is no justice–judgment conflict). Note also that fairness or reasonableness is not the only attribute making an alternative a prominent one (see Pruitt, 1982, pp. 57–58).

HELMUT LAMM • Institut für Psychologie, Universität zu Köln, 5000 Köln 41, West Germany.

Austin and Tobiasen (1982), writing about justice in intimate relationships, note that "many marriage counselors and family therapists train their clients to think in exchange and fairness terms" so that "conflict can be managed more effectively" (p. 242). Lamm, Kayser, and Schwinger (1982) analyze the role of justice norms in reducing a party's initial level of demand, thus reducing the magnitude of conflict.

Several experiments on negotiation show that under certain conditions the assumption of justice motivation—in particular, the assumption that parties desire to divide an externally provided reward equally among each other—enables better prediction of the outcome of a negotiation (see Lamm, 1975, pp. 48–49, 83–86, 94, 111, 117, 169).

Only a few authors have noted that justice considerations may foster conflict and impede conflict resolution. According to Scanzoni (1972, pp. 70–71), husband–wife conflict emerges when a partner feels treated unjustly (". . . exploited by unfair demands"). He analyzes "the chain of events *between* perceived inequities, conflict, *and* whatever follows" (p. 79). In Holm (1970), "justice fanaticism" (defined as a need for justice regarding the distribution of resources in one's social environment) is seen as a basic factor affecting both the level of demand by the active party and the acceptance and/or rejection of that demand by the passive party in a conflict of interest.[2]

This chapter will explore the role of justice considerations in preventing and mitigating as well as in eliciting and exacerbating conflict.

Interpersonal Conflict: Definition, Delimitation, and Analytic Approach

Definition of Conflict

For the present analysis, (dyadic) conflict is said to be given when a person (A) and another person (B) have directed acts (e.g., utterances) at each other that are incompatible in their behavioral implications. In particular, attention will focus on the case where a request[3] by A is rejected by B.[4]

---

[2]The importance of structural conflict (Peterson, 1983) for the content of justice considerations has been elaborated by Greenberg & Cohen (1982). The justification function of justice considerations has been discussed by Mikula (1984). Austin and Tobiasen (1982) have analyzed procedural justice and conflict resolution in legal contexts. The "theory of procedure" proposed by Thibaut and Walker (1978) has some important commonalities with the present framework.

[3]The term *request* is used here broadly to denote any proposal, directed by a person to another, expressing a desire for some (change in) behavior on the latter's part. Thus,

The primary concern here will be with conflict of interest, where (a share of) a valued resource is requested by A and rejected by B. I will deal with *cognitive conflict*—that is, situations where persons A and B have manifested mutually incompatible cognitions—only to the extent that it plays a part in the conflict of interest as just defined.[5]

Types of Conflict of Interest

For the present purposes I will distinguish only between two types of conflict of interest. In the *unilateral-request* situation, one party (A, the active party) takes the initiative, directing a request at another (B). The *bilateral-request* situation has two variants. In the competitive type, the two parties compete for the same scarce resource (e.g., a parking space). In the cooperative type, the two parties have the joint goal of reaching a mutual arrangement but they have opposite preferences as to the contents of that arrangement (i.e., the terms of the agreement). For example, A wants to sell his used car and B wants to buy a used car: they have a cooperative goal of arriving at a mutual deal but conflicting interests concerning the price.

---

despite its connotation of humility, a request here may also stem from the person with the stronger power position (e.g., by virtue of his role) in the given relationship. Power differences do play an important part in the way justice considerations enter into conflict processes but this will have to be neglected here (cf. Cohen, Chapter 4, this volume). Note further that in an actual communication, wording such a request in terms of "entreaty," "request" (in the narrow sense), "proposal," "demand," or "command" may have different psychological implications for the addressee and thus may be used for tactical purposes by a requester. The success of such a maneuver depends, among other things, on the justice considerations elicited in the addressee.

[4]In this chapter I will only consider conflicts in which the initial request is egoistic, that is, it is designed by A to fulfill a need *of his* (or his constituents). In other words, I am speaking only of conflicts in which the resource requested by A is intended for his own consumption (or for the consumption of others he is representing) but not eventually for consumption by B. Thus I am not including cases like these: (a) A parent asks his child to hand him his money so he (the parent) can save it for the child, who would spend it too quickly. (b) A spouse asks his depressed partner to relinquish the sleeping pills.

[5]Any particular instance of "justice conflict" (see following) may involve cognitive conflict (defined as conflict over "what is true"). Thibaut and Walker (1978) deal with the interrelations of cognitive conflict and conflict of interest. Hammond and Brehmer (e.g., Brehmer and Hammond, 1977) have investigated the processes of, and the factors affecting, the resolution of cognitive conflict, and have analyzed its role in conflict of interest. Their research paradigm involves two persons who bring into the situation different positions on a judgmental issue (e.g., how democratic is a certain country), their positional differences being due, for example, to the different weights they give to criteria underlying such judgments.

These different types or subtypes may occur in the same interaction episode, and one type may become transformed into another one in the course of the interaction.

My main emphasis here will be on the unilateral-request conflict, because this type has been rather neglected in social-psychological research. Thus, the analysis will focus primarily on the unilateral-request situation, neglecting in part the peculiarities of the bilateral-request type. Again for reasons of space, the focus will be more on party A (the requester) than on party B. Much of the analysis will, however, apply to both A and B.

The Process of Conflict Resolution

The whole sequence of behaviors elicited by two incompatible acts (e.g., a request by A and its rejection by B) is said to constitute a *controversy*. Several stages of a controversy may be distinguished. These may be outlined as part of a descriptive analysis of the (unilateral-request type of) conflict.

Stage 0: Party A has an interpersonal desire (involving an image of a state of affairs for whose realization he sees a behavior X on the part of B as necessary or instrumental).

Stage 1: (a) Party A directs a request (R_x) at party B; this may be accompanied by (b) influence behaviors (designed to be instrumental toward B's accepting the request) and by (c) emotional-expressive behaviors.

Stage 2: (a) Party B states his acceptance or rejection of the request, possibly with conditions for entire or partial acceptance (e.g., a request by himself); this may be accompanied by (b) influence behaviors (designed to make A accept B's response) and (c) emotional-expressive behaviors. In the case of unconditional acceptance, there is no conflict.

Stage 3: Parties A and B exchange behaviors that may involve (a) requests and modified requests, (b) influence behaviors, (c) emotional-expressive behaviors, and (d) problem-solving behaviors designed to find a mutually acceptable solution to the conflict.

Stage 4: The controversy is over when it is clear (e.g., through communication between the parties) that there will be no further requesting or influencing behaviors related to the original issue.

A few comments on this simplified scheme are necessary. First, not all of these stages and behaviors will actually occur in any given conflict. Also, a full conflict is not given until stage 2, if B rejects A's request. Finally, I have not mentioned any covert events (e.g., cognitions—such as "justice thoughts"—and feelings), which play an important part in controversies.

INTERPERSONAL JUSTICE

The Concept and Its Principal Aspects: Interpersonal Comparison and Entitlement/Obligation

Interpersonal justice concerns the comparative treatment of individuals. A comparative treatment is considered just when it is deemed to be "right" (i.e., socially approvable). Thus, two key aspects of interpersonal justice are social comparison and entitlement/obligation (on the part of a potential receiver/allocator).

In the following discussion I will distinguish between intradyadic comparison (in which one conflict party compares himself with the other conflict party) and extradyadic comparison (in which, for example, the requesting party compares himself with an outside person).

The Justice Argument: Its Elements and Structure

Table 1 presents the various elements of a (complete) justice argument for the unilateral-request type of conflict. Together, they define the justice argument. The three major components are: the *justice appeal* (justice should guide behavior in the given situation); the *justice account* (in which A demonstrates that B's accepting his request would be an act of justice and his rejection an act of injustice); and the *proposition of action obligation* in which A concludes—from the two foregoing—that B has an obligation to act as requested.

The first two of these major components contain *factual assertions* (in particular, observational assertions in which certain attributes or quantities are said to be present or absent) and *normative assertions* (postulating the socially accepted validity or priority of basic rules to guide behavior).

A central element in the justice argument is the *justice judgment* (No. 8). It is the result of a complex chain of cognitive processing containing both assertions of content (factual and normative) and logical reasoning. No wonder there are many occasions for errors in thinking, and also for disagreement among two parties, because the latter may have different perceptions, recollections, values, and different current interests (motivations). The case of disagreement with regard to justice judgments will receive special attention later.

No fixed temporal sequence is suggested by the order in which the elements are listed in Table 1. Further, note that the term *argument* does not exclusively refer to the overt verbal behavior of a party, because some or all of its elements may remain covert: the argument may be entertained merely in the mind of a conflict party.

TABLE 1. Elements of the Justice Argument in the Case of Extradyadic Comparison when Person A (Recipient) Requests a Resource (X) from Person B (Allocator)

Name of element	Description
A. Justice appeal	
1. Assertion of general justice priority	"Justice—and not (only) liking—should govern the comparative behavior of persons of category K (e.g., mother) toward persons of category L (e.g., her children)"
2. Factual assertion of category membership[a]	"You belong to category K" "C and I belong to category L"
3. Assertion of particular justice priority (Conclusion from 1 & 2)	"Justice should govern your comparative behavior toward me and C"
B. Justice account	
4. Assertion of general priority of a certain justice principle[b]	"In contexts of type S, that is, having the characteristics[c] (a) (concerning attributes of allocator) (b) (concerning attributes of recipients) (c) (concerning attributes of resource) (d) (concerning attributes of situation) justice means (primarily) that comparative treatment be governed by the principle of (e.g.) strict equality."
5. Factual characterization of given context	"The present context has characteristics (a), (b), (c), and (d)"
6. Assertion of particular priority of a certain justice principle (Conclusion from 4 & 5)	"In the present context justice means strictly equal treatment"
7. Comparative fact assertion	"C has received X from you"
8. Justice judgment (Conclusion from 6 & 7)	"It would be just if you gave me X" (and/or:) "It would be unjust if you did not give me X"
C. Proposition of action obligation	
9. (Conclusion from 3 & 8)	"You have an obligation to give me X"

[a]"Category" here is very close to "social role." This implies that if conflict parties are not in some kind of social role relationship (broadly defined)—and be it only the role of fellow human being—justice will not be seen to be obligatory.

[b]I am presupposing here that a person has a notion of what form justice should take in a context such as the given one. That "form" can be said to be a justice principle (or distribution rule). Several classifications of such justice principles have been offered, the most familiar in justice research being the strict equality, equity (or contribution), and need principles (e.g., Deutsch, 1975; for a more differentiated list of distributive justice rules, see Reis, 1984). Much research has concerned the conditions under which one of these rules will be preferred by allocators or observers (see Mikula, 1980).

[c]It is not suggested that a conflict party attends to all the four classes of characteristics (or some other classification of characteristics). A frequent case is that in which person A invokes a certain justice principle (e.g., one that supports his request), without attention to any conditions necessary for the principle to be accepted as valid. Person B will then point to certain characteristics of the present context by virtue of which the validity of the proposed justice principle is to be disputed. (Here we have an instance of justice conflict.) For example, a pupil (A) requests something from his teacher, invoking the equality principle and pointing to the fact that another pupil has been granted the same request (number 7). The teacher may reply that equal treatment is not obligatory in the present context because a certain attribute is not given (e.g., the teacher notes that he is the tutor of the other pupil but not of A; or he notes that the other pupil has "earned" the granting of the request through good homework, thereby asserting a different justice principle).

Table 1 addresses only the case of extradyadic comparison (e.g., when a son demands something from his father and is trying to buttress his request by pointing out that his brother has previously received the requested resource). This restriction is due only to reasons of easier formulation and space limitation. The analysis applies also to the case of intradyadic comparison. The interesting differences in the effects of these two kinds of comparison for our topic cannot be pursued here.

JUSTICE CONSIDERATIONS IN INTERPERSONAL CONFLICT: CONDITIONS OF OCCURRENCE AND EFFECTS

The term *justice consideration* is used to encompass any ideas or statements connected with justice (as defined above). Thus, justice considerations may be present covertly (as justice thoughts in the mind of a conflict party) or overtly (as justice statements constituting part of the conflict parties' verbal exchange). Taking up these two levels separately in the two main parts of this section, I will attempt to describe their types, suggest some principal conditions under which they occur, and— as the main focus of interest—analyze their effects on conflict resolution. In this section I will consider only the (simpler) situation (or stage) in which no disagreement on B's part is manifest concerning A's justice-related statements. The case of disagreement will be discussed in the section on justice conflict.

A first classification of justice considerations corresponds to the various elements of the justice argument. We may distinguish among a justice appeal, a justice account, and a proposition of action obligation. Further, we may distinguish beween factual assertions and normative assertions. And we may distinguish between various justice principles.

A second distinction is between justice considerations involving intradyadic comparisons and those involving extradyadic comparisons. Table 1 is concerned with the latter. It is plausible to assume that B's psychological reactions are different when he hears a comparison (e.g., an assertion of being advantaged) involving a third person than one involving himself. Generally speaking, the second type is probably more psychologically consequential as it touches on the relationship between A and B.

A third distinction is between the justice considerations of the active and of the passive party. For reasons of space, in most of the subsequent discussion attention will focus on the active party (A), but in general the analysis holds also for B (e.g., with appropriate substitution of the term *request* with "rejection of A's request").

A final classification of justice considerations is into self-serving and other-serving ones. The justice considerations entertained by A are defined as self-serving when speaking for his request, and as other-serving when speaking against his request.[6] A hypothesis on self-serving bias will be presented later.

AT THE INTRA-INDIVIDUAL LEVEL: JUSTICE THOUGHTS

Conditions of the Occurrence of Justice Thoughts

A justice thought may occur because an interpersonal comparison has imposed itself. For example, A observes C receiving X from B, triggering in himself a desire for X (e.g., through a sense of "relative deprivation").

The more usual case is presumably that in which A entertains a desire that could be fulfilled through an appropriate act on B's part. Now, A may feel the need to buttress a respective request vis-à-vis B, which occasions a (covert) search for supporting information, justice considerations constituting one type of relevant information. However, it may also occur to A that his request—if granted—would create a state of imbalance (in his favor), which in turn may generate in him ideas on how to create anticipatory justice (e.g., through promising future reciprocation).

Persons vary in the strength of what might be called a "justice filter," through which they put any request that they might direct to another, testing its moral acceptability. As justice arguments also contain judgments of fact, reality provides another filter, which might be called the "reality test" (for example, concerning the truth of the "comparative fact assertion"). On the result of this test depends, of course, the viability of the argument for use as an influence instrument vis-à-vis the opposite party.

In sum, the occurrence of justice thoughts depends on the situation and on the person. A more detailed discussion—which also would specify the conditions of occurrence of various types of justice considerations—is beyond the limits of this chapter.

Effects of Justice Thoughts

Assumption of a Bias toward Self-Serving Justice Thoughts. As a general hypothesis it is suggested that in (potential) interpersonal conflicts, self-serving justice thoughts are more likely to occur than other-serving ones.

---

[6]This definition seems appropriate here as we are concerned with egoistic requests (see footnote 4). In other contexts a justice consideration supporting one's request may well constitute support for the other's interests.

This hypothesis derives from the assumption that in any situation individuals are more likely to consider and process information that is helpful to furthering their own need satisfaction. Thus, a person (A) entertaining a request will consider information that is apt to help making that request successful. And a person (B), confronted with a request implying some cost for him, is more likely to search for information that may help him to ward off the request than for information that would help support the request. The exceptions—the limiting conditions—to the above general hypothesis linking self-interest and justice considerations would be particularly worthwhile to study. (See the last section of this chapter for further relevant discussion.)

Some conditions can be hypothesized to affect the bias toward self-serving justice thoughts. First, the greater one's ego-involvement (i.e., the stronger A's need for X, and the greater B's cost in granting X) the stronger will be that bias. Second, the stronger one's (general) justice motive, the more "objectively" will he scan his memory and/or the environment for justice-relevant information bearing on voicing a request (in the case of A) or on accepting or rejecting a request (in the case of B).

How Do Self-Serving and Other-Serving Justice Thoughts Affect Conflict Resolution? Self-serving justice considerations on the part of A/B (initiator/recipient of a request) are likely to facilitate the occurrence of conflict and to impede its resolution (because they are likely to strengthen the respective party's insistence/resistance tendency), whereas other-serving justice considerations are likely to impede the occurrence of conflict and to facilitate its resolution (because they are likely to weaken one's insistence/resistance tendency).

The twin constructs of insistence tendency and resistance tendency seem useful with a view to tying the present framework to theories of action or decision making. The term *tendency*, referring to the resultant of forces disposing one to act in a certain direction, is due to the theorizing of Atkinson and his associates (e.g., Atkinson & Birch, 1978).

The effect of justice considerations on conflict (and conflict resolution) may be mediated through various psychological processes, for example, greater assurance on A's part that his request is morally acceptable.

What factors affect the extent to which any given self-serving justice thought in fact enhances conflict? One important aspect is likely to be the subjective validity of the justice consideration (e.g., A's subjective certainty that his justice judgment is correct); another would seem to be the subjective importance of the particular justice issue (e.g., how important is it to A that there generally be equal treatment in the given respect).

Furthermore, the awareness of being treated unjustly (in particular, less favorably than another) may be accompanied by negative emotions (e.g., anger), which impede conflict resolution. Negative emotions are especially likely to be present when the justice consideration was the occasion for the request (and thus for the conflict) in the first place, as in Scanzoni's (1972) analysis of marital conflict. The kind and intensity of negative emotions triggered by the awareness of (unfavorable) injustice depends on many factors, including the attribution of causality regarding the injustice. The more the injustice is attributed to the opposite party, seen to be under the latter's control, and seen as intentional, the more likely is the awareness of injustice accompanied by negative emotions, especially anger (cf. Cohen, 1982; Greenberg, 1984; Hassebrauck, 1984; Utne & Kidd, 1980).

AT THE INTERINDIVIDUAL LEVEL: JUSTICE STATEMENTS

To this point, attention has been focused on justice considerations as they occur merely in the mind of a conflict party. The question now becomes, When will justice thoughts be expressed, and what are the likely effects of such justice statements? Usually in a conflict—or, more generally, in a request situation—not all of the elements of the full justice argument will be voiced (either because the speaker does not have the complete argument in his mind or is unable to present them in a coherent way—perhaps because of emotional arousal—or because he intentionally suppresses some of the elements). Part of the justice-related verbal exchange will consist in the other party asking for substantiation (e.g., for a fuller justice account) or voicing disagreement with one or more of the propositions contained in A's justice statement (see the section on justice conflict).

Conditions of Occurrence of Justice Statements

Two kinds of justice statements can be distinguished: those constituting instrumental behavior and those constituting emotional-expressive behavior. This distinction does not imply two discrete forms of behavior but refers to the degree to which a particular justice statement is under rational control (in the sense of means–ends calculations) versus under emotional (arousal) control.

The Justice Statement as Instrumental Behavior. As with any behavior under rational control, the individual will consider the consequences of voicing a justice statement and the likelihood of these consequences. The consequence of primary interest for A is getting his request fulfilled. As a general hypothesis it is suggested that an individual will use a justice statement when, overall, its anticipated effect of furthering his conflict goal outweighs any other possible negative effects (such as creating additional conflict if the other party disagrees with the justice judgment, or generating reactance on the part of the other, or causing the other to "leave the field").

The Justice Statement as Emotional-Expressive Behavior. The more person A is emotionally aroused—for whatever reason (including, of course, anger about having received unjust treatment)—the more likely he will be to express the thoughts that are dominant in his mind concerning his request; and the less likely will he be to consider objectively the possible consequences of such verbal acts. In the present context this means that once there is (as assumed here) a self-serving justice consideration, the more likely will one be to voice it when emotionally aroused.

An additional hypothesis is that with increasing level of arousal the justice argument will be voiced in a more truncated form, and cognitively simpler elements will be voiced (in particular, those constituting end assertions—Nos. 3, 8, and 9 in Table 1—instead of those providing reasons). In the extreme form, this becomes manifest in the reproach "you are being unjust" as a simple expression of deprivation for which the addressee is seen as responsible.

Effects of Justice Statements

A justice argument is a complex type of persuasive communication. Thus, in a detailed analysis of the conditions under which such a communication affects the recipient's beliefs (here: B's justice judgment) and behavior (B's compliance with A's request), it would be important to apply the research on attitude change, with special attention to the attitude–behavior relationship (see Cialdini, Petty, & Cacioppo, 1981, for a recent review). Concerning the latter, a particularly interesting case is the one where B remains personally unconvinced and yet complies in view of possible sanctions from an (actual or imagined) audience sharing A's justice views.

A few questions worthy of research follow. At which point should the justice argument be introduced in order to be optimally effective? (Before, along with, or after the request?) How does the temporal order of elements within the justice argument affect the other's reaction? What effects does it have if one or more of the elements are missing from the justice statement? What are the comparative effects of the different elements (stated singly or in various combinations)?

Special note should be made of the possibility that B claims that he does not have the resources necessary for carrying out the requested action. For example, if the requested action involves motor behavior, information, or money, person B may simply not, at the time given, have available the physical ability, information, or money. Thus, although he acknowledges the action obligation, he may plead a lack of capability. Alternatively B may point to his lack of ability and assert that therefore A is not being fair in demanding this respective action. This may generate a "justice dispute" (to be discussed later).

There are some not so obvious possible psychological effects of a justice argument on the recipient. Because a justice argument implies that not fulfilling the request would mean upholding an unjust state of affairs, it conveys a message of moral insufficiency. Thus there is in fact an implied threat to B's self-esteem and potentially his social esteem. However, fulfilling a request under such conditions may have attributional consequences such that B sees himself as thereby acknowledging that there was indeed a state of injustice and, further, that he himself was responsible for that injustice. In sum, the justice argument is a message that may convey rather unpleasant connotations to a sensitive B. It is suggested that this creates in him a state similar to psychological reactance—a desire to reinstate his freedom (for positive self-perception) by refusing (or delaying) acceptance of the request; it may also result in negative feelings vis-à-vis A (Brehm, 1966).

Of course, negative affect may also be aroused in B through (a) the sheer experience of the threat of having to give up something, as entailed by the justice statement; and (b) the cognitive incongruence engendered by the reception of a justice statement that is at odds with his own preexisting beliefs.

In sum, a justice argument is accepted only under special conditions. Due to the implications of a (self-serving) justice argument for its recipient—namely, he would have to act against his immediate interest— his dominant response (in the sense of the first impulse) is to reject the requester's justice-related assertions and to scan his memory and/or the environment selectively for counterarguments. Thus, a justice argument is quite likely to result in justice conflict.

JUSTICE CONFLICT

TYPES AND PSYCHOLOGICAL CONCOMITANTS OF JUSTICE CONFLICT

The parties may disagree on any of the nine kinds of assertions contained in the (complete) justice argument. (To be sure, some of these are logically linked with each other, but others are mutually independent.) These may be divided into factual assertions (Nos. 2, 5, and 7), normative assertions (Nos. 1 and 4), and combinations of these two

(Nos. 3, 6, 8, and 9). The processes involved in factual and normative disagreements will differ in some respects, related to the distinction between normative and informational influence (Deutsch & Gerard, 1955).

From another perspective, we may, in some cases, speak of attributional conflict (in the larger sense), namely whenever the disagreement is over an attributional judgment (cf. Cohen, 1982). It may stem from the "fundamental attributional bias" (Ross, 1977), by which a person's attributional beliefs are brought in line with his needs. For example, in No. 5, the disagreement might lie in the parties' different recollections regarding their causal contributions to the resource of which A is requesting a share.

For reasons of space I will limit myself largely in the following to disagreement concerning justice judgment, neglecting disagreement concerning the priority of justice (Nos. 1–3).

Concomitants

The awareness of justice-judgment conflict may elicit (interrelated) reactions at different levels: cognitive (e.g., covert information processing on the source of the discrepancy), affective (e.g., disappointment, negative interpersonal feelings), and behavioral (e.g., asking for substantiation, attempts at persuasion). The cognitive and affective reactions may operate as determinants of the controversy in their own right and they may also affect the behavioral reactions. The latter constitute the justice dispute.

THE JUSTICE DISPUTE

Descriptive Analysis

A justice dispute is one type of controversy. It refers to all behaviors, verbal and nonverbal, that are related to the justice disagreement. It may involve instrumental behaviors (e.g., persuasion attempts) as well as emotional-expressive behaviors. Attention is focused here especially on the *justice-judgment* dispute.

In an ideal type of justice-judgment dispute, one party gives his own account of his justice judgment and asks the other party to do likewise. The two justice accounts would contain information on all of the elements noted in Table 1.

In an actual dispute the justice account will be more fragmentary. Hence the other party may ask one to be clearer and to provide additional information; he may voice disagreement, provide counterinformation, and so on. In addition, there may be emotional-expressive reactions accompanying any of the assertions at the verbal and the nonverbal level.

All of this occurs along with the behaviors constituting the primary controversy (conflict of interest). However, the justice dispute may become autonomous and be uncoupled; depending on the centrality of the justice issue, this conflict may become more important and more consuming to the parties than the primary conflict (of interest), especially when basic justice principles and their applicability are at issue.

The justice conflict becomes more complex when one or both of the parties change the levels at which comparisons are made—usually going from the more specific (e.g., where single instances of transaction are compared and balanced against each other) to the more general (where, in the extreme case, the justice inherent in the entire relationship history is at issue). This may involve new justice issues and thus new justice-judgment conflicts.

The Outcome of Justice Conflict and Its Determinants

Outcome, in the narrow sense, here refers to change in the two parties' positions on the judgmental issue at hand when the justice dispute has ended. The two simplest possible outcomes are no change (continuing disagreement) and agreement (one party accepts the other's position, or both accept a modified judgment).

In both cases there may also be covert changes (e.g., regarding judgmental certainty; note also the possibility of overt acceptance but internal nonacceptance of the other's justice judgment).

A primary determinant of agreement likelihood is the persuasiveness of the other's justice-related communication. This was considered earlier when focusing on effects of justice statements. In the present case, where two discrepant positions have been voiced, the communications from both parties may be persuasive (e.g., well reasoned and articulated). This would make agreement rather less likely if both are highly committed to their positions (i.e., if there is high commitment to the underlying values and/or interests and if there are strong needs to present an image of consistency).

Commitment may be considered as an intervening variable that is related to other factors. Some of these will be mentioned in the following in terms of tentative hypotheses. A justice-judgment dispute is more likely to end in agreement when (a) the disagreement is over factual (versus normative) justice issues, (b) the justice principle in question is not central to a party, (c) a party's confidence in his judgment is low, and (d) the primary conflict issue is not important. The rationale and the limiting conditions for these hypotheses cannot be explicated here, for reasons of space.

Finally, the parties' readiness to publicly change their justice positions may be affected by the psychological concomitants (especially affective ones) of the awareness of justice-judgment conflict, mentioned earlier.

It is emphasized that the above factors are not mutually independent and that they may operate interactively in any particular case.

SIGNIFICANCE OF JUSTICE CONFLICT FOR THE OUTCOME OF THE PRIMARY CONFLICT

The justice conflict and the way it is handled may affect the outcome of the primary conflict (a) directly, through the quasi-logical consequences resulting from the outcome of the justice-judgment conflict; and (b) indirectly, through the psychological concomitants of the justice conflict and of the ensuing dispute. Only the former will be considered here.

As regards justice-judgment conflict, it seems helpful to distinguish between parties' public positions and private positions on the judgmental issue. There are four combinations of the two pairs of alternatives (if we consider the reaction of B): B accepts A's justice judgment (a) publicly and also privately, (b) publicly but not privately, (c) privately but not publicly, (d) neither privately nor publicly. (Of course, these are not the only possible outcomes concerning the justice-judgment issue; there is, after all, some room for acceptance of the other's judgment after a certain amount of revision by the latter. And there is also the possibility that no unambiguous statement of position regarding the justice judgment has been made.) I will compare only the two consonant cases (a) and (d). What, then, are the consequences for the resolution of the primary conflict when the justice-judgment conflict ends in agreement (e.g., B comes to accept A's justice argument), as compared to when disagreement persists?[7]

The answer is not simply that B, having accepted A's justice judgment, will also accept the action obligation and act as requested, thus solving the primary conflict. Whether he accepts the action-obligation conclusion depends on how compelling the justice argument is, that is, on the priority that B gives to justice in guiding his behavior (elements

---

[7]The conditions under which B's acceptance of A's justice judgment also leads to yielding on the request have been taken up earlier, when discussing the effects of justice statements (in the absence of justice conflict). Strictly considered, the present discussion concerns only factors affecting the significance of B's acceptance of A's justice judgment after prior disagreement—over and above the factors holding for the previous case.

1–3 in Table 1). Further, such acceptance depends on whether there are other behaviors, more preferable (e.g., less costly) to him, through which he could serve justice. Thus B might come to offer something else, comparable in value, to A. This might end the conflict (if A is satisfied) or it might lead to additional verbal exchange and bargaining. As noted above when discussing the effects of justice statements, the factors affecting the attitude–behavior relationships would have to be considered in a complete discussion of the effects of justice agreement on conflict resolution (i.e., on action such as compliance and request withdrawal).

CONCLUSIONS

In the case of justice conflict, what effects will self-serving justice statements introduced by A have on conflict resolution? I will compare each of the two varieties of this situation constituted by the two possible outcomes (agreement and continuing disagreement) with the case where no justice statements at all were introduced by A. A requester often faces this decision situation (where the risky alternative is that of introducing a justice statement). The rationales for the following general hypotheses will be left largely unexplicated as these hypotheses are conclusions from the earlier discussion.

First, consider the (presumably more likely) case where the justice conflict does not end in agreement. In this case conflict resolution will be impeded.

Now consider the (less likely) case where the justice conflict does end in agreement. Let us first presuppose that party B is the one who comes to accept—privately and publicly—A's justice judgment. In this case conflict resolution will be facilitated, mainly because B will feel pressure to comply and (if he cannot comply for lack of resources) he will be motivated to engage in joint problem-solving discussion.

Let us now presuppose that party A is the one who comes to accept the other's justice position. Here there is also ground for expecting conflict resolution to be facilitated, but less so than in the first case, because A's initial motivation for the request is likely to persist (except when his request was occasioned by justice considerations in the first place). Hence A might turn to other arguments (e.g., the social responsibility norm) or perhaps even to stronger pressure behaviors (e.g., threat) in order to ensure compliance.

As suggested earlier, agreement over matters of justice on which a dispute has arisen is an unlikely outcome (and hence, by the way, a third party may be necessary), and continuing disagreement the more likely one. If that is so, then justice considerations that engender justice conflict are generally more likely than not to impede conflict resolution.

Going a step further, I submit that the introduction of justice statements is more likely than not to engender justice conflict. If this is so, then—overall—we must conclude that (self-serving) justice statements are more likely to impede than to facilitate conflict resolution.

Yet the picture may not be so gloomy, as justice considerations brought into a conflict (or potential conflict) are not always egoistic; they may be motivated by other than egoistic concerns.

THE ROLE OF DIFFERENT JUSTICE MOTIVATIONS[8]

Justice Considerations Motivated by Self-Interest

When the primary motivation is self-interest, a party selectively (but not necessarily in a calculated way) generates information (e.g., social comparisons) apt to legitimize his position vis-à-vis the other party and/or to delegitimize the other's position. As discussed above such thoughts and statements will impede conflict resolution directly by strengthening a person's tendency to defend his interest, and indirectly through negative sentiments arising when parties disagree in their justice-related judgments.

Justice Considerations Motivated by Genuine Moral Concern

When the genuine desire for justice is the primary motivation underlying justice considerations, no global prediction as to their effect on conflict resolution seems possible at first glance. Here the information processing is unselective in so far as it is guided primarily by one's basic general convictions concerning justice. Such neutral justice considerations, on the one hand, provide a filter preventing one's egoistic desires from being translated into unfairly high demands on another person. On the other hand, they may give a person the legitimated courage for voicing his request (or for his rejection of the other's request) and for upholding that position during a controversy. This may create conflict in the first place, and delay subsequent conflict resolution. By the same token, however, a person may feel compelled by justice considerations

---

[8]These motivations, to be defined below, may be present in the same instance of conflict. For example, party A may see himself as using a given justice argument, supporting his request, for the sake of justice (genuine moral concern), and (perhaps at a later stage) for the sake of helping the other to accept a "solution" to their "joint problem." It would seem worthwhile to investigate how conflict parties and observers assign given justice arguments (in particular, justice judgments) to these three motive classes.

to refrain from voicing a request (when he thinks that would be unfair), thus precluding conflict (and perhaps any interaction). And, just as important, the recipient of a request may feel compelled by genuine moral concern to yield to the other's request even when that is personally quite unpleasant.

In the case where the (morally motivated) justice consideration happens to support one's own position, conflict resolution may be impeded—and even more strongly than if it were (merely) motivated by self-interest—when the opposite party does not come to agree with one's justice position. Especially when B refuses to accept the proposition of action obligation (number 9 in Table 1), A will experience moral outrage, engendering negative affect that would impede conflict resolution. Or again, when both A and B are motivated by genuine moral concern (in the extreme case, by justice fanaticism) and they disagree as to which justice principle is applicable in their particular situation (see Table 1, number 4), the justice dispute may become uncoupled from the primary conflict and the negative affects may be particularly intense.

Justice Considerations Motivated By a Problem-Solving Orientation

The third type of motivation is of particular relevance in a type of situation that has so far received little attention: the bilateral-request conflict. In this situation the parties recognize that they have a joint problem, whose solution—if both parties are to be satisfied—requires that they find a mutual arrangement. Now justice rules may provide a foundation from which such an arrangement can be derived. These rules may be distributive justice norms written into various laws and similar social statutes (e.g., inheritance laws), or existing in unwritten form in a social community,[9] or they may be dyad-specific rules developed in the course of the dyad's history—in written form (as in the case of a marriage contract) or in unwritten form.

Clearly, in this case conflict resolution is facilitated by justice considerations of the kind described. Of course, various conditions must be met in any specific case of conflict for the parties to turn to justice norms in the first place and for the facilitating effect in fact to obtain. For example, an adverse circumstance would occur if the parties disagreed regarding the interpretation of a particular norm; however, this

[9]In the competitive case, two examples are (a) the rule that he who comes first has the right to the parking space, and (b) the throwing of a coin to guarantee each an equal chance for obtaining the scarce resource. In the cooperative case, two examples are (a) the rule that a concession made in the course of the negotiation should be reciprocated, and (b) the rule that each should benefit equally from the bargaining deal.

still leaves the possibility of turning to a third party to settle the latter dispute. Also, when there are marked power differences, the weaker party is more likely, and the stronger party less likely, to entertain, invoke, and be persuaded by, justice considerations (see Cohen, Chapter 4, this volume). This would seem especially to apply to the competitive type of situation.

As noted earlier, the distinction between unilateral-request and bilateral-request conflict may fade away in any given instance. For example, a conflict episode may start with a unilateral request (e.g., that the other person do a certain piece of work) and trigger off a controversy that, in a later episode, may turn the conflict into a bilateral-request type, where both parties come together in search of a solution to "their problem"; the original issue has turned into the more general issue of finding an arrangement (e.g., how generally to divide up work duties). This later, bilateral, episode may involve the application of a justice norm (as outlined above), and it may also involve the negotiating of a dyad-specific norm concerning such matters for the future.

CONCLUDING REMARKS

The present chapter represents merely a first step in studying the role of justice considerations in interpersonal conflict. The domain of the analysis has been limited in various ways. I have focused exclusively on distributive justice, to the neglect of procedural justice, which is important in conflict resolution. In addition, I have largely limited myself to one type of conflict situation (unilateral request). Further, I have focused on the active (requesting) party in a conflict, and have not systematically discussed differences between initiator and recipient of the request as regards the role of justice considerations.

On the other hand, the present framework has a broader domain of application than indicated so far, as it may prove useful in analyzing justice-related thinking and communication in situations other than conflict. Further, this framework might be fruitfully extended to intergroup conflict.

There is little if any empirical research bearing directly on the two questions that are central to the present topic: (a) when do justice considerations (thoughts and statements) occur, and what are they like? and (b) what are the functions (effects) of justice considerations?[10] Linked together, these two foci—the descriptive and the functional—lead to a

---

[10]Most relevant to the present, communication-oriented, approach is the research by Herrmann and Winterhoff on types of verbal requests and styles of argumentation (Herrmann, 1982, Chapter 6; Winterhoff-Spurk & Herrmann, 1981).

decision-making analysis (e.g., under what conditions will a party use justice statements, and to what ends?). The differentiation into emotional-expressive and instrumental justice statements is relevant along this line, where the ultimate goal would be to help conflict participants become more aware of the beneficial and detrimental powers of justice considerations and thus help them use and deal with them more judiciously.

Acknowledgments

I thank Peter Schettgen and Ulrike Six for helpful comments on earlier drafts. I am particularly grateful to Hans Werner Bierhoff and to Ron Cohen for many suggestions that helped improve this chapter.

REFERENCES

Atkinson, J. W., & Birch, D. (1978). *Introduction to motivation* (2nd ed.). New York: Van Nostrand.

Austin, W., & Tobiasen, J. (1982). Moral evaluation in intimate relationships. In J. Greenberg & R. L. Cohen (Eds.), *Equity and justice in social behavior* (pp. 217–259). New York: Academic Press.

Brehm, J. W. (1966). *A theory of psychological reactance*. New York: Academic Press.

Brehmer, B., & Hammond, K. R. (1977). Cognitive factors in interpersonal conflict. In D. Druckman (Ed.), *Negotiations: Social-psychological perspectives* (pp. 79–103). Beverly Hills, CA: Sage.

Cialdini, R. B., Petty, R. E., & Cacioppo, J. T. (1981). Attitude and attitude change. *Annual Review of Psychology, 32,* 357–404.

Cohen, R. L. (1982). Perceiving justice: An attributional perspective. In J. Greenberg & R. L. Cohen (Eds.), *Equity and justice in social behavior* (pp. 119–160). New York: Academic Press.

Deutsch, M. (1973). *The resolution of conflict: Constructive and destructive processes*. New Haven: Yale University Press.

Deutsch, M. (1975). Equity, equality, and need: What determines which value will be used as the basis of distributive justice? *Journal of Social Issues, 31,* 137–149.

Deutsch, M., & Gerard, H. B. (1955). A study of normative and informational influences on social judgment. *Journal of Abnormal and Social Psychology, 51,* 629–636.

Greenberg, J. (1984). On the apocryphal nature of inequity distress. In R. Folger (Ed.), *The sense of injustice: Social psychological perspectives* (pp. 167–186). New York: Plenum Press.

Greenberg, J., & Cohen, R. L. (1982). Why justice? Normative and instrumental interpretations. In J. Greenberg & R. L. Cohen (Eds.), *Equity and justice in social behavior* (pp. 437–469). New York: Academic Press.

Hassebrauck, M. (1984). *Emotionale Konsequenzen distributiver Ungerechtigkeit* [Emotional consequences of distributive injustice]. Regensburg: Roderer.

Herrmann, T. (1982). *Sprechen und Situation* [Speech and situation.]. Berlin: Springer-Verlag.

Holm, K. (1970). *Verteilung und Konflikt* [Distribution and conflict]. Stuttgart: Enke.

Holmes, J. G., & Miller, D. T. (1976). Interpersonal conflict. In J. W. Thibaut, J. T. Spence, & R. C. Carson (Eds.), *Contemporary topics in social psychology* (pp. 265–307). Morristown, NJ: General Learning Press.

Lamm, H. (1975). *Analyse des Verhandelns* [Analysis of negotiation]. Stuttgart: Enke.

Lamm, H., Kayser, E., & Schwinger, T. (1982). Justice norms and other determinants of allocation and negotiation behavior. In M. Irle (Ed.), *Decision making: Social-psychological and socio-economic analyses* (pp. 359–410). Berlin: De Gruyter.

Mikula, G. (1980). On the role of justice in allocation decisions. In G. Mikula (Ed.), *Justice and social interaction* (pp. 127–166). Bern: Huber; New York: Springer.

Mikula, G. (1984). Justice and fairness in interpersonal relations: Thoughts and suggestions. In H. Tajfel (Ed.), *The social dimension: European developments in social psychology* (Vol. 1, pp. 204–227). Cambridge: Cambridge University Press.

Peterson, D. R. (1983). Conflict. In H. H. Kelley, E. Berscheid, A. Christensen, J. H. Harvey, T. L. Huston, G. Levinger, E. McClintock, L. A. Peplau, & D. R. Peterson, (Eds.), *Close relationships* (pp. 360–396). New York: W. H. Freeman.

Pruitt, D. G. (1972). Methods for resolving differences of interest: A theoretical analysis. *Journal of Social Issues, 28*, 133–154.

Pruitt, D. G. (1982). *Negotiation behavior*. New York: Academic Press.

Reis, H. T. (1984). The multidimensionality of justice. In R. Folger (Ed.), *The sense of injustice: Social psychological perspectives* (pp. 25–61). New York: Plenum Press.

Ross, L. (1977). The intuitive psychologist and his shortcomings. In L. Berkowitz (Ed.), *Advances in experimental social psychology* (Vol. 10, pp. 173–220). New York: Academic Press.

Scanzoni, J. (1972). *Sexual bargaining*. Englewood Cliffs, NJ: Prentice-Hall.

Thibaut, J. W., & Walker, L. (1978). A theory of procedure. *California Law Review, 66*, 541–566.

Utne, M. C., & Kidd, R. F. (1980). Equity and attribution. In G. Mikula (Ed.), *Justice and social interaction* (pp. 63–93). Bern: Huber; New York: Springer.

Winterhoff-Spurk, P., & Herrmann, T. (1981). *Auffordern bei der Gewinnaufteilung* [Stating requests in allocation situations]. Unpublished manuscript, Universität Mannheim, West Germany.

Chapter 4

Power and Justice in Intergroup Relations

RONALD L. COHEN

INTRODUCTION

Why do victims of injustice seem so rarely to challenge, rebel against, or press for systematic change in the factors responsible for their condition? This chapter explores certain aspects of this question, employing a wide variety of evidence from the social psychological literature on justice and revolutionary coalitions. Before proceeding, two potential objections to the perspective taken here must be mentioned.

First, one potential objection concerns an assumption implicit in the question: that victims of injustice only rarely challenge or press for systematic change. It is possible to point to dramatic instances of extreme injustice and degradation in which attempts at collective challenge were absent (cf. Hochschild, 1981; and especially Moore, 1978), but it is difficult to specify the characteristics of "significant collective challenge." In addition, as more historical information becomes available on these instances, many more examples of individual and collective resistance come to light. Such information provides an important corrective to depictions of the unjustly disadvantaged as docile or willingly accepting of their fate, but the question posed here retains its force.

RONALD L. COHEN • Social Science Division, Bennington College, Bennington, VT 05201.

Second, it might be argued that the question assumes some objective, or at least widely agreed upon, meaning of injustice. A related version of this concern is the assertion that it substitutes the judgment of the observer for the judgment of the person whose conduct is under examination. There should be little doubt that these dangers exist, but if, as so much contemporary social psychological theorizing suggests, people's conduct is only meaningful in terms of the understanding they have of it, then the failure to act in situations where it seems reasonable to expect action is as much in need of explanation as the expected action. This realization, and its consequences, are especially important when matters of power, domination, and justice are at stake. So, although there are dangers in assuming that "real injustices exist" and that the absence of attempts to alleviate them needs to be understood, there is a different set of dangers attendant upon the assumption that injustices exist primarily (or only) in the eyes of the beholder and that only what is easily describable as overt action can be understood. If social psychological work on these issues is to avoid "employing justice in the service of sustaining the existing arrangements of social power and privilege," (Sampson, Chapter 5, this volume) precisely the question posed here, with its dangers, must be considered.

It must also be examined systematically. The position taken in this chapter is that individuals and groups with the power to make crucial allocative decisions also have at their beck and call other resources that inhibit those with less power from developing certain understandings and from taking the collective action that might follow from those understandings. The major sections of the chapter will focus on three different sets of processes through which the reproduction of injustice occurs: (a) the masking of group differences in power, (b) the use of divisive tactics, and (c) the introduction of symbols of the just consideration of conflicting interests. Before getting to those discussions, it is necessary to offer a short, and critical, discussion of the ways in which the relationship between power and justice has been addressed in recent social psychological work.

JUSTICE AND POWER

In a recent chapter on justice, Hogan and Emler (1981) criticize current psychological work on justice as inappropriately focused on distributive justice. They suggest this focus is misguided for several reasons, one of which is particularly important here:

> [D]istributive justice . . . reflects a power holder's view of the world. How to distribute resources defensibly is a problem that concerns deans, parents, political leaders, and other persons who must keep peace among the flock

> that they tend. They are concerned with keeping the system running. The members of the flock are concerned with keeping themselves running—they rarely consider how to allocate the available resources fairly. They are primarily interested in getting their fair share, and this is quite a different issue. (p. 129)

Hogan and Emler (1981) argue not only that the problems of distributive justice are the problems of powerholders, but that it is their unique concern.

> Not only are power holders concerned with distributive justice, but they must also have power at their disposal to enforce its claims. In short, distributive justice is linked to power in that it is a principal concern of fair-minded power holders, and power is necessary to ensure that the requirements of distributive justice are met. (p. 141)

Members of the flock are not interested in distributive justice, only their own well-being. Leaders are not interested in distributive justice either; they are concerned primarily about being able to defend their distributive decisions in order to "keep peace."

There is a great deal of evidence that contradicts the picture Hogan and Emler (1981) paint of "the flock." At the same time, they have identified a crucial fact often overlooked in discussions of distributive justice: those who distribute resources have considerable power over those to whom resources are distributed. Those in power have an interest in "keeping the system running," and, in order to do so, must limit disruptions. However, at the same time that Hogan and Emler call attention to this crucial fact, their imagery diverts their and our attention from considering the implications of the structure of power.

"Keeping peace among the flock" suggests both a paternalistic concern on the part of the powerful, and a childlike innocence and ignorance of the responsibilities of power by the powerless. In addition, the imagery suggests that each member of the flock has interests that conflict with the interest of others ("keep peace among the flock"), but not with the powerful. The person or group in power is portrayed without interests except the performance of the allocative function. One must somehow imagine that deans, parents, political leaders, and owners and managers of profit-making enterprises (a category curiously absent from Hogan and Emler's list) merely "preside" over a set of distributional practices. Somehow we are to imagine leaders who merely want to keep a system running, a system in which their own position and interests are not involved, and to imagine a flock of followers motivated primarily by their own self- and selfish interests.

This is powerful imagery, and in certain respects it may capture the understanding those with different amounts of power bring to situations involving the allocation of scarce and valuable resources. But one must ask whether it is an accurate description of these situations.

A significant portion of the argument made later is that those with real interests to hide will invoke precisely this imagery of the disinterested, neutral, and impartial presider, or more accurately, judge. This attempt is described very accurately by Edelman (1977):

> For authorities and dominant social groups, political situations that call atten-
> tion to adversary interests and to the forms of power available to the inter-
> ested groups are risky. . . . The employment of force to suppress resistance
> or dissent engenders fears of the arbitrary and despotic use of power . . .
> [However] by clouding the recognition of adversary interests, by presenting
> authorities as helping and rehabilitative, it symbolizes the constriction of elite
> power within narrow limits. Public attention then focuses on procedures
> rather than outcomes, so that the power to coerce, degrade, and confuse
> dissidents is greater. (pp. 133–134)

The attempt made in the present chapter to demonstrate the ways in which the powerful exercise their power to forestall ameliorative action against injustice by the powerless owes a great deal to Lukes's (1975) discussion of power. In other words, I attempt here to discover in the social psychological literature on justice evidence of ways in which action against injustice is forestalled by the success of the powerful in prevailing in conflicts of interest over scarce and valuable resources, in excluding certain issues and potential actors from the arena of public debate, and in influencing 'and shaping the desires of the powerless so as to affect their understanding of their identities and interests.

PRIVATE PROBLEMS AND PUBLIC ISSUES

Under what conditions will an unjustly treated group act to rectify that injustice? It seems important to distinguish among three types of issues: (a) to what extent does the group define its condition as unjust? (b) to what extent is mobilization and collective action possible? and (c) what are the likely outcomes, positive and negative, of such mobilization? Each of these issues presents the members of unjustly treated groups, as individuals and as groups, with a set of considerations.

The large research literature stimulated by equity theory demonstrates that an unjustly disadvantaged individual may respond in several different ways. The person may revise the initial cognitive appraisal of the situation; this may involve a reinterpretation of his or her outcomes, identity, or previous actions. It can also involve a shift in the focus of the standard chosen for comparison; whereas someone may feel unjustly treated compared to person X, no such unjust treatment will be experienced in comparison to person Y. Unjustly disadvantaged individuals may also "leave the field," or "exit." Each of these options (identified by equity theory; Walster, Walster, & Berscheid, 1978) changes the situation in some way, but none corresponds to overt action directed at overcoming the injustice. Much of the literature on the individual's response to injustice should serve as a reminder of the variety of options available to someone confronting an unjust disadvantage, though "options" hardly seems appropriate as a description of someone with few resources confronting an injustice.

There is another important finding in the literature on individual responses to unjust disadvantage. Research designed to distinguish between private and public responses suggests that people are aware of what is expected of someone confronting an injustice, and they usually report beliefs and feelings that conform to those expectations. Rivera and Tedeschi (1976) demonstrated that unjustly advantaged subjects publicly report the predicted guilty discomfort, but privately experience pleasure, happiness, and satisfaction. Montada's work (Chapter 7, this volume) also suggests that at least some people report discomfort, sometimes in the form of existential guilt, at realizing the unjust disadvantage of others, but whether this publicly communicated guilt is also experienced privately is not clear.

There seems to be no experimental work comparable to the Rivera and Tedeschi (1976) study that focuses on unjustly disadvantaged subjects. It seems reasonable to suggest a similar discrepancy between their public reports and private feelings and beliefs. Because the expression of negative affect is generally regarded unfavorably, particularly when it might be directly expressed toward present others, private feelings of anger at unjust treatment may well be stronger than public expressions of such anger would suggest. In addition, public expression of guilt over one's unjust advantage often is accompanied by the knowledge that one's advantage came at the expense of another's unjust disadvantage. Such knowledge would provide even more reason for a public expression of guilt and discomfort. On the other hand, public expression of anger over one's unjust disadvantage may have no other social support or validation; it may be seen as "sour grapes," or as improper and undue attention to selfish or self-interested concerns. Thus, it may be interpreted as an expression of dissatisfaction, not injustice, as Hogan and Emler's (1981) characterization of the flock clearly suggests.

Finally, it is important to remember that the allocations that produced unjust advantage and disadvantage are structurally situated. In the type of situation being considered here, someone produced those allocations, had the power to do precisely that. Challenging that power by publicly objecting to the allocation requires, or is at least likely to stimulate, consideration of possible retaliation. Whereas both the unjustly advantaged and unjustly disadvantaged might consider the possibility of retaliation by an allocator, the fact that the allocator has "erred" in their favor is likely to make the advantaged less concerned about retaliation than those for whom the error produced an unjust disadvantage. These considerations obtain when a third party performs the allocation; when the allocator and the unjustly advantaged are one and the same, the consequences of possible retaliation are even clearer. Mikula's intriguing research (Chapter 6, this volume) confirms the thrust of these suggestions: in recalling their own experiences of injustice, people often report injustices perpetrated on them by those with greater power, and in none of those instances reported were attempts to persuade the other to rectify the injustice successful.

There is one more reason to expect that direct expressions of anger by the unjustly disadvantaged will be a rather pale reflection, in incidence and intensity, of their private reactions. It seems reasonable that both those advantaged and those disadvantaged by injustice would be aware of the discrepancy between the public and private reactions of each. This suggests that, though they might hear the unjustly advantaged proclaim their concern and guilt, the unjustly disadvantaged may be skeptical about the sincerity of those expressions. They might believe, and the available data support the validity of such a belief, that public expressions of concern over injustice by individuals (and groups) that benefit from them are not to be counted on. Furthermore, calling attention to this very fact publicly might itself be seen negatively, as ungrateful criticism of those who express sympathy. If this line of reasoning makes sense, it also seems reasonable to suggest that the unjustly advantaged (correctly) believe the unjustly disadvantaged to be more angry and indignant than the latter were demonstrating publicly. As a consequence, the advantaged might be convinced of the desirability and the necessity of close surveillance and restriction of the disadvantaged (cf. arguments of this sort by Dinnerstein, 1976, with regard to sexist injustice; and by Kovel, 1971, with regard to racist injustice).

The argument here has been that individuals as individuals confronted with their own unjust disadvantage may have strong feelings and thoughts about rectifying that injustice at the same time that they deny these feelings and thoughts public expression. At least some, and perhaps most, of the injustices suffered by individuals are the result of their social location in groups. All of the considerations that lead unjustly treated individuals to be wary of objecting publicly also confront individuals as members of groups subjected to collective injustices. As individuals, and as potential members of coalitions mobilized for action against these injustices, they confront several issues that highlight the role of powerful, advantaged individuals and groups. They must consider: (a) the legitimation of the structure of power; (b) mobilization for collective action; and (c) manipulation of the symbols of justice. Each will be considered in turn.

THE EFFECTS OF POWER

ENDORSEMENT, AUTHORIZATION, AND LEGITIMATION

One way to understand the processes by which the powerful structure situations to forestall collective action on the part of the less powerful is to examine the way in which power has been legitimized in the settings employed by social psychologists to study distributive justice. Despite their many differences, all the paradigms employed in this research lead subjects to understand that some identifiable person or persons has allocated a store of scarce and valuable resources among two or more recipients. What is always (with the exceptions to be noted below) background to this understanding is the process by which the power to allocate these resources was determined. Researchers are interested in how subjects will react to a distribution already determined, or how they will allocate resources themselves; what is necessary is that subjects accept as unquestionable the in-place distribution of allocative power.

Although the complete argument requires more attention than it can be given here (see Cohen, 1982, for a more complete version), the central point is that in order for them to focus their attention on the allocation of monetary resources that is the researcher's concern, subjects must be led to accept as legitimate, as just, the distribution of power within which the monetary allocation takes place. This is accomplished in most cases by convincing subjects either that the distribution of power was chance determined, or that in some central respect, it *is* equal.

In research on the mobilization of revolutionary coalitions, to be examined more fully in the next section, the structure of allocative power is not equal or randomly assigned but constructed on the basis of the bogus results of a prior test taken by all subjects. In one of these studies (Lineweber, Barr-Bryan, & Zelditch, 1980; cited in Zelditch, Harris, Thomas, & Walker, 1981), all subjects in each experimental group were assigned randomly to their positions except for the one chosen to wield allocative power; this person was ostensibly selected on the basis of a demonstration of superior ability on a task. Compared to a condition in which there was no such explanation of the structure of allocative power, subjects in this condition were significantly less likely to propose a change in the structure of power.

This suggests that subjects' understanding of the structure of allocative power can affect their reactions to that structure, and presumably to the subsequent allocations made within its parameters. However, postexperimental interviews with subjects revealed that they did not *personally* believe in the legitimacy of the unequal distribution of power;

> they felt the [ability] task was too simple . . . but they did not attempt to change the structure. . . . because they felt that, in an experiment, rules made by and beliefs held by *E* were valid, hence binding on them . . . they felt that in some sense *E*'s authority *backed* the normative order. (Zelditch *et al.*, 1981, p. 37; emphasis in original)

Thus, the provision of what was intended to be a justificatory explanation of an unequal distribution of allocative power increased subjects' acceptance of that structure, but it did so *not* because subjects judged the structure to be a just one. Rather, this acceptance rested on subjects' belief that this structure was supported by someone more powerful than they. Zelditch and his colleagues (1981; following Dornbusch & Scott, 1975) call this process *authorization*. What the experimenter appears to have done in this and similar studies was to "authorize" the structure of power, which, in turn, increased subjects' acceptance of it in spite of the fact that the subjects were not convinced that the structure was just. Authorization also seemed to induce subjects to believe that others in similar, subordinate positions, their peers, supported the structure of allocative power. Authorization, therefore, created the expectation of *endorsement*, the support of the structure by peers (cf. work on leadership endorsement, Tyler, Chapter 16, this volume).

These considerations suggest that the structure of power significantly affects both the allocation of material resources and the reaction to previously existing resource distributions. Subjects in research on distributive justice construct or react to distributions, at least in important part, as a consequence of how they understand the distribution of power and how they understand it to have come into existence. Those understandings are themselves the result of inferences drawn by subjects about the beliefs and values held by those who occupy positions of power, inferences drawn as a result of the information those occupying the powerful positions have presented. Endorsement of a resource distribution, or more cautiously, absence of public objection to a resource distribution, may be the result of subjects' own beliefs about justice, their beliefs about what the structure of power suggests are the beliefs of those with power, or some interaction between the two. If endorsement of resource distributions is subject to these forces, so, too, should be acquiescence and active opposition.

These considerations suggest, once again, the importance of strategic (what have been called utilitarian and organizational; Lawler, 1983) issues that interact with concerns about justice in determining the occurrence of endorsement, acquiescence, and opposition. The relative importance of grievances based on (for example) justice and the strategic issues that are, to a large extent, constituted in terms of the structure of power, is a central concern of the *resource mobilization* perspective on social movements. Whether, as that perspective emphasizes, "grievances are relatively constant . . . and movements form because of long-term changes in group resources, organization, and opportunities for collective action" (Jenkins, 1983, p. 530), or whether grievances based on justice are more central, the role that they play needs closer examination.

REVOLUTIONARY MOBILIZATION

That role has been examined in the literature on revolutionary coalitions. Many studies in this tradition demonstrate that members of a group who feel they have been unjustly treated will act together, coalesce, to reallocate collective resources (e.g., Lawler, 1975; Ross, Thibaut, & Evenbeck, 1971; Webster & Smith, 1978). For example, Webster and Smith (1978) found that the two members of a three-person group who were treated unjustly by the third-person leader agreed to reallocate collective resources, and did so primarily on those trials on which the leader most clearly violated an accepted standard of justice. When the leader conformed to the justice standard, very few coalitions occurred.

In addition to demonstrating the willingness of unjustly treated subordinates to revolt against an unjust leader, more recent research has focused on the tactics leaders may employ to prevent such revolts (e.g., Lawler, 1983). It seems reasonable to assume that as subordinates who are unjustly treated contemplate mobilization of a revolutionary coalition, those responsible for the injustice contemplate action to preempt such an occurrence (Cook and Hegtvedt's contribution to this volume presents some evidence on actual power use).

Work on the mobilization of revolutionary coalitions does not focus on the types of coalitions that are likely to form when opportunities are present, but rather on when they form. Coalitions are conceived as joint actions by two or more actors against a specified target; a revolutionary coalition is conceived more specifically as joint action by subordinates against those in authoritative positions (cf. Lawler, 1975). Thus, revolutionary coalitions can occur only in a system of structured inequality, where more powerful and less powerful actors, superordinates and subordinates, confront each other in interaction.

Much of this research focuses not only on the tendency toward revolutionary coalitions stimulated by unjust treatment, but on the effects of other situational and structural variables that might mediate the relationship between injustice and mobilization. Michener and Lyons (1972) focused on triads in which the leader appropriated an unjustly

large proportion of collective resources for herself. Although a manipulation of potential upward mobility for subordinates had no direct effects,
the extent of support or criticism of the leader ostensibly conveyed by
one of the subordinates had striking effects on the attitudes and behavior
of the other. When another subordinate conveyed dissatisfaction with
the leader's behavior and a judgment that it had been unjust, subjects
themselves were very critical of the leader and advocated a significantly
greater allocation in favor of the subordinates than when another subordinate supported the leader's actions. Here is another clear demonstration of the impact of peer support—endorsement—on revolutionary
mobilization.

Two aspects of this study are particularly noteworthy. First, consider the interpretation of the data. Subordinates judged the leader and
her behavior as more unjust after receiving similar judgments from a
peer than after receiving word that the peer supported the leader. This
motivated greater efforts at establishing a revolutionary coalition to reallocate resources away from the leader and toward the subordinates as
a whole. Because the study employed no baseline condition in which a
peer's support or challenge was absent, it is not clear whether the peer's
opinion released a previously held but inhibited justice judgment for
public expression, or changed subjects' minds about what the leader's
behavior actually represented. Whichever is the case, social influence or
disinhibition, or some interaction of the two, injustice produced more
revolutionary coalitions when there was peer support for them and for
the appropriately justificatory justice judgment than when such support
was lacking.

The second aspect of this study that is important, particularly for
interpreting other, similar research and for generalizations to situations
involving collective injustices, is that all subordinates were treated equally
unjustly. Each received an identically unjust low outcome from the leader.
In addition, possibilities for coalitions were restricted in that subordinates knew that the only allowable proposals were those that reallocated
equal amounts to both subordinates. This identical treatment by the
leader may have contributed to the frequency of revolutionary coalitions
and to the strength of the coalitions recommended by emphasizing subordinates' sense of shared fate.

Whether revolutionary coalitions of this type would have mobilized
in the absence of such emphasis on shared fate and common interests
is not clear. However, there are some indications in the resource allocation literature of the specific ways in which leaders' equal or unequal
allocations affect subordinates. First, it is widely accepted that differential allocations, primarily allocations based on manipulated task performance, maintain or enhance status distinctions among recipients,

create strained interpersonal relations, and encourage the emergence of competitive orientations. Equal allocations, particularly when they occur in the presence of manipulated performance differences but elsewhere as well, tend to accentuate similarity and commonality among recipients, minimize status differences that may exist, and (may) increase both solidarity and the quality of relations among recipients (some of this research is discussed in Deutsch, Chapter 1, this volume; see also Mikula, 1980).

Second, there is experimental evidence that people expect differential allocations to increase conflict and hostility among recipients (Leventhal & Michaels, unpublished data reported in Leventhal, Karuza, & Fry, 1980, p. 179), and that, when told to prevent conflict, people reduce differences in the allocations that recipients receive. The data that provide the clearest support for this latter contention (Leventhal, Michaels, & Sanford, 1972) suggest that people see increasing the equality of allocations as a way to prevent conflict among recipients and between recipients and allocator. Such data would seem to be reasonably valid indicators, not only of the beliefs people hold about the consequences of different allocations, but of the consequences they have for conflict, and thus, coalition. The inductions in the Michener and Lyons (1972) study may have simultaneously increased the prospects for conflict between groups (i.e., between the leader and the subordinates), and decreased the likelihood of conflict among subordinates, thus increasing the likelihood of revolutionary coalitions.

Subsequent research on revolutionary coalitions employs a paradigm similar to that employed by Michener and Lyons (1972). Fictitious triads are created in which a leader is distinguished from two subordinates. The leader is "chosen" on the basis of an ability test that supposedly establishes his or her authority to allocate resources for the subsequent performance of the triad as a whole. An unjust allocation between leader and subordinates is then created, and the subordinate subject is asked to express attitudes toward the leader and the allocation, and is given the opportunity to initiate, or to respond to the other (fictitious) subordinate's proposal to create, a coalition.

A study by Lawler (1975) confirms the validity of the suggestions made earlier concerning the effects of differential outcomes to subordinates. Although manipulated differences in the status of, and the resources given to, the two subordinates did not affect coalition frequency or intensity, the manipulation did affect the degree to which subordinates perceived themselves to have common interests: Subordinates treated identically saw their interests as more similar than subordinates treated differently. Lawler was also able to demonstrate that subordinates in the inequity condition responded by mobilizing

revolutionary coalitions because, in addition to the anger it produced
toward the leader, inequity created expectations of mutual support for
a coalition which, in turn, led to more and more severe revolutionary
coalitions:

> It is not only dissatisfaction that is important to coalitional responses to
> inequity, but the fact that subordinates expect others to share their disen-
> chantment and be receptive to mobilizing insurgent action. Inequity probably
> increases subordinates' sense of "common position" vis-à-vis a leader and
> engenders a "class consciousness" that is reflected in mutual expectations of
> support. (Lawler, 1975, p. 177)

Inequity of the type produced here, equally unjust treatment of
two subordinates, apparently creates expectations of mutual support for
revolutionary coalitional action. It seems reasonable to expect that when
that support is forthcoming, when the expectation is confirmed, a coalition is likely. However, when that support is not forthcoming, for
whatever reason, a subordinate is in a quandry: "Why does the other
person, treated identically to me, not agree, and not propose some
retaliatory or ameliorative action?" It seems reasonable that the absence
of expected validation for the judgment of injustice, and for the ameliorative action that judgment would support, would inhibit one's tendency
to publicize a private judgment of injustice, thus imperiling the emergence of a framework conducive to collective action (cf. Gamson, Fireman, & Rytina, 1982).

Lack of expected support from peers treated equally unjustly,
therefore, can create the impression of endorsement where none exists.
But given the interest that those with allocative power have to defend,
it seems unreasonable to suppose they would not contribute to the
impression of endorsement. More recent research on revolutionary coalitions has examined some of the ways in which leaders act to preempt
the emergence of revolutionary coalitions. One can distinguish two different types of tactics leaders might employ for this purpose. The first
involves the strategic employment of unequal allocations of resources,
apart from any other considerations leaders might have for employing
them.[1] Such allocations might, if the earlier work on allocations can be
counted on for support, interfere with the development of a sense of
common interests. The second involves the strategic use of other resources
at the leader's disposal to threaten or to reward subordinates. Such use
of coercive power may attempt to prevent subordinate action by conveying the likelihood of future punishment, and complementary use of

---

[1]Some of the work discussed by Deutsch in his chapter for this volume suggests that this
consideration is based on a myth, a convenient one for leaders to endorse, to be sure.

reward power may attempt to absorb potential opposition by holding out the promise of future rewards.

Any action a leader takes with respect to subordinates, allocative or nonallocative, is reasonably labeled *divisive* if it is directed at only some of the relevant subordinates, and *nondivisive* if directed at all subordinates. Lawler (1983) suggests that these two types of tactics differ in the extent to which they bear on subordinates' common interests: "a divisive tactic (whether threat or co-optation) is designed to alter the relationship of subordinates by undermining their common interests" (Lawler, 1983, p. 89). Although this is true, what is additionally the case (and focused on here) is that such divisive tactics (may) alter subordinates' relationships by changing the way in which they conceive their interests (cf. Gaventa, 1980; Lukes, 1975).

Note that it is a combination of threat and cooptation that the district attorney offers to the suspects in the prisoners' dilemma, and although the tactics are directed at both, each of the suspects operates in ignorance of this fact. Thus, the tactic is a divisive one, one clearly meant to undermine the suspects' common interest and their understanding of those interests; the tactic is successful, at least in part, precisely for these reasons.[2]

Research on the use of divisive co-optation tactics suggests that they weaken subordinates' conceptions of common interest and reduce the likelihood of subsequent revolts (Lawler, 1975; Lawler, Youngs, & Lesh, 1978). The research also suggests that cooptation is most effective when the target is offered some future personal gain from a leader strongly committed to the offer. Co-optation also appears most effective when the consequences of the alternative to accepting the offer, specifically the consequences of coalitional mobilization, are unclear.

A recent study in this tradition (Lawler, 1983) compared the effectiveness of divisive threats and divisive co-optation in preventing revolutionary coalitions. Co-optation proved more effective than threat, although both tactics produced a conflict of interest among subordinates. Furthermore, the targets and nontargets of both tactics identified the target as the more powerful of the two subordinates. Perhaps the singling out of a subordinate, whatever the nature of that singling out, increases his or her importance and potential power among the subordinate group as a whole.

How does cooptation act to prevent revolutionary coalitions, and why is it more effective in doing so than threat? Whereas subordinates

---

[2]See Sommer, 1982, for a discussion of the extent to which this creates, even for the relatively powerful district attorney, a dilemma of his or her own, one that arises when the opportunity for the suspects to reestablish contact and form a coalition returns.

in all conditions of Lawler's (1983) study, targets and nontargets of threats and co-optation, were very critical of the leader, the targets of co-optation were least critical of all. Thus, co-optation may achieve its effect by weakening the target's reasons for joining the coalition.

Unjust treatment seems to provide a normative justification for revolt, and no less than any other subordinate, the target of co-optation expects the nontarget peer to press for precisely this action. However, the co-optation tactic appears to provide its target with reason for doubting the normative justification for revolt, even though by failing to join a coalition, the target gives tacit approval (silent endorsement) to the leader's unjust treatment and demonstrates a lack of concern for, and apparent solidarity with, fellow subordinates.

Thus, although clear collective injustice created by a leader at the expense of subordinates creates angry judgments of injustice, and expectations of mutual support for revolutionary coalition mobilization, other aspects of the leader's powerful position provide him or her with resources to forestall the formation of such coalitions. Results from this body of literature do not permit a confident judgment about how the possession of such capacities, and their exercise, achieves its effect. It may do so by affecting subordinates' judgments of the gains and losses to be achieved by joint action, by influencing subordinates' beliefs about the difficulty of organizing such action, and by affecting the very way subordinates conceive of their interests and the claims that can be made for them on the basis of justice.

THE SYMBOLS OF JUSTICE

To this point, I have tried to identify some important ways in which the powerful encourage the powerless to acquiesce in their unjust treatment, (a) by their influence on the views the powerless have about the distribution of power, its structure and rationale; and (b) by their allocative and tactical conduct, which serves to undermine the beliefs the powerless have about their own common fate and interest, and the likelihood they will be able to mount an effective challenge. Both of these operate to prevent the emergence of collective action by the victims of injustice.

Most of the emphasis has been on processes involving action by the powerful that creates attitudes and objective conditions that prevent collective action. But because many of the situations in which such conduct occurs require a belief that a shared understanding unites those in, and out of, positions of power, this emphasis has overlooked an important fact: the powerless are often invited to participate, to voice concerns and state preferences, to present and defend claims, in the areas where allocative decisions are made. To a large extent, such processes are important guarantors of rights that are important to defend. My discussion in the present section is in no way meant to question the importance of such processes in defending the interests of the less powerful.

However, what I do want to suggest is that the specific processes guaranteeing those interests may mask a darker side of relationships between the powerful and the powerless, one in which subtle manipulation of the conceptions held by the powerless is effected by employing the symbols of justice. By assimilating characteristics of a process in which conflicting claims are resolved by a neutral, disinterested third party illustrated by the blind goddess of justice or the prototypical judge, procedures that permit the participation of the powerless in allocative and other decision making may obscure and reproduce the very injustices their implementation was (partially) designed to alleviate.

> Because participation symbolizes democracy, it systematically clouds recognition of conflicting interests that persist regardless of negotiation. The adoption of formal procedures for direct or indirect participation in decisions conveys the message that differences stem from misunderstandings that can be clarified through discussion or that they deal with preferences that are readily compromised . . . such routines perpetuate and legitimize existing inequalities in influence, in the application of law, and in the allocation of values. (Edelman, 1977, p. 126)

The way in which such procedures may work can be gleaned from recent work on procedural justice (some of which is discussed in Tyler's contribution to this volume). Most of this work is based on Thibaut and Walker's (1975) efforts to understand the appeals of various dispute resolution processes in legal settings. Thibaut and Walker's work demonstrates convincingly that procedures that permit those pressing claims a participatory voice are preferred to those procedures that permit no such participation. More specifically, satisfaction with verdicts is greater among defendants allowed to present evidence on behalf of their own claim than among those with no such opportunity (e.g., LaTour, 1978; Walker, LaTour, Lind, & Thibaut, 1974); similar effects are observed on defendants' ratings of the fairness of verdicts. So strong is the effect that it appears even where subjects believed themselves innocent but were found guilty.

Important extensions of this work into other institutional arenas have been made more recently. In a series of studies, Tyler has shown that procedural justice has important effects on evaluations of the police (Tyler & Folger, 1980), student evaluations of teachers and citizen evaluations of political leaders (Tyler & Caine, 1981), and defendants' evaluations of their courtroom experiences (Tyler, 1984). This work demonstrates both that beliefs about the justice of the procedures through

which resources are allocated serve to legitimize the institutional structure in which those procedures are embedded, and that procedures that
provide some degree of participation are seen as more legitimate than
those that do not. The most recent study in this tradition (Tyler, Rasinski,
& Spodick, 1985) confirms the previous findings and suggests that in
the political arena there is an important legitimating function played
merely by the ability to speak, whether or not the opportunity for speech
has some instrumental role in influencing decisions.

In addition to the work in legal and quasi-legal dispute resolution
settings, and in the political arena, work on voice and procedural justice
has explored the legitimizing function of the opportunity to speak in
research modeled on business and industrial organizations (e.g.,
deCarufel & Schopler, 1979; Folger, 1977; Folger, Rosenfield, Grove, &
Corkran, 1979). In ways very similar to the effects demonstrated in legal
and political arenas, this work demonstrates that those with voice (here,
the ability to send a message expressing a belief about one's unjust
treatment) are more satisfied with their outcomes, and consider them
more just, than those with identical outcomes but no such voice.

What is crucial to the present discussion is that it is *only* in the
work modeled on business and industrial organizations that a very different effect sometimes appears. Under two conditions to be specified
in the following, the provision of voice may backfire: subjects provided
an opportunity to speak are less satisfied with their outcomes, and consider them less just, than do subjects receiving the same outcomes but
having no opportunity to speak. I have argued more extensively elsewhere (Cohen, 1985) that this is because subjects in this research, and
people more generally, understand the nature of power and allocations
(and the issues of justice to which they are related) differently in the
legal and political arenas than they do in the economic arena.

As suggested previously, voice "backfires"—produces less legitimation rather than more—under two conditions: (a) where the subject
learns that peers confirm his or her judgment that the payment received
was unjust; and (b) where the subject receives increased outcomes in
subsequent allocations made by the employer. In both cases, some form
of social validation, endorsement when it comes from peers, and something approaching authorization when it comes from the employer, makes
the unjustly treated less likely to accept continued injustices.

Why do unjustly treated people appear to accept decisions in which
they believe they have had a voice consistently in legal and political
arenas and only inconsistently in economic settings? I believe this is
because the economic settings on which the research has been modeled
involve hierarchical industrial and business settings where there is a
fundamental division between the employers who control profit-oriented
organizations and employees who are remunerated for their labor. In

settings such as these, it is more difficult to assume, as it appears many do in imagining the ideal-typical judge, that those in powerful positions are merely presiding over a decision that allocates scarce and valuable resources. Rather, the person making the decision has interests that conflict with the interests of the others most directly involved. Voice sometimes backfires, I am arguing, because those to whom it is provided are wary of accepting the apparent claim to disinterestedness and impartiality the offer to listen seems to convey.

Whatever the motives of those who make allocative decisions may be, if those decisions directly affect their own material well-being at the same time they affect the material well-being of others, and if there is some measure of incompatibility in (at least these) material interests, then voice can be, and I am arguing here that it is, seen as co-optation. If those with little power believe the offer to "hear them out" is nothing more than an attempt to "cool them out" (Goffman, 1952), they may well be less persuaded of the justice of their condition than they would have been without the offer. They may well suspect that the introduction and operation of such procedures was intended to give the appearance of due consideration by an unbiased authority, but that in profit-oriented business enterprises, allocative decisions about wages made by owners and managers are likely to be less than unbiased and duly considerate of their (partially) opposing interests. Interesting in this regard is that the two questionnaire items that correlated most closely with defendants' judgments of the distributive and procedural justice of their own trials in Tyler's (1984) work concerned whether the "judge [took] enough time to consider your case carefully" and whether the judge was "unbiased" (p. 68). In situations in which people cannot respond to these questions affirmatively, they may doubt how well minimal forms of participation serve their interests.

Forms of voiced participation, then, may be introduced for the symbolic value they have in conveying due consideration, lack of bias, and the kind of disinterested presiding Hogan and Emler's (1981) depiction of the leader as shepherd suggests. Such procedures seem to work to legitimize structures of power where the less powerful are more convinced of shared interests with the more powerful, such as in court and in certain political arenas, but they work less well at legitimizing the structure of power where interests more clearly conflict.

CONCLUSION

Though social psychologists working in this area have been slow to recognize the implications of this fact, justice concerns the legitimation of differential holdings of, and access to, resources by groups differing in social power. Not only the structure of social power, but the resource allocations made through procedures and decision-making structures that constitute that structure of power, require legitimation conceived in terms of justice. We have been too ready to assume that the absence of public objection by those groups with less is a reflection of their endorsement of their position and the structure of power that gives it meaning.

This chapter has tried to address several of the ways groups with power exercise it to maintain and solidify their advantage. Power consists of the ability to prevail in overt contests over scarce resources, to constitute the agenda for public debate, and to exert a disproportionate effect over the way groups understand their identities and interests. The social psychological evidence described in this chapter demonstrates some of the ways those with greater power are able to make allocative decisions in a way that prevents the less powerful from mounting effective challenges: differences in power are masked, recognition of common identity and interest among the powerless is inhibited, and the symbols of justice are displayed to portray the current structure of power between groups as agreed upon and in the common interest of all. This is no conspiracy theory of power; nor is it a suggestion that justice is always and necessarily used as a cover for private interest. It is, however, a deeply felt call to investigate how fundamental concerns for social justice find their way so rarely onto agendas of widespread public debate. Hannah Pitkin (1981) describes well two ways in which the very concept of justice can facilitate the required transition from private to public. By transforming

> "I want" into "I am entitled," a claim . . . becomes negotiable by public standards . . . [and a previously] inarticulate and perhaps even unexpressed private "No!" becomes a claim: "No one should be treated like this!" The transformation releases passion . . . in the cause of principle, of justice, of the community. (pp. 347–348)

Acknowledgments

For their comments on an earlier version of this chapter, I would like to thank Tom Tyler, Jerry Greenberg, Thomas Schwinger, and Helmut Lamm.

REFERENCES

Cohen, R. L. (1982, June). *Distributive justice and power: Preliminary considerations*. Paper presented at the Conference on New Directions in Psychological Aspects of Justice, Nags Head, NC.

Cohen, R. L. (1985). Procedural justice and participation. *Human Relations, 38*(7), 643–663.

deCarufel, A., & Schopler, J. (1979). Evaluation of outcome improvement resulting from threats and appeals. *Journal of Personality and Social Psychology, 37*, 662–673.

Dinnerstein, D. (1977). *The mermaid and the minotaur: Sexual arrangements and human malaise.* New York: Harper Colophon.

Dornbusch, S. M., & Scott, W. R. (1975). *Evaluation and the exercise of authority.* San Francisco: Jossey-Bass.

Edelman, M. (1977). *Political language: Words that succeed and policies that fail.* New York: Academic Press.

Folger, R. (1977). Distributive and procedural justice: Combined impact of "voice" and improvement on experienced inequity. *Journal of Personality and Social Psychology, 35*, 108–119.

Folger, R., Rosenfield, D., Grove, J., & Corkran, L. (1979). Effects of "voice" and peer opinions on responses to inequity. *Journal of Personality and Social Psychology, 37*, 2253–2261.

Gamson, W. A., Fireman, B., & Rytina, S. (1982). *Encounters with unjust authority.* Homewood, IL: Dorsey.

Gaventa, J. (1980). *Power and powerlessness: Quiescence and rebellion in an Appalachian valley.* Urbana, IL: University of Illinois Press.

Goffman, E. (1952). On cooling the mark out. *Psychiatry, 15*(4), 451–463.

Hochschild, J. H. (1981). *What's fair? American beliefs about distributive justice.* Cambridge, MA: Harvard University Press.

Hogan, R., & Emler, N. P. (1981). Retributive justice. In M. J. Lerner & S. C. Lerner (Eds.), *The justice motive in social behavior: Adapting to times of scarcity and change* (pp. 125–143). New York: Plenum Press.

Jenkins, J. C. (1983). Resource mobilization theory and the study of social movements. *Annual Review of Sociology, 9*, 527–553.

Kovel, J. (1971). *White racism: A psychohistory.* New York: Pantheon.

LaTour, S. (1978). Determinants of participant and observer satisfaction with adversary and inquisitorial modes of adjudication. *Journal of Personality and Social Psychology, 36*, 1531–1545.

Lawler, E. J. (1975). An experimental study of factors affecting the mobilization of revolutionary coalitions. *Sociometry, 38*, 163–179.

Lawler, E. J. (1983). Cooptation and threats as "divide and rule" tactics. *Social Psychology Quarterly, 46*, 89–97.

Lawler, E. J., Youngs, G. A., & Lesh, M. (1978). Cooptation and coalition mobilization. *Journal of Applied Social Psychology, 8*, 199–214.

Leventhal, G. S., Karuza, J., Jr., & Fry, W. R. (1980). Beyond fairness: A theory of allocation preferences. In G. Mikula (Ed.), *Justice and social interaction* (pp. 167–218). New York: Springer-Verlag.

Leventhal, G. S., Michaels, J. W., & Sanford, L. (1972). Inequity and interpersonal conflict: Reward allocation and secrecy about reward as methods of preventing conflict. *Journal of Personality and Social Psychology, 23*, 88–102.

Lineweber, D., Barr-Bryan, D., & Zelditch, M., Jr. (1980). *Effects of a legitimate authority's justification of inequality on the mobilization of revolutionary coalitions.* Unpublished manuscript, Laboratory for Social Research, Stanford University.

Lukes, S. (1975). *Power: A radical view.* London: Macmillan.

Michener, H. A., & Lyons, M. (1972). Perceived support and upward-mobility as determinants of revolutionary coalition behavior. *Journal of Experimental Social Psychlogy, 8*, 180–195.

Mikula, G. (1980). On the role of justice in allocation decisions. In G. Mikula (Ed.), *Justice and social interaction* (pp. 127–166). New York: Springer-Verlag.

Moore, B., Jr. (1978). *Injustice: The social bases of obedience and revolt*. White Plains, NY: M. E. Sharpe.

Pitkin, H. F. (1981). Justice: On relating private and public. *Political Theory, 9*(3), 327–352.

Rivera, A. N., & Tedeschi, J. T. (1976). Public versus private reactions to positive inequity. *Journal of Personality and Social Psychology, 34*, 895–900.

Ross, M., Thibaut, J., & Evenbeck, S. (1971). Some determinants of the intensity of social protest. *Journal of Experimental Social Psychology, 7*, 401–418.

Sommer, R. (1982). The district attorney's dilemma: Experimental games and the real world of plea bargaining. *American Psychologist, 37*, 526–532.

Thibaut, J., & Walker, L. (1975). *Procedural justice*. Hillsdale, NJ: Erlbaum.

Tyler, T. R. (1984). The role of perceived injustice in defendants' evaluations of their courtroom experience. *Law and Society Review, 18*(1), 51–74.

Tyler, T. R., & Caine, A. (1981). The influence of outcomes and procedures on satisfaction with formal leaders. *Journal of Personality and Social Psychology, 41*, 642–655.

Tyler, T. R., & Folger, R. (1980). Distributional and procedural aspects of satisfaction with citizen–police encounters. *Basic and Applied Social Psychology, 1*, 281–292.

Tyler, T. R., Rasinski, K., & Spodick, N. (1985). The influence of voice upon satisfaction with leaders: Exploring the meaning of process control. *Journal of Personality and Social Psychology, 48*, 72–81.

Walker, L., LaTour, S., Lind, E. A., & Thibaut, J. (1974). Reactions of participants and observers to modes of adjudication. *Journal of Applied Social Psychology, 4*, 295–310.

Walster, E., Walster, G. W., & Berscheid, E. (1978). *Equity: Theory and research*. Boston: Allyn & Bacon.

Webster, M., Jr., & Smith, J. E., Jr. (1978). Justice and revolutionary coalitions. *American Journal of Sociology, 84*, 267–292.

Zelditch, M., Jr., Harris, W., Thomas, G. M., & Walker, H. A. (1981). *Decisions, nondecisions, and metadecisions* (Technical Report No. 78). Stanford, CA: Laboratory for Social Research, Stanford University.

Part II

THEORETICAL PERSPECTIVES ON JUSTICE

Chapter 5

Justice Ideology and Social Legitimation

A REVISED AGENDA FOR PSYCHOLOGICAL INQUIRY

EDWARD E. SAMPSON

Many issues involving justice are contained in the following situation: "John receives a salary of $3.50 per hour." In its present form, however, we cannot answer the central question, whether this situation is just or fair, without having more information. As we reflect on the kinds of additional information we require, we realize that questions of justice cannot be answered with psychological information alone. We must also attend to features of the larger social world in which the justice-making process resides (see Berger, Zelditch, Anderson & Cohen, 1972; Jasso & Rossi, 1977).

The typical psychological study of justice takes for granted the background framework of the society in which the work is carried on, and so leaves unexamined the very conditions that we need to examine in order truly to understand how justice operates. For example, in varying the individual's contribution to a task in order to study how outcomes are allocated, the researcher already assumes a societal framework in which a contribution principle operates. Although this frame may currently be valid in the researcher's society or in that segment under study, when it is taken for granted so that conclusions about individual choice are drawn, our understanding of the justice-making process is not enriched.

EDWARD E. SAMPSON • The Wright Institute, 2728 Durant Avenue, Berkeley, CA 94704.

OVERVIEW

In the following chapter, I examine several ideas, some of which I have previously presented (e.g., Sampson, 1983), and others that I am as yet able to present in only a preliminary way. The intent of this overview is to help channel the direction and flow of these ideas so that my position is reasonably clear.

Four themes govern this work. First, justice-making is a process rooted in collective social life and cannot meaningfully be reduced to individual psychological dynamics. Second, to ignore this first point, as much work on the social psychology of justice has done, is to enter the arena of ideology and to fail thereby to achieve an understanding of genuine justice in human affairs. Third, the latter requires both a radical transformation in our understanding of the nature of personhood and a commitment to search for an objective, social basis for justice to replace our predilection for subjective, individual dynamics (see Horkheimer, 1974, for further discussion of this objective-subjective distinction). Fourth, I suggest that this objective basis lies in the social practices of caretaking and receiving, which provide a standard to be applied in judging whether or not something is just, as well as an antidote to our current tendency, in merely describing the status quo, to normalize current injustices.

PERSONHOOD AND JUSTICE

The tendency to psychologize justice is part of the larger cultural understanding of the nature of persons. Although it would take me too far afield to expand on this idea in the present chapter (see Sampson, 1985, for a more complete discussion of this point), in my view, our cultural ideal of personhood derives from our preferences to seek order and coherence by means of personal control and mastery. Personhood is thereby defined in terms designed for control and mastery: that is, as a self-contained, firmly individuated agent in charge.

Therefore, when we discover a justice principle within the minds of individuals, we fail to see that the individual is more like a medium through which the society speaks than the agent in charge who does the speaking. In the former, mediated view, we may reasonably ask individuals about justice principles in order to map out the justice for-mulations that exist within a given society or societal subgroup. And, we may reasonably ask about the processes by which people learn, retain, and act on justice principles. We are in error, however, if we attribute the bases of these principles to the individual as such.

When psychology seeks to discover universal social principles whose origin purportedly lies within the individual, psychology takes what to me is a fatal plunge into a region that contributes more to ideology than to genuine understanding. To assume that our findings reveal something fundamental about the individual as such is to reproduce the underlying social form, concealed however, as though it were a necessary and inevitable matter of individual psychological functioning. On the other hand, when we concentrate on the manner by which people learn social principles, we are less likely to assume the individual to be the locus of these principles, and are thus less suceptible to ideological distortion.

Our currently dominant conception of personhood contributes to this ideological distortion and thwarts the achievement of real justice. A self-contained personhood ideal (e.g., Sampson, 1977) excludes the larger web of interconnections among persons and between persons and the rest of nature on which any genuine justice must be based. When the boundaries of the person dwell firmly at skin level and go no further, the chances for including the larger whole of humanity and nature into our concerns is not likely.

For psychology to understand and realize genuine justice, it must reconceptualize personhood and its understanding of the role of persons-in-the-world. This is not an easy reconceptualization. The concept of personhood that dominates Western psychology derives from a given social form and contributes to sustaining that form. Hence to reconceptualize personhood is to fly in the face of the society that not only affirms one conception but employs that conception in order to carry out its serious business.

THE PERSONHOOD IDEAL

The currently dominant conception of personhood is well summarized by the cultural anthropologist Clifford Geertz (1979) in the following passage:

> the Western conception of the person as a bounded, unique, more or less integrated motivational and cognitive universe, a dynamic center of awareness, emotion, judgment and action organized into a distinctive whole and set contrastively both against other such wholes and against a social and natural background is, however incorrigible it may seem to use, a rather peculiar idea within the context of the world's cultures. (p. 229)

Geertz's conclusions were based on his work in Bali and Java. The paper by Shweder and Bourne (1982) comparing American with Oriyan (Indian) concepts of persons, as well as Miller's (1984) replication and extension of this work on another Indian population, confirm Geertz's analysis. The Western conception of the person is described as a contextually free and autonomous abstraction, governed by an egocentric rather than a sociocentric or more organic world premise.

As Shweder and Bourne conclude, whereas the Westerner is likely to describe so-and-so as being "a principled person," their Oriyan sample is more likely to say, "he does not disclose secrets" (p. 125). Where we see a selfish man, they see someone who "is hesitant to give away money to his family" (p. 125). In summary, "Oriyas tell you what someone has done . . . Americans tell you what is true of what someone has done" (p. 116).

This bounded, Western conception of personhood directs psychology's works and leads it to search for the governing agency within the person. We restrict our understanding to the seemingly autonomous, contextually independent entity, the well bounded, self-contained individual; we slough off or ignore the social forces that interpenetrate and inhabit the individual. An alternative view would see persons more as media than as agents. This does not demean or lessen their importance; it relocates the individual within the social world and studies the manner by which the social world inhabits that individual.

JUSTICE

Let me illustrate this point briefly by means of some of psychology's work on justice. In presuming the relative autonomy of the individual, certain psychologists study justice principles as though these were derivatives of human mental functioning. For example, equity becomes a cognitive necessity, an attribute of the way the human mind works, rather than a feature of the social system. Or, the developmental sequence whereby justice principles are learned takes on the aura of an inevitable progression of the human mind, rather than the unfolding story of the encounter between the person and a particular society (e.g., Damon, 1981). Or, the demand for a just world is treated as an abstract property of the individual's mind, a kind of psychic equation. Whenever the equation is not satisfactorily solved, tension results and motivates the individual to balance the equation by mentally restoring a just world, even derogating those who get less by believing them to be deserving of what they get.

In noting these examples, I am not questioning the empirical findings that often support each approach. I am questioning the location of these as psychological principles rather than as social principles that individuals learn and in terms of which they function in their daily lives. These are not psychological inevitabilities, therefore, but social principles that serve certain functions and meet certain social needs, perhaps on behalf of the domination of certain groups over others (see Sampson, 1983).

Let me also be quick to say that there are those psychologists of justice who have been more sensitive to the social world than the examples I have chosen here to illustrate my point would seem to indicate (e.g., Deutsch, 1975; Lerner, 1981; Leventhal, Karuza, & Fry, 1980; Mikula, 1980). Although each gives us a sense of the social within what would otherwise appear to be purely psychological functioning, for the most part, once these obligatory bows towards society have been taken, the majority then return to treating justice and decisions about its form as though these were matters of individual psychology rather than the enduring marks of society, serving its larger purposes, often far removed from matters of genuine justice in human affairs.

My concern is with what ensues once justice principles, which do indeed dwell within the minds of individual members of society, are presumed to be a function of those individual minds rather than of the social justice-making process. This is part of a larger concern with the ideological outcomes that appear whenever a social fact is transmuted into a matter of psychological agency.

Whenever we presume that a social process is derivative of a psychological act of individual agency, we conceal the underlying interests that are served by that social process. Our focus on individual psychology deflects our attention away from the underlying process that thereby passes unscathed by any critical insights. One of the best examples of what I mean comes from the psychology of blaming.

To blame the victim or hold the individual responsible, that is, deserving, of her or his fate, as the work of Ryan (1971), Lerner (e.g., Lerner & Miller, 1978), Caplan and Nelson (1973) and Schuman (1982), among others, have observed, is a central belief that helps keep those whose lot in life is minimal in a state of quietly depressive acceptance. They blame themselves for their fate, never looking beyond and into the social system that helped deal them their hands of failure. This psychologizing of blame works on behalf of sustaining a social arrangement that benefits from never having its processes carefully scrutinized, as the search turns inward towards the individual. Much of the psychotherapy business builds on this framework, treating the individual for social ills and thereby perpetuating the illusion of full-blown individual agency.

Psychology must examine both the social bases of the justice-making process, which Mikula, Leventhal and others have so properly encouraged us to do, and the underlying legitimating role that this process serves, by which certain arrangements of power and privilege are sustained, whereas others are denied any current validity. Psychology helps affirm those unexamined relationships by deflecting our attention and framework of understanding away from society and into the heart and mind of the individual.

ENLARGING PERSONHOOD

A further aspect of my concern with the psychologizing of justice goes well beyond the preceding and takes us into the realm of morality and its realization under differing conditions of personhood. Geertz's work once again introduces a different possibility for understanding ourselves and others that illustrates what I mean.

Employing Schutz's (1970–1971) distinction among types of person–other relationships, Geertz speaks of people who are our contemporaries and consociates (we and they generally share the same time, and with the latter, the same space as well); our predecessors (they once lived but no longer do); and our successors (they are the generations still to be born). Geertz finds that the Balinese treat all persons as consociates. In other words, successors and predecessors are considered to be living and vital members of the current community. The Balinese concept of personhood thereby reaches out beyond our own time–space framework to embrace predecessors and successors in its web. Consider the consequences of this concept of personhood for justice as compared with its achievement under our own self-contained understanding.

Whereas we tend to exclude both predecessors and successors from our judgments about whether or not something is just, among those cultures whose conception of personhood includes such persons as active consociates, this kind of exclusion could never be legitimately sustained. We could even further expand this alternative conception by following those Native American cultures for whom nature is likewise included as a living entity with subject-like qualities. Here we see how a justice that excluded nature could never be legitimate.

My point is not merely to observe that cultures differ in their understandings of personhood, but that these differences create approaches to justice that also differ from our own in ways central to genuine justice in human affairs. Our exclusionary concept of personhood achieves an egocentrically based sense of justice. Is it not possible that real injustices are created by such an exclusionary conception? When we restrict our definition of justice to the parties involved in the immediate transaction, for example, we may create a short-term sense of justice and yet fail to establish a justice that encompasses those generations still to come. Our actions would differ significantly if those yet unborn generations were living parts of our current everyday world and experience.

In one sense, psychology should not be criticized for uncritically adopting its own culture's framework as its own. In another sense, however, when we adopt our own cultural perspective uncritically and proclaim its principles of justice as though they conveyed an abstract and essential truth, then we may inadvertently perpetuate injustices in the name of sustaining current arrangements.

TOWARD AN OBJECTIVE BASE FOR JUSTICE

Every response of justice is an answer to the legitimacy claims of a given social order and its arrangements of power and privilege. To conclude that a situation is just is to conclude that voluntary assent not requiring blatant coercion has been employed to gain the citizenry's acceptance of societal principles and practices.

The legitimacy of a social arrangement of privilege and power is crucial to social cohesion or to social disruption. People are bound together by consensually shared agreements or rent asunder by their absence. A society's allocation of power and privilege is held to be legitimate (i.e., right and proper), whenever the claim of justice can be affirmed. Allocations that grant more power, prestige, respect, and special privileges to some rather than others, are accomplished by responding to any challenges that may arise by turning to the concept of justice.

John gets more than Jane because. . . . The completion in this instance adopts some kind of justice principle that legitimates the allocation that gives more to John. Once legitimacy can be established, acceptance follows. People will agree without further challenge or accept the arrangement with no doubts about its rightness because they believe it to be legitimate, thus morally proper and binding. Justice serves this legitimating function, answering potentially disruptive complaints of unfairness by its cohesion-creating response.

BASES OF LEGITIMATION

What is it that permits people to rest rather than do battle once justice has conferred legitimacy on a social form? To phrase this question somewhat differently, is there a general underlying agreement that enfolds other, more particularistic agreements, and without which those others could not work?

The point is an important one that has historically been answered in a variety of different ways. My assumption is that there is an "objective something" that unites people together; that this something forms the cement of all human sociation; and that this something preexists any later agreements that people develop. Indeed, those later agreements presuppose this objective something. This primary agreement is usually implicitly assumed whenever other agreements are employed. Thus this objective something is not just another category of justice; it is the frame within which justice is to be measured and finally redeemed.

In other words, I am searching for an underlying, objective principle by which all other principles that employ justice to legitimate social arrangements can be redeemed. This is a search for a general social interest that underlies and forms the basis for the more particularistic interests that specific principles represent.

To preview the direction of my own thoughts, I will suggest that this underlying agreement resides within the social institution of caretaking and receiving. The bond that unites people, that provides the basis whereby all other principles can be redeemed and found congruent or wanting, lies within this social institution. A justice principle not based on caretaking and receiving is not fundamentally just. In order to achieve the cohesion-creating, legitimate quality of justice, principles that provide specific benefit to some seek to wrap themselves (albeit implicitly) in the mantle of the primary institution of caretaking and receiving. We do a grave disservice to the concept of justice, however, when we dignify other justice principles as though they occupied the same deep status as the justice frame based on caretaking and receiving.

Those familiar with Gilligan's work (e.g., Gilligan, 1977; Pollak & Gilligan, 1982) will note both similarities and differences with my own claims. Gilligan and I agree both in emphasizing a moral dimension to justice and in differentiating between two contrasting principles: one based on connectedness and interpersonal responsibility, the other based on protecting boundaries and separations. We differ, however, in that I have claimed that the latter cannot serve as the fundamental, objective ground for justice. In my view, justice must be grounded in matters of caretaking. Space limitations do not permit me to do more than introduce these points of similarity and difference at this time.

This was only a preview. Before moving further into this discussion, let us first review several other efforts to define that objective something that joins people together.

Relativistic Approaches

It is best to begin with those approaches that, like Weber's (1946), assume that there is no singular underlying framework to legitimate the social bond, but rather shifting standards as a function of social history.

I would include Lerner's (e.g., 1981) efforts here, even though his concern is less with social history than the individual's developmental history.

Weber emphasizes the shifting historical standards that redeem legitimacy claims by means of charisma, tradition, or impersonal, legal agreements. In our current society, people are comforted primarily by claims that presume a rational-legal basis for legitimacy. Attempting to redeem legitimacy by turning to tradition or charisma would be unsettling because such claims violate current legitimation standards.

We should be persuaded, therefore, that something is just on the basis of rational arguments and discourses. Insofar as rationality is currently defined primarily in terms of standards of efficiency and technical usefulness for mastery and control (e.g., see Habermas, 1971, 1975; Horkheimer, 1974; Horkheimer & Adorno, 1972), this suggests that the most compelling current basis for accepting justice as legitimate is the view that argues on behalf of its being the best way to accomplish essential societal goals. Indeed, this is precisely the position argued in Davis and Moore's (1945) classic, functionalist theory of social stratification and also seems to be at the center of several more psychological analyses of justice (e.g., equity theory).

For example, we claim that it is unfair to distribute goods equally when differential contributions to a task have been made because equality in this case will undermine the motivation of individuals to continue making essential contributions if their efforts go unrewarded. Or, we suggest that because people must learn to delay immediate gratification in order to gain pleasure later, they learn a personal contract (e.g., Lerner, 1981) in which they agree to endure some costs now in anticipation of receiving their well-deserved benefits later. In time, this generalizes to become a social contract in which they learn that the most efficient way to get their own deserving met is to work with others to get their deserving accomplished.

If we add Lerner's analysis of the interpersonal bases of justice to Weber's, we come upon a further view of the role of justice in legitimation. Lerner outlines three kinds of relationship, identity, unit, and nonunit, which provide the templates to organize the child's experiences of others via empathy (identity), via similarities (unit), or via differences (nonunit). He suggests that justice principles vary as a function of the kind of relationship that exists. For example, treating others as persons (identity or unit) may lead to a justice of equality or need, whereas treating others as positions (nonunit) may lead to a justice of equity.

In terms of my analysis, I assume that these interpersonal templates establish different criteria whereby a justice principle becomes legitimate. What is considered to be legitimately just in a relationship of identity differs from what is considered legitimately just in a nonunit relationship.

Singular and Universal Themes

Others have turned to a variety of more singular and universalistic principles, including reason, power, social contract and a host of non-rational theses in their search for the cement of sociation.

Reason has been a long-time favorite since the ancient Greeks and Romans. Cicero (cited in Klapp, 1973), for example, emphasized the central role that reason and discourse played in providing the bond that joined persons and that made humanity distinct from the other beasts who lacked this ability.

Power theories have also held substantial appeal. The real source of human bonding is located in the power of one group to impose its will over another. Machiavelli (1532/1950) offers one of the finest statements of this perspective, turning however, more to the notion of cunning than brute force. Both Hobbes (1690/1904) and Marx (1867–1879/1925–1926) also stressed the role of power in undergirding social agreements, though for Marx, this was a condition to be undone, not to be left untouched.

Social contract theorists, whether Hobbesian or Lockean (1690/1960) have likewise found substantial support throughout history. Hobbes' views are generally well known. The fundamental selfishness of humanity creates the need for social agreements that allow peaceful coexistence rather than the otherwise inevitable war of all against all.

Locke offers a more generous outlook on the nature of humanity and the ensuring social contract that joins people together. All people share certain natural rights and the commonsense ability to judge what fits and what violates these natural rights. Rousseau (1762/1961) also argued on behalf of natural law and natural rights, but unlike Locke, who saw the state as the vehicle to guarantee their attainment, Rousseau saw the state as a source of distortion and nature as the locale within which justice and harmony could obtain.

Nonrational approaches to human sociation have also flourished throughout human history. Adam Smith (1759/1966) among others (e.g., Kropotkin, see Allport, 1954), emphasized sympathy as a kind of innate governing mechanism that permitted the agreements to be reached that made society possible. Freud (1922) emphasized the binding force of the libidinal instinct as the basis for all human sociation, but only when it was deflected into identifications rather than directly expressed. For Trotter (1916), the root of human sociation lay in a herding instinct. With

Tarde (1903), humanity's innate capacity to imitate provided the basis for human social life.

CRITIQUE

My dissatisfaction with these points of view has motivated my own efforts, still preliminary in form, to recommend a different foundation for human sociation and thus for the legitimizing role of justice in human affairs.

The approach that includes Weber's, among others, strikes me as too relativistic to warrant the founding status that I am seeking. The tendency is to accept the current structure of society, for example its rational-legal or nonunit, contractual base, and presume that this adequately resolves all questions of legitimacy. This however, merely describes contemporary social life, not necessarily its underlying basis. We still must critically evaluate a rational-legal principle against a more profound, objective standard that captures the strongly moral sense that the use of justice for legitimation conveys.

I also find self-interest theories, from Hobbes to equity, unsatisfactory. The underlying quality of justice involves a moral feeling that transcends mere self-interest. Although self-interest may predominate in our current social life, this does not necessarily recommend it as the basis for the underlying agreement on which human society is formed.

A further dissatisfaction involves the fact that many of the preceding approaches, and indeed, the majority of psychology's analyses, adopt too individualistic a perspective to provide the basis for what is fundamentally a social process. These begin within the psyche of the individual and then assume that the social bond somehow springs from individual psychology. It is my firm belief, shared with others (e.g., Mead, 1934; also Marx, 1867–1879/1925–1926; and Vygotsky, 1978), that the reverse is the actual state of affairs. Justice making is a social process; our search must begin within the social world, not within the world of the individual's psychology.

Finally, I need to be clear at least about my intent, if not my present ability, to convince. Something that is as deeply persuasive as justice is in legitimating a social arrangement cannot be merely relative and ever shifting. Justice principles must be founded on a more fundamental stratum of human social life. Justice principles must address issues that all human societies confront, and, I believe, focus on cooperation and general community interest rather than competition or individual self-interest.

CARETAKING AND RECEIVING

I suggest that the most fundamental arena in which justice emerges as a social concept lies within the sphere of caretaking and receiving. The most fundamental human agreement in which justice first appears is not a personal contract established by the individual, but rather a societally shared agreement regarding caretaking and receiving. Only in this sphere will we find the fundamental trust that appears when justice works to achieve legitimacy; only here will we find something more fundamental than the instrumental rationality conveyed by other formulations; only here will we find the profoundly affective quality that grounds justice in morality and legitimacy.

Agreements about caretaking and receiving, in particular of the newly born, are basic to the survival of the newborn and to the perpetuation of the human community. Caretaking and receiving establishes the first arena within which questions involving justice emerge as well as the locus for its intensely affective quality. Viewed more abstractly, the justice of need more than any other form appears in the context of caretaking and receiving and thus founds the meaning of justice in human affairs.

If the sense of fairness originates in notions of nurturing and responsibility, then a contributive notion of deserving is less central than a more deeply engraved sense of having needs met, of feeling reasonably secure, safe, and comfortable. This intensely affective and bonding experience of well-being and belongingness accounts both for the durability of justice and its ability to communicate the end of doubt that legitimacy represents.

I am not describing the empirically observed variations in the degree to which caretaking actually provides for the newly born's needs. I am arguing that institutionalized practices of caretaking and receiving introduce the first and most fundamental basis for justice within society and establish the foundation for all later meanings and experiences of justice. I am further suggesting an answer to the questions of why justice plays a key role in social legitimation and why justice has its intensely moral quality. Other bases of justice must reach the foundation of caretaking or run the risk of failing to achieve these enduring and legitimating qualities.

VULNERABILITY TO IDEOLOGY

It almost goes without saying that the potent role that justice plays in social legitimation readily lends itself to the possibility that justice principles will serve the interests of current patterns of domination. This is what I mean when I speak of the vulnerability of justice to ideology. How tempting for those who benefit from a particular arrangement of power and privilege to believe deeply that they deserve their exalted position. How much easier it is for them to sleep peacefully at night when they realize that those less fortunate than they are likewise wrapped safely in the belief of deservingness for their lesser fate. I am not describing a hypothetical scenario, but a currently commonplace situation.

One need not be a politically radical social analyst to reach these kinds of conclusions. In my several other publications, but especially my recent book, *Justice and the critique of pure psychology* (1983), I explored this theme and do not wish to repeat myself endlessly over again here. I would like, however to combine this notion of the special vulnerability of justice to ideology with my final point, the role of psychology in all of this.

PSYCHOLOGY AND THE REPRODUCTION OF INJUSTICE

Psychology plays an important role in sustaining contemporary society. Along with other, similar disciplines, psychology occupies a position in the machinery of social reproduction. In saying this, I do not mean that this little island of research in the midst of the larger fabric of social life, in and of itself, bears total responsibility for the shape of society. This would be a patently absurd position, and one which I do not take.

It is my contention, however, that psychology contributes to the essential conceptual underpinnings that support the larger social world. I am simply making the same kind of observation that others (e.g., Bhaskar, 1979; Giddens, 1979) have also made: namely, that any social practice requires the underlying support of understanding and self-understanding that permits persons to carry out their social functions. Social actors function in the light of their understanding of the meaning of what they are doing. This is what implicates the discipline of psychology in ideology.

My concerns with social change or what I term a transformative relationship between psychology and society, derive from a deeply held belief in the fundamental absence of justice within the world today. I am not suggesting that the lot of humanity has been without significant improvement over the last several centuries. I am stating my belief that the concept of justice has been employed more vigorously in the service of sustaining unjust arrangements that benefit a few at the expense of many, than it has become a real condition of life for the majority of the world's peoples.

This is not some abstract philosophical or psychological argument. I am describing what anyone can know: wasting and hungry peoples wander homelessly while others feast; death and destruction in the name of preserving peace too often translates into the preservation of the rights of one nation to plunder another's resources for the former's gain; destruction of an environment that is not understood as another rightful claimant in the court of justice; creation and deployment of weapons whose purpose can never be seriously construed as serving the interests of human freedom and the attainment of justice for all.

My concerns are complex. They join an interest in the attainment of justice with my concern about the role that psychology plays in this drama. I am not foolish enough to believe that a more transformative psychology would create a just world. I am foolish enough, however, to believe that a psychology whose primary contributions are to social reproduction plays a much too significant role in sustaining injustice. I am not optimistic, however, about psychology's own transformation. We are too embedded in the heart of the current patterns of advanced Western society to prove to be the locus for a dramatic turnaround. On the other hand, there remain those in the field who sense the possibilities for a new direction and who even now are working to map its shapes and forms.

CONCLUSION

This has been a critical piece rather than one that, strictly speaking, is theoretical. Whereas the latter, if done well, should lead to several directly testable hypotheses, the former is less likely to generate more research than to raise questions about the way things are currently being done within the field. It may prove helpful if I conclude this chapter with a brief rundown of the kinds of implications, both for our "doing business as usual" and for research possibilities that I see embodied in this preliminary critical analysis.

1. We must be alert in our works on justice to the ever present possibility that rather than finding justice through our efforts we have employed justice in the service of sustaining the existing arrangements of social power and privilege. I have strongly suggested that the latter is an inappropriate role for the science of social psychology to play.

2. My emphasis on caretaking as a root for justice in human affairs suggests both a past-oriented, historical hypothesis and a future-directed possibility. Do we find greater harmony and less internal strife within societies that attend to the caretaking of those less fortunate or in need when compared with those societies in which power and privilege are

more centralized in the hands of a few? How does our own current society rate as regards its caretaking and what does this imply for its future stability?

3. Would a deeply probing examination of persons' beliefs about the legitimacy of social arrangements reproduce the current social patterns of domination or uncover a set of values more sensitive to the caretaking- and need-related themes that I have stressed? Research on this point runs into the problem of ideology and its deep seating within the minds of societal members.

4. This then brings me to a final point. To uncover levels beyond ideology requires what I can only refer to as a deep probing that goes past a mere description of the status quo. The research techniques required here are more in the clinician's kit than the survey researcher's, and yet, these are precisely the kinds of methodology needed for a critical social psychology of justice.

REFERENCES

Allport, G. W. (1954). The historical background of modern social psychology. In G. Lindzey (Ed.), *Handbook of social psychology* (Vol. 1, pp. 3–56). Cambridge, MA: Addison-Wesley.

Berger, J., Zelditch, M., Jr., Anderson, B., & Cohen, B. P. (1972). Structural aspects of distributive justice: A status-value formulation. In J. Berger, M. Zelditch, Jr., & B. Anderson (Eds.). *Sociological theories in progress* (Vol. 2, pp. 119–146). Boston, MA: Houghton Mifflin.

Bhaskar, R. (1979). *The possibility of naturalism.* Atlantic Highlands, NJ: Humanities Press.

Caplan, N., & Nelson, S. D. (1973). On being useful: The nature and consequences of psychological research on social problems. *American Psychologist, 28,* 199–211.

Damon, W. (1981). The development of justice and self-interest during childhood. In M. Lerner & S. Lerner (Eds.), *The justice motive in social behavior* (pp. 57–72). New York: Plenum Press.

Davis, K., & Moore, W. E. (1945). Some principles of stratification. *American Sociological Review, 10,* 242–249.

Deutsch, M. (1975). Equity, equality and need: What determines which value will be used as the basis of distributive justice? *Journal of Social Issues, 31,* 137–149.

Freud, S. (1922). *Group psychology and the analysis of the ego.* London: International Psychoanalytical Press.

Geertz, C. (1979). From the native's point of view: On the nature of anthropological understanding. In P. Rabinow & W. M. Sullivan (Eds.), *Interpretive social science* (pp. 225–241). Berkeley, CA: University of California Press.

Giddens, A. (1979). *Central problems in social theory.* Berkeley, CA: University of California Press.

Gilligan, C. (1977). In a different voice: Women's conceptions of the self and of morality. *Harvard Educational Review, 47,* 481–517.

Habermas, J. (1971). *Knowledge and human interests.* Boston, MA: Beacon Press.

Habermas, J. (1975). *Legitimation crisis.* Boston, MA: Beacon Press.

Hobbes, T. (1904). *Leviathan*. Cambridge: University Press. (Original work published 1651)
Horkheimer, M. (1974). *Eclipse of reason*. New York: Seabury.
Horkheimer, M., & Adorno, T. (1972). *Dialectic of enlightenment*. New York: Seabury.
Jasso, G., & Rossi, P. H. (1977). Distributive justice and earned income. *American Sociological Review, 44*, 639–651.
Klapp, O. E. (1973). *Models of social order*. Palo Alto, CA: National Press Books.
Lerner, M. J. (1981). The justice motive in human relations. In M. Lerner & S. Lerner (Eds.), *The justice motive in social behavior* (pp. 11–35). New York: Plenum Press.
Lerner, M. J., & Miller, D. T. (1978). Just world research and the attribution process: Looking back and ahead. *Psychological Bulletin, 85*, 1031–1051.
Leventhal, G. S., Karuza, J., & Fry, W. R. (1980). Beyond fairness: A theory of allocation preferences. In G. Mikula (Ed.), *Justice and social interaction* (pp. 167–218). Bern: Huber.
Locke, J. (1960). *Two treatises of government*. Cambridge: Cambridge University Press. (Original work published 1690)
Machiavelli, N. (1950). *The prince and The discourses*. New York: Modern Library. (Original work published 1532)
Marx, K. (1925–1926). *Capital: A critique of political economy* (3 Vols). Chicago, IL: Kerr. (Original work published 1867–1879)
Mead, G. H. (1934). *Mind, self and society*. Chicago, IL: University of Chicago Press.
Mikula, G. (1980). On the role of justice in allocation decisions. In G. Mikula (Ed.), *Justice and social interaction* (pp. 127–166). Bern: Huber.
Miller, J. G. (1984). Culture and the development of everyday social explanation. *Journal of Personality and Social Psychology, 46*, 961–978.
Pollak, S., & Gilligan, C. (1982). Images of violence in Thematic Apperception Test stories. *Journal of Personality and Social Psychology, 42*, 159–167.
Rousseau, J. J. (1961). *The social contract*. London: Dent. (Original work published 1762)
Ryan, W. (1971). *Blaming the victim*. New York: Vintage Books.
Sampson, E. E. (1977). Psychology and the American ideal. *Journal of Personality and Social Psychology, 35*, 767–782.
Sampson, E. E. (1983). *Justice and the critique of pure psychology*. New York: Plenum Press.
Sampson, E. E. (1985). The decentralization of identity: Towards a revised concept of personal and social order. *American Psychologist, 40*, 1203–1211.
Schuman, H. (1982). Free will and determinism in public beliefs about race. In N. R. Yetman & C. H. Steele (Eds.), *Majority and minority: The dynamics of racial and ethnic relations* (3rd ed., pp. 345–350). Boston, MA: Allyn & Bacon.
Schutz, A. (1970–1971). *Collected papers* (3 Vols). The Hague: Martinus Nijhoff.
Shweder, R. A., & Bourne, E. J. (1982). Does the concept of the person vary cross-culturally? In A. J. Marsalla & G. M. White (Eds.), *Cultural conceptions of mental health and therapy* (pp. 97–137). Dordrecht, Netherlands: D. Reidel.
Smith, A. (1966). *Theory of moral sentiments*. New York: Kelley. (Original work published 1759)
Tarde, G. (1903). *The laws of imitation*. New York: Holt.
Trotter, W. (1916). *Instincts of the herd in peace and war*. New York: Macmillan.
Vygotsky, L. S. (1978). *Mind in society*. Cambridge, MA: Harvard University Press.
Weber, M. (1946). *From Max Weber: Essays in sociology*. H. H. Gerth & C. W. Mills (Eds.), New York: Oxford University Press.

Chapter 6

The Experience of Injustice

TOWARD A BETTER UNDERSTANDING OF ITS
PHENOMENOLOGY

GEROLD MIKULA

"The more to a man's disadvantage the rule of distributive justice fails of realization, the more likely he is to display the emotional behavior we call anger" (Homans, 1961, p. 75). This proposition of Homans (1961), his related analyses, and Adams' (1965) seminal work on inequity were the main stimuli for the development of a new area of social psychological inquiry dealing with justice and injustice. Considerable progress has been made in this field, as documented in several recent books (e.g., Folger, 1984; Greenberg & Cohen, 1982; Lerner & Lerner, 1981; Mikula, 1980). However, as Deutsch (1983) has correctly pointed out recently, "there is practically no research relating to the phenomenology of injustice, to the actual experiences of people who inflict injustice or to those who suffer injustice" (p. 312). There is very little evidence on the quality of emotions that follow perception of an injustice (see Greenberg's 1984 review of what evidence there is); the same holds for the cognitive processes elicited by the perception of an injustice. Several authors (e.g., Cohen, 1982; Kayser & Schwinger, 1982; Mikula, 1984; Utne & Kidd, 1980) have suggested that attributional thoughts will be elicited and mediate the reactions to a perceived unjust event. Empirical data are lacking here too, however.

GEROLD MIKULA • Karl-Franzens-Universität Graz, Institut für Psychologie, A-8010 Graz, Austria.

One major reason for our poor knowledge of what people think and feel when they confront an unjust event lies in methodological difficulties. To learn about these processes one must rely on subjects' self-reports, which are of questionable validity. However, if we really want to proceed in our understanding it is important to study what people think and feel when they confront an unjust event, and how these cognitions and feelings mediate their final reactions. The bias toward rigorous methodology should not prevent the relevant research from being conducted, even if the data collected are not as pure as one would like them to be.

The present chapter reports several studies that move in this direction. Two different methodologies have been used to collect empirical data on the nature of experiences of injustice and their consequences. The first consists of retrospective reports of unjust events people have actually confronted. The second methodology consists of a passive role-playing technique. Subjects are given descriptions of the unfair treatment of a person and are asked to place themselves either in the role of the unfairly treated person or in the role of an unaffected observer of the unfair event. Then they have to record their feelings and thoughts in the situation described. Because of space limitations and the preliminary nature of this research, it seems appropriate to focus the discussion on the methodologies used and on the main results obtained. The implications of the results for future research and a proper conceptualization of injustice experiences also will be suggested.

RETROSPECTIVE REPORTS ON EXPERIENCES OF INJUSTICE

The main reason for analyzing retrospective reports is to collect information on unjust events people actually confront in their daily lives. In typical social psychological studies of injustice, subjects are confronted with situations the experimenter believes to be unjust (e.g., inequitable payment). Even if subjects are later asked to rate the fairness or unfairness of the situation, very little is known about how relevant and common the situation is for the subjects. In contrast, the present approach provides information about actual, common, and relevant experiences of injustice. Furthermore, by using this approach, it should be possible to learn about the most typical social settings in which people feel unjustly treated. We also can learn about the events and treatments people especially feel to be unfair, and how they react to injustices in their daily lives. As such, this approach should yield richer information than usually collected in experimental settings.

PROCEDURE

Subjects were students in various psychology classes at the University of Graz, Austria. Participants were asked to take part in a research program on experiences of injustice by reporting an unjust event they had actually confronted as victims. Specifically, the subjects were instructed to describe how and when the event occurred, what actually happened, and what exactly they felt to be unjust. Then they were asked to report as completely as possible: (a) their thoughts and feelings in the situation they described; (b) whether (and if so, what) consequences had resulted and what action they had taken in response to their unjust treatment; and (c) if their view of the event has changed subsequently, and if so, how it changed.

Fifty-seven reports were collected from 180 students solicited. Thirty-nine of the subjects were females, 18 males; their mean age was 22.28 (range was 18 to 43). Subjects' reports ranged from about 300 to 1200 words in length. The period of time that had passed since the events described had taken place varied considerably; about 23% of the events dated back less than 1 month, about 30% up to 1 year, and 35% more than 1 year (the maximum was 15 years).

RESULTS

As the size of the available sample was rather small ($N = 57$), no statistical analyses were conducted. Rather, an attempt was made to summarize systematically the information in a descriptive way.

Social Settings

In a first step, the social settings in which the unjust events occurred were analyzed (see Table 1). Approximately one third of the reported events (31.58%) took place at a school or university. The next two most frequently mentioned social settings were the family (24.56%) and the job or work place (14.04%). The remaining events were evenly distributed over interactions with friends (10.53%), various public settings (e.g., shopping, traffic, public transportation; 8.77%), lodging (problems with neighbors, roommates, landlords; 8.77%), and, finally, authorities and administrative institutions (1.75%). These types of settings seem to cover the most essential areas of our subjects' lives. If one were to ask groups of people other than students to report on their experiences of injustice, it is likely that some of these same settings would not be mentioned or would be mentioned less frequently (e.g., school/university), and that

TABLE 1. Frequencies of Social Settings and Eliciting Events Reported by the Subjects

	School/ university	Family	Work place	Friends	Public setting	Lodging	Authorities/ administration	Totals
Unjustified accusations and blame	2	6	3	2	2	3		18(31.58%)
Unfair grading, lack of recognition of performance or effort	12	1	1					14(24.56%)
Violations of promises and agreements		1	1	1		1		4(7.02%)
Unfair punishment		2						2(3.51%)
Not conceding one's error	1		1					2(3.51%)
Unconscionable demands				2				2(3.51%)
Betrayal of confidence				1			1	2(3.51%)
Giving orders in an inappropriate tone	1				1			2(3.51%)
Meddling in one's business		1						1(1.75%)
Cheating					1			1(1.75%)
Withholding rights one feels entitled to		1						1(1.75%)
Ruthless or illegal misuse of high status and power					1			1(1.75%)
Mixed and ambiguous cases	2	2	2			1		7(12.29%)
Totals	18 (31.58%)	14 (24.56%)	8 (14.04%)	6 (10.53%)	5 (8.77%)	5 (8.77%)	1 (1.75%)	57(100.00%)

the frequencies of other settings would increase (e.g., authorities and administrative institutions).

Authority Relationship

The next variable to be analyzed, the authority, power, or status relationship between the perpetrator of the injustice and the victim, is partly correlated with the social setting. All reported events in the school setting and the authorities setting, as well as the overwhelming majority of cases in the family (84.62%) and at the work place (88.89%), were characterized by a power or status differential favoring the perpetrator. In contrast, in the friendship setting both persons had equal power and status. Approximately equal numbers of equal and unequal relationships were reported in the public setting and in those concerning lodging. Independent of the social setting, the perpetrator had more power or higher status than the victim in 73.68% of the reported unjust incidents. One can assume this to be quite typical for reports of unjust events.

Eliciting Events

A closer inspection of the events that were reported to have elicited the experiences of injustice revealed that the subjects used the term *injustice* much more freely than social scientists usually do.[1] Nevertheless, many of the types of events described (see Table 1) are consistent with the scientific understanding of justice. The most frequently reported events were instances of unjustified accusation and blaming (31.58%). They occurred in nearly all types of social settings. The second most frequent category (24.56%) refers to unfair grading or lack of recognition of performance and effort. Of course, this category is most typical for the school/university setting. Violations of promises and agreements constitute a third category (7.02%), one which was observed in nearly all settings. Beyond these three types, a number of other categories were observed only one or two times in the present sample: unfair punishment; failure to admit an error; unconscionable demands; betrayal of confidence; giving orders in an inappropriate tone; meddling in one's business; cheating; withholding rights to which one feels entitled; and, finally, ruthless or illegal misuses of one's high status and power. Six of the reported events consisted of a mixture of two or three of the

---

[1]For example, one of our subjects felt it to be unjust that his mother-in-law poked her nose into his business, thus getting on his nerves.

previously mentioned categories. One event could not be unambigiously classified even with the help of this category system.

Consequences and Reactions

Attention was next focused on the reported consequences of, and the actions taken by the victims in response to their unfair treatment.[2] Looking through the protocols, it seemed appropriate to distinguish among seven types of consequences. The first category refers to subjects' attempts to convince the perpetrators to modify their decision or action, and to attempts to explain and justify one's own preceding actions. Twenty-eight subjects (49.12%) reported reactions of this type. However, 20 of them admitted that their attempts were unsuccessful; only 5 subjects reported success.[3] Three additional subjects mentioned that they considered intervening but, ultimately, did not do so. The second category consists of punishment in the form of insulting or taking revenge on the perpetrator. Ten subjects (17.54%) reported that they actually did so and eight additional subjects reported that they had considered punishment. The third category includes responses such as actively avoiding future contact, actively breaking off the relationship with the perpetrator, and leaving-the-field reactions. Six subjects (10.53%) reported actual responses of this type, and eight additional subjects (14.03%) mentioned that they had considered this possibility. A fourth category included those responses in which the victims reported actually seeking advice, support, or consolation (6 cases; 10.53%), or considered doing so (1 case). Compared to these first four types of reactions, the remaining three categories consisted of more passive responses or consequences. Nine subjects (15.79%) reported that the quality of their relationship with the perpetrator declined as a consequence of the unjust actions, 7 subjects (12.28%) reported some form of passive resistance, and 12 (21.05%) subjects explicitly mentioned that they resigned themselves to their fates.

In response to the question of whether, and if so, how the subject's view of the event had changed since it happened, only 12 subjects mentioned that they no longer felt they had been unjustly treated. Thirty-four subjects explicitly stated that their view had not changed since the event. Some of them admitted, however, that they no longer felt angry (five cases), or that they now perceived the event as being far less important (five cases).

---

[2]Subjects could report, of course, more than one consequence or action. Therefore, the percentage numbers reported below do not add up to 100%.

[3]It is interesting to note that in all successful attempts, the victim was equal in power and status to the perpetrator.

Emotional Responses

The final step in analyzing subjects' protocols was to study the emotional responses reported. To arrive at a meaningful category system the explicit remarks regarding emotional responses in the protocols of the first 32 subjects (consisting of 38 different emotional terms), were judged by 6 persons. These individuals (mainly staff members from the Department of Psychology, University of Graz) were asked to categorize the emotional terms into meaningful classes. They were allowed to use as many categories as they felt necessary. Although the number of proposed categories varied between five and eight, generally speaking, there was an impressive agreement among the judges. Combining their suggestions, it seemed most appropriate for present purposes to distinguish among five different categories of emotion, which were then used to classify the emotional remarks in all 57 protocols.

The first category included emotional responses like anger, rage, and indignation—emotions reported by 68.42% of the subjects.[4] Typical examples of reactions assigned to the second category are getting upset, feeling aroused, butterflies in the stomach, and increased heartbeat. This category of arousal responses and physical symptoms was relevant for 12.28% of the subjects. The third category included all those emotional responses related to being perplexed, dumfounded, surprised, bewildered, cohfused, and shocked. Emotional reactions of this type were reported by 29.82%. The fourth category consisted of more passive reactions such as feeling helpless, despair, miserable, wretched, self-pity and resignation. One third of the subjects in our sample mentioned experiencing such emotions. The fifth and final category refers to emotional responses suggesting a negatively evaluated preceding action by another person. It consists of emotional responses like being disappointed, aggrieved, and feeling hurt, and is relevant for 28.07% of the subjects.

Objectivity of Coding

To test the objectivity of the various category systems employed in these analyses, an untrained coder was asked to recode all 57 protocols. With a single exception, the interrater agreements proved to be satisfactorily high. Agreement was 96.49% for the social setting, 98.25% for the status or power relationship, 80.70% for the eliciting events, and

---

[4]Most of the subjects reported more than one single emotion (up to 6, $M = 2.6$), sometimes from the same and sometimes from different categories. Therefore, the percentages do not add up to 100%.

79.59% for the emotional responses. With regard to the reported consequences and reactions, the agreement was no more than 59.76%.

Discussion

The analyses of the retrospective reports on unjust events provided an impressive amount of information and demonstrated the usefulness of this methodological approach. However, until more extended and more systematic follow-up studies can be conducted, the results obtained should be taken cautiously for the following reasons. First, the number of reports analyzed so far is rather small. Second, the return rate in this investigation was very low—slightly below one third. Third, nothing is known about why the subjects chose to report the particular events they did. Finally, as the present investigation used only university students as subjects, one should be cautious about generalizing the findings too freely. This seems especially important with regard to the observed types of events eliciting the experience of injustice, and the social settings in which they occurred. Despite these limitations, it seems appropriate to discuss some of the major implications of the results for future research and theory building.

There is an obvious discrepancy between the unjust events reported by our subjects and the situations of injustice normally examined in previous research. Those types of injustice that were studied most frequently in the past—unfair payment and unjust distributions of material goods—were hardly mentioned in the present investigation. Rather, the majority of events reported consisted of unjustified accusation and blaming, unfair grading, and lack of recognition of performance or effort by teachers or parents. As students were used as subjects in the majority of previous studies and in the present investigation, the discrepancy just mentioned challenges the validity and generalizability of the results obtained in the past. Future studies should carefully try to use unjust events and social settings that are familiar and relevant to the subjects under investigation. It is only then that we can expect to obtain valid responses from our subjects.

The great variety of unjust events reported in the present investigation suggests the need to analyze more closely the similarities and differences among them. Perhaps it will be possible with appropriate methodologies to arrive at a meaningful taxonomy of events and treatments that are experienced as unjust or unfair. Such a taxonomy could contribute considerably to a refined conceptualization of injustice experiences.

The consequences of the unjust events reported by the subjects, and the data on whether and how their view has been changing since the event, disagree with the theoretical assumption of equity theory

(Adams, 1965) that unjustly treated people always restore justice either behaviorally or cognitively. According to the present data, only very few people were successful in their attempts at behaviorally restoring justice. Nevertheless, the majority of our subjects did not change their view of the event and still felt that they had been unjustly treated.[5]

Finally, the emotional responses reported agree quite well with the propositions of Homans (1961), Adams (1965), and Walster, Walster, and Berscheid (1978): feelings of anger, rage, and indignation constitute the type of emotions mentioned most frequently and by the largest proportion of the subjects. However, one should not overlook the fact that many other—and phenomenologically quite different—emotions were also reported (e.g., surprise, helplessness, and aggrievement). If this finding can be replicated, it suggests that the emotional processes accompanying experiences of injustice deserve to be treated more carefully in our conceptualization of injustice than they have been in the past.

ROLE-PLAYING INVESTIGATION 1

The role-playing studies were conducted to explore in more detail the cognitive processes and emotional reactions that are elicited by the perception of an unjust event. In addition, an attempt was made to examine possible differences between a person in the role of victim and a person in the role of an unaffected observer. Several authors (e.g., Deutsch, 1985; Mikula, 1984; Reis, 1984) have suggested that the perspective or role an individual takes in relation to an unjust event (i.e., whether one is the perpetrator, the victim, or an unaffected observer) might make a difference in the perception and experience of this event. The main focus of the following discussion is the analysis of the reported cognitions and feelings rather than the differences between victims and observers. Nevertheless, these differences will also be mentioned.

The usefulness of a role-playing methodology to uncover the cognitions following the perception of an unjust event was first assessed in an already published investigation by Mikula and Schlamberger (1985). The subjects in this study, students at Austrian high schools, were given a short description of an incident of an unjust treatment of a student by his or her teacher. Depending on the experimental condition, they were led to place themselves either in the role of the victim of the injustice

---

[5]Of course, one could argue that this follows from the instruction used in our study, because events that are no longer considered unjust would not be events that are reported. The plausibility of this argument is weakened, however, by the fact that 12 subjects did report events they no longer felt to be unjust.

or that of an unaffected fellow student observing the event. They were then asked to record all questions and thoughts that came to their minds in the situation described.

Subjects' reports were partitioned into single units of cognitions, coding separate units whenever the content of the reported idea changed. On this basis, about 390 different responses were identified. Then, a coding system was developed to classify the reported cognitions into meaningful categories. On the basis of theoretical considerations and the observed responses, the following three categories were defined: action-related questions and thoughts, attributional questions and thoughts, and assessments and evaluations. The category of action-related cognitions included remarks about actions planned by the individual as well as explicit remarks concerning the hopelessness of acting against the injustice. The attributional category included mainly questions about possible causes and attempts at explanation. The third category included evaluations of the teacher and his or her action, assessments of the situation, and assessments of potential consequences for the teacher and the teacher–student relationship.

Approximately 98% of the responses could be classified using this category system. The intercoder agreement among the authors (Mikula and Schlamberger) and three untrained coders was 80% to 85%. Approximately 47% of the coded remarks consisted of evaluations and assessments; action-related thoughts made up approximately 31%; and attributional questions and thoughts accounted for 22% of the observed responses. Compared to those in the observer role, subjects in the victim role reported significantly more attributions (1.39 vs. 0.73) as well as action-related thoughts (2.15 vs. 0.73), and significantly fewer assessments and evaluations (2.11 vs. 3.12).

Generally speaking, the role-playing methodology proved useful and provided interesting results. There are, however, several shortcomings of this study. First, only one scenario describing an unjust event was used. Therefore, nothing is known about whether the results obtained can be generalized to other events of injustice. Second, the rather small number of subjects ($N = 72$) made it impossible to establish more narrowly defined categories of responses, as their frequencies of occurrence would have been too small. Third, the instructions used in this investigation stressed only cognitions, such as questions and thoughts, and did not explicitly solicit reports of emotional reactions. As a result, very few emotional remarks were observed. (One can assume this to be quite atypical of experiences of injustice.) Finally, it would have been interesting to collect additional information from the subjects about how they perceived the situation described. Given these arguments, it seemed appropriate to conduct a second and more extended investigation using the same methodology.

ROLE-PLAYING INVESTIGATION 2

The second investigation involved 316 Austrian high school students between 16 and 20 years of age ($M = 17.25$). Data from 38 subjects (about 12%) had to be excluded from the analyses; two subjects refused to participate, eight subjects discussed problems of injustice on a general level, and 28 subjects changed the perspective to which they were assigned.[6] Thus, the final sample consisted of 278 subjects (144 females and 134 males); 149 played the role of a victim and 129 played the role of an unaffected observer.

Five different scenarios of injustice were employed, all related to the school setting. One scenario was the same as that in the first investigation; the other four were concerned with grading problems, unjustified accusation or blaming, and lack of recognition of a pupil's effort or performance by a teacher.[7] The events described in these scenarios were selected on the basis of informal interviews with students regarding frequently occurring unjust events.

Subjects were given one of two versions of one of the five scenarios describing the situation either from the perspective of the victim or an unaffected fellow student observing the event. They were asked to try as hard as possible to put themselves in the described situation and to write down how they would feel and what would go through their minds in the situation. After reporting their cognitions and feelings, the subjects were asked to answer a variety of questions. Among other things they were asked to rate: (a) the effect to which the event caused them to feel aroused, annoyed, disappointed, depressed, and helpless; (b) how unjust they felt the situation to be; (c) how frequently they had been confronted with a similar situation in the past; and (d) the degree to which they empathized with the victim in the story.

CATEGORIES OF COGNITIONS AND FEELINGS

As the sample size and, consequently, the number of observed responses, was much larger in this second investigation than in the first, it was possible to arrive at a more detailed coding system including a larger number of more narrowly defined categories. Many of these categories cannot be subjected to statistical analyses because they were too infrequently observed. Nevertheless, they are informative since they

[6]It is interesting to note that these changes of perspective were distributed very unevenly. Twenty-six subjects moved from the perspective of an observer to that of a victim and only two subjects changed in the opposite direction.

[7]A description of the scenarios is available from the author.

contribute to a more detailed and vivid description of the phenomenology of experiences of injustice. The major types of responses and the more narrowly defined categories within the same type of responses are described in the following. Examples are given in Table 2.

Attributional Questions and Thoughts

As in the first study, one type of response was concerned with attributional questions and thoughts. Within this type, four different categories could be distinguished: (a) attributional questions concerning possible causes, reasons, and explanations of the perpetrator's (teacher's) unfair action or decision (*Attr?*); (b) causal attributions providing explanations of the event or of the perpetrator's action or decision (*Attr*); (c) attributions of responsibility to the victim (*Resp*); and (d) explicit denials of responsibility of the victim and attributions of responsibility to other persons or events that imply the innocence of the victim (*N-Resp*).

Action-Related Thoughts

The second major type of responses observed are action-related thoughts of various sorts. It seemed appropriate to distinguish the following categories: (a) thoughts concerned with active intervention and attempts to restore justice, assist the victim, and mount collective actions of all students in the class (A_{rest}); (b) thoughts concerned with punishment of the perpetrator by insulting him or taking revenge (A_{pun}); (c) thoughts concerned with more passive responses to the unfair treatment (A_{pass}); (d) thoughts concerned with opposition against or transgression of a prohibition that has been unfairly issued by the perpetrator (A_{opp}); (e) thoughts concerned with asking the advice of other persons, looking for others' confirmation of one's own point of view, and searching for relevant information to assess the situation properly (A_{inf}); (f) thoughts concerned with encouraging other people to act against the unfair action or decision (A_{enc}); (g) thoughts concerned with actions which should be undertaken by others without any active participation of the subjects (A_{other}); and (h) action-related thoughts that do not fit into any of the previously mentioned categories (*A?*).

Nonacting

As opposed to the first investigation, thoughts concerned with nonacting (*N-Act*) were treated as a separate category this time. Included are explicit remarks on nonacting and reflections on the impossibility or hopelessness of acting against the injustice.

TABLE 2. Examples of Response Classifications

Category	Examples
	I. Attributional questions and thoughts
1. *Attr?*	"Why me?"; "Why doesn't he believe in me?"; "What does she have against him?"; "Is she angry at me?"; "How can he do anything like that?"; "Did she do this on purpose?"
2. *Attr*	"Perhaps she doesn't like me"; "He is biased"; "He is in a bad mood"; "I'm sure it was a mistake."
3. *Resp*	"It's his own fault"; "I should have learned more."
4. *N-Resp*	"I can't help it"; "But I studied so much"; "It's not the student's fault."
	II. Action-related thoughts
1. A_{rest}	"I'll go to the teacher and tell him . . ./ ask him why . . ."; "I won't stand for it"; "We should stick together"; "I'll help the student to convince the teacher"; "She has my full support."
2. A_{pun}	"I'll show her"; "I'll get back at him"; "I'll make her look ridiculous"; "I'll tell him off."
3. A_{pass}	"I'll let him know that I'm angry"; "I won't cooperate in class"; "I'll laugh at her contemptuously"; "I'll be stubborn."
4. A_{opp}	"I'll go out although it is not allowed."
5. A_{inf}	"I'll discuss the matter with my friend"; "I'll ask the advice of other teachers"; "I'll find out if it's legally allowed"; "I'll compare the tests of the two students."
6. A_{enc}	"I'll have my parents come to school"; "I'll ask the class representatives to speak with the teacher"; "I'll encourage the student to protest against the decision."
7. A_{other}	"The victim should not stand for that"; "Other students should speak with the teacher"; "My mother will surely take care of that."
	III. Nonacting
1. *N-Act*	"You can't do anything about it"; "It does not pay to do anything about it"; "I don't care enough to do anything about it"; "I guess I'll finally get used to it"; "I think it's better if I let things be."
	IV. Reflections, evaluations, and assessments
1. E_p	"That's mean"; "The teacher (this decision) is unfair"; "He is a pig"; "Arse-holes!"
2. R_s	"He should keep his word"; "The same two tests should be graded equally"; "A teacher should only claim a thing like that if she can prove it"; "I ask myself what I studied for"; "Forbidding us to go out is no proper educational method."
3. R_g	"It's always the same"; "That's typical of teachers (our school system); "Teachers are . . ."; "There is no justice in the world."
4. C_v	"I'll have to study harder the next time"; "What happens if I fail the examination"; "The student will be in trouble with her parents."
5. C_p	"He will have troubles"; "The students will lose faith in the teacher"; "I'll never forgive him."
6. *Pd*	"That's not so bad"; "I could not care less about it"; "Don't worry."
	V. Imaginary aggressions
1. *Aggr*	"I could wring this teacher's neck"; "Aggression toward the teacher."
	VI. Empathic responses
1. *Emp*	"I sympathize (have compassion) with my fellow student"; "The victim will naturally be angry"; "The victim does not understand why . . ."; "If I were the victim I would . . ."

Reflections, Evaluations, and Assessments

The fourth type of remark includes reflections, evaluations, and assessments. These can be subdivided into the following six categories: (a) evaluations of the perpetrator or of his or her decision (E_p); (b) reflections on the immediate event or situation (R_s); (c) more general reflections (R_g) stimulated by the immediate event, but mainly concerned with more general topics (e.g., the school system, teachers in general, injustice in general); (d) reflections on long-lasting consequences of the event for the victim (C_v); (e) reflections on long-lasting consequences of the event for the teacher (perpetrator) or the teacher–student relationship (C_p); and (f) remarks playing down the importance of the event (*Pd*).

Emotional Responses

The next type of response concerns emotional reactions (*Emo*) and has been divided into six categories. The first five of them correspond to those that have been developed on the basis of our analyses of subjects' descriptions of actually occurring unjust events: E_1—anger, rage; E_2—getting upset, physical symptoms; E_3—surprise; E_4—helplessness, depression; and, E_5—disappointment, feeling aggrieved. Beyond this, very few remarks on feelings of envy (E_6) were observed.

Imaginary Aggressions

Additionally, imaginary aggressions (*Aggr*) were treated as a separate category.

Empathic Responses

A final category of remarks was defined for various types of empathic responses of observer subjects (*Emp*), such as compassionate reactions, speculations on the victim's feelings or cognitions, and remarks of the type "If I were . . . I would . . ." regarding acting, nonacting, emotions, and aggressions.

Noncoded Remarks

Not covered by this classification system and, therefore, omitted from further analyses were remarks on the scenarios (e.g., "That's a very realistic example"), communications to the experimenter (e.g., "The same happened to me once"), and those reflections in which subjects, feeling they had inadequate information about the specific details of the event, rehearsed various alternative possibilities (e.g., "It depends on the concrete circumstances: if the victim were my friend, I would . . . If, however, I don't like him, I would . . . "). Taken together, there were 57 such remarks. Of the remaining 1,406 remarks, only 24 (1.70%) could not be categorized according to the category system.

OBJECTIVITY OF CODING

The objectivity of coding was tested by asking a doctoral student, who was unaware of the specific aims of the study, to recode 40 randomly selected protocols, after receiving a detailed description of the category system and some brief training with 8 additional protocols. The intercoder agreement was 87.28% concerning the partitioning of subjects' reports into single units of cognitions, and 82.63% regarding the categorization of the units. If one counts only disagreements regarding the type of responses and neglects disagreements regarding the various categories within the same type of responses (e.g., A_{rest} vs. A_{pun}), agreement regarding categorization improves from 82.63% to 88.42%.

RESULTS

Table 3 shows the frequency of occurrence of the various types and categories of responses. As can be seen, about one half (50.29%) of all coded responses are reflections, evaluations, or assessments. Within this type of cognition, reflections on the event (23.08%) and evaluations of the perpetrator (15.34%) were most frequently observed. Action-related thoughts constituted 16.40% of the total of observed responses. The most frequently occurring category of these types of cognitions were thoughts of restoring justice (9.94%). All other categories were far less frequently observed. Attributional questions and thoughts were reported approximately as often as action-related thoughts; they constituted 15.12% of all coded remarks. Attributional questions (4.47%) and causal attributions (6.46%) were more frequent than responsibility attributions (1.85%) and denials of responsibility (2.34%). The observed emotional responses (8.03%) overwhelmingly belonged to the categories of anger, rage, indignation (4.40%), and disappointment or feeling aggrieved (1.70%). Empathic reactions (3.69%), which naturally occurred only with observer subjects, thoughts on nonacting (3.41%), and imaginary aggressions (1.35%) complete the total of coded responses.

Many of the categories of responses were too infrequently observed to be treated separately in statistical analyses. Therefore, and in order to compare the results of both investigations, the more narrowly defined categories of the second investigation were combined into larger units

TABLE 3. Frequencies of Categories of Responses

Types and categories of responses	Frequency	%
Attributional questions and thoughts		
Attributional questions ($Attr?$)	63	4.47
Causal attributions ($Attr$)	91	6.46
Responsibility attributions ($Resp$)	26	1.85
Denials of responsibility ($N\text{-}Resp$)	33	2.34
Total	213	15.12
Action-related thoughts		
Attempts at restoring justice (A_{rest})	140	9.94
Punishment (A_{pun})	28	1.99
Passive resistance (A_{pass})	13	0.92
Opposition against prohibition (A_{opp})	5	0.36
Seeking for information (A_{inf})	16	1.14
Encouraging others (A_{enc})	14	0.99
Actions others should undertake (A_{other})	11	0.78
Ambiguous cases ($A?$)	4	0.28
Total	231	16.40
Thoughts on nonacting ($N\text{-}Act$)	48	3.41
Reflections, evaluations, assessments		
Evaluations of the perpetrator (E_p)	216	15.34
Reflections on the event (R_s)	325	23.08
Generalized reflections (R_g)	54	3.84
Consequences for the victim (C_v)	48	3.41
Consequences for the perpetrator (C_p)	25	1.78
Playing down (Pd)	40	2.84
Total	708	50.29
Emotional responses		
Anger, rage (E_1)	62	4.40
Physical symptoms (E_2)	8	0.57
Surprise (E_3)	9	0.64
Helplessness, depression (E_4)	8	0.57
Disappointment, feeling aggrieved (E_5)	24	1.70
Envy (E_6)	2	0.14
Total	113	8.03
Imaginary Aggressions ($Aggr$)	19	1.35
Empathic Reactions (Emp)	52	3.69
Uncoded responses	24	1.70
Total	1408	100.00%

resembling the categories of the first investigation as closely as possible. Thus, all types of attributional cognitions were treated as one single category, the remarks on nonacting were added to the category of action-related thoughts, and all reflections, evaluations, and assessments, as well as the empathic reactions were combined. As opposed to the first investigation, the emotional responses (also including the imaginary aggressions) were considered as an additional fourth category. An analysis of variance, with the type of response, the subjects' perspective, sex, and the scenarios treated as independent variables, revealed two significant main effects, for perspective, $F(1, 258) = 9.77$, $p < .01$, and type of response, $F(3, 774) = 151.52$, $p < .01$, both of which are qualified by the two-way interaction of these two variables, $F(3, 774) = 9.60$, $p < .01$. This interaction shows that, compared to those in the observer role, subjects in the victim role reported significantly fewer reflections (2.48 vs. 3.02) and significantly more action-related thoughts (1.31 vs. .66). The observed difference with regard to attributional thoughts, .87 for victims versus .64 for observers, fell short of being significant. Finally, emotional responses occurred significantly more frequently with victims (.70) than with observers (.24). Neither the scenarios given to the subjects nor the subjects' sex showed any significant effects.

DISCUSSION

The cognitions observed, and their frequencies, agreed quite well with those of the first investigation using the same methodology. Both investigations show that the major type of cognitive activity involved reflections on and evaluations of the event. Attributional cognitions are also of importance, as several authors have suggested (e.g., Cohen, 1982; Utne & Kidd, 1980). However, they are not nearly as prominent in thought as one might have expected, given the writings of these authors. Action-related thoughts occur at least as frequently as attributional thoughts. This evidence, and the great variety of categories of responses observed within the major types of cognitions, suggest that we will need more detailed and complex models than those proposed until now to appropriately depict what is going on in people's minds when they confront an injustice.[8] Future analyses should focus on the temporal structure of the various types and categories of thoughts and how they relate to each other.

[8] One should be cautious, however, about generalizing from the present results that people always think as much when confronting an unjust event as they did in the present studies. The hypothetical nature of the role-playing studies might have increased the cognitive activity of our subjects (cf. discussion of Greenberg, 1984, of the possibility of mindless reactions to injustice).

The differences observed between victims and observers are also impressively similar to those of the first investigation using the role-playing technique. Apparently, victims are more personally involved than are observers. Preliminary analyses of the rating data that are relevant to this point corroborate this interpretation. Victim subjects empathized more strongly with the unjustly treated person in the story, perceived the event as more unjust, and described themselves as being more aroused, annoyed, disappointed, depressed, and helpless than did the observer subjects. This agrees well with the propositions of previous writers (e.g., Mikula, 1984; Walster *et al.*, 1978) and suggests that it will be necessary to consider the perspective a person holds in relation to an unjust event as an additional variable in our theorizing on injustice. This holds, of course, not only for victims and observers but also for the perspective of the perpetrator (cf. Deutsch, 1985).

The next results to be discussed are those regarding acting and nonacting. The remarks on the impossibility or hopelessness of acting against the unfair treatment, which were observed in the role-playing studies, demonstrate that a number of people resigned themselves to what had happened. These people neither said that no injustice occurred at all nor did they play down the importance of the event.[9] Rather, they felt the event to be unfair but simply did not consider acting against it. This evidence agrees with the results obtained in the retrospective reports. Contrary to what is assumed by earlier theorists (e.g., Adams, 1965), resignation to one's fate seems to be a feasible alternative to restoring justice either by compensatory actions or by cognitive distortions (cf. Greenberg, 1984).

If we look at the full range of the action-related thoughts observed in the role-playing studies, and the actions mentioned in the retrospective reports, it seems appropriate to distinguish between four· major types of behavioral responses to an unjust event: (a) attempts to restore justice, either by one's own intervention or by seeking support from others; (b) punishment of the perpetrator, either in an active way or in form of passive resistance;[10] (c) leaving-the-field reactions; and (d) resignation. Our theoretical models of injustice will have to consider all these options of responding and specify the (situational and person-specific) conditions associated with their occurrence. Perhaps, it might

---

[9]There is no significant correlation between the remarks on nonacting and those playing down the importance of the event.

[10]One might argue that punishment of the perpetrator is a subcategory of restoring justice rather than an independent category of response. However, punishment can restore justice only in the sense of equity; it does not change the victim's treatment by the perpetrator. Thus it seems more appropriate to distinguish between these two options of behavioral response to an unjust event.

be helpful in this task to borrow from research findings and theorizing on coping with stressful events other than injustice.

The final topic to be discussed are the emotional responses.[11] The kinds of emotions observed agree well with those found in the retrospective reports. Reactions of anger and rage were again most frequently mentioned. This evidence lends support to the propositions of prominent theories of injustice (e.g., Adams, 1965). However, the consistent occurrence of additional emotions suggests that it will be necessary to consider them too in our conceptualization of injustice experiences. The categories of emotions observed seem to reflect different aspects and different phases of a rather complex emotional process that is elicited by the perception of an injustice.[12] It is tempting, of course, to speculate about what such a temporal sequence of emotions could look like. The first position in such a sequence presumably would be occupied by reactions of surprise (E_3). Reactions of arousal (E_2) seem to be located appropriately at the second position. The third position might be reasonable for emotions like disappointment and feeling aggrieved (E_5). Finally, depending on the coping strategy of a certain individual, either responses of anger and indignation (E_1) or the more passive emotional reactions of feeling depressed and helpless (E_4) would occur at the fourth position. Needless to say, the methodologies used in our investigations are far too crude to provide the information needed to substantiate any model of the sequential nature of emotions. However, the suggestion to adapt a process model to depict the emotional reactions to injustice might be fruitful.

CONCLUSION

The methodologies employed in the investigations described in this chapter have proven to be useful and have provided interesting data on the nature of experiences of injustice. In addition, the methodologies complement each other quite well. The role-playing technique yields data on spontaneous reactions to imagined unjust events, whereas the responses obtained with the retrospective reports are nonspontaneous

[11]Their number was indeed higher in the second than in the first investigation, but it was still rather low. This may be a consequence of the role-playing technique and the hypothetical nature of the unjust event. Another plausible explanation is that existing emotional expressions were not properly coded by the judges, who classified only emotions mentioned explicitly. Other remarks, which implicitly indicated an emotional state of the subject, were not considered in order to minimize subjective interpretation as far as possible.

[12]I am grateful to Klaus Scherer for calling my attention to this possibility.

but deal with unjust events actually experienced. Consistency in the results that were obtained with the two methods (e.g., those with regard to the emotional and the behavioral responses to injustice) lend considerable support to their validity. They also demonstrate the usefulness of a variety of methodologies, a variety that may be especially useful whenever the topic to be explored is one as complicated and difficult to grasp as injustice.

What, then, follows from the results of these studies? In my opinion, they suggest that the experience of injustice would be appropriately conceptualized as a multifaceted process of interrelated sequences or subprocesses of cognitions, emotions, and action tendencies (or actions). What cognitions, emotions, and actions specifically occur in a certain case will depend, in part, on the event that elicited the perception of injustice, and the circumstances given (e.g., the power relationship between the people involved and/or the degree to which the event occurred unexpectedly). Those responses that occur later in the sequences will be additionally determined by preceding cognitive, emotional, and behavioral responses. Finally, it seems reasonable to assume that individual differences will explain a considerable amount of variance.

If one agrees to such a conceptualization of experiences of injustice, the implications for future research are quite clear. First, we would have to develop a taxonomy of major types of events that elicit the perceptions of injustice. Second, we would have to analyze in detail the interrelationships existing between certain cognitions, emotions, and actions (or action tendencies), both within and between the three subsystems of the process. Third, we should try to identify typical sequential patterns of eliciting events (and circumstances given, as noted earlier), cognitions, feelings, and actions. Fourth, and finally, it would be useful to explore individual differences with regard to typical patterns of responding to an injustice.

The studies that were reported in this chapter should be regarded as merely first steps in this direction. However, in my view, they proved to be promising. Thus, I hope that others will follow in these steps.

Acknowledgments

I am indebted to Norbert Haider for his assistance in collecting and analyzing most of the data reported in this chapter. For providing additional help, thanks are also extended to Gerda Nittel, Birgit Petri, Gerhard Ruenstler, and Walter Naehrer. Last but not least, I am grateful to Lita Furby and the editors of this volume, Hans Werner Bierhoff, Ronald Cohen, and Jerry Greenberg, for their helpful comments on an earlier version of this chapter.

REFERENCES

Adams, J. S. (1965). Inequity in social exchange. In L. Berkowitz (Ed.), *Advances in experimental social psychology* (Vol. 2, pp. 267–297). New York: Academic Press.

Cohen, R. L. (1982). Perceiving justice: An attributional perspective. In J. Greenberg & R. L. Cohen (Eds.), *Equity and justice in social behavior* (pp. 119–160). New York: Academic Press.

Deutsch, M. (1983). Current social psychological perspectives on Justice. *European Journal of Social Psychology, 13*, 305–319.

Deutsch, M. (1985). *Distributive justice: A social psychological perspective.* New Haven, CT: Yale University Press.

Folger, R. (Ed.). (1984). *The sense of injustice: Social psychological perspectives.* New York: Plenum Press.

Greenberg, J. (1984). On the apocryphal nature of inequity distress. In R. Folger (Ed.), *The sense of injustice: Social psychological perspectives* (pp. 167–186). New York: Plenum Press.

Greenberg, J., & Cohen, R. L. (Eds.). (1982). *Equity and justice in social behavior.* New York: Academic Press.

Homans, G. C. (1961). *Social behaviour: Its elementary forms.* New York: Harcourt, Brace & World.

Kayser, E., & Schwinger, T. (1982). A theoretical analysis of the relationship among individual justice concept, laymen's social psychology, and distribution decision. *Journal of the Theory of Social Behaviour, 12*, 47–51.

Lerner, M. J., & Lerner, S. C. (Eds.). (1981). *The justice motive in social behavior.* New York: Plenum Press.

Mikula, G. (Ed.). (1980). *Justice and social interaction.* New York: Springer-Verlag.

Mikula, G. (1984). Justice and fairness in interpersonal relations: Thoughts and suggestions. In H. Tajfel (Ed.)., *The social dimension: European developments in social psychology* (pp. 204–227). Cambridge: Cambridge University Press.

Mikula, G., & Schlamberger, K. (1985). What people think about an unjust event: Toward a better understanding of the phenomenology of experiences of injustice. *European Journal of Social Psychology, 15*, 37–49.

Reis, H. T. (1984). The multidimensionality of justice. In R. Folger (Ed.), *The sense of injustice: Social psychological perspectives* (pp. 25–61). New York: Plenum Press.

Utne, M. K., & Kidd, R. F. (1980). Equity and attribution. In G. Mikula (Ed.), *Justice and social interaction* (pp. 63–93). New York: Springer-Verlag.

Walster, E., Walster, G. W., & Berscheid, E. (1978). *Equity: Theory and research.* Boston, MA: Allyn & Bacon.

Chapter 7

Thinking about Justice and Dealing with One's Own Privileges

A STUDY OF EXISTENTIAL GUILT

LEO MONTADA, MANFRED SCHMITT, and
CLAUDIA DALBERT

THE CONCEPT OF EXISTENTIAL GUILT

Resources are distributed unequally. Differences in wealth, prestige, education, freedom, or power are common, within and between families, organizations, social classes, countries, and so forth. Historians, social philosophers, sociologists, and psychologists have often examined how people deal with being disadvantaged: When do they consider their lot unjust and possibly suffer from it? When do they tend to act against perceived injustice? When do they put their lot into perspective and justify it? Theories of social conflict, of revolution, and of envy have analyzed inequalities from the viewpoint of the disadvantaged.

By contrast, relatively little is known about the perspective of the privileged. Do they enjoy their privileges? Do they fear losing their advantages? Do they deny or justify their favorable lot? Certainly, various doctrines of justice offer ample arguments that can be used by the advantaged to justify their privileges. But what happens if someone fails

LEO MONTADA, MANFRED SCHMITT, and CLAUDIA DALBERT • Fachbereich I—
Psychologie, Universität Trier, Postfach 3825, 5500 Trier, West Germany. This research
was supported by a grant from the Stiftung Volkswagenwerk (VW-Foundation).

to justify his favorable lot without having to renounce his preferred principles of justice, or the facts? In such cases, a person should experience conflict and feel uneasy about his advantages.

We have begun research on the phenomena of uneasiness caused by one's own privileges and on the attempt to cope with this uneasiness. Our first study, from which the data presented in this chapter stem, was focused on *existential guilt*. We conceive existential guilt as an intra- and interindividually varying disposition to react with feelings of guilt to perceived differences between one's own favorable lot or position (i.e., one's own privileges) and the unfavorable lot of others.

We believe existential guilt to be a likely reaction whenever the following four conditions are met. First, one's own advantages must be seen to result from controllable distributions that need to be justified. Second, one must assume a causal relationship between one's own privileges and the unfavorable situation of others, that is, the lot of the disadvantaged must either be regarded as a direct or indirect consequence of one's own privileges, or it must be open to improvement by means of redistribution. Third, there must be some doubt concerning the justice of the discrepancies between one's own and others' situations. Different principles of distributive or procedural justice may cast doubts on the legitimacy of a distribution. Finally, the privileged person must feel solidarity with, and responsibility or even sympathy for, the disadvantaged. This points to the question of where the boundaries of a community are seen, within which solidarity and justice may be claimed. These boundaries may be narrow (e.g., the nuclear family), or they may be so broad as to incorporate the entire human race, including subsequent generations.

In the past, psychology has not been interested much in the concept of existential guilt. Theoretical elaborations are lacking as are operationalizations of the concept and sound empirical research. Nevertheless, analogies can be found in psychiatric case descriptions, that is, in analyses of guilt feelings experienced by survivors of catastrophes (Lifton, 1967) or concentration camps (von Bayer, Haefner, & Kisker, 1964; Chodoff, 1976; Ostwald & Bittner, 1976). Survivors sometimes feel guilty toward the dead. Why? Perhaps because surviving is seen as violating solidarity or equality in bad fate.

Hoffman (1976) was the first theorist to use the concept of existential guilt in a broader sense: not only may survival promote feelings of guilt, certain favorable circumstances in life may cause them as well. Not only might those who lose their lives in a catastrophe be considered victims, but potentially all individuals who are undeservedly underprivileged. In this conceptual framework Hoffman interpreted the political activities of America's (radical) white youth during the sixties, when members of the white middle class fought for the civil rights of blacks and against the continuation of the Vietnam War (Haan, Smith, & Block, 1968; Keniston, 1968).

The preceding conceptualization of existential guilt raises a number of empirical questions. First, by means of what cognitive-defensive strategies can someone protect himself against feelings of existential guilt when confronted with his own privileges vis-à-vis the unfortunate lot of others? In particular, how effective are denial of the existence of inequality or of differences in privileges, justification of one's own advantages by attributing them to internal causes, such as effort or aptitude, and justification of inequality by attributing the disadvantages of others to themselves, for example, to their laziness or lack of ability? Second, how important is adherence to a particular principle of distributive justice in understanding whether one's own privileges require justification and lead to existential guilt if justification fails? Third, what role does perceived control over the distributive process play in existential guilt? Does perceived control enhance feelings of existential guilt if justice is seen to be violated? Fourth, what role does generalized denial of responsibility for the fate of the disadvantaged play? Does it, as we assume, moderate the effects of perceived injustice on existential guilt? Fifth, does existential guilt vary with attitudes toward the disadvantaged? Sixth, does belief in a just world (Lerner, 1980) immunize someone against existential guilt? Does this effect vary depending on how important or central issues of justice are seen to be? Finally, is it possible to demonstrate the construct validity of existential guilt (a) by distinguishing it from empathic distress, and (b) by relating existential guilt to social and political attitudes and behavior?

COPING WITH ONE'S OWN PRIVILEGES: AN EMPIRICAL STUDY

Our empirical study on these questions is focused on three groups of disadvantaged people: (a) people living in developing countries, (b) the handicapped, and (c) Turkish guest workers in West Germany.[1] These

[1]There are many Turkish guest workers living in Germany with their families, mainly blue collar workers with permission to stay and jobs for a restricted period of time. Although they earn the same as Germans in the same jobs, they are considered relatively poor because they send a lot of money home to their relatives in Turkey, they usually have large families, they live in overcrowded dwellings, and so forth. Because they remain in Germany for a limited period of time only, they have not accumulated property in the way most Germans do. Moreover, they have no rights of political participation, which is becoming more and more of a problem. Of course, these Turkish people may compare

three groups were chosen because most West Germans live under much better conditions than those people do.[2] No assessment was made of the living conditions of our subjects to ensure their privileged situation compared to the living conditions of the three groups of underprivileged selected.

SAMPLE

Three hundred and forty subjects with a mean age of 36.1—ranging from 16 to 70 years—took part in the study. Sixty-two percent were male. Higher levels of formal education were somewhat overrepresented. Most subjects (88%) described their income as sufficient or better.

About half of the sample were randomly drawn residents of an urban area; the remaining subjects were selected from organizations that, because of their programs or activities, expect their members to have either a low or a high tendency to experience existential guilt.

RESEARCH INSTRUMENTS

Because we were unaware of any research on existential guilt and its relationship to the variables specified above, all research instruments had to be constructed (cf. Dalbert, Montada, Schmitt, & Schneider, 1984; Montada, Schmitt, & Dalbert, 1983). Because we were interested primarily in interindividual differences in dispositional existential guilt and their relation to other constructs, mainly derived from theories of justice and prosocial behavior, our approach fits well into a personological framework. As is common in this framework, all variables were assessed by questionnaires.

The target variable, existential guilt, and six other variables were measured with an existential guilt inventory. This instrument consists of nine short stories or scenarios describing the disadvantages of (a) people in developing countries, (b) handicapped people, and (c) Turkish guest

themselves to other Turkish people in Germany or to reference groups in Turkey. Therefore, they may not consider themselves disadvantaged. However, our study is not focused on the self-perception of the Turkish, but on the perceptions and evaluations of Germans.
[2]The present study was focused on existential guilt toward anonymous groups. We assume that feelings of existential guilt may arise toward individual persons as well. For example, a German blue collar worker may have a bad conscience when he observes that his Turkish colleague has to perform the most difficult jobs; or a husband may feel guilty when he becomes aware of his wife being frustrated because she had to give up her professional career for the sake of the family and the children; or the son of a rich family may feel guilty when entering a famous college whereas his friend cannot enroll because of financial reasons.

workers in West Germany. The stories clearly emphasize the large discrepancy in desirability of living conditions between the disadvantaged, that is, the characters of the story, and the reader. Each story is followed by a list of seven different thoughts representing cognitive/emotional reactions to it; only five of these are mentioned here. They are conceived as indicators of the following constructs: (a) *existential guilt* (EG): bad conscience, feelings of guilt, feelings of injustice resulting from the comparison of one's own privileges with the fate of underprivileged people; (b) *denial of discrepancies* (DD): denial of or attempts to play down the discrepancies between one's own privileges and the situation of the disadvantaged; (c) *justifying one's own privileges as deserved* (PD): causal attribution of one's own favorable lot to internal factors, such as aptitude or effort or inherited rights; (d) *justifying the disadvantaged's fate as self-inflicted* (SI): causal attribution of the underprivileged's unfavorable lot to themselves, for example, to their incompetence; (e) *empathic distress* (ED): compassion toward the underprivileged.

Subjects were asked to rate on a 6-point scale ranging from "very likely" to "very unlikely" the probability that they would have each particular thought as a reaction to the content of the story.

All statistical analyses reported in the following are based on individual average scores across the nine stories. Intra- and interindividual differences concerning the three groups of disadvantaged will not be reported in this chapter because the primary concern here is to address general relationships between existential guilt and other variables. Internal consistency (Cronbach's alpha) of these five scales, each comprising nine items, is as follows: EG (.89), DD (.76), PD (.86), SI (.79), ED (.84).

The descriptions and statistical properties of the questionnaires developed to measure all other variables will be presented in the sections that deal with their relationship to existential guilt.

COGNITIVE ANALYSIS OF INEQUALITY AND EXISTENTIAL GUILT

We expected existential guilt to be most likely for those subjects who did not use any of the three defensive strategies mentioned: denial of discrepancy (DD), justifying one's own privileges (PD), and justifying the disadvantaged's lot (SI).

The data supported this hypothesis. The three predictor variables (DD, PD, SI) and the criterion variable (EG) were dichotomized at their medians. The contingency table analysis results in a significant chi square for the entire table and for the predictor combination DD-PD-SI (see Table 1). Existential guilt is most likely for subjects who do not deny

TABLE 1. Contingency Table Analysis of the Predictor Variables DD, PD, SI, and the Criterion Variable EG (All Variables Dichotomized at Their Median)

			EG+			EG−			
DD	PD	SI	f_o	f_e	χ^2	f_o	f_e	χ^2	Total
+	+	+	45	51.2	.75	56	49.8	.77	101
+	+	−	3	7.6	2.78	12	7.4	2.86	15
+	−	+	6	9.6	1.35	13	9.4	1.38	19
+	−	−	8	6.6	.30	5	6.4	.31	13
−	+	+	12	12.2	.06	10	10.9	.07	22
−	+	−	6	7.6	.34	9	7.4	.35	15
−	−	+	5	8.1	1.19	11	7.9	1.22	16
−	−	−	69	52.2	5.41*	34	50.8	5.56*	103
Total			154			150			304[a]

[a]In this and all subsequent tables, N is reduced due to missing data.
*$p < .05$

the discrepancies, do not justify their own privileges, and do not hold the disadvantaged responsible for their fate.

DISTRIBUTIVE JUSTICE AND EXISTENTIAL GUILT

Differences in privileges may be judged differently depending on the principle of distributive justice underlying the evaluation.

Based on results of a previous study (Schmitt & Montada, 1982), we constructed short scales to measure generalized preference for the equity and the need principle. Those preferring the equity principle were expected to have few difficulties justifying existing inequalities in contrast to people considering the need principle just.

The equity scale (EY) consists of nine items meant to represent preference for input–output proportionality as a just distribution rule, for example, "I consider an employer to act justly if during times of slow business he dismisses the least productive employees first." Subjects had to indicate how much they agreed with the statements on 6-point Likert scales. Considering the small number of items, internal consistency of the scale is acceptable (Cronbach's alpha = .76).

The need scale (NE) consists of six items meant to represent a preference for distributions based on recipients' needs, for example: "If two friends own a sailboat together, I feel it would be fair if they paid for all expenses according to their income." Internal consistency of the scale is acceptable (alpha = .79).

The relationships of these two justice variables to existential guilt and to the defensive cognitions are consistent with our expectations. Although the contents of the two justice scales have no commonalities with the contents of the nine scenarios of the existential guilt inventory, the correlations are significant and substantial. For example, the correlation between equity (EY) and justification of one's own privileges as deserved (PD) amounts to .46 ($p < .001$), whereas the correlation between the need principle (NE) and PD equals .06 ($p = .16$); existential guilt (EG) is correlated positively with NE ($r = .46$, $p < .001$) and negatively with EY ($r = -.12$, $p = .019$).

THE ROLE OF PERCEIVED CONTROL

Our conceptual analysis of existential guilt suggests that perceived control over redistribution may be a crucial factor in addition to the evaluation of inequality in terms of justice. *Subjectively perceived control* (PC) was assessed with a scale of nine items referring to the same groups of disadvantaged people and to the same privileges as the nine stories of the existential guilt inventory. Each item consists of a question asking subjects whether they see options or means for themselves to improve the unfavorable lot of the disadvantaged mentioned. Subjects answer these questions by indicating on a 6-point Likert scale the amount of influence they believe they would have if they wanted to change the situation. For example: "(Even) if I wanted to, I could exert no (. . . a lot of) influence on the bad housing situation of Turkish guest workers in West Germany." Subjects were not asked if they were motivated or willing to exert influence but only if they could exert influence if they wanted to. The internal consistency of the scale is high (alpha = .89).

In addition to a positive correlation between perceived control (PC) and existential guilt ($r = .27$, $p < .001$), we expected PC to act as a moderator of the (positive) effect of need (NE), and the (negative) effect of equity (EY), on existential guilt (EG). Perception of high control should enhance these two effects, whereas perception of little control should lower them. Concerning equity, perceived control should corroborate the view that everyone is the master of his or her own fate. On the other hand, the perception of control over redistribution should increase the sense of being responsible for reestablishing justice, which according to the need principle is considered violated.

This hypothesis was tested via multiple regression analysis with NE, EY, and PC as predictors and EG as the criterion variable. In addition to NE, EY, and PC, their products (NE $\times$ EY, NE $\times$ PC, EY $\times$ PC, NE $\times$ EY $\times$ PC) were included as predictor terms to test the interaction hypothesis (see Cohen, 1978). As can be seen in Table 2, PC indeed acts

TABLE 2. Multiple Regression from EG on NE, EY, PC, and Their Products (Accepted Model; All Variables Ranging from 1 to 6; $N = 268$)

Predictor term[a]	R	R^2	r	b	$\hat{\sigma}_b$	F	df	p
NE	.46	.21	.46	.92	.21			
PC	.48	.23	.25	−.50	.28			
EY	.49	.24	−.11	−.35	.31			
NE × EY	.50	.25	.29	−.14	.05	6.72	1/262	<.05
EY × PC	.51	.26	.14	.18	.07	5.97	1/262	< .05
Intercept				2.46				

[a]Total $F = 18.79$; $df = 5/262$; $p < .01$. Model equation: $E(EG|NE,EY,PC) = 2.46 + .92NE − .50PC + (−.35 − .14NE + .18PC)EY$.

as a moderator variable but only with respect to EY. Additionally, NE serves as a moderator of EY.

The model equation at the bottom of Table 2 allows for the computation of conditionally expected values of EG for all values of NE, EY, and PC (cf. Steyer, 1985).[3] Existential guilt is highest for those who simultaneously consider the need principle as very just, reject the equity principle as very unjust, and believe themselves to have high control over redistribution. On the other hand, those who have a very favorable attitude toward the equity principle score high on perceived control, and reject the need principle as unjust, are least likely to experience existential guilt.

FELT RESPONSIBILITY FOR AND ATTITUDE TOWARD THE DISADVANTAGED

We have argued that existential guilt presupposes solidarity with, responsibility and even sympathy for the disadvantaged. Theory and research on the context-specific preference for justice principles (e.g., Deutsch, 1975; Schmitt & Montada, 1982) make it clear that the need principle is considered particularly appropriate whenever the social context of the conflict is characterized by interpersonal responsibility.

Responsibility denial (RD) as conceptualized by Schwartz (e.g., 1977) may serve as an indirect indicator of how narrowly someone sets the boundaries for solidarity and responsibility. Consequently, responsibility

[3]All coefficients in this chapter are based on scale scores that were computed as individual item means. Scores can range from 1 to 6. Coding of all variables in this chapter is such that a low numerical value represents a high substantive value. For example, EG = 1 represents the highest amount of existential guilt possible, PC = 6 means the lowest amount of perceived control possible. This coding is important for the understanding of both conditional effects and conditional values.

denial should determine whether need (NE) is considered appropriate to evaluate the justice of a situation. Although NE was assessed only in a generalized form, the assessment of RD was specific to groups of the disadvantaged. Therefore, we expected a curvilinear moderator effect of RD on the dependency of existential guilt on NE, and for the following reasons. A moderate degree of responsibility denial may well indicate an ambivalent opinion with respect to solidarity. In such cases of indecision (i.e., whether or not to exclude the disadvantaged from one's community), more generalized beliefs like NE should be relied on to evaluate the situation, and NE should therefore become a more influential source of variance in existential guilt. By contrast, low *or* high degrees of RD indicate clear decisions. In such cases, reference to more general opinions or beliefs such as NE should be less important for the generation of existential guilt.

Similar to Schwartz (e.g., 1977), *responsibility denial* (RD) was conceptualized as a tendency to play down others' needs or misery, explain them as self-inflicted, point to the responsibility of others, claim that help is not possible, or apply any other similarly defensive perception or evaluation. Each of the three parts of the RD scale focuses on one of the three groups of the disadvantaged considered. Each part consists of 12 items, such as the following concerning the handicapped: "Many handicapped exaggerate their problems," or "I can't see why individual citizens should care about the problems of the handicapped; that's the business of the Federal Government." Again, subjects had to indicate on a 6-point Likert scale how much they agreed with the statements. Internal consistencies of the three parts of the scale are high, ranging from .85 to .93. As they were highly intercorrelated, average scores were computed for further data analysis. In a formal sense, the hypothesis concerning the moderating effect of RD on the relationship between NE and EG corresponds to a quadratic moderator function (cf. Bartussek, 1970). Again, multiple regression analysis served to test the hypothesis. As can be seen from Table 3, the partialed product of NE and RD^2 (NE × RD^2) accounts for a significant proportion of the variance in existential guilt (EG).

The conditional regression effects of NE (given RD) are consistent with our hypothesis. Attitude toward the need principle is most important as a predictor of existential guilt for those subjects who deny responsibility to a moderate degree and least important for those who either deny responsibility a great deal or very little.[4]

---

[4]Given RD = 2.5, 3, 4, 5, and 5.5, the respective effects of NE on EG amount to .11, .36, .53, .25, and −.06. These values of RD were chosen to take into account the

TABLE 3. Multiple Regression from EG on NE, RD, RD^2 and Their Products (Full Model; All Variables Ranging from 1 to 6; $N = 299$)

Predictor term[a]	R	R^2	r	b	$\hat{\sigma}_b$	F	df	p
NE	.41	.17	41	−2.84	1.25			
RD	.51	.26	−.38	−5.23	2.02			
NE × RD	.53	.28	.18	1.74	.59			
RD^2	.53	.29	−.39	.63	.24			
NE × RD^2	.56	.31	−.02	−.22	.07	10.55	1/293	< .01
Intercept				12.47				

[a]Total $F = 26.39$; $df = 5/293$; $p < .01$. Model equation: $E(EG|NE,RD) = 12.47 - 5.23RD + .63RD^2 + (-2.84 + 1.74RD - .22RD^2)NE$.

Besides responsibility denial, attitudes toward the disadvantaged (AU) were considered as indirect indicators of a disposition to experience solidarity and responsibility. Among other instruments (e.g., social distance scales), we used adjective lists to assess AU. This measure is, as expected, significantly and substantially correlated with existential guilt ($r = .50$, $p < .001$). There are no interaction effects of AU with any other justice variable predicting existential guilt.

BELIEF IN A JUST WORLD AND EXISTENTIAL GUILT

According to Lerner (e.g., 1977), many people seem motivated to hold the view that the world is a just one where everyone gets what he or she deserves. When these people encounter injustice, they experience a conflict between reality and their belief. This conflict may be resolved either by intervention, for example, by trying to reestablish justice, or, if that seems impossible, too costly, or aversive, by cognitive reevaluation or reorganization. Many puzzling phenomena begin to make sense when analyzed in this framework (see also Lerner, 1980).

Belief in a just world would seem to provoke denial of the injustice of obvious inequalities of the type depicted in the scenarios of our existential guilt inventory. Therefore, belief in a just world should be correlated positively with the three defensive strategies, denial of

skewed distribution of RD (most of our subjects tended not to deny responsibility, $\overline{RD} = 4.38$).

discrepancies (DD), justification of own privileges (PD), justification of the disadvantaged's fate as being self-inflicted (SI), and negatively with existential guilt.

Because a German translation of Rubin & Peplau's (1975) just world scale achieved poor reliability and consistency scores (Dalbert, 1982), two new scales were developed, one assessing a *general belief in a just world* (GJW) (e.g., "I believe that in general people get what they deserve") and a second assessing *specific belief in a just world* (SJW) that relates to the three groups of underprivileged people at issue (e.g., "I believe that in West Germany Turkish employees are not disadvantaged"). GJW consists of six items (alpha = .88), SJW of eight (alpha = .82). Subjects responded by indicating the extent of their agreement with the statement on a 6-point Likert scale.

We expected the specific belief in a just world (SJW) to be more strongly related to the defensive strategies (DD, PD, SI) than the general belief in a just world (GJW) because of content similarities. The data confirm the expectation as well as the hypothesis stated previously: the correlation between general belief in a just world (GJW) and existential guilt is negative. Though significant, it is not impressive ($r = -.10, p < .05$). The correlations between GJW and the defensive strategies are much higher: DD ($r = .47, p < .001$), PD ($r = .52, p < .001$), SI ($r = .45, p < .001$). As expected, all correlations were higher when belief in a just world was assessed specifically (SJW): EG ($r = -.37, p < .001$), DD ($r = .62, p < .001$), PD ($r = .64, p < .001$), SI ($r = .57, p < .001$).

The Moderating Role of Centrality of Justice

It seems reasonable to assume that the relation between belief in a just world and existential guilt is not constant across all groups of people but itself depends on moderator variables, such as the centrality of justice as part of one's self-concept. It seems unlikely that people to whom justice issues are very important could easily claim the world to be just when confronted with obvious inequalities. On the other hand, those for whom justice is less central should have fewer difficulties in warding off feelings of existential guilt by means of conceiving the world as a just place. In addition to this interaction effect, we expected a main effect of *centrality of justice* (CJ) on existential guilt because we assume people for whom issues of justice are important to be more sensitive to inequalities. A five-item scale (e.g., "There is almost nothing that infuriates me as much as injustice") was devised to test these hypotheses. Subjects had to indicate on a 6-point Likert scale how much they felt these statements described them. Internal consistency of the scale is low, though acceptable if the shortness of the scale is considered (alpha = .73).

As before, the interaction hypothesis stated previously was tested via multiple regression analysis. Only specific belief in a just world (SJW) was included. The results of this analysis are reported in Table 4.

As hypothesized, the partialed product (SJW × CJ) is significant and substantial in size. The direction of the interaction effect is consistent with our expectations; that is, the more central justice is, the weaker is the effect of belief in a just world on existential guilt. On the other hand, if justice is of little importance to someone (CJ = 6), existential guilt will strongly depend on specific belief in a just world (b_{SJW} = −1.75; see the model equation at the bottom of Table 4). Even though "main effects" may not be interpreted if significant interaction effects exist, the correlation between centrality of justice and existential guilt (r = .31, $p <$ .001) supports the second part of our hypothesis.

A PREDICTIVE MODEL FOR EXISTENTIAL GUILT

To this point, we have identified several variables on which existential guilt seems to depend. However, we have not taken all the interrelations among these variables into account. Indeed, our interpretation would be more sound if we could demonstrate these reported effects to be independent of each other. Therefore, a multiple regression analysis was performed with all the predictor variables discussed so far, including the significant products (DD, PD, SI, NE, EY, PC, RD, AU, GJW, SJW, CJ, EY × PC, NE × EY, NE × RD^2, SJW × CJ). In addition, the German

TABLE 4. Multiple Regression from EG on SJW, CJ, and Their Product
(Full Model; All Variables Ranging from 1 to 6; N = 253)

Predictor term[a]	R	R^2	r	b	$\hat{\sigma}_b$	F	df	p
SJW	.37	.14	− .37	.26	.21			
CJ	.49	.24	.31	1.95	.44			
SJW × CJ	.52	.27	.07	− .33	.09	12.48	1/249	< .01
Intercept				1.00				

[a]Total F = 31.02; df = 3/249; $p <$ .01. Model equation: E(EG|SJW,CJ) = 1.00 + 1.95CJ + (.26 − .33CJ)SJW.

version of the Crowne and Marlowe (1960) social desirability scale (Lück & Timaeus, 1969) was included as a predictor variable. Existential guilt (EG) served as the criterion variable.

The results of this stepwise analysis (forward selection) are presented in Table 5. Remarkably many predictors survive this analysis: attitudes toward the underprivileged (AU), need principle (NE), responsibility denial (RD), centrality of justice (CJ), specific belief in a just world (SJW), and justification of one's own privileges as deserved (PD). Three of the five variables dealing with justice exert an independent effect on existential guilt (NE, SJW, CJ); equity and the general belief in a just world do not account for a significantly independent portion of the variance in existential guilt in addition to the other predictors. Two of these three justice scales have no commonalities in content with existential guilt (recipients and resources to be distributed). This strengthens the theoretical interpretation of these correlations, as they cannot be accounted for by shared content variance. Even though none of the interaction effects survived this rigorous test of their significance, we still believe in their value for conceptual clarification.

DISCRIMINATING EXISTENTIAL GUILT FROM EMPATHIC DISTRESS

The proportion of variance in existential guilt (EG) accounted for by the six significant predictor variables is remarkable. However, there is one single variable, empathic distress (ED), that accounts for more variance in EG than these six predictors taken together. ED was assessed

TABLE 5. Multiple Regression from EG on All Potential Predictors Measured and Some of Their Products (Accepted Model; All Variables Ranging from 1 to 6; $N = 273$)

Predictor term[a]	R	R^2	r	b	$\hat{\sigma}_b$	F	df	p	beta
AU	.50	.25	.50	.62	.10	39.74	1/266	< .01	.32
NE	.61	.37	.44	.28	.05	34.53	1/266	< .01	.29
RD	.64	.40	−.41	−.31	.08	17.68	1/266	< .01	−.21
CJ	.66	.43	.32	.24	.07	12.68	1/266	< .01	.17
SJW	.66	.44	−.36	−.20	.08	5.77	1/266	< .05	−.17
PD	.67	.45	−.15	.13	.06	3.99	1/266	< .05	.13
Intercept				1.23					

[a]Total $F = 35.52$; $df = 6/266$; $p < .01$.

by the existential guilt inventory. The correlation between EG and ED is as large as .73. Does this mean that empathic distress and existential guilt are not distinguishable, or that they are caused by one single underlying latent variable? We believe the answer is no.

There is a clear conceptual difference between the two. Empathic distress may be caused solely by the misery of others, whereas existential guilt requires in addition the perceived injustice of one's own privileged situation. However, a high correlation between EG and ED is hardly surprising. We think that existential guilt requires solidarity and sympathy with the underprivileged as a prerequisite. Empathic distress might be a good indicator of such solidarity and sympathy.

In addition to these conceptual arguments, there is relevant evidence in our data on the discriminant validity of existential guilt. First, as expected, more variance in EG (26%) than in ED (15%) can be accounted for by the linear combination of need principle, equity principle, and personal control. Justice considerations and perceived control over redistribution are much less predictive of empathic distress than of existential guilt. Second, the correlation between specific belief in a just world and existential guilt is higher ($r = -.36, p < .001$) than the correlation between SJW and ED ($r = -.12, p = .019$). Again, justice considerations seem to be more important for the development of existential guilt than for the presence of empathic distress. Third, whereas the defensive strategies (DD, PD, SI) and their interaction are significant predictors of existential guilt ($R = .29, p < .001$), none of them correlates significantly with empathic distress. Empathic distress may arise independently of whether the inequality seems justified or not; this is not true for existential guilt that is unlikely if these defensive arguments are favored. Fourth, if perceived control (PC) is added as a predictor to DD, PD, and SI, their multiple correlation with EG increases to $R = .40$ ($p < .001$), whereas the multiple correlation of DD, PD, SI, and PC with ED still remains insignificant. Again, perceived control affects existential guilt but not empathic distress, a result which corresponds to Hoffman's conceptual analyses (Hoffman, 1982). Finally, some items of the scale measuring responsibility denial (RD) stated that the state and professional welfare organizations, rather than individual citizens, are responsible for improvements in the situation of the underprivileged. The combination of these items to a reduced scale did not correlate with empathic distress ($r = .01$), but with existential guilt ($r = -.23, p < .001$). This result is totally in line with our theoretical considerations: whereas existential guilt depends on one's own perceived responsibility for the unfavorable lot of others, empathic distress does not. Taken together, this evidence supports the claim that empathic distress and existential guilt are more than just two sides of the same coin.

CRITERION GROUP VALIDITY OF EXISTENTIAL GUILT

So far, the argument for the construct validity of existential guilt has relied on its specific relations to other constructs focused on the discrepancy between one's own privileges and the unfavorable lot of others. There are also data demonstrating the construct validity of existential guilt based on its relation to membership in criterion groups and criterion behavior.

Research has repeatedly found that liberals more frequently evaluate social inequalities as unjust than conservatives, who, as the concept "conservative" implies, tend to justify or play down inequalities (e.g., Sandberger, 1982). Included in our sample were several groups that can be ordered according to their *political liberalism/conservatism* (L/C). The presumably most conservative group emcompasses members of *Burschenschaften*, which are student fraternities with distinctively conservative opinions on the justice of existing differences (L/C = 1), followed by members of the CDU (Christian Democratic Union), the more conservative of the four main political parties in West Germany (L/C = 2). Members of the SPD (Democratic Socialists), the *Grüne* (Environmentalists), and members of various *Bürgerinitiativen* (formal action groups committed to the peace movement or to environmentalist organizations) were considered the least politically conservative subjects (L/C = 4). All remaining subjects, probably very heterogenous in political thinking, were assigned a L/C value of three (L/C = 3). Statistical significance of the differences in existential guilt among these groups was tested via one-way analysis of variance. The results of this analysis are given in Table 6.

Differences in existential guilt among groups are consistent with expectations. However, only the most conservative group (student fraternity) differs significantly from the other groups who do not differ in EG from each other significantly.

TABLE 6. One-Way Analysis of Variance on EG between Four Groups Differing in Political Conservatism/Liberalism

Group (L/C) =)	n	$\overline{EG}$	$s\overline{EG}$	$\hat{\sigma}\overline{EG}$	Significant difference (LSD, $p < .01$, two-tailed) to group 1	2	3	4
1	50	4.01	1.16	.16				
2	41	3.13	.97	.15	*			
3	213	3.07	.99	.07	*			
4	23	2.89	1.12	.23	*			

Another criterion behavior to which existential guilt should be related is *commitment to and active support of underprivileged people.* We assume that existential guilt is not only a reaction to perceived injustice (to one's own advantage) but also a motivation to relieve one's guilty conscience. As an indicator of such motivation we have considered endeavors to reestablish justice. Our sample included members of several nonprofessional organizations committed to helping disadvantaged people. Some of these organizations focus their activities on the three groups of disadvantaged people we considered in our study (i.e., people from developing countries, the handicapped, Turkish guest workers in West Germany); other organizations have a more general social commitment. As expected, the difference in existential guilt between subjects belonging to one of these groups and uncommitted subjects is very significant ($t_{327} = 4.1$, $p < .01$). However, taken absolutely, the difference is not very large (approximately one half of a standard deviation). This might be explained by the guilt-reducing effect of adequate social commitment.

CONCLUDING REMARKS

In most societies, people strive for privileges, advantages, and status. Often, they are not only proud of successes but pleased about social and economic luck. Upward mobility is a strong and widespread motive. However, in addition to the motive to maximize personal gains, there must be a fundamental motive for justice (Lerner, 1980). Without assuming such a motive, feelings of existential guilt would be difficult to explain.

The more equality is taken into consideration in thinking about justice, the more troubling large inequalities in the distribution of social goods may become. The questions addressed in our research are, How do people cope with their own obvious and substantial advantages? When do they "plead guilty" to having taken advantage undeservedly? and, When do they apply various defensive strategies to justify the status quo?

A primary goal of this chapter was to clarify the concept of existential guilt and its theoretical network, especially certain prerequisite conditions, such as preference for the need principle, lack of justifications of discrepancies, lack of responsibility denial, and lack of belief in a just world.[5] The overall meaning of empirical relationships between

[5]Because the description of populations was not the main purpose of this chapter, means and other descriptive statistics of existential guilt and its correlates have not been presented and discussed.

existential guilt and its correlates (including the interaction effects) seem to support the validity of the construct and the hypothesized theoretical network.

A second aspect of validity was addressed by the question of how well existential guilt can be differentiated from empathic distress. Though highly correlated, these two variables are clearly distinguishable. They have different and theoretically meaningful relationships. As expected, existential guilt covaries to a higher degree than empathic distress with attitudes toward justice principles, "defensive" justifications of discrepancies, belief in personal control, and belief in just world. It is argued that empathic distress itself is a contributing (if not a necessary) condition for existential guilt. A person who is indifferent or derogatory or hateful toward the disadvantaged will hardly feel existential guilt. But there are further conditions that are necessary to transform empathic distress into existential guilt.

This evidence for the validity of the concept and its measurement should encourage further research. As we have only indirect evidence that existential guilt may instigate actions on behalf of the disadvantaged (actually, on differences between criterion groups), we will have to learn more about the consequences of, and the strategies of coping with, existential guilt. Evidence from experimental research leads to the expectation that guilt feelings dispose people to prosocial actions (e.g., Tobey-Klass, 1978) which might take the form of giving away some of one's own goods or making a plea for some redistribution. Certainly there are social conflicts whose solution requires some amount of redistribution of duties, wealth, power, freedom, income, and so forth. Therefore, future research on existential guilt should include additional target groups (e.g., the unemployed, female employees, members of future generations as potential victims of today's exploitation of natural resources).

Prosocial action is not the only way to cope with one's own advantages. For example, a critique of society's value system may be another, and sometimes relatively inexpensive, strategy to free oneself of guilt feelings without a concrete personal commitment.

Although we have identified some strategies employed to avoid or free ourselves from guilt feelings, we have to study these processes and their outcomes in more detail. Moreover, we have to look at what happens when prosocial commitment is very costly and guilt defensive strategies are not successful. Certainly existential guilt may become a virulent or even a dangerous feeling. As the justice of differences may always be questioned, one's own advantages can never be justified beyond any doubt. Those who fail to convince themselves that their advantages are justified (e.g., earned or socially functional) should experience a permanent conflict: either they give up their advantage or they violate their personal norms of justice. That is the type of conflict out of which neuroses might develop.

REFERENCES

Bayer, v., W., Haefner, H., & Kisker, K. P. (1964). *Psychiatrie der Verfolgten* [Psychiatry of the persecuted]. Berlin: Springer.

Bartussek, D. (1970). Eine Methode zur Bestimmung von Moderatoreffekten [A method to determine moderator effects]. *Diagnostica, 66,* 57–76.

Chodoff, P. (1976). The German Concentration Camp as a psychological stress. In R. H. Moos (Ed.), *Human adaptation: Coping with life crises* (pp. 337–349). Lexington, MA: D. C. Heath.

Cohen, J. (1978). Partialed products are interactions; partialed powers are curve components. *Psychological Bulletin, 85,* 858–866.

Crowne, D. P., & Marlowe, D. (1960). A new scale of social desirability independent of psychopathology. *Journal of Consulting Psychology, 24,* 349–354.

Dalbert, C. (1982). *Der Glaube an eine gerechte Welt: Zur Güte einer deutschen Version der Skala von Rubin and Peplau* [The belief in a just world: On the quality of a German version of Rubin and Peplau's scale.] (Berichte aus der Arbeitsgruppe "Verantwortung, Gerechtigkeit, Moral" Nr. 10). Trier: Universität Trier, FB I—Psychologie.

Dalbert, C., Montada, L., Schmitt, M., & Schneider, A. (1984). *Existentielle Schuld: Ergebnisse der Item- und Skalenanalysen* [Existential guilt: Results of item- and scales analyses.] (Berichte aus der Arbeitsgruppe "Verantwortung, Gerechtigkeit, Moral" Nr. 24). Trier: Universität Trier, FB I—Psychologie.

Deutsch, M. (1975). Equity, equality, and need: What determines which value will be used as the basis of distributive justice? *Journal of Social Issues, 31,* 137–149.

Haan, N., Smith, M. B., & Block, J. (1968). Moral reasoning of young adults: Political-social behavior, family background, and personality correlates. *Journal of Personality and Social Psychology, 10,* 183–201.

Hoffman, M. L. (1976). Empathy, role-taking, guilt, and development of altruistic motives. In T. Lickona (Ed.), *Moral development and behavior* (pp. 124–143). New York: Holt, Rinehart, & Winston.

Hoffman, M. L. (1982). Development of prosocial motivation: Empathy and guilt. In N. Eisenberg (Ed.), *The development of prosocial behavior* (pp. 281–313). New York: Academic Press.

Keniston, K. (1968). *Young radicals: Notes on committed youth.* New York: Harcourt, Brace, & World.

Lerner, M. J. (1977). The justice motive: Some hypotheses as to its origins and forms. *Journal of Personality, 45,* 1–52.

Lerner, M. J. (1980). *The belief in a just world: A fundamental delusion.* New York: Plenum Press.

Lifton, R. (1967). *Death in life: Survivors of Hiroshima.* New York: Random House.

Lück, H. E., & Timaeus, E. (1969). Skalen zur Messung Manifester Angst (MAS) und Sozialer Wünschbarkeit (SDS-E and SDS-CM) [Scales for measuring manifest anxiety (MAS) and social desirability (SDS-E) and SDS-CM]. *Diagnostica, 15,* 134–141.

Montada, L., Schmitt, M., & Dalbert, C. (1983). *Existentielle Schuld: Rekrutierung der Untersuchungsstichprobe, Erhebungsinstrumente und Untersuchungsplan* [Existential guilt: Sampling method, measurement instruments, and design] (Berichte aus der Arbeitsgruppe "Verantwortung, Gerechtigkeit, Moral" Nr. 20). Trier: Universität Trier, FB I—Psychologie.

Ostwald, P., & Bittner, E. (1976). Life adjustment after severe persecution. In R. H. Moos (Ed.), *Human adaptation: Coping with life crises* (pp. 361–371). Lexington, MA: D. C. Heath.

Rubin, Z., & Peplau, L. A. (1975). Who believes in a just world? *Journal of Social Issues, 31*, 65–89.

Sandberger, J. U. (1982). *Between legitimation and critique on West German intellectuals' beliefs, norms, and evaluations of social inequality.* Konstanz: Universität Konstanz, Zentrum I Bildungsforschung, Sonderforschungsbereich 23, Arbeitsunterlage 73.

Schmitt, M., & Montada, L. (1982). Determinanten erlebter Gerechtigkeit [Determinants of perceived justice]. *Zeitschrift für Sozialpsychologie, 13*, 32–44.

Schwartz, S. H. (1977). Normative influences on altruism. In L. Berkowitz (Ed.), *Advances in experimental social psychology* (Vol. 10, pp. 221–279). New York: Academic Press.

Steyer, R. (1985). Causal linear stochastic dependencies: An introduction. In J. R. Nesselroade & A. von Eye (Eds.), *Individual development and social change: Explanatory analysis* (pp. 95–124). New York: Academic Press.

Tobey-Klass, E. (1978). Psychological effects of immoral actions: The experimental evidence. *Psychological Bulletin, 85*, 756–771.

Chapter 8

Rethinking Equity Theory

A REFERENT COGNITIONS MODEL

ROBERT FOLGER

Equity theory (Adams, 1965; Walster, Berscheid, & Walster, 1973) seems to have outlived its usefulness. Can it—should it—be revised or reconceptualized? This chapter argues that there is a basis for rethinking equity theory and that such an enterprise is a worthwhile precursor to further research on the psychology of injustice.

A recent issue of the *Industrial-Organizational Psychologist* contained an article by John Miner (1984) entitled "The Unpaved Road over the Mountains: From Theory to Applications." In it Miner evaluated various theories in industrial/organizational (I/O) psychology and organizational behavior (OB) according to their usefulness. His evaluative categories were *useful, question mark,* and *not so useful.* Miner rated equity theory in the bottom, least useful, category. Certainly it is easy to understand the disdain of I/O and OB practitioners for a theory that, as Miner puts it, "has never . . . been brought to a specific application" (p. 12).

But lack of applicability may not be the root cause of equity theory's troubles (e.g., see Furby, 1986). Some of the current neglect of equity theory might simply be the result of greater interest in other kinds of issues. For example, current interest in social cognition (see Fiske & Taylor, 1984) has shifted attention away from many traditional theories. I think social cognition research also invites a return to such classic problems as the relationship between cognition and affect, however,

ROBERT FOLGER • A. B. Freeman School of Business, Tulane University, New Orleans, LA 70118.

and I think one of equity theory's focal concerns—affective reactions to perceived injustice—can be recast in a useful way by drawing from the social cognition literature.

Independent of having lacked an applied focus or having been displaced by "hotter" topics, equity theory has also suffered from certain conceptual shortcomings. Three that stand out can be described briefly as follows (cf. Folger, 1984a).

1. The essence of equity is that across persons, there should be a comparable rate of compensation for contributions to an exchange (an equivalent outcome/input ratio). This focus on contributions has been challenged by those who suggest that attention to need, and provision of equal outcomes to all, are alternative justice principles (e.g., Deutsch, 1975; Lerner, 1974; Leventhal, 1976). The argument is that these alternative principles are sometimes used, and that equity theory does not accomodate them without making the concept of inputs vacuous and chamelion-like (e.g., Furby, 1986; Reis, 1984). Later I will argue that we should abandon the notion of inputs and replace it with a focus on the conditions that lead to outcomes. This strategy shifts attention away from the specific criteria used for awarding outcomes, which will tend to differ from situation to situation anyway. Instead it draws attention to the perceived causal process behind a given outcome, and particularly to "social accounts" (cf. Bies, in press) that are offered as reasons and justifications for the process.

2. Equity also fails to characterize justice adequately because the theory only specifies a criterion for *distributive* fairness, or the fairness of amounts received. The theory is incomplete because it overlooks *procedural* fairness, or the fairness of procedures that brought about a given outcome. Again this problem is amenable to my strategy of focusing attention on the perceived causal elements leading up to an outcome, because procedures represent one category of such elements. And again I will be emphasizing that perceptions of fairness are heavily influenced by such things as the reasons and justifications supplied for using one procedure rather than another.

3. Adams (1965) explicitly noted that people can respond to an injustice in a variety of ways. The problem is that his theory was not very explicit about predicting when people will respond one way rather than another. This problem will continue to haunt us for a long time, but I think we can make some headway on it in the process of addressing the other two previously described problems. My approach is to specify as carefully as possible the determinants of a particular type of emotional experience—one we can describe in terms such as moral outrage, righteous indignation, or simply resentment (cf. Crosby, 1976). The point is that we should first identify when this emotion is felt strongly and when

weakly or not at all. Once we can reliably find ways of having the emotion "turned on and off," we will be in a better position to investigate how it is channeled in various ways when it is "on" (see also Mark & Cook, 1979; Mark & Folger, 1984).

LEVELS OF REFERENT OUTCOMES

Suppose you do not get what you deserve. Regardless of whether the distributive rule being violated is equity, equality, or need, you are apt to feel resentful. Regardless of which rule was broken, the point is that what happened is not what ought to have happened. When you feel resentful, your thinking is inherently referential—your frame of reference for evaluating what happened consists of a mental comparison to what might have happened instead . . . if only things were as they should have been. Such thoughts, then, are *referent cognitions*, involving the psychology of "what might have been."

Research on social cognition has produced some work that helps characterize this mode of thought, particularly the work by Kahneman and Tversky (1982). The Kahneman–Tversky analysis does not assume referential thinking has to be initiated by social comparison or the violation of previous expectations. Consider, for example, the following demonstration study that Kahneman and Tversky conducted. They had students read a vignette about two men, Crane and Tees. Crane and Tees were riding to the airport together in a limousine. They were going to different locations, so they were booked on different flights. Both planes, however, were scheduled to leave at the same time. The limousine did not get to the airport until 30 minutes *later* than this time, and both men missed their flights as a result. But Crane's plane had left on time (30 minutes before the limousine got the airport), whereas Tees learned that his flight's takeoff had been delayed until just 5 minutes before the time he arrived.

Under these circumstances, who gets more upset: Crane or Tees? When Kahneman and Tversky asked their subjects this question, 96% said "Tees." Kahneman and Tversky argued that the "psychological distance" to a preferred outcome—the distance between the *actual outcome* of missing the flight and the simulated or *referent outcome* of making the flight—was smaller for Tees than for Crane.

By addressing additional aspects of psychological distance, I have formulated a referent cognitions theory (RCT) that expands the Kahneman–Tversky analysis (see also Folger, 1984b, 1986, in press). For one thing, Kahneman and Tversky only wrote about psychologically "close" comparisons between reality and a favorable alternative. Psychological closeness is a function of the ease with which an alternative state of affairs can be imagined. Clearly the most salient alternatively imaginable outcome is not always better than one's actual outcome (e.g., Tees might learn that his plane, which he just missed, crashed on takeoff). RCT thus makes a distinction between *high* referent outcomes and *low* referent outcomes. A high referent outcome is an imaginable outcome that represents a more favorable state than reality (e.g., I got $5; I can easily imagine ways I might have gotten $10 instead). A low referent outcome represents a state that is not any better than reality (e.g., I got $5, and nothing I can imagine could have gotten me any more than that).

EFFECTS OF REFERENT AND LIKELIHOOD COGNITIONS

The Crane and Tees example lends itself to other variations, one of which illustrates a second element of the RCT model—the perceived *likelihood of amelioration* (referent outcome level being the first element). Obviously we might assume that Tees's reaction to his barely missed flight would vary depending on the availability of other flights. Thus RCT distinguishes between a *low* likelihood of amelioration (e.g., Tees needs to make a meeting, and no other flight will get him there in time) and a *high* likelihood of amelioration (e.g., another flight is leaving in 20 minutes, and it will allow him to make the meeting easily). The point is that the level of current outcomes may under some circumstances be considered transient (and hence relatively unimportant), especially if there is a strong chance they will soon be replaced by much better outcomes (cf. Folger, Rosenfield, & Rheaume, 1983). Why be upset about minor setbacks today if tomorrow looks rosy?

Researchers deriving predictions based on equity theory, so far as I know, have not been cognizant that two people may respond differently to the same level of current inequity if they have different impressions of what the future holds. Adding this RCT element makes for an improvement over equity theory, which has no provision for differences in perceived likelihood of amelioration. RCT assumes that if two workers are inequitably underpaid to the same degree, for example, the worker who perceives the greater probability of the inequity's being ameliorated will express less resentment.

An experiment (Folger, Rosenfield, Rheaume, & Martin, 1983) has shown that in addition to this main effect of likelihood, the two RCT elements (likelihood and referent outcomes) also interact in their effect on resentment. All subjects in the experiment worked on two different tasks. Feedback from one, the "incentive" task, was used to manipulate likelihood. Feedback from the second, the "nonincentive" task, was used to manipulate referent outcomes.

The subjects (psychology students) worked on the incentive task first. They were told that their scores on this task would determine whether or not they received a bonus reward (an extra "unit" of experimental credit to be added to their course grades). They also learned that if they failed initially, there would be another chance later (after an interpolated round of trials on the nonincentive task). All were told they had failed, so the subsequent chance to try again later represented the prospects for amelioration. Subjects in the high-likelihood conditions received an indication that they were virtually certain to win later, whereas subjects in the low-likelihood conditions were led to believe they were virtually certain to lose.

Subjects then worked on the nonincentive task. They had been told performance on this task would not count toward the bonus. They were also told, however, that for another group of subjects the procedure had been reversed (i.e., some other subjects had been randomly assigned this second task as the one that counted). Performance feedback from the nonincentive task indicated what would have happened if that assignment had been different: high-referent subjects were told they would have won, whereas low-referent subjects were told they would have lost. A questionnaire (containing measures of anger and resentment) was administered at this point, prior to the round of trials on which subjects thought they would get to try again on the incentive task.

The results confirmed RCT predictions. High-likelihood subjects were significantly less resentful than low-likelihood subjects. This effect is hardly surprising; it shows that those who thought they would eventually get the bonus were happier than those who thought they would not. Thus a low likelihood of amelioration is a necessary condition for resentment, a point that equity theory overlooks. But it is not a sufficient condition for maximal resentment. Maximal resentment also requires a high-referent outcome. The illustration of this point is that within the low-likelihood conditions, low-referent subjects expressed significantly less resentment than high-referent subjects—which produced a referent × likelihood interaction.

"If only . . . " thoughts are at the heart of the RCT framework, but such thoughts can be provoked in a variety of ways. In the experiment just described, for example, the high-referent subjects thought they would have won if only they had been assigned differently. Notice they also thought that some other subjects had been assigned differently. Nevertheless, an important way in which RCT represents a rethinking of equity theory is that RCT specifies social comparison is not a necessary aspect of referential thinking. Other data (Folger, Rosenfield, Rheaume, & Martin, 1983) show that an additional source of resentment can be previously held expectations—including expectations based on a promise made to the subject alone, so that no other subject's situation is comparable.

In addition, further data (Folger, Rosenfield, Rheaume, & Martin, 1983) show resentment can also be affected by referent outcomes that are only imagined, having neither been available to anyone else nor ever been expected by the subjects personally. Thus RCT provides a means for considering *internal standards* of justice, an issue raised in discussions of ways equity theory should be modified (e.g., Austin & Susmilch, 1974; Austin, McGinn, & Susmilch, 1980; Lane & Messé, 1972; Messé & Lane, 1974; Messé & Watts, 1983; Pritchard, 1969; Weick, 1966; Weick & Nesset, 1968). The RCT framework is explicit in stipulating that past experience and previously held expectations are not the only possible sources of internal, nonsocial standards of comparison. Vividly imagined alternative outcomes can also be a source of comparative judgment even when no one may have had any actual experience with such outcomes— such as when these outcomes are implied by the messages of ideological statements about the ways things ought to be done (cf. Fine, 1979; Martin, Chapter 17, this volume).

LEVELS OF JUSTIFICATION

Consideration of "the way things ought to be done" also relates to another element of the RCT model, the element of justification. In terms of the Crane and Tees example, this element takes into account that although Tees might well be highly upset because of just missing his plane, whether or not he will be resentful should depend on the reason why the limousine was late. That is, resentment should vary as a function of whether there was a good reason or a bad reason for the delay. RCT makes a distinction, therefore, between high and low levels of justification for the circumstances that led to the outcomes actually received. In the RCT terminology, circumstances that are instrumental in leading to outcomes are called *instrumentalities*. RCT focuses attention on the extent to which instrumentalities are justified, particularly in the form of reasons offered or arguments made in an attempt to produce such justification (see also Bies, in press). This focus contrasts with that of equity theory.

Equity theory uses the term *outcome* to refer to the level of benefit or harm received. The term itself, however, has further implications that have been overlooked. Specifically, the term implies an end result, the final stage of some process, an effect of causal factors and background conditions. Assume that a concatenation of processes/factors/conditions is perceived as having been instrumental to the occurrence of a given outcome; then any or all elements of this concatenation might have a bearing on the justifiability of that outcome. My argument is that equity theory has been overly restrictive in focusing attention on only one such element, namely the level of entitling "inputs" a person has contributed to some exchange.

Consider an example Furby (in press) has used in arguing that people react differently to unfulfilled expectations depending on the reasons given. The example pertains to an employee who expects to be paid on the first of the month but is not. Furby argued that if company records had been destroyed by fire that morning, the employees would not feel unjustly treated. Similarly, two people might be inequitably underpaid to the same degree, and yet the two would react differently if one person knew there was an unavoidable problem responsible for the inequity (e.g., records destroyed by fire) and the other did not know the reason for the inequity, or thought that the explanation offered was not a sufficient justification of the circumstances.

The focus on instrumentalities also serves to distinguish resentment and feelings of injustice from mere discontent or dissatisfaction. Specifically, this distinction relates to the different effects of outcome and instrumentality comparisons. When a person's referent outcome represents a more favorable state of affairs than the actual outcome received, dissatisfaction results. This dissatisfaction, however, may or may not be accompanied by resentment. Resentment is a separate issue that hinges on perceptions of instrumentalities and the nature of their justification.

Instrumentalities can be evaluated comparatively in the same fashion as outcomes. That is, a counterpart to the actual/referent outcome comparison exists in the form of a comparison beween actual and referent instrumentalities. *Actual instrumentalities* are the events, circumstances, conditions, processes, and actions of various parties that are perceived as having been responsible for the outcomes actually received. *Referent instrumentalities* are the parallel features of an alternatively imagined world, a mental construction of the way things might have operated instead (e.g., if a different policy had been implemented, a different procedure followed). The implication of a comparison between these instrumentalities is that actual outcome-producing circumstances may appear unjustifiable to the extent that the imaginable circumstances seem more reasonable, appropriate, and socially acceptable. Comparison between referent and actual instrumentalities is the basis for feelings of injustice comprising resentment and righteous indignation (cf. Folger, Rosenfield, & Robinson, 1983).

It is certainly possible to imagine referent outcomes without imagining referent instrumentalities, but I think it is more likely for referent outcomes to be dwelt on (ruminated about) when plausible referent instrumentalities capable of producing such outcomes are easy to imagine. I also think there is a tendency, once a desirable end result has been contemplated, to consider what it would take to bring about such a result. When the desired result does not match existing realities, the question "why not?" can thus be answered by comparing plausible means for achieving the desired result with the means that were in fact enacted. In this means–ends analysis, a key consideration is the legitimacy of the means that were enacted, vis-à-vis the legitimacy of the alternative means. If referent instrumentalities appear more legitimate than actual instrumentalities, then any unfavorable comparison between referent outcomes and actual outcomes will transcend mere discontent and will move toward moral outrage.

Note also that when outcomes are allocated by a decision maker, certain decision-making styles may implicitly invoke a comparison to more ideal styles as referent instrumentalities. Much of the literature on procedural justice, for example, suggests that when decisions are made without consultation they seem procedurally unfair (see Folger & Greenberg, 1985, for a review applicable to perceptions of injustice in the workplace). Presumably this lack of procedural fairness stems from recognition of a principle that decision makers should allow people who will be affected by the decision to have some voice in the decision-making process (cf. Folger, 1977; Thibaut & Walker, 1975, 1978).

Thus procedures without "voice" (cf. Hirschman, 1970) may implicitly invoke consideration of systems that have voice, the latter serving as a comparison set of referent instrumentalities. Other kinds of implicit procedural comparisons may be common as well. My emphasis on the importance of reasons and explanations, for example, suggests that an arbitrary decision-making style—a style that shows little interest in providing any justification for one's actions—is likely to be perceived as socially unacceptable. Leventhal (1980) lists additional procedural principles whose violation would presumably constitute grounds for making actual instrumentalities (the violation) seem unjustifiable relative to the referent instrumentalities (the normatively approved practice of following the principle in question).

DISTRIBUTIVE AND PROCEDURAL EFFECTS

Because RCT focuses attention on the justifiability of instrumentalities, it also makes procedural justice a central issue. Instrumentalities are the events and circumstances leading up to outcomes. Among these instrumentalities, procedures (e.g., rules and regulations, decision-making practices, mechanisms of implementation) are often the focus of special attention. They are often figural, even when other aspects of the situation (the ground against which this figural element stands out) may have been more causally instrumental. Thus, although the development of hypotheses pertaining to the perceived fairness of procedures is a worthwhile endeavor in and of itself (e.g., see Thibaut & Walker, 1978), the RCT framework emphasizes that there can be an intimate connection between procedural justice and distributive justice as well. Hence there are additional grounds for rethinking equity theory, which is silent on the subject of procedural justice.

Rather than state the nature of the relationship between procedural and distributive justice in the abstract, let me illustrate that relationship by describing results from a recent experiment (Folger & Martin, 1985). This experiment manipulated referent outcomes in terms of previously held expectations. Subjects heard that there would be an opportunity for a highly advantageous bonus. Half thought a stringent requirement would probably make them ineligible for this opportunity, whereas the remainder thought they were assured of the opportunity. The experimenter subsequently canceled the bonus opportunity. This cancellation made a low-referent outcome salient to the "ineligible" subjects: considering what might have happened, they would simulate not receiving the bonus even under the alternatively imaginable case of no cancellation. On the other hand, the cancellation made a high-referent outcome salient to the subjects who had previously been "assured" of the bonus opportunity: under the imaginable no-cancellation scenario, they presumably would have gotten the bonus.

Subjects were working alone on a bogus task when they learned about the cancellation. The announcement came in the form of a note (allegedly from the experimenter) slipped under the door of the cubicle in which the subject was working. Half received a note in which the experimenter simply stated that "I've decided" not to allow the bonus opportunity; this message established the low-justification conditions. The remaining subjects, who were in the high-justification conditions, learned that the cancellation was due to an equipment failure (cf. the fire-damage example of Furby, 1986). (Note that the likelihood of amelioration was held constant at a very low level, because no future opportunities existed.)

The RCT prediction is that resentment should show the effects of a referent × justification interaction. That is, resentment should be maximized when referent outcomes are high (the subject had firmly expected to be able to participate) and the justification for actual outcomes is low (the first experimenter's procedure involved an arbitrary, unilateral decision to break a promise). Note also that when the referent outcome is low (the reward opportunity is not salient because eligibility requirements are extremely strict), the procedural justifications for the first experimenter's actions are largely irrelevant with respect to one's own outcomes, because the bonus was not a very likely opportunity in the first place.

These predicted effects were confirmed (see also Folger, Rosenfield, & Robinson, 1983). Table 1 shows the means from a composite index of anger and resentment. (These means come from half the conditions of the study, the "ordinary context" conditions; the remainder of the design is described in the next section.) The referent × justification interaction was significant, as was the difference beween the low- and high-referent means within the low-justification conditions. Notice two things: (a) the interaction was produced by a significantly greater amount of resentment occurring in the low-justification, high-referent cell; and (b) resentment was absent in the low-justification, low-referent cell.

These results fit RCT predictions but are nevertheless problematic. The problem is the reaction of the low-justification, low-referent subjects. They expressed less resentment than their high-referent counterparts, as predicted. What is problematic is that they were not more resentful than subjects in either of the high-justification conditions—even though they learned about an arbitrary change in the procedures. It is as if they were completely outcome oriented and oblivious to procedural improprieties. Or to put it another way, it is as if employees under a dictatorial manager, whose decision-making style is totally arbitrary and autocratic, would tolerate this style and allow the manager to act with impunity—sans complaint—simply because he or she "hasn't yet done anything to hurt me personally." Surely people are not always so oblivious to procedural improprieties. The question is, When do people pay attention predominantly to procedures?

TABLE 1. Discontent as a Function of Referent
Outcomes and Justification, within Ordinary-
Context Conditions

Referent outcomes	Justification	
	Low	High
Low	1.2	0.8
High	4.3	0.4

Note. Higher numbers indicate greater anger and resentment, as measured by a composite index of responses to the following question: "How do you feel as the result of the way you were treated by the experimenter?"

CONTEXT EFFECTS

The portion of the Folger and Martin design shown in Table 1 represents the ordinary context of a standard laboratory study, and in this context resentment ratings produced a referent × justification (or outcome × procedure) interaction. If people are not always oblivious to procedural improprieties, then in a different type of context we might instead get only a justification main effect. That is, we should expect to find contexts in which people would give overriding importance to procedural considerations. In such contexts, people might express equally strong amounts of resentment regardless of whether their referent outcomes are high or low.

This speculation was the basis for a manipulation of context in the Folger and Martin study. In the context of an ordinary laboratory study, the experimenter's failure to use a well-justified procedure does not have very significant implications: the procedure has a socially isolated, one-time-only effect. Suppose instead we portray the role of experimenter as a position that entails enduring responsibilities. It then becomes an analog of positions occupied by authorities in social institutions. Attaining such positions often requires receiving some degree of formal or informal endorsement from one's constituents.

Constituents of social institutions sometimes know that a person is eligible for a position of enduring responsibility, and then are asked whether they would vote this person into office—or hire this person for a position. I argue that procedural considerations are likely to dominate the constituents' responses when they are asked to indicate their degree of endorsement for a candidate. The endorsement context makes it more important to assess the person's use of procedures, the person's decision-making style, and so forth. These issues become important because evidence of procedural impropriety violates the trust essential to a position of enduring responsibility.

This argument is supported by evidence from the political science literature on trust in government and its leaders (as reviewed by Tyler & Caine, 1981). The evidence is that citizen support for authorities depends more on believing that government leaders and institutions use fair procedures than on any specific one-shot outcome. Tyler and his colleagues have extended the evidence for this procedural-justice main effect to leadership endorsement in a variety of institutions, including teacher ratings and evaluations of judges (Tyler, 1984; Tyler & Folger, 1980; Tyler, Rasinski, & Spodick, 1985).

None of this previous research has varied the context within a single study. Instead, the research has shown that a particular type of questionnaire item, a leadership endorsement item, is the most likely to be predominantly influenced by procedural rather than outcome considerations. The Folger and Martin study was designed to show that if you vary the context, you can get different responses to the same item. The study used mood items, including anger and resentment. The manipulated difference between contexts was the difference between (a) merely reporting mood, and (b) knowing that the mood reported would affect whether or not someone was hired.

The subjects in the Folger and Martin study had been given different instructions at the beginning of the experiment to create these contexts. The subjects were students taking introductory psychology. All knew ahead of time that each experiment during the semester would conclude with a questionnaire assessing their reactions to it. For half the subjects, the session began with an innocuous reminder about this "departmental questionnaire"; these ordinary-context subjects (see Table 1) read that it was intended merely to get an indication of psychology students' feelings about experiments. The remaining subjects, who were in the endorsement-context conditions, read that their experimenter had applied for the position of research assistant in charge of running experiments for the psychology department, and that their questionnaire responses would influence the hiring decision.

Table 2 shows the results from the endorsement conditions. In particular, the means represented are from mood items (anger and resentment) that these subjects thought would be used to help determine whether their experimenter was hired for the research assistantship. The only finding obtained was a significant main effect of procedural justifications. Notice that this procedural-justice main effect was obtained because the low-justification, low-referent subjects expressed as much resentment as their high-referent counterparts.

The Folger and Martin results (Tables 1 and 2) show that procedural justification has overriding impact in endorsement contexts. Two sets of ancillary data also bear on this finding. The first comes from an

TABLE 2. Discontent as a Function of Referent
Outcomes and Justifications, within Endorsement-
Context Conditions

Referent outcome	Justification	
	Low	High
Low	3.7	0.9
High	3.1	1.0

Note. Higher numbers indicate greater anger and resentment, as measured by a composite index of responses to the following question: "How do you feel as the result of the way you were treated by the experimenter?"

additional item included on the questionnaire. After having given their mood responses, subjects read the following statement: "Suppose the department were hiring someone as a paid research assistant in charge of running experiments." They were then asked, "Is your experimenter someone you would recommend to be hired, under these circumstances?" (circumstances the endorsement subjects thought were operative). On this one questionnaire item alone, the responses of both the ordinary and endorsement subjects produced a procedural-justice main effect.

The second set of ancillary data has a bearing on the underlying psychological mechanism responsible for the predominant attention to procedure in endorsement contexts. Earlier I characterized endorsement contexts as those in which positions of enduring responsibility are involved. When someone is considered for such a position, constituents should tend to think beyond their own outcomes and recognize that the outcomes of other people are at stake. When someone commits a procedural impropriety, endorsing that person for a position of responsibility entails placing other people's outcomes in jeopardy. My argument is that low-justification, low-referent subjects in the endorsement conditions tended to think about the social consequences of the experimenter's decision-making style. Their counterparts in the ordinary-context conditions apparently did not consider the implications for other people's outcomes until prompted by the last questionnaire item, which did raise the issue of enduring consequences—although only in a hypothetical "suppose" fashion.

The ancillary data relevant to this argument were collected from a survey of other introductory psychology students in a subsequent semester. The survey noted that the psychology department planned to use a standardized questionnaire at the end of each experiment conducted that semester. Allegedly this departmental questionnaire would be used to assess student reactions to experiments, and this vaguely stated purpose was the only instructional set contained on half the surveys. The other half of the surveys, however, contained an additional sentence giving an example of one specific use of the questionnaire that was possible. The example was that the questionnaire might be used to help determine whether an experimenter was hired as a research assistant in charge of conducting experiments for the department of psychology.

Given those contrasting instructions (presence vs. absence of the hiring example), students were asked to indicate the extent to which each of several features of experiments "represents an important consideration affecting your responses to such a questionnaire." Imbedded among filler items was the following key feature that served as the dependent measure: "the welfare of other subjects who will have the same experimenter." Consistent with the interpretation of a hiring decision as a context that makes collectivity-oriented concerns salient, the instructional set produced a main effect on this item alone: students whose survey instructions contained the hiring example rated other subjects' welfare as being an important consideration significantly more than did students whose instructions had not contained that example.

My hunch is that consideration of others' welfare is only one of at least two features making an endorsement context distinctive. A second is that this context makes salient the broader time course of outcomes, because one's endorsement has implications for how long a given person stays in a position of authority or how long a given institution can maintain the consensual support necessary for its effectiveness. A broadened temporal perspective would help account for Alexander and Ruderman's (1983) finding that procedural considerations had more impact than distributive considerations on measures pertaining to supervisor evaluation and trust in management. Especially interesting in light of equity theory's neglect of procedural justice is that the same effect was also found on measures of job satisfaction. This suggests that global evaluations of one's work situation take into account more than current pay; in the context of ongoing employment, management philosophy and procedural regulations color one's impression such that job discontent can persist despite currently favorable outcomes. If the instrumentalities are untrustworthy, then there is little security in short-term gains. This reasoning also suggests that procedural considerations might sometimes dominate distributive considerations even in a laboratory study— if the study involved an ongoing interaction with an allocator and a series of outcomes.

SUMMARY AND CONCLUSION

Several points summarize how RCT provides useful ways of rethinking equity theory. The common focus is on specifying when people will resent an injustice (or a "disadvantageous inequity"). Equity theory (Adams, 1965) uses four terms to define the basis for a sense of injustice and the accompanying potential for resentment: Person's outcomes, Person's inputs, Other's outcomes, and Other's inputs. Rather than a comparison between "Person" and "Other," RCT defines the basis for resentment as consisting of the comparison between reality (what happened) and an alternatively imaginable referent state (what might have happened instead). Thus the first distinguishing feature of the RCT terms is that they do not necessitate social comparison.

The second distinguishing feature is that RCT assumes outcomes are evaluated in terms of their relationship to any and all background instrumentalities. An advantage of defining injustice in terms of instrumentalities rather than inputs is that the RCT approach is more inclusive. This inclusiveness has been discussed in terms of the RCT provision for procedural justice considerations, whereas equity theory ignores procedural justice. Furthermore, RCT specifies that the justifiability of various instrumentalities is critical, whereas equity theory identifies inputs as the only source of justification (i.e., an outcome is justified to the extent that a person's inputs entitle him or her to receive this outcome). RCT emphasizes that justifiability can vary as a function of reasons for what happened—reasons that are independent of levels of entitling inputs. Recall, for example, how Furby (in press) noted that the presence versus the absence of a fire would affect the reasonableness of nonpayment. Suppose I have contributed certain inputs that entitle me to receive certain outcomes from you. If you do not give me what I am entitled to, my reaction will vary depending on the reason why you failed to do so (e.g., whether or not fire-related damage was responsible for the nonpayment).

Of course, fire-related damage might only give you an excuse for not having paid me yet. The example thus highlights another advantage of RCT over equity theory, namely that the former (but not the latter) takes into account the prospects for amelioration. The data indicate that differences in the perceived likelihood of amelioration do have a profound effect on people's tendencies to express resentment.

For the last point of differentiation, I want to note that equity theory portrays perceived injustice as arising only within a single context, namely the context of a social exchange. I believe we should seek to identify different contexts, and the Folger and Martin (1985) results indicate that contextual factors are important. Even if we restrict ourselves to outcomes received via an exchange (and I think equity theory is limited in that respect more than RCT), we should have reason to suspect that not all exchanges are alike. The Folger and Martin study, for example, showed that it makes a difference whether the person with whom one is in an exchange relationship does or does not come to be perceived as someone eligible for a position of enduring responsibility.

In concluding, let me suggest how RCT opens up new areas for research, whereas equity theory seems to have led to premature closure on the nature of injustice. RCT is both theory and framework. As theory, it has yielded predictions that have been confirmed empirically. As framework, it points to several topics for future research.

The first pertains to the nature of referent outcomes: How and when do they become salient? What makes them psychologically "close"? Current research in social cognition is a rich source of hypotheses related to these issues (e.g., Kahneman & Tversky, 1982).

A second topic is the likelihood of amelioration. RCT has treated likelihood as being a matter of a simple probability estimate, and research has only operationalized the all-or-none extremes. Between these two extremes, is there a linear, curvilinear, or step-function relationship between perceived likelihood and expressed resentment? Does resentment vary only as a function of the perceived *probability* of amelioration, or is the *source* of amelioration taken into account as well (e.g., intended amelioration by the original harm doer vs. from some other source)? What factors determine the relevant time span for prospects of amelioration?

The nature of justifications constitutes a third topic. What makes for good justification? Is poor justification better than no justification at all? Separate theories of procedural justice will be helpful in addressing such issues as when outcome concerns predominate and when the use of a fair procedure suppresses resentment no matter how poor the outcome. Work on attribution of moral responsibility and on the giving of social accounts as excuses will also be helpful.

Finally, there is a fourth area of issues that is not implied by any of the three RCT elements considered separately but that emerges from the $2 \times 2 \times 2$ matrix they entail. This area pertains to a differentiation among coping responses. Not getting what we want is something with which we will all have to cope, and it makes for an overly simplistic theory to imply that the nature of our responses is adequately summarized by the presence or absence of resentment. RCT specifies that maximal resentment will be produced by the combination of a high level of referent outcomes, a low level of justification for the enacted instrumentalities, and a low level of likelihood regarding the prospects for amelioration. What responses other than resentment are elicited when, for example, one of these conditions is met but the other two are not? (See Mark & Folger, 1984, for suggestions regarding a taxonomy of coping responses.)

The RCT framework has already provided, I believe, an indication that it is useful to rethink equity theory rather than abandon the issues the theory had raised. I hope I have also indicated that there are many more unanswered questions yet to be addressed.

REFERENCES

Adams, J. S. (1965). Inequity in social exchange. In L. Berkowitz (Ed.), *Advances in experimental social psychology* (Vol. 2, pp. 267–299). New York: Academic Press.
Alexander, S., & Ruderman, M. (1983, August). *The influence of procedural and distributive justice on organizational behavior*. Paper presented at the meeting of the American Psychological Association, Anaheim, CA.

Austin, W., & Susmilch, C. (1974). Comment on Lane and Messé's confusing clarification of equity theory. *Journal of Personality and Social Psychology, 30,* 400–404.

Austin, W., McGinn, N. C., & Susmilch, C. (1980). Internal standards revisited: Effects of social comparisons and expectancies on judgments of fairness and satisfaction. *Journal of Experimental Social Psychology, 16,* 426–441.

Bies, R. J. (in press). The predicament of organizational injustice: Interpersonal and affective processes. In B. M. Staw & L. L. Cummings (Eds.), *Research in organizational behavior* (Vol. 9). Greenwich, CT: JAI Press.

Crosby, F. (1976). A model of egoistical relative deprivation. *Psychological Review, 83,* 85–113.

Deutsch, M. (1975). Equity, equality and need: What determines which value will be used as the basis for distributive justice? *Journal of Social Issues, 31,* 137–149.

Fine, M. (1979). Options to injustice: Seeing other lights. *Representative Research in Social Psychology, 10,* 61–76.

Fiske, S., & Taylor, S. E. (1984). *Social cognition.* Reading, MA: Addison-Wesley.

Folger, R. (1977). Distributive and procedural justice: Combined impact of "voice" and improvement on experienced inequity. *Journal of Personality and Social Psychology, 35,* 108–119.

Folger, R. (1984a). Emerging issues in the social psychology of justice. In R. Folger (Ed.), *The sense of injustice: Social psychological perspectives* (pp. 3–24). New York: Plenum Press.

Folger, R. (1984b). Perceived injustice, referent cognitions, and the concept of comparison level. *Representative Research in Social Psychology, 14,* 88–108.

Folger, R. (1986). A referent cognitions theory of relative deprivation. In J. M. Olson, C. P. Herman, & M. P. Zanna (Eds.), *Relative deprivation and social comparison: The Ontario symposium* (Vol. 4, pp. 33–55). Hillsdale, NJ: Erlbaum.

Folger, R. (in press). Relative deprivation and referent cognitions: Reformulating the preconditions of resentment. In J. C. Masters & W. P. Smith (Eds.), *Social comparison, relative deprivation, and social justice: Theoretical, empirical, and policy perspectives.* New York: Plenum Press.

Folger, R., & Greenberg, J. (1985). Procedural justice: An interpretive analysis of personnel systems. In K. Rowland & G. Ferris (Eds.), *Research in personnel and human resources management* (Vol. 3, pp. 141–183). Greenwich, CT: JAI Press.

Folger, R., & Martin, C. (1985). *Relative deprivation and referent cognitions: Distributive and procedural justice effects.* Manuscript submitted for publication.

Folger, R., Rosenfield, D., & Rheaume, K. (1983). Roleplaying effects of likelihood and referent outcomes on relative deprivation. *Representative Research in Social Psychology, 13,* 2–10.

Folger, R., Rosenfield, D., Rheaume, K., & Martin, C. (1983). Relative deprivation and referent cognitions. *Journal of Experimental Social Psychology, 19,* 172–184.

Folger, R., Rosenfield, D., & Robinson, T. (1983). Relative deprivation and procedural justification. *Journal of Personality and Social Psychology, 45,* 268–273.

Furby, L. (1986). Psychology and justice. In R. L. Cohen (Ed.), *Justice: Views from the social sciences.* New York: Plenum Press.

Hirschman, A. O. (1970). *Exit, voice and loyalty: Responses to declines in firms, organizations, and states.* Cambridge, MA: Harvard University Press.

Kahneman, D., & Tversky, A. (1982). Availability and the simulation heuristic. In D. Kahneman, P. Slovic, & A. Tversky (Ed.), *Judgment under uncertainty: Heuristics and biases* (pp. 201–208). New York: Oxford University Press.

Lane, I. M., & Messé, L. A. (1972). Distribution of insufficient, sufficient, and oversufficient rewards: A clarification of equity theory. *Journal of Personality and Social Psychology, 31,* 228–233.

Lerner, M. J. (1974). Social psychology of justice and interpersonal attraction. In T. L. Huston (Ed.), *Foundations of interpersonal attraction* (pp. 331–351). New York: Academic Press.

Leventhal, G. S. (1976). Fairness in social relationships. In J. W. Thibaut, J. T. Spence, & R. C. Carson (Eds.), *Contemporary topics in social psychology* (pp. 211–239). Morristown, NJ: General Learning Press.

Leventhal, G. S. (1980). What should be done with equity theory? In K. J. Gergen, M. S. Greenberg, & R. H. Willis (Eds.), *Social exchange: Advances in theory and research* (pp. 27–55). New York: Plenum Press.

Mark, M. M., & Cook, T. D. (1979). Relative deprivation: When does it lead to anger, achievement, or disengagement? *Alternatives: Perspectives on Society and Environment, 8*, 13–17.

Mark, M. M., & Folger, R. (1984). Responses to relative deprivation: A conceptual framework. *Review of Personality and Social Psychology, 5*, 192–218.

Messé, L. A., & Lane, I. M. (1974). Rediscovering the need for multiple operations: A reply to Austin and Susmilch. *Journal of Personality and Social Psychology, 30*, 405–408.

Messé, L. A., & Watts, B. L. (1983). Complex nature of the sense of fairness: Internal standards and social comparison as bases for reward evaluation. *Journal of Personality and Social Psychology, 45*, 84–93.

Miner, J.B. (1984, February). The unpaved road over the mountains: From theory to applications. *The Industrial-Organizational Psychologist, 21*(2), 9–20.

Pritchard, R. D. (1969). Equity theory: A review and critique. *Organizational Behavior and Human Performance, 4*, 176–211.

Reis, H. T. (1984). The multidimensionality of justice. In R. Folger (Ed.), *The sense of injustice: Social psychological perspectives* (pp. 25–61). New York: Plenum Press.

Thibaut, J. W., & Walker, L. (1975). *Procedural justice: A psychological analysis*. Hillsdale, NJ: Erlbaum.

Thibaut, J. W., & Walker, L. (1978). A theory of procedure. *California Law Review, 66*, 541–566.

Tyler, T. R. (1984). The role of perceived injustice in defendants' evaluations of their courtroom experience. *Law and Society Review, 18*, 101–124.

Tyler, T. R., & Caine, A. (1981). The influence of outcomes and procedures upon satisfaction with formal leaders. *Journal of Personality and Social Psychology, 41*, 642–655.

Tyler, T. R., & Folger, R. (1980). Distributive and procedural aspects of satisfaction with citizen–police encounters. *Basic and Applied Social Psychology, 1*, 281–292.

Tyler, T. R., Rasinski, K., & Spodick, N. (1985). Influence of voice on satisfaction with leaders: Exploring the meaning of process control. *Journal of Personality and Social Psychology, 48*, 72–81.

Walster, E., Berscheid, E., & Walster, G. W. (1973). New directions in equity research. *Journal of Personality and Social Psychology, 25*, 151–176.

Weick, K. E. (1966). The concept of equity in the perception of pay. *Administrative Science Quarterly, 11*, 414–439.

Weick, K. E., & Nesset, B. (1968). Preferences among forms of equity. *Organizational Behavior and Human Performance, 3*, 400–416.

Part **III**

NORMS AND JUSTICE

Chapter 9

Social Context and Perceived Justice

HANS WERNER BIERHOFF, ERNST BUCK, and
RENATE KLEIN

INTRODUCTION

Contemporary research on fairness and justice has focused on the situational determinants of the relationship between performance and reward. Social psychologists have emphasized the influence of contributions of the group members on the reward distribution. In contrast to this major interest area in justice studies, the influence of the reward allocation on the inferred input level of the group members has received relatively little attention.

Allocation decisions may resemble the equity or proportionality principle (allocating according to equal outcome–input ratios among group members), the equality principle (allocating equally among group members), and the need principle (allocating according to individual needs). In addition, other distribution rules may be available (e.g., "take more/ give less" and "take all"; Kayser & Schwinger, 1982: Lerner, 1981).

In the discussion that follows, two restrictions should be noted. First, only the allocation of material rewards will be considered. Second, only the equity principle and the equality principle will be discussed. In the present chapter we attempt to break new ground in justice research in two ways: first, by varying equity and equality independently (cf.

HANS WERNER BIERHOFF, ERNST BUCK, and RENATE KLEIN • Fachbereich Psychologie der Philipps-Universität Marburg, D-3550 Marburg/Lahn, West Germany.

Brickman & Bryan, 1976) with regard to social.context, and second, by focusing on backward inferences from rewards to contributions.

JUSTICE IN INTERPERSONAL RELATIONS: EQUITY OR EQUALITY

Two distribution rules are near universal: the equity rule and the equality rule. In fact, both rules are applied in similar social situations. Lerner (1981) distinguishes between acquisition processes (i.e., vicarious dependency, convergent goals, or divergent goals) and the perceived relation to others (i.e., identity, unit/similarity, or nonunit). Where there is the perception of similarity and convergent goal acquisition, either equity or equality is expected. Which of the two principles is more likely to be employed will depend on the focus of attention. When attention is focused on goals, cooperative relationships and the equity distribution rule should be the emergent activities. When the focus is the interpersonal relationship, a team relation as well as the equality rule should emerge.

In terms of theory, a competition between the equity and the equality principle can be expected in many areas. For example, what does it mean to establish equal opportunities for education? The equity principle favors the selection and promotion of the best students. On the other hand, the equality principle argues for the compensation of unequal sociocultural conditions and even reverse discrimination. The complex issues involved in this controversy are discussed more fully by Sampson (1981).

The equity principle appears to be one widely used script for the distribution of rewards. The principle states that members of a group should allocate rewards in proportion to the contribution of each person. Each person derives his or her satisfaction from the fact that group members receive shares proportional to their contributions.

The equality principle appears to be another widely used script for the distribution of rewards. This principle states that members of a group should allocate resources to self and others equally. Each person derives his or her satisfaction from the fact that each member of the group receives an equal share.

The equity rule requires prior knowledge of the contributions of the group members, whereas the use of the equality rule does not rest on such knowledge. In addition, the equity principle is more appropriate when differences among people are stressed, whereas the equality principle is more appropriate when the equality of, and similarity among, people is emphasized. These and other differences between the two allocation principles are summarized in Table 1 (cf. Leventhal, Karuza, & Fry, 1980; Mikula, 1980).

One factor that may affect how allocations are made is the nature of the relationship among the people involved (Austin, 1980). According to this view, the use of a distribution rule depends on the type of interpersonal relationship. Studies of the effects of the relationship have indicated that, in a variety of conditions, having information on the social context can influence what is perceived as just (Mikula & Schwinger, 1978; Schmitt & Montada, 1982).

The most commonly used laboratory paradigm for studying the effects of such factors on perceived justice involves providing subjects with information on the performances of different people and on the context (e.g., the relationship between them), and then assessing preferences for equity and equality as allocation rules. Using this general procedure, various investigators have found that the type of interpersonal relationship will influence people's choice of an allocation rule (Austin, 1980; Austin & McGinn, 1977; Benton, 1971; Debusschere & van Avermaet, 1984; von Grumbkow, Deen, Steensma, & Wilke, 1976; Lerner, 1974; Major & Adams, 1983; Reis & Gruzen, 1976; Sagan, Pondel, & Wittig, 1981; Schmitt & Montada, 1982; Shapiro, 1975).

Shapiro (1975) crossed the usual manipulation of performance (i.e., high vs. low) with two levels of expectation of future interaction: expected and not expected. High performers preferred equality over equity when future interaction was expected and equity over equality when no future interaction was expected. Low performers preferred equity regardless of their expectations of future interaction. Von Grumbkow et al. (1976) had impartial subject-allocators observe two students coding questionnaires for about half an hour; one student coded 70 questionnaires, and the other, 30. Half the allocators expected future interaction with the students, whereas the other half did not. Results indicated that the low

TABLE 1. Properties of Equity and Equality

	Equity	Equality
Prior knowledge of performances	Necessary	Not necessary
Emphasis on individual differences	Yes	No
Domain	Economic, scientific, and technical productivity	Mutual support, close relationships
Consequences	High individual efficiency, alienated work	Interpersonal harmony, solidarity

input student was given more, and the allocation was more in accordance with the equality rule, when future interaction was expected. In summary, high performers and observers anticipating future interaction are more inclined to prefer the equality principle, whereas low performers—and high performers and observers anticipating no future interaction—are inclined to prefer the equity principle.

Benton (1971) compared three types of children's interpersonal relations: friend, nonfriend, and neutral. Girls accepted equity allocations with nonfriends, whereas they preferred equality allocations with neutral classmates or friends. Comparable results were obtained by Austin (1980). Although the Shapiro study suggests that the expectation of future interaction is one factor that can instigate adherence to the equality norm, the studies by Benton (1971) and Austin (1980) show that nonfriendship increases the acceptance of equity allocations. Both articles suggest that closer interpersonal relations facilitate the use of the equality principle.

This assertion is supported by the results of three studies by Lerner (1974). In these studies, children worked alone or as a team. All subjects later allocated rewards in a dyad. Children who worked alone preferred the equity rule more than children who worked in a team. One distinguishing feature of the team situation is that it places the subject in a setting in which group cohesiveness is high. As such, it seems plausible that variables associated with feelings of "we-ness" and solidarity foster the application of the equality rule. Whereas status congruence among co-workers defines group relations in terms of harmony and equality, economic situations focus the attention on productivity and performance.

Reis and Gruzen (1976) suggested that the experimenter has a role similar to an employer in defining the situation as an economic setting. Therefore the subjects should follow the equity norm when the experimenter is aware of their allocations, but should adhere to the equality norm when his or her co-workers are aware of the allocations. Reis and Gruzen's findings were consistent with these predictions and the argument that self-presentation plays an important role in determining decisions. In short, allocators will adhere to that norm that promises to maximize the social approval of relevant others.

The implication that closer interpersonal relations favor the use of the equality rule is also suggested by the results of a study by Debusschere and van Avermaet (1984). These authors distinguished two social contexts, one in which the relationship among group members was described as long lasting and harmonious, the other in which future interaction was not expected and performance maximization was stressed. It was assumed (cf. Leventhal, Karuza, & Fry, 1980) that these two experimental conditions would provide a distinction between the two justice principles. Subjects in the more harmonious context distributed the rewards more in correspondence with the equality rule and less in correspondence with the equity rule than subjects in the performance orientation context. In summary, equality seems to be the appropriate form of distributive justice in close relationships (Kidder, Fagan, & Cohn, 1981, p. 238).

EQUITY VERSUS EQUALITY AND RESPONSE TO REWARD ALLOCATION

Brickman & Bryan (1976) reasoned that equity and equality describe independent justice orientations. Because performance information and outcomes affect perceived justice in combination, it is reasonable to separate experimentally the adherence to the equity rule and the equality rule.

To distinguish between these two principles, Bierhoff (1982) reported the results of three studies that extended the work of Lerner (1974) on equity and equality among children. Although following the same general approach, these studies differed from Lerner's in employing students rather than children as subjects, and in using written scenarios. The most important change was the inclusion of the Brickman and Bryan (1976) paradigm which permits the independent variation of equity and equality (see Figure 1).

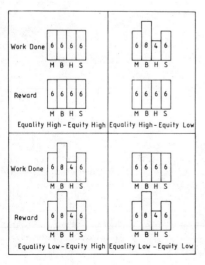

FIGURE 1. Equity and equality as a function of contributions and rewards. In the upper part of each quadrant the amount of work done by each of four persons (M, B, H, S) is represented. In addition, the reward received by each person is specified. If the height of the bars in the performance diagram coincides with the height of the bars in the reward diagram, the equity principle was applied. If the height of the bars in the reward diagram is equal, the equality principle was applied.

Bierhoff's (1982) three studies employed a 2 × 2 × 2 between-subjects design that systematically varied social context (team/nonteam), the extent to which equity was fulfilled (high/low), and the extent to which equality was fulfilled (high/low). The subjects were presented with a written account of the contributions and outcomes of four school-girls and their cooperative or competitive work relationship. The rewards were chips that could later be exchanged for toys. Subjects' evaluation of the teacher who allocated the rewards constituted the primary dependent variable.

The evaluation of the teacher varied as a function of equality, $F(1, 73) = 38.48$, $p < .001$. Those who received equality information were more likely to approve the teacher ($M = 21.10$) than subjects who received the violation-of-equality information ($M = 8.26$). In addition, a significant main effect of equity was obtained, $F(1,73) = 10.54$, $p < .001$. However, this effect was qualified by an interaction between equity and team, $F(1,73) = 7.51$, $p < .01$. As shown in Figure 2, the manipulation of the equity rule made a difference only in the nonteam condition. Simple effect analyses revealed that in the nonteam condition subjects evaluated the teacher lower when she violated the equity norm. The simple effect was not significant in the team condition.

Two additional studies (Bierhoff, 1982) replicated this pattern of results. One study employed the 2 × 2 design in a team context. The only significant result obtained was an equality effect, $F(1, 26) = 68.79$, $p < .001$. The mean evaluation score for the high equality condition was 29.78, and the mean score for the low equality condition was 8.88. The other study employed the 2 × 2 design in a nonteam context. Once again, subjects receiving equality information rated the teacher more

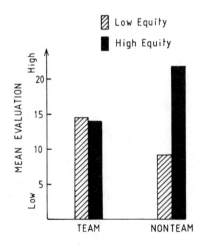

FIGURE 2. Mean evaluation of allocator as a function of equity and team. Subjects' evaluation scores were obtained by summing the values of four scales. The four items concerned approval of what the teacher did, perceived fairness, and whether the teacher was a clever person and a good person. All items were rated on 11-point scales (0 = lowest evaluation, 10 = highest evaluation). The scales loaded high on a factor-analytic dimension of teacher evaluation.

favorably (M = 26.09) than did other subjects (M = 12.34), F (1, 20) = 17.01, p < .001), and subjects receiving the high equity information gave more favorable ratings (M = 23.84) than those in the low equity condition (M = 14.59), F (1, 20) = 7.70, p < .05.

What stands out most clearly in these data is that the evaluation measure related consistently and quite strongly to the equality manipulation. On the other hand, differences between the equity conditions were found only when a nonteam context was specified. These results replicate the findings of Lerner (1974) and are consistent with the results of Brickman and Bryan (1976), because the latter reported two main effects for equity and equality in a nonteam context.

GENDER DIFFERENCES REVISITED: RESPONSE TO EQUITY AND EQUALITY

Sex of subject appears to have an influence on allocation decisions (Austin & McGinn, 1977; Callahan-Levy & Messé, 1979; Leventhal & Lane, 1970; Major & Adams, 1983; Sagan, Pondel, & Wittig, 1981). The most common finding to date has been that males prefer an equity norm, whereas females prefer an equality norm. This finding seems limited to certain circumstances. For example, the typical pattern of sex differences was not found when a stereotyped feminine task was used (Reis & Jackson, 1981).

Recent theorizing and research has dealt with confounding influences on sex differences. For example, Callahan-Levy and Messé (1979) disentangled self-allocations from other-allocations, which are interconnected in a zero-sum situation. Other researchers observed that the male preference for equity divisions was restricted to stereotyped male tasks (Reis & Jackson, 1981). In addition, Major and Adams (1983) distinguished between gender and interpersonal orientations of allocators because males usually have a more instrumental orientation than females. Another important question is whether sex differences are focused on the equity principle or the equality principle. By disentangling the two principles, it is possible to distinguish between gender effects on equity and equality.

What explains gender differences in justice research? To answer this question two lines of research must be considered. On the one hand, groups of women tend to be oriented toward social concerns in zero-sum situations (Hottes & Kahn, 1974). In general, women seem to be more interested in interpersonal harmony and solidarity than men. On the other hand, variables that foster concern with interpersonal harmony (e.g., anticipation of future interaction) are positively correlated with a preference for the equality principle. Integrating these two lines of research, one might propose that women adhere more to the equality norm and less to the equity norm than men.

To test this hypothesis, Bierhoff and Renda (1985) crossed sex of subject with the basic 2 (equity) × 2 (equality) design. Data from 158 13th graders and university students revealed two significant main effects, for equality, F (1, 142) = 62.04, $p < .001$ ($M_{\text{High Equality}}$ = 22.05, $M_{\text{Low Equality}}$ = 10.11), and for equity, F (1, 142) = 18.51, $p < .001$ ($M_{\text{High Equity}}$ = 19.53. $M_{\text{Low Equity}}$ = 12.92).

In addition, there was a significant interaction between gender and equity, F (1, 142) = 6.067, $p < .05$, but no significant interaction between gender and equality, $F < 1$. As can be seen in Figure 3, this interaction arises from a tendency for males to evaluate the allocator more positively when she follows the equity rule than when she violates the equity rule, whereas this difference is reduced for females. This interpretation is confirmed by simple effect analyses. The simple effect was highly sig-. nificant for males, F (1, 142) = 22.74, $p < .001$, but not for females, F (1, 142) = 3.42, ns. Therefore, it seems reasonable to conclude that males emphasize the evaluative difference between high equity and low equity more than females. However, this conclusion is based only on the evaluation of female allocators.

The analysis to this point may help explain why gender differences are prevalent in justice research and why they are not fully understood. They are prevalent because equity is preferred by males more than by females. They are not fully understood because both the equality

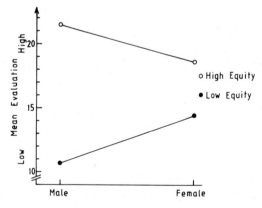

FIGURE 3. Mean evaluation of allocator as a function of subject's gender and equity of allocation. Higher values indicate higher evaluation.

component and the equity component are involved and because the modifying influences of sex roles (Callahan-Levy & Messé, 1979; Taylor & Hall, 1982) on equity and equality have not been taken into account.

A word of caution is in order here. Reviews of the literature on sex differences in allocation behavior show that female allocators divide rewards less in agreement with the equity rule than male allocators do (Kahn, O'Leary, Krulewitz, & Lamm, 1980; Major & Deaux, 1982). This is especially true when allocators divide rewards between themselves and others and when their input is higher than the input of their co-workers. In addition, females reward themselves less than males do (Callahan-Levy & Messé, 1979). As Major and Deaux (1982) have emphasized, these sex differences are related to a specific research paradigm.

The allocation of rewards must be distinguished from the evaluation of allocators. Although allocation of rewards and evaluation of allocators may correspond (see Callahan-Levy & Messé, 1979), the theoretical explanations of allocation behavior and allocation evaluations may differ. For example, whereas allocations create facts, evaluations comment on facts. Evaluations of allocators may be more dependent on sex role orientations than allocations of rewards, because the allocation situation may minimize the impact of gender differences and sex roles on dependent variables (see Kourilsky & Kehret-Ward, 1984; Major & Adams, 1983). In contrast, evaluations of the allocator may be more directly related to attitudes, values, or sex role orientations. In their recent study, Major and Adams (1983) found no relationship between the femininity subscale of the Personal Attribute Questionnaire (Spence & Helmreich, 1978) and allocations of money to self and co-worker, although sex differences in accordance with previous results were found. This failure to find a significant relationship with sex role orientation indicated that sex differences were not mediated by sex role orientation. Further research is needed to explore the possibility that sex role orientations are predictors of justice considerations when evaluative ratings of fairness or evaluations of allocators are obtained.

THE OTHER WAY AROUND

There would appear to be many occasions in everyday life where people have more information about others' outcomes than they do about the performances or contributions to which those outcomes are related. For example, rough indicators of income and prosperity are likely to be known to members of the community at large. Contrast this with how little observers are likely to know about the interdependence of occupational roles and what constitutes a good performance in such roles. Although observers may have some crude information, they can only speculate as to what individual contributions or levels of performance actually are.

People may not always engage in the cognitive activity necessary for such an inference. They may be more likely to use outcome information as the basis for a reversed equity script: those who have more must have performed better (Bierhoff, 1984). Surprisingly little research effort has been directed toward clarifying the relation between outcomes and inferred levels of performance. This reversed perspective seems to have some practical and theoretical importance. During our daily activities the performance level is hard to identify; the reward allocation is more transparent.

It seems reasonable to argue that equity and equality rules are used to infer the level of performance on the basis of rewards. A recent study (Bierhoff & Kramp, 1982) demonstrated that rewards may instigate backward inferences regarding contributions on the basis of justice rules. Subjects read an account of the rewards given to four girls and of their work relationship (i.e., cooperative or competitive). Rewards were described as having been distributed equally or unequally (see Figure 4), and the work relationship of the four girls was described as either team (i.e., cooperative) or nonteam (i.e., competitive). The rewards were chips that could later be exchanged for toys, and the reward received by each

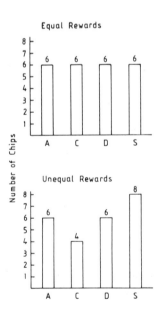

FIGURE 4.   Equal and unequal reward diagrams. The reward received by each of four persons (A, C, D, S) is specified.

person was specified. The dependent variables were subjects' probability rankings for 10 specified performance configurations. The four primary configurations represent four degrees of skewness (i.e., 0, 2, 4, and 6) and are depicted in Figure 5.

Three predictions were made and tested in this study. First, it was predicted that a tendency to invoke the equity rule would be elicited by the unequal reward diagram; that is, subjects would infer that an equivalent performance diagram fits the reward diagram. Therefore, the 4-diagram should be judged most likely, the 0-diagram should be judged least likely, and the 2-diagram and 6-diagram should be ranked halfway between these extremes.

Second, it was predicted that a tendency to invoke both the equity rule and the equality rule would be elicited by the equal reward diagram. Therefore, the 2-diagram should be judged most likely. The equity rule implies in this case (equal reward configuration!) equal contributions. On the other hand, the equality principle implies, as a backward inference rule, unequal contributions. This is so because the equality rule—independent of the equity rule—may be invoked when unequal contributions are given. Equal contributions correspond with equal rewards due to the equity principle. As a consequence, the equality rule has a distinct identity only when it is applied to unequal contributions. An observer who infers unequal contributions on the basis of equal rewards in essence is saying that the allocator has invoked the equality rule in addition to and beyond the equity rule. Therefore, someone who makes the assumption that unequal contributions lie behind equal rewards invokes the equality principle. This is so because the use of the equality principle in the other direction (from contributions to rewards) implies that unequal contributions are rewarded equally. As a compromise

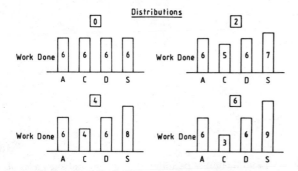

FIGURE 5.   Comparison of performance diagrams. The work done by each of four persons (A, C, D, S) is specified. The degree of skewness of each of the four diagrams is represented by the difference between highest and lowest bar (0, 2, 4, 6).

between the equity principle (saying contributions are equal) and the equality principle (saying contributions are at least moderately unequal), a moderate inequality of contributions should be inferred.

Finally, it was predicted that the 0-diagram and the 2-diagram would be judged most likely, and the 4-diagram and the 6-diagram would be judged least likely, under team instructions as opposed to nonteam instructions. This prediction was derived from the assumption that team instructions facilitate the instigation of an equality orientation.

Subjects were 80 psychology students at the University of Marburg, whose participation partially fulfilled a course requirement. The first question of interest is whether the unequal reward diagram succeeded in eliciting an equity orientation, which would be reflected by a greater willingness to choose the 4-diagram as most likely. The data were analysed using a 2 × 2 × 4 analysis of variance with repeated measures on the last factor: equal/unequal reward diagram × team/nonteam × degree of skewness (0, 2, 4, 6). Simple effects were computed on the four levels of the skewness factor in order to contrast the equal condition with the unequal condition and the team condition with the nonteam condition (Winer, 1971, pp. 530 ff.). In addition, Newman-Keuls tests were used to compare the repeated measures with each other. Finally, a trend analysis (Keppel, 1973, pp. 416 ff.) was performed within the repeated measures.

The analysis of variance revealed a significant equality × skewness interaction, $F (3, 216) = 30.61$, $p < .001$. As portrayed in Figure 6, this interaction reflects the fact that the profiles deviate from each other. Simple effects indicate that all four contrasts are significant ($p < .01$).

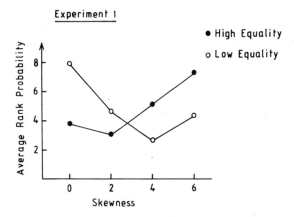

FIGURE 6.   Likelihood rankings as a function of performance diagram and skewness of reward diagram in Experiment 1; $n = 40$ in each condition. Lower rankings indicate higher probabilities.

Newman-Keuls tests reveal that the first hypothesis is confirmed: within the unequal condition, the 0-diagram is significantly less likely than all other diagrams, whereas the 4-diagram is significantly more likely than all other diagrams ($p < .01$). The quadratic component is highly significant, $F (1, 39) = 50.27$, $p < .001$. In addition, the linear component is significant, $F (1, 39) = 20.04$, $p < .001$.

Additional Newman-Keuls tests reveal that in the equal condition the mean rankings of the 0-diagram and the 2-diagram are not significantly different from each other, whereas the 4-diagram and the 6-diagram are significantly different from the 0-diagram and the 2-diagram and from each other ($p < .01$). Thus, the second hypothesis receives marginal support in the Newman-Keuls analysis. Further support comes from the fact that the quadratic component is highly significant, $F (1, 39) = 19.50$, $p < .001$. In addition, the trend analysis indicates that the linear component of the equal profile is significant, $F (1, 39) = 20.51$, $p < .001$.

These results were replicated in a second study (see Figure 7). Procedures were similar to those in Experiment 1, but the dependent measures were modified. Subjects were asked to estimate the likelihood (on 11-point rating scales from 0 = very unlikely, to 10 = very likely) that each of the four diagrams shown in Figure 5 was the origin of the specified reward distribution. Thirty subjects provided data in each of the four conditions of the 2 (equal/unequal) × 2 (team/nonteam) between-subjects design. The results of the analysis of variance were consistent with those obtained in Experiment 1: the analysis revealed a significant equality × skewness interaction, $F (3, 336) = 7.44$, $p < .001$, once again confirming the first hypothesis. The second hypothesis also received

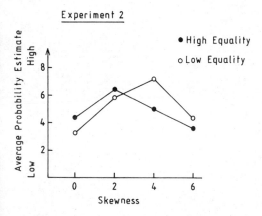

FIGURE 7. Likelihood estimates as a function of performance diagram and skewness of reward diagram in Experiment 2; $n = 60$ in each condition. Higher ratings indicate higher probabilities.

some support: a Newman-Keuls test revealed that in the equal condition the mean probability estimates of the 0-diagram and the 2-diagram were significantly different from each other ($p < .01$).

The third hypothesis states that the 0-diagram and the 2-diagram would be judged more likely under team than under nonteam instructions, whereas the reverse would be true for the 4-diagram and 6-diagram. The analysis of variance (Experiment 1) indicated that the predicted effect was obtained (see Figure 8). A significant team × skewness interaction was found, $F (3, 216) = 3.95$, $p < .01$. Simple effect analyses revealed that only at the 0-level were mean values in the team condition and the nonteam condition significantly different ($p < .01$). This pattern of results was replicated in Experiment 2 (see Figure 9). Suffice it to say that the team × skewness interaction was significant, $F (3, 336) = 3.40$, $p < .05$, and that simple effect analyses revealed that only at the 0-level were mean likelihood estimates significantly different ($p < .05$). In summary, the third hypothesis received qualified support in both experiments. What makes the results convincing is the fact that the same pattern of results emerged in two independent experiments. Given the fact that replicability of results is essential for social psychological research, this consistency is promising.

JUST WORLD, EXPECTATIONS, AND SCRIPTS

These experiments have touched on issues pertinent to just world theory and expectation-states theory. Just world theory (Lerner & Miller, 1978; Lerner, Miller, & Holmes, 1976) has been proposed to account for

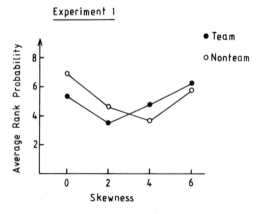

FIGURE 8.   Likelihood rankings as a function of team and skewness of reward diagram in Experiment 1; $n = 40$ in each condition. Lower rankings indicate higher probabilities.

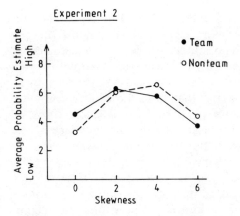

FIGURE 9. Likelihood estimates as a function of team and skewness of reward diagram in Experiment 2; $n = 60$ in each condition. Higher ratings indicate higher probabilities.

the perceived consistency between outcomes and contributions. The theory asserts that "individuals have a need to believe that they live in a world where people generally get what they deserve" (Lerner & Miller, 1978, p. 1030).

Numerous studies in the just world paradigm have found that people derogate innocent victims. In addition, Lerner (1965) demonstrated that a person who had been awarded payment by chance was rated as having contributed more to a group task. In this study, subjects observed two co-workers. Half of the subjects heard that Tom would be paid; the other half was told that Bill would be paid. All subjects later rated the workers' contribution to the task. According to just world theory, the worker who earned the money should have been viewed as more productive. This is precisely what occurred.

The above line of reasoning is consistent with the results of the unequal conditions of Experiment 1 and Experiment 2 (Bierhoff & Kramp, 1982). One additional feature of the present work is that results from the equal condition have indicated that equal rewards are inferred to be the result of equal contributions as well as of unequal contributions. The just world effect occurred only for those subjects who had previously been told that the rewards were unequal (as in the study by Lerner, 1965).

Expectation-states theory (Berger, Rosenholtz, & Zelditch, 1980; Berger, Fisek, Norman, & Wagner, 1983) is a model about status characteristics and holds that specific performance expectations are attached to specific status characteristics. The theory suggests that outcome differences involve differential performance expectations. Rewards function as performance cues, because specific status characteristics are assumed to be associated with levels of performance at specific tasks.

"The distance between positions A and B is assumed to depend on the relative *expectation advantage* of the actors in these two positions" (Berger *et al.*, 1980, p. 489; emphasis in the original). If reward is a status characteristic, we should find that higher rewards are associated with better performances.

An initial test of the proposition that outcome differences elicit differential performance expectations was performed by Cook (1975). In her "undefined-equity condition" subjects received no feedback about their performances in the first phase of the experiment. However, during a second phase of the experiment they were given higher rewards than their co-workers. It was assumed that this reward differential would function as a performance cue indicating that the subject performed better than her co-worker. Due to lack of a control group the results must be interpreted with caution. Mean allocations to self indicated that the undefined-equity condition resulted in self-allocations that were nearly as high as in a "defined-equity condition." In the latter condition subjects were informed during phase 1 that their ability in the task was definitely higher than the ability of their co-worker. The actual distribution of rewards was the basis of the performance expectations that had a similar—although somewhat weaker—effect on reward allocations as did objective evidence of ability differences. These results point in the same direction as the backward inferences of our subjects, because unequal rewards were taken as evidence for unequal performances.

Our experimental data do not support one theory over the other. As a matter of fact, just world theory and expectation-states theory make identical predictions with regard to backward inferences from unequal rewards to performance. However, it is possible to contrast the two theories in terms of the additional predictions they make. For example, expectation-states theory includes the assumption that multiple status characteristics are combined and that inconsistency in status characteristics may increase the use of the equality principle (Berger, Rosenholtz, & Zelditch, 1980). In contrast, just world theory contains no assumptions with regard to persons who get more than their co-workers on one occasion and less on other occasions. One might extrapolate from the theory that such inconsistencies threaten the belief that people get what they deserve. It is unclear, however, what type of justice response would follow.

One main difference between the two theories lies in the emphasis on the just world motive that finds no equivalent in expectation-states theory. It seems reasonable to argue that the theories complement each other. Whereas just world theory explains why individuals are motivated to prefer evaluations that are consistent with status characteristics, expectation-states theory does not locate the stability of status organizing processes in the individual but in the social system. From the perspective of systems theory (Luhmann, 1973), status organizing processes are the results of information processing that is determined by the necessity to reduce the high complexity of social reality. Although the theoretical origins of just world theory and expectation-states theory are psychological and sociological, respectively, they converge in their implications for social perception in general, and especially with regard to performance expectations formed on the basis of reward configurations.

A related theoretical framework is script theory (Abelson, 1976, 1981, 1982), proposed to account for schematic information processing. Scripts are "organized bundle[s] of expectations about an event sequence" (Abelson, 1982, p. 134), and scripts can facilitate the interpretation of behavior of others. If subjects are responding to the outcome diagram on the basis of equity and/or equality scripts, then the results in the equal and unequal reward conditions can be predicted. The reasoning is that unequal rewards activate the equity script, whereas equal rewards activate both the equality script and the equity script. The latter prediction can be derived from the fact that equal rewards can be the result of allocations on the basis of the equity principle (when equal contributions are given) *and* on the basis of the equality principle (when equal or unequal contributions are given). In the case of unequal contributions, the equality principle is the justice rule that justifies equal rewards. In the case of equal contributions, the equity rule and the equality rule justify equal rewards. This reasoning invites research employing fine-grained analyses of the cognitive processes involved.

In the introduction two restrictions were mentioned with regard to the scope of the present research. First, the experiments reported dealt with the exchange of material rewards. Resource theory (Foa & Foa, 1980) distinguishes six types of resources that vary on the dimensions of particularism and concreteness. Foa and Foa suggest a number of exchange rules that specify the relationships among the resource classes. Resources that are similar (e.g., on the dimension of particularism) are assumed to be exchanged with one another. For example, money, information, and goods constitute one cluster in which exchanges of one type of resource with another are likely. The results that were obtained in the present research for material rewards can be most easily generalized to the resource classes within this cluster of universal resources. To a lesser degree, the results can be generalized to the resource classes of status and services, respectively.

The second restriction was that only the equity rule and the equality rule were discussed. It is interesting to note that in school settings or in work relationships equity and equality are the justice principles that immediately come to mind. Other principles, for example the need principle, seem to be noticed only if relevant cues are available that make clear that special circumstances are present. This reasoning seems to be valid for unit relationships (cf. Kayser & Schwinger, 1982; Lerner, 1981) where the goals of the group members are convergent rather than divergent. In such a context, special cues (e.g., needs) must be present so that other justice rules (instead of equity and equality) are taken into consideration.

Backward inferences may be hindered if cues indicate that the need principle was used as a basis of the reward distribution. In addition, the evaluation of an allocator who violates the equity and equality rule might be changed from negative to positive if relevant cues suggest that he or she followed the need principle. This is only a speculation, but it seems reasonable to suggest that the need principle can be accepted as a justification for reward distributions that violate the justice rules that are usually applied in unit relationships. Further research must investigate the conditions under which the need principle is superimposed as a justified rule in cooperative relationships (for related research, see Schwinger, Chapter 11, this volume).

SUMMARY

In everyday life allocators often have the choice between the equity rule and the equality rule. Whereas the equity principle seems to be more appropriate when individual differences are emphasized, the equality principle is associated with similarity and solidarity among coworkers.

Research reported here was designed to investigate whether the type of interpersonal relations influences the evaluation of allocators who violate one or both distribution rules. Results from this research show that allocators who follow the equality rule are evaluated more positively than allocators who violate the equality rule. More interestingly, the violation of the equity rule was evaluated negatively only when the work relationship was described as a nonteam situation. Therefore, it seems reasonable to assume that allocation differences found in earlier studies between team and nonteam conditions are caused by the situation-dependent use of the equity principle. In addition, results indicate that the use of equity is evaluated differently by males and females.

The data suggest that situational cues are potentially important for persons in determining their preference for allocation rules and in inferring expected contributions when only the reward distribution is known. The results of two experiments indicated that backward inferences from reward configurations to performances followed the equity rule if the rewards were unequally distributed. Equal rewards were interpreted to be the result of moderately unequal contributions.

Further research should seek to provide more direct evidence on the influence of implicational scripts. On the one hand, there is good reason to expect that implicational scripts will be closely related to situational determinants, such as type of interpersonal relationship and inequalities of contributions and outcomes. On the other hand, there are reasons to disentangle equity and equality. Empirical evidence indicates that perceived justice depends on the complex interaction of justice scripts, situational demands, and gender.

Acknowledgments

The authors wish to express their sincere gratitude to Ronald Cohen for his considerable advice and helpful comments.

REFERENCES

Abelson, R. P. (1976). Script processing in attitude formation and decision making. In J. S. Carroll, & J. W. Payne (Eds.), *Cognition and social behavior* (pp. 33–45). Hillsdale, NJ: Erlbaum.

Abelson, R. P. (1981). Psychological status of the script concept. *American Psychologist, 36*, 715–729.

Abelson, R. P. (1982). Three modes of attitude-behavior consistency. In M. P. Zanna, E. T. Higgins, & C. P. Herman (Eds.), *Consistency in social behavior. The Ontario Symposium* (Vol. 2, pp. 131–146). Hillsdale, NJ: Erlbaum.

Austin, W. (1980). Friendship and fairness: Effects of type of relationship and task performance on choice of distribution rules. *Personality and Social Psychology Bulletin, 6*, 402–408.

Austin, W., & McGinn, N. C. (1977). Sex differences in choice of distribution rules. *Journal of Personality, 45*, 379–394.

Benton, A. (1971). Productivity, distributive justice, and bargaining among children. *Journal of Personality and Social Psychology, 18*, 68–78.

Berger, J., Rosenholtz, S. J., & Zelditch, M. (1980). Status organizing processes. *Annual Review of Sociology, 6*, 479–508.

Berger, J., Fisek, M. H., Norman, R. Z., & Wagner, D. G. (1983). The formation of reward expectations in status situations. In D. M. Messick & K. S. Cook (Eds.), *Equity theory: Psychological and sociological perspectives* (pp. 127–168). New York: Praeger.

Bierhoff, H. W. (1982). Sozialer Kontext als Determinante der wahrgenommenen Gerechtigkeit [Social context as a determinant of perceived justice]. *Zeitschrift für Sozialpsychologie, 13*, 66–78.

Bierhoff, H. W. (1984). Sozialpsychologie [Social psychology]. Stuttgart: Kohlhammer.

Bierhoff, H. W., & Kramp, P. (1982). Rückschlüsse auf Leistungsverteilungen bei vorgegebenen Gewinnaufteilungen [Backward inferences to contributions on the basis of reward allocations]. *Proceedings of the 24th Meeting of Experimental Psychologists*, 247. Trier: University of Trier.

Bierhoff, H. W., & Renda, O. (1985). *Absolute und relative Gleichheit, Ressourcenklasse, sozialer Kontext und Geschlechtsunterschiede* [Equality, equity, type of resources, social context, and gender differences]. Unpublished manuscript, Philipps University, Department of Psychology, Marburg.

Brickman, P., & Bryan, J. H. (1976). Equity versus equality as factors in children's moral judgments of thefts, charity, and third-party transfers. *Journal of Personality and Social Psychology, 34,* 757–761.

Callahan-Levy, C. M., & Messé, L. A. (1979). Sex differences in the allocation of pay. *Journal of Personality and Social Psychology, 37,* 433–446.

Cook, K. S. (1975). Expectations, evaluations and equity. *American Sociological Review, 40,* 372–388.

Debusschere, M., & van Avermaet, E. (1984). Compromising between equity and equality: The effects of situational ambiguity and computational complexity. *European Journal of Social Psychology, 14,* 323–333.

Foa, B. E., & Foa, U. G. (1980). Resource theory. In K. J. Gergen, M. S. Greenberg, & R. H. Willis (Eds.), *Social exchange* (pp. 77–94). New York: Plenum Press.

Grumbkow, J. von, Deen, E., Steensma, H., & Wilke, H. (1976). The effect of future interaction on the distribution of rewards. *European Journal of Social Psychology, 6,* 119–123.

Hottes, J., & Kahn, A. (1974). Sex differences in a mixed-motive conflict situation *Journal of Personality, 42,* 260–275.

Kahn, A., O'Leary, V. E., Krulewitz, J. E., & Lamm, H. (1980). Equity and equality: Male and female means to a just end. *Basic and Applied Social Psychology, 1,* 173–197.

Kayser, E., & Schwinger, T. (1982). A theoretical analysis of the relationship among individual justice concepts, layman's social psychology, and distribution decisions. *Journal for the Theory of Social Behavior, 12,* 47–51.

Keppel, G. (1973). *Design and analysis: A researcher's handbook.* Englewood Cliffs, NJ: Prentice-Hall.

Kidder, L. H., Fagan, M. A., & Cohn, E. S. (1981). Giving and receiving. Social justice in close relationships. In M. J. Lerner & S. C. Lerner (Eds.), *The justice motive in social behavior* (pp. 235–259). New York: Plenum Press.

Kourilsky, M., & Kehret-Ward, T. (1984). Kindergarteners' attitudes toward distributive justice: Experiential mediators. *Merrill-Palmer Quarterly, 30,* 49–64.

Lerner, M. J. (1965). Evaluation of performance as a function of performer's reward and attractiveness. *Journal of Personality and Social Psychology, 1,* 355–360.

Lerner, M. J. (1974). The justice motive: "Equity" and "parity" among children. *Journal of Personality and Social Psychology, 29,* 539–550.

Lerner, M. J. (1981). The justice motive in human relations: Some thoughts on what we know and need to know about justice. In M. J. Lerner, & S. C. Lerner (Eds.), *The justice motive in social behavior* (pp. 11–35). New York: Plenum Press.

Lerner, M. J., & Miller, D. T. (1978). Just world research and the attribution process: Looking back and ahead. *Psychological Bulletin, 85,* 1030–1051.

Lerner, M. J., Miller, D. T., & Holmes, J.G. (1976). Deserving and the emergence of forms of justice. In L. Berkowitz, & E. Walster (Eds.), *Advances in experimental social psychology* (Vol. 9, pp. 133–162). New York: Academic Press.

Leventhal, G. S., & Lane, D. W. (1970). Sex, age, and equity behavior. *Journal of Personality and Social Psychology, 15,* 312–316.

Leventhal, G. S., Karuza, J., & Fry, W. R. (1980). Es geht nicht nur um Fairneβ: Eine Theorie der Verteilungspräferenzen [Beyond fairness: A theory of allocation preferences]. In G. Mikula (Ed.), *Gerechtigkeit und soziale Interaktion* (pp. 185–250). Bern: Huber.

Luhmann, N. (1973). *Vertrauen* [Trust]. Stuttgart: Enke.

Major, B., & Adams, J. B. (1983). Role of gender, interpersonal orientation, and self-presentation in distributive-justice behavior. *Journal of Personality and Social Psychology, 45,* 598–608.

Major, B., & Deaux, K. (1982). Individual differences in justice behavior. In J. Greenberg & R. L. Cohen (Eds.), *Equity and justice in social behavior* (pp. 43–76). New York: Academic Press.

Mikula, G. (1980). Zur Rolle der Gerechtigkeit in Aufteilungsentscheidungen [On the role of justice in allocation decisions]. In G. Mikula (Ed.), *Gerechtigkeit und soziale Interaktion* (pp. 141–183). Bern: Huber.

Mikula, G., & Schwinger, T. (1978). Intermember relations and reward allocations: Theoretical considerations of affects. In H. Brandstätter, J. H. Davis, & H. Schuler (Eds.), Dynamics of group decisions (pp. 229–250). Beverly Hills, CA: Sage.

Reis, H. T., & Gruzen, J. (1976). On mediating equity, equality, and self-interest: The role of self-presentation in social exchange. *Journal of Experimental Social Psychology, 12,* 487–503.

Reis, H. T., & Jackson, L. A. (1981). Sex differences in reward allocation. Subjects, partners, and tasks. *Journal of Personality and Social Psychology, 40,* 465–478.

Sagan, K., Pondel, M., Wittig, M. A. (1981). The effect of anticipated future interaction on reward allocation in same- and opposite-sex dyads. *Journal of Personality, 49,* 438–449.

Sampson, E. E. (1981). Social change and the contexts of justice motivation. In M. J. Lerner & S. C. Lerner (Eds.), *The justice motive in social behavior* (pp. 97–124). New York: Plenum Press.

Schmitt, M., & Montada, L. (1982). Determinanten erlebter Gerechtigkeit [Determinants of perceived justice]. *Zeitschrift für Sozialpsychologie, 13,* 32–44.

Shapiro, E. G. (1975). Effects of expectations of future interaction on reward allocations in dyads: Equity or equality. *Journal of Personality and Social Psychology, 31,* 873–880.

Spence, J. T., & Helmreich, R. L. (1978). *Masculinity and femininity.* Austin, TX: Texas University Press.

Taylor, M. C., & Hall, J. A. (1982). Psychological androgyny: Theories, methods, and conclusions. *Psychological Bulletin, 92,* 347–366.

Winer, B. J. (1971). *Statistical principles in experimental design* (2nd. ed.). New York: McGraw-Hill.

Chapter 10

Levels of Interest in the Study of Interpersonal Justice

HARRY T. REIS

The period following 1976 ought to have been the halcyon years of equity theory. The year 1976 stands as a landmark, because in that year, *Advances in Experimental Social Psychology* devoted an entire volume to equity theory, the only time since its inauguration in 1964 that a single issue has been so dedicated. The reason for this unprecedented attention was the "new mood of optimism [that] is emerging in social psychology." This hopefulness sprang from the promise of equity theory, because "equity theory was developed in the hope of providing the glimmerings of the general theory that social psychologists so badly need." (Both quotes, Berkowitz & Walster, 1976, p. xi.) In other words, it was thought, by the editors as well as many other researchers at the time, that equity theory might be the general systems theory that would provide a framework for conceptualizing most aspects of social relations. In so doing, the theory would make available an integrated structure for the myriad of minitheories and isolated experimental phenomena that then predominated the literature.

As this chapter is written nine years later, it seems to me that equity theory proper is mostly of historical interest. It was never laid to rest by a final battle of empirical discomfirmation; instead, it seems to have slipped away quietly through benign (albeit affectionate) neglect. The nature of this demise is well illustrated by the history of the debate

HARRY T. REIS • Department of Psychology, University of Rochester, Rochester, NY 14627.

over the proper mathematical form of the equity equation. Adams (1965) originally proposed that in order for equity to occur, the following equation must hold:

$$\frac{O_p}{I_p} = \frac{O_a}{I_a}$$

(where O = outcomes, I = inputs, $_p$ refers to the person and $_a$ refers to the other). It is not clear whether Adams meant this formula to be heuristic, as Aristotle did, or a mathematical necessity. Nevertheless, the early and middle 1970s saw a flurry of published and unpublished papers arguing about precise amendments to the above formulation (e.g., Harris, 1976; Walster, 1975). This line of writing ended abruptly when George Bohrnstedt, then the editor of *Social Psychology Quarterly*, declared a moratorium on papers concerning the mathematics of the equation. This halt was intended to last until the demonstrated empirical utility of the equation for predicting and understanding human behavior in actual justice situations had progressed to the point where the mathematical fine points justified further attention (Bohrnstedt, 1982). Such evidence has not been forthcoming, and the issue would seem to be moot.

Whatever the mathematical weaknesses of equity theory were, they diverted attention from the more consequential problems the theory had. Many commentators have already spoken eloquently of these difficulties (e.g., Deutsch, 1985; Wexler, 1983). My primary purpose in this chapter is not to dwell on the shortcomings of equity theory. Indeed, an historical perspective suggests that we might evaluate equity theory in terms of its seminal value, for which it would receive high grades, and not on the validity of its specific propositions. Instead, I would like to highlight a fundamental problem that pervaded equity theory, as well as other contemporaneous theories of justice, and then use this point as the springboard for describing a multidomain approach to the study of interpersonal justice. The problem is this: in the zeal to provide a general systems theory applicable across the realm of social psychology, the various propositions of equity theory became so general that their operational limits became difficult to define and their hypothetical implications became impossible to disconfirm. Three examples may help illustrate my contention.

1. Equity theory was formulated as a motivational theory, in that individuals were said to strive for equity, as well as to seek restitution whenever inequity occurred. Perhaps as a consequence, the distinction between equity as a motivating force and as a normative pattern for regulating outcome distribution was not made explicit. Because norms arise from the nature of social interdependence (Deutsch, 1985; Sampson,

1969) and help to determine its form in the future, the role of the social context in defining standards of distributive justice was not systematically integrated.

2. Although equity was defined as outcomes proportional to inputs, in the attempt to include the many varieties of social interdependence within its purview, most any arrangement could be evaluated as equitable, given an appropriately selective constellation of weighted inputs and outcomes. Thus, when other scholars noted that egalitarian groups would tend to ignore inputs and instead allocate outcomes equally (Sampson, 1969), this state could be portrayed as equitable because the relevant inputs were the fact of simple group membership and not individual productivity (Walster & Walster, 1975). Likewise, the justice of need could be construed as equitable if inputs were assessed in terms of dependence on others. As critics have noted (e.g., Deutsch, 1985), allowing such transformations makes the theory tautological. More subtlely, such breadth redefines the term *equitable* as a general synonym for fair, leaving the precise concept of proportionality unaddressed.

3. The broad concept of equity, once again in its attempt to be general, failed to establish, specify, and differentiate the classes of phenomena to which the theory was meant to pertain. Numerous domains were lumped together within the same terms: monetary and nonmonetary outcomes, motives, attitudes, emotional experiences, perceptions, and philosophical beliefs. Although these categories are undoubtedly related to one another, lumping them together under singular principles is likely to obscure full understanding of the broader concept. A theory that identifies domain-specific principles, accounting for the relationship of phenomena across domains, is more likely to be empirically verifiable and pragmatically applicable.

In short, my thesis will be that proper understanding of a complex multifaceted concept, such as interpersonal justice, requires first distinguishing the various domains of the phenomenon from one another. Only then can the appropriate level for each empirical operation, theoretical question, or applied problem be concisely identified. To be optimistic, I believe this sort of differentiation has begun in the last few years, albeit unsystematically, and that is one major reason why the new direction of research, labeled interpersonal justice, offers more promise than its predecessor, equity theory, did.

LEVELS OF INTERPERSONAL JUSTICE PHENOMENA

There are many possible schemes for subdividing the phenomena in which interpersonal justice researchers are interested. For example, one might distinguish between beliefs and actual behavior, between cognitive evaluations and emotional reactions, or between activities that involve continued sequences of interaction or distinctly separable points in time. Although all of these categorizations might be appropriate in a complete Linnaean taxonomy of justice, I will focus primarily on a set of hierarchical discriminations that separates phenomena that are, at least in their psychological processing, fundamentally discrete. The overall scheme will be presented briefly first. Subsequently, each aspect of the model will be discussed in some detail, as well as its connection to the other levels.

A simple depiction is presented in Figure 1. The first tier distinguishes studies concerned with the justice motive from those dealing with the specific rules that instantiate the general principle (e.g., proportionality, equality, need, impartial procedures). The justice motive refers to the desire to participate in social interactions that can properly be called just. It acts as a motive in the full psychological sense of that term, in that it impels certain behaviors, be they proactive (as in the case of distributing outcomes) or reactive (as in the case of redressing or rationalizing an existing injustice). Although there is great heuristic danger in positing a special motive as the origin for every class of human activity, the evidence for conceptualizing justice as a peripheral motive is clear (see the following). Support for this contention stems from two lines of investigation. One line demonstrates that the desire for just relations, however they might be operationalized, is a consistent and pervasive ambition in many walks of life (Hochschild, 1981; Lerner & Lerner, 1981). This goal is not easily reducible to a sublimated version of other, better established, social motives. Second, a number of studies document the impact of the justice motive by demonstrating the behavioral consequences of making it more or less salient (Lerner, 1980; Mikula, 1973; Reis & Burns, 1982).

The other major category of Figure 1 concerns specific principles

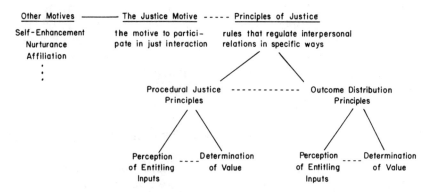

FIGURE 1. Levels of interest in justice phenomena.

of justice that operationalize the general concept. These principles regard antecedents and consequences of various schemes for regulating social interaction, more particularly those that mediate access to mutually desired outcomes (Deutsch, 1985; Haan, 1978). It is useful to think of allocation schemes, such as equality or need, as socially regulating rules because they prescribe how individuals ought to treat one another in the context of attaining life's benefits. For example, the need rule stipulates that people should attend to one another's needs, and attempt to satisfy them (see Schwinger, Chapter 11, this volume). From the standpoint of Figure 1, it is important to note the conceptual independence of these specific principles from the more general desire to achieve justice. After all, there are many rules that might be used by persons seeking a just end, varying as a function of cultural imperatives (Gergen, Morse, & Gergen, 1980), situational factors (Deutsch, 1985), and individual or group preferences (Major & Deaux, 1982). Many theorists have already argued persuasively that variations in interpersonal orientation affect the specific principle that will be seen as just (Lerner, Miller, & Holmes, 1976; Reis, 1984; Schwinger, Chapter 11, this volume). Although these rules differ meaningfully, they are all, in their proper context, perceived as fair, and consequently can gratify a salient justice motive.

What is the import of this distinction? For one, it suggests that two people can desire justice, yet seek it in different forms. In real life, such differences of opinion produce conflict. But there is an equally important implication for justice research. If the same goal can engender different distributions, and if by extension, the same allocations can arise from different motives, then it is impossible to infer which motive is operative from a specific pattern of outcomes. Yet it is common in the literature to examine variations in the distribution of rewards and costs, using the findings to defend inferences about the justice motive. The result is a potentially misspecified conclusion that may slant our understanding of justice off the mark.

In a subsequent section, I will argue that other motives in addition to justice (e.g., conflict avoidance, self-presentation) occur in typical research. For the present, one striking example demonstrates the necessity for keeping separate the justice motive and actual allocation patterns. Using standard hypothetical allocation-to-others scenarios, Harris and Joyce (1980) asked subjects to divide a partnership's financial earnings among its members. These subjects favored equality, a result which, given the tendency to infer motive from allocations, might be attributed to the group-harmony enhancing value of equality as a justice rule. However, Harris and Joyce also asked other judges given the same information to distribute expenses rather than outcomes. In this case, proportionality was the simpler calculation, and it was preferred. Thus, the study demonstrates not an inherent preference for one or another rule, but rather that mathematical simplicity is a factor in standard allocation procedures. Note that their instructions asked subjects "to be as fair as possible." Assuming subjects strove for this goal, inferences about the concrete form this desire takes would appear to be tenuous.

The next subdivision in Figure 1 distinguishes justice principles that focus on procedural issues from those that concern the distribution of outcomes. Procedural justice refers to the manner in which the claims of contending parties are considered, independent of the ultimate resolution (Thibaut & Walker, 1975). Outcome distribution rules regard the rewards and costs that accrue, independent of how they were attained. Focusing on a distinction between procedural and outcome justice as a special tier in Figure 1 is somewhat arbitrary, inasmuch as they represent not fundamentally disparate concerns, as did the justice motive and specific rules, but rather two general subclasses within which all of the specific principles can be placed. Nevertheless, the importance of separating procedural and outcome issues has been indicated clearly in theoretical, empirical, and practical analyses (Greenberg, Chapter 18; Tyler, Chapter 16, this volume). For example, it is obvious that deserved outcomes may result even when procedures are perceived to be unfair, as in the case of vigilante-style retaliation. Similarly, fair procedures can lead to unfair outcomes, such as when legal trials are decided on the basis of technicalities and not on the merits of the case. Philosophers disagree markedly as to which feature is the more crucial element of justice *per se* (see Kaufmann, 1973; and Rawls, 1971, for discussions of this issue). These treatises notwithstanding, empirical studies demonstrate that perceptions of *both* procedural and outcome justice affect overall satisfaction, although they operate independently (Lind, Kurtz, Musante, Walker & Thibaut, 1980; Tyler, 1984).

As with specific rules and the justice motive, the failure to distinguish procedural rules from outcome distribution principles may create conceptual confusion. However, because these are parallel factors, both of which are pertinent to all distributive justice situations, the problem is more likely to be one of underspecification than misleading inferences. An example may be helpful. As Tyler (1984) noted, many psychological and political theories assume that satisfaction is solely a function of outcomes, either in absolute terms or relative to some comparison standard. Consequently, research designs that only assess perceived outcomes overlook the simultaneous impact of procedural considerations, and, more importantly, fail to identify any processes that depend on the interaction of outcome and procedure. Such interactions have often been demonstrated in experimental studies. For instance, Folger (1977) demonstrated that perceived fairness was greater for constant outcomes if the recipient had a voice during allocations (voice was seen as procedurally fairer than no voice), whereas increasing outcomes were seen as fairer if the recipient had no voice.

The problem may be greater in naturalistic studies that rely on naturally occurring variations in procedural and outcome justice, rather than manipulating them orthogonally. In many of these studies, outcome levels and procedural factors have been shown to influence each other directly. For example, Tyler (1984) examined the mediating role of perceived procedural and outcome fairness on court evaluations by defendants who had been tried for traffic violations and misdemeanors. Among many results, he found that outcomes relative to expectations affected perceived procedural fairness, which in turn influenced ratings of the court and judge. This indirect effect is noteworthy because it indicates how the failure to consider both factors might overlook an important aspect of the process. That is, relative outcomes related to satisfaction by virtue of the procedural justice mediating factor. If procedural justice had been omitted from the analyses, this would have been taken as evidence of an outcome justice effect, a conclusion that is incorrect.

To return to Figure 1, the final differentiation elaborates the operation of each justice principle. I will use outcome distribution rules for convenience. A specific division of rewards requires two judgments. First, allocators must decide what the relevant parameters are; second, they must assess each recipient's standing on those parameters. In Figure 1, the choice of parameters is referred to as a "determination of value" because allocation norms are statements that stipulate the particular characteristics entitling an individual to the desirable commodities that a society controls. For example, the Protestant ethic asserts that rewards should go to those who work hard (Weber, 1904). Hence, effort is given ascribed value. The proportionality rule dictates, somewhat vaguely, that inputs are to be rewarded. Allocators must decide which inputs are pertinent, be they effort, time, units produced, contributions to the group's output, and so forth. This decision affirms the dominant values of the group, and it also influences how group members will orient their activities. However, were all participants in an exchange to concur that effort is to be the basis of reward, they might still disagree about the level of effort, and hence entitlement, of each person. That is why the evaluation of particular inputs must be distinguished from the determination of value. Minimally, the prevalence of egocentric biases, demonstrated in many areas of social psychology, indicates that actors tend to evaluate their own inputs more highly than do interaction partners or impartial observers. Ross and Sicoly (1979) have shown, for example, that when both spouses' assessments of their personal contribution to the marriage are summed, the total usually exceeds 100%. The justice literature is also replete with evidence of egocentric biases, as in the robust tendency of subjects to perceive deviations from equity as less unfair when in a favorable direction than when they are unfavorable (Austin & Walster, 1974), or in the tendency to attribute causality for an accident externally to the extent that they might be blameworthy (Shaver, 1970).

Indeed, egocentric biases in the application of justice rules are so well established that they are essential to many philosophical theories of justice. Rawls' (1971) theory of justice stipulates that for a distributive system to be truly fair, the choice of a specific rule must be made behind a "veil of ignorance," so that no one can know how they might fare under each rule and thereby be biased to favor it. Rawls also implies that the perception of specific cases will be influenced by its outcome implication for allocators. Thus, it is clear that factors affecting the determination of value and the assessment of entitling inputs play a major role in the theory and practice of justice. Then it is perhaps surprising that little social psychological research has explicitly differentiated these two components, despite the fact that the failure to do so may yield ambiguous generalizations. Two empirical examples may highlight this point.

The first concerns sex differences in reward allocations. A number of studies have shown that under certain conditions, females' allocations tend toward equality, whereas males' generally lean toward proportionality (Major & Deaux, 1982). The usual explanation of this difference is that women prefer equality as a social norm, implying that they value productivity less and group harmony more than males do (the determination of value component in Figure 1). But the same allocation difference would also result if women evaluated performance levels less extremely, either because of lesser self-enhancement in the case of self-allocations, or because of less polarized evaluations of others' performance (Major, McFarlin, & Gagnon, 1984). In other words, equality might result not from a normative preference, but from the perception that participants did not differ much in their work. Given the theoretical and applied value of understanding why males' and females' allocation behavior differs, it would be important to distinguish these components.

The second example is meant to be generic of studies that investigate systematic preferences in allocation behavior by having subjects divide a monetary sum among workers differing in various criteria. In the interest of modesty, I will describe one of my own studies (Reis, Haddad, Levine, & Shanab, 1981). Business students in the United States, Jordan, and Brazil were given a fixed sum of money to allot among eight hypothetical blue-collar employees varying in performance, effort, need, and responsiveness to pay changes. One of the findings, shown in Table 1, was that American subjects differentiated *less* between the high

TABLE 1. Percentage of Total Payment Allocated to Differing
Performers

	Brazil	Jordan	U.S.	Perceived value
Low performance	8.28	10.73	11.01	B>J>U
High performance	16.71	14.27	13.99	
Low effort	9.57	10.31	10.49	B>J=U
High effort	14.91	14.68	14.52	
Low need	11.53	12.25	12.47	B>J>U
High need	13.47	12.75	12.52	
Low responsiveness	13.03	12.33	12.27	B<J=U
High responsiveness	11.97	12.67	12.73	

Note. All differences are significant at $p < .05$ or less in one-way analyses of variance. There were four recipients in each category, hence percentages sum to 25% (within rounding error). B, J, and U refer to Brazil, Jordan, and the United States.

and low extremes of each factor than did Jordanians (for performance and need) and Brazilians (on all four factors). Our goal was to be able to conclude that in the United States, contrary to popular assumptions, these four factors are perceived to be less valuable, whereas other principles (e.g., solidarity) have more merit. However, our results might also mean that American judges saw the levels of these factors as less variable. Perhaps American workers naturally vary more, so that the same hypothetical information is perceived to be relatively less extreme. If this is true, identical cultural values would yield less divergent allocations. Although the results of this study may still be interesting, the unfortunate implication is that we cannot tell which factor is causally responsible.

Other examples might be given to demonstrate the need for precise empirical differentiation of the factors in Figure 1. The overall point is reminiscent of Thorngate's (1976) postulate: no theory is simultaneously general, simple, and accurate. Given that interpersonal justice spans a realm of phenomena that are by definition general, and given the obvious necessity of being correct, our theories will have to be complex. One foundation for such complexity is that presented above: careful delineation and differentiation of variables dealing with distinguishable aspects of the general phenomenon.

In the remainder of this chapter, I would like to illustrate the utility of this scheme in a different manner: by discussing each of these domains separately, in the hope of depicting the disparate processes that come together when we try to act justly.

SPECIFIC DOMAINS

THE JUSTICE MOTIVE

As noted earlier, there is conceptual danger in positing a motive whenever an originating force is needed to explain certain behaviors. Then why is it necessary to posit a justice motive? Essentially because justice is a broadly defined goal for which people strive actively and consistently across varied settings, resource classes, and interaction types. Undoubtedly this striving is the result of socialization, or more precisely, the cognitive representations that accompany learning to delay gratification and act interdependently with others. Some theorists also see justice as having a universal or innate genesis (e.g., Lerner, 1977; Walster, Berscheid, & Walster, 1973). This claim is unnecessary to argue for a justice motive, although it may be correct. Instead, the basis for the motive is its breadth and pervasiveness as an impelling force, as well as the theoretical value that derives from considering justice as a unitary process. Other discussions have attempted to characterize the justice motive as a transformation of more generally accepted motives, such as power (Walster & Walster, 1975), impression formation (Tedeschi & Lindskold, 1976), or self-enhancement (Walster et al., 1973). Although these motives are relevant in the development and operation of the justice motivation (see the following), each one independently cannot account for the full range of phenomena that constitutes interpersonal justice.

What, then, is the nature of the justice motive? It is first necessary to specify its place in the hierarchy of motives. In a recent book, Aronoff and Wilson (1985) distinguish between core needs and peripheral, or acquired, motives. Core needs refer to internal forces driving the organism to seek specific environmental events. Peripheral motives are integrated patterns of learned responses to subsets of the events that activate primary needs. In other words, peripheral motives are subordinate categories of motivated behavior, general enough to denote organized, frequent actions, yet narrower in scope than the primary needs from which they derive. A key feature of Aronoff & Wilson's framework is that the individual's experience shapes the nature and salience of peripheral motives, so that socialization and life events play a large part in determining which motives will be most powerful for which persons.

In this perspective, justice is best conceptualized as a peripheral motive. Three of Aronoff & Wilson's primary needs are implicated—control over experience, love and belonging, and esteem—although on conceptual grounds, the role of control appears predominant. The notion that the desire for justice helps individuals ensure control over their outcomes has recently been presented by Mikula (1984) and Reis (1984), and is in fact inherent in Lerner's (1977) personal contract. Common to these schemes is the idea that participating in just exchanges fosters assurance that the rewards to which one is entitled will be received. In fact, Lerner's (1977) seminal discussion of the justice motive proposes that the internal representation of this premise as a personal contract forms the basis of all future justice behavior. Given that most individuals possess a global sense of their own personal deserving, however ill-defined this sense may be, treating others fairly is both a necessary and sufficient qualification for anticipating fair treatment in return. Thus, a sense of justice structures the environment in a manner that lessens anxiety over receipt of future outcomes.

Elsewhere, I have argued that the developmental process of acquiring the concept of justice requires internalizing the belief that one's actions fulfill the above provisions (Reis, in press). In adults, believing oneself to be just affords a sense of long-term control, over and above that engendered in specific interactions that may be more or less ambiguous. After all, the details of exactly how many units of outcomes each person merits are often unclear (as Figure 1 implies). Because claims accompanied by the stamp of legitimacy are more likely to be successful, some degree of strategic distortion may be expected, within the latitude of acceptance for a fair exchange. Some theorists take this tendency to mean that the control justice affords is to legitimize self-aggrandizement in a socially acceptable manner. However, this interpretation is belied by noting that to the extent that perceptions of justice are shared, cooperative interaction occurs efficiently and autonomously, resulting in increased outcomes for all parties. In other words, self-aggrandizement interferes with coordinated action. Furthermore, most studies that demonstrate self-serving biases in claims of justice also find cognitive distortions justifying those claims. Insofar as the justice motive is concerned, the key requirement is the self-perception of having fulfilled the terms of a fair exchange, whatever they may be.

Two other primary needs play a role in the development and mature operation of the justice motive. The first, love and belonging, is relevant essentially because most standards of justice regulate interaction in ways that are intended to facilitate coaction and group well-being. Acting justly helps form and preserve satisfying social relationships. Of course, parents often make love contingent on various forms of justice, such as sharing. The second category, esteem needs, implies that recognition by self and others as a morally worthy person reinforces fair behavior. Behaving fairly so as to be seen as a "good child" is a well-established stage of moral development (Damon, 1977), and self-presentation may affect adults similarly (Reis, 1981). Although belonging and esteem have a part in establishing justice as an independent motive, they are secondary to control for two reasons. First, they often motivate actions inconsistent with the justice motive, without requiring cognitive reconciliation. Second, the justice motive and its attendant consequences may be derived exclusively from control needs. That is, both the benefits of group belonging and being seen as a righteous person facilitate fulfillment of the personal contract, thereby enhancing a sense of control over exchange processes. Consequently, it seems more parsimonious to view control as the primary need from which justice arises.

Integration with Other Peripheral Motives

If justice is to be conceptualized as a peripheral motive, its interaction with other peripheral motives must be noted. This is illustrated in the left-hand portion of Figure 1. Individuals have goals other than justice: self-enhancement, affiliation, dominance, self-presentation, to name but a few. The extent to which each influences behavior is determined by their relative salience, itself a function of the situation, the relationship, the person, and his or her interaction goals. Thus, when the justice motive is operative, its actual impact is modified by integration with other relevant motives.

This process is more than weighted algebra. There are many acceptable principles of justice, each of which fosters a different type of interdependence or social goal. The dilemma of choosing between the justice motive and some other motive is no dilemma at all if a principle exists satisfying the latter goal that also may appropriately be perceived as just. For example, if both justice and intimacy were salient, an equal division of costs and rewards would accomplish both goals. On the other hand, allocators seeking justice and dominance might rely on the proportionality principle when their own performance was superior. From these examples, it may be inferred that the justice motive is flexible, requiring only that the selected rule be consistent with an existing standard of fairness. This flexibility imbues justice with the capability of operating in a sophisticated, situation-specific manner, incorporating legitimate factors such as history, intention, cultural goals, and so forth.

In part, this is why two concepts often linked to justice in lay analyses, frustration (Deutsch, 1985), and relative deprivation (Crosby, 1976), must be considered independent of justice. Frustration or relative deprivation need not be perceived as unjustified, and relative advantage need not be seen as fair. As both of the previously cited authors have noted, when an unfavorable position is also believed to be unjust, it produces stronger feelings of indignation, more active attempts at redress, and probably a greater likelihood of effective resolution. As a result of cognitive distortion, or perhaps strategic gamesmanship, a wanted outcome is often presented as deserved. But the fact that relative deprivation may or may not be perceived as justified, and that the degree of justification leads to different responses, supports the contention that the desire for justice and the desire for specific outcomes are conceptually distinct. Consequently, a full understanding of responses to disadvantageous outcomes requires examination of the entire constellation of operative motives. The justice motive refers to the desire that justice be done. Its specific form may be modified by other contextually salient motives.

One methodological implication of this distinction is that research designed to examine the nature of justice behavior may more nearly reflect other motives. For example, it is often presumed in reward allocation studies that subjects' distributions indicate what they believe would be fair in that situation. However, other goals may also be salient: impressing the experimenter, avoiding conflict with peers, making as much money as possible, and so on. Unless the experimental design or subjects' self-reports establish the prepotency of justice as a goal, it is impossible to know whether justice or other social motives are responsible for the results. Evidence for this point comes from two studies, one conducted with adults (Mikula, 1973) and one with children (Nelson & Dweck, 1977). In both cases, subjects in one condition were asked to try to be fair; for subjects in the other condition, this instruction was omitted. Allocations tended toward proportionality when fairness was an explicit goal, but they deviated toward equality when it was not. Although it might be tempting to conclude that equality was the preferred form of justice in the latter condition, it seems more plausible to posit that subjects were simply more concerned with satisfying their peers than they were with justice.

Justice Principles as Different Forms of Social Interdependence

Principles of justice are codified representations proposing how people ought to live and work together. That is, if interpersonal relations are viewed as a systematic pattern of altering by coaction the outcomes that would be received from solitary action (Kelley & Thibaut, 1978), then justice rules stipulate the terms for mutually acceptable exchanges. Deutsch (1985; Chapter 1, this volume) expressed this point in his "crude law" of social relations: that justice principles embody existing patterns of interdependence, and help mold new relationships into similar forms. Somewhat more specifically, Haan (1978) asserted that principles of justice arise from agreements between individuals about how conflicts over responsibilities and limited resources are to be regulated. That is, consensually acknowledged beliefs minimize the potential for conflict, and facilitate cooperation action. Justice rules are more than cultural philosophies, however. For one thing, by specifying what ought to be done to attain desired outcomes, they engender particular kinds of interactions and relationships. Moreover, because justice rules are typically taught as being morally correct (Walster & Walster, 1975), such patterns of interaction are seen as desirable and become the dominant mode of the culture or group. To paraphrase Piaget (1965), moral judgments represent the logic of social understanding.

A few brief examples may make this point clear. A culture in which the essential resources for survival were extremely scarce might emphasize rules favoring the welfare of the group over the welfare of the individual, so that wasteful conflict would be minimized. Similarly, a proportionality rule is likely in a hierarchically stratified society in which status is based on achievement and performance. On the other hand, an obligation standard might be appropriate in a society requiring cooperative interaction, yet not having the potential to monitor and punish violations. These principles also apply in dyadic relationships. For example, reciprocity works well in acquaintanceships, but intimate friendship depends on a needs focus (Clark, 1985). This is because reciprocity precludes a caring, nurturant person focus, whereas a needs emphasis encourages it.

If justice rules describe patterns of social interdependence, then there should be as many justice rules as there are varieties of interdependence. Yet, the history of social psychological research into justice rules has been more limited. Among social psychologists, Homans (1961) first suggested proportionality. Subsequently, Sampson (1969) proposed that equality was also important, leading many researchers for a time to see "equity versus equality" as the allocator's dilemma. Deutsch (1975) joined the needs rule to the list, followed by Lerner, Miller, and Holmes (1976), who added justified self-interest, Darwinian justice, and social obligations. A wider perspective was recommended by Leventhal (1980), whose Justice Judgment Model proposed that various rules are weighted in any situation to arrive at a useful metric, but this model also implied that there were still more possibilities than the above six.

In research reported elsewhere (Reis, 1984), Leventhal's point was combined with our belief that many other forms of interdependence have, at some time or in a particular context, properly been labelled instantiations of justice. A list of 17 principles was derived from folklore, law, history, philosophy, and social psychology (see Table 2). Each identifies a specific recipe for outcome distribution. Moreover, each has been described by its proponents as just, fair, or morally correct in some way. The list is hardly exhaustive; however, in its range of alternatives, many

TABLE 2. Seventeen Distributive Rules

---

1. When it is necessary to choose between a harmful outcome for oneself or someone else, one is justified in choosing the harmful outcome for the other person.
2. A person is justified in always making sure that his or her own needs are met first.
3. People should help others who need their assistance without expecting benefits in return.
4. Only when resources are scarce is one justified in being primarily concerned with one's own welfare.
5. The welfare of the group is more important than the welfare of any individual member.
6. Outcomes should be based on the results of people's actions, irrespective of their intentions.
7. Anyone who does a favor for someone else is justified in expecting a favor in return.
8. Rewards and benefits should be distributed strictly according to the laws and rules applicable in that situation.
9. In any situation, rewards or benefits should be divided equally among the participants regardless of their individual contributions.
10. People are responsible for living up to the moral principles of any groups to which they voluntarily belong.
11. One should do good things for other people for its own sake, irrespective of what they might receive in return.
12. As long as one adheres to the rules and laws governing a situation, one is justified in maximizing one's own interests within those rules.
13. People have the responsibility to live up to their own moral principles.
14. Those in power are justified in using their power to further their own interests.
15. In any situation, people should receive rewards or benefits proportional to what they have contributed.
16. Rewards should be distributed on the basis of the needs of the recipients, rather than their contributions.
17. People ought to fulfill the needs of those to whom they have an obligation through duty, contract, or promise.

---

significant viewpoints are represented. The purpose of this list was not sophisticated pedantry. Rather, we sought to identify the dimensions that people use to understand justice. If there are at least 17 possible strategies for allocating rewards, a cognitive schema would preclude the burdensome task of weighing each alternative in every instance. Identifying the phenomenology of this structure may be useful in helping us understand how people think about principles of justice, how they select from among the numerous possibilities, and how they apply these principles.

The 17 principles listed in Table 2 were examined in two multidimensional scaling studies (for more information and exact results, see Reis, 1984). Three dimensions emerged from this analysis (prototypic examples are given in Table 3):

1. Complex entitlement-determining procedures favoring long-term gratification versus simple outcome-focused rules favoring immediate gratification

TABLE 3. A Three-Dimensional Categorization of Distributive Justice Norms

	Self-perspective		Group/other perspective	
	Procedural focus Long-term gratification	Outcome focus Immediate gratification	Procedural focus Long-term gratification	Outcome focus Immediate gratification
Status assertion	Criterion-referenced exchange: proportionality	Hedonic self-interest: own needs	Impersonal exchange: laws, actions, not intentions	Self-preservation attenuated by group concern: own needs if resources scarce
Status neutralization	Self-centered idealism: own moral principles	Paternalism	Universal idealism: good for its own sake, help without return	Nurturance and solidarity: needs, equality

    2. Status-assertion versus status-neutralization

    3. Self-focused perspective versus group–other perspective

The first dimension most strongly differentiated contract (17), group welfare (5), and proportionality (15) from the various own gratification rules (1,2,4,14), needs (16), and equality (9). This first dimension was empirically labeled as proceduralism and delay of gratification. Principles that base outcome entitlement on relatively complex criteria that ultimately benefit the entire group are pitted against a set of doctrines that focus on relatively concrete, immediate divisions of outcomes. A proportionality rule requires assessment and enforcement of criteria that ultimately would have the effect of increasing group productivity. Contracts also benefit a group in the long run by establishing procedures on which individuals can rely. Kaufmann (1973), among others, has noted that explicit procedures are in the long-term interest of a just society. On the other hand, own gratification ignores long-term implications (i.e., anarchy, lack of cooperation) and focuses on immediate gratification instead. It is interesting to note that needs and equality load similarly on this dimension. Perhaps this is because neither demands a focus on complex, goal-driven procedures, instead apportioning outcomes either on the basis of their value to the recipient or irrespective of differential entitlement.

The fact that this dimension differentiated rules with a strong procedural component from those that focus more apparently on outcomes supports the distinction between procedural and outcome justice made in the literature and in Figure 1. This is not to imply that procedural justice is the opposite of distributive justice. Indeed, we argued earlier that they are conceptually independent. Rather, a given rule must by its definition focus either on procedures or outcomes. To the extent that one factor is implicated, the other is not. This is precisely why rules that focus on procedural justice do not guarantee fair outcomes: in dealing with the fairness of the procedures, the resulting outcomes are ignored. Similarly, consideration of whether an outcome is deserved or not overlooks the procedures that spawned them. Parenthetically, it should come as no surprise that proportionality possesses relatively more of a procedural focus than equality or need. Proportionality requires procedures, often complex, to assess inputs. Equality and need dole out rewards in straightforward, outcome-focused ways.

The second dimension contrasted impersonally based rules that enhance status differentials with those that minimize status differences between individuals. Status-asserting interactions create, enhance, or perpetuate distance between people, in terms of their standing on a status hierarchy and their access to material outcomes (Deaux, 1977). Proportionality (15) does this by linking rewards to productivity. So do actions, not intentions (6) and laws (8), in that they disregard the unique aspects of the person, basing entitlement on impersonal positions that could be filled just as well by any other individuals. Status-neutralizing behaviors minimize existing differences by establishing nurturant bonds and stressing the intrinsic worth of every person. Equality (9), need (16), and doing good for its own sake (11) clearly fulfill this function. So do one's own moral principles (13), in that it places the personal beliefs of eachindividual on an equal footing. Inasmuch as many distributive justice studies examine the relation of allocation patterns to independent and dependent variables that explicitly concern stratification and solidarity, it is reassuring that this dichotomy was prominent in our analysis.

The final dimension was one of perspective. Awareness of the rights and viewpoints of others, Machiavellianism, and humanitarianism all differentiated justice rules on opposing ends of this scale. As Table 3 shows, one pole included norms based on a self-focused perspective, such as one's own needs (2, 12), own principles (13) and expecting a favor in return (7). That proportionality (15) resides on this pole, although weakly, perhaps indicates an egocentric expectation that one's own contributions will tend to yield greater rewards for oneself. Focusing on the perspective of others characterized the other pole of this dimension. Significant exemplars were good for its own sake (11), help without return (3), needs (16), laws (8), group welfare (5), and one's own needs when resources are scarce (4). Of course, self–other focus has a rich history in other areas of psychology as well (for example, empathy and perspective-taking skills, group task performance, social influence, self-awareness, altruism).

The present choice of dimension labels and exemplars should not be taken too literally. Including other principles of justice would change these interpretations somewhat, and more precise labels are likely to be found in future studies. However, to the extent that this analysis identifies eight discrete justice prototypes, a corresponding variety of inter-dependent patterns of social exchange can be articulated. Table 3 depicts these types. Following Deutsch's crude law (1985; Chapter 1, this volume), it can be expected that each of these principles would result in substantially different social interactions and relationships. The empirical yield of this exercise may not only be in identifying the dimensions that characterize people's concepts of justice, but also in suggesting significant categories that have not yet received attention in justice research. The causes and consequences of the distribution patterns contained in some of the cells of Table 3 are well known (e.g., proportionality, needs/equality). Investigation of the remainder awaits future studies.

DETERMINATION OF VALUE AND PERCEPTION OF INPUTS

Justice principles are abstract statements about entitlement. The concrete application of these principles to specific instances requires two additional judgments. First, it must be decided which particular actions exemplify the concept stated in the general rule. For example, in the case of proportionality, decisions about what constitutes an input are necessary. In a factory, hours worked, quality of product, quantity of output, helpfulness to other workers, seniority, flexibility of skills, or long-term potential all might be considered inputs deserving of reward. This is a determination of value in the sense that persons in control of outcomes choose the input characteristics that entitle desired rewards, and those that do not. Some justice principles, such as equality, demand less explication on this factor, because they deal simply with outcome. Yet even in this instance, some dimensions will be weighted heavily, others not at all. Co-workers following an equality norm are probably very concerned about the equality of their salaries, but less so about their supervisor's esteem for each of them.

The second judgment in the application of a justice rule evaluates each participant's standing on the relevant dimensions. Having decided that quality of publications is to be the basis of academic salaries, for example, deans and departmental chairpersons must then assess each faculty member's publications. As discussed earlier, egocentric biases often greatly affect this stage of the justice judgment process. Moreover, inherent subjectivity in many criteria may add substantial error.

Despite its relevance for a wide variety of applications, little research has focused on this distinction. One exception is the line of investigation deriving from Foa and Foa's (1976) discussion of resource classes. They discuss six classes of inputs and rewards: love, status, information, money, goods, and services. Although the preceding argument dictates an even finer subdivision, a helpful start is provided by this research, notably in the finding that the categories are not mutually interchangeable. From the standpoint of outcome justice principles, a number of studies have examined input parameters and reward allocations. However, it is often impossible to separate value determinations from input perceptions, rendering interpretations ambiguous. In the procedural justice field, few studies have attempted to systematically determine what factors lead to perceptions of procedural justice. A recent study by Barrett-Howard and Tyler (1986) offers a promising start in this direction.

Finally, it must be noted that practitioners in the art of conflict resolution stress the distinction between norm selection and input assessment. Braiker and Kelley (1979) note the importance of norm setting in marital conflict. This process helps establish the value of activities each spouse performs for the other. Walster, Walster, and Berscheid (1978) suggest 22 such contributions and 24 such outcomes. Conflict may still arise, however, when partners disagree about the existing level of each factor. Similar principles operate in organizational conflict. For example, the process of arbitration often explicitly acknowledges the value-determination–input-assessment distinction, such as when baseball players and management may agree about a player's statistics, but disagree over their worth to the team. Alternatively, players and management may concur that leadership is valuable, yet quarrel over a given player's role. Either way, resolution is facilitated by distinguishing the two issues from each other.

POSTSCRIPT

In a convention paper (Reis, 1979), I once argued that justice research was progressing very much like a child going through the Piagetian stages of learning. In mastering an unknown object, a child first explores any aspects of the object that come to mind, hoping to discover its properties. Next, the child assimilates what has been observed to existing categories, that is, testing how the object is like various other objects, already well known. Finally, the child accommodates to the new object by detecting its unique qualities and learning how it can best be utilized.

Social psychological investigations often follow a similar trajectory, and appropriately so. First we explored the various properties of interpersonal justice, albeit without any theoretical expectations of what might be found. The attempt to apply existing established theories to justice was next. I refer to the use of dissonance-like drive reduction concepts and general reinforcement principles in the development of equity theory. It is only lately that researchers have begun to accommodate to the phenomenon of justice itself—that is, to determine its unique properties and to discover new principles that best describe its origin and operation.

The taxonomy presented in this chapter is but one framework for distinguishing the varied and complex behaviors subsumed under the rubric of interpersonal justice. It is meant to facilitate the accommodation stage. Taxonomies are not theories, nor do they explain the operation or interaction of their components. However, the absence of an organizing framework can obscure general principles and relationships that may be helpful. The range of research covered under the heading of interpersonal justice is broad indeed, as this volume demonstrates. This breadth makes the topic exciting, important, and challenging to investigators. It also implies the need for theories that acknowledge variability and diversity in domain and organizing principles. To the extent that the different phenomena of justice are distinguished, yet placed in their proper place with regard to one another, it will be possible to conceive theories that are simultaneously general, complex, and accurate.

REFERENCES

Adams, J. S. (1965). Inequity in social exchange. In L. Berkowitz (Ed.), *Advances in experimental social psychology* (Vol. 2, pp. 267–299). New York: Academic Press.

Aronoff, J., & Wilson, J. P. (1985). *Personality in the social process.* Hillsdale, NJ: Erlbaum.

Austin, W., & Walster, E. (1974). Reactions to confirmations and disconfirmations of expectancies of equity and inequity. *Journal of Personality and Social Psychology, 30,* 208–216.

Barrett-Howard, E., & Tyler, T. R. (1986). Procedural justice as a criterion in allocation decisions. *Journal of Personality and Social Psychology, 50,* 296–304.

Berkowitz, L., & Walster, E. (1976). Preface. In L. Berkowitz & E. Walster (Eds.), *Advances in experimental social psychology* (Vol. 9, p. xi). New York: Academic Press.

Bohrnstedt, G. (1982). Editorial footnote. *Social Psychology Quarterly, 45,* 126.

Braiker, H. B., & Kelley, H. H. (1979). Conflict in the development of close relationships. In R. L. Burgess & T. L. Huston (Eds.), *Social exchange in developing relationships* (pp. 135–168). New York: Academic Press.

Clark, M. S. (1985). Implications of relationship type for understanding compatibility. In W. Ickes (Ed.), *Compatible and incompatible relationships* (pp. 119–140). New York: Springer-Verlag.

Crosby, F. (1976). A model of egoistical relative deprivation. *Psychological Review, 83,* 85–113.

Damon, W. (1977). *The social world of the child.* San Francisco: Jossey-Bass.

Deaux, K. (1977). Sex differences. In T. Blass (Ed.), *Personality variables in social behavior* (pp. 357–377). Hillsdale, NJ: Erlbaum.

Deutsch, M. (1975). Equity, equality, and need: What determines which value will be used as the basis of distributive justice? *Journal of Social Issues, 31,* 137–149.

Deutsch, M. (1985). *Distributive justice.* New Haven, CT: Yale University Press.

Foa, E. B., & Foa, U. G. (1976). Resource theory of social exchange. In J. Thibaut, J. Spence, & R. Carson (Eds.), *Contemporary topics in social psychology* (pp. 99–131). Morristown, NJ: General Learning Press.

Folger, R. (1977). Distributive and procedural justice: Combined impact of "voice" and improvement on experienced inequity. *Journal of Personality and Social Psychology, 35,* 108–119.

Gergen, K. J., Morse, S. J., & Gergen, M. (1980). Behavior exchange in cross-cultural perspective. In H. Triandis & R. W. Brislin (Eds.), *Handbook of cross-cultural psychology.* Boston, MA: Allyn & Bacon.

Haan, N. (1978). Two moralities in action contexts: Relationships to thought, ego-regulation, and development. *Journal of Personality and Social Psychology, 36,* 286–305.

Harris, R. J. (1976). Handling negative inputs: On the plausible equity formulae. *Journal of Experimental Social Psychology, 12,* 194–209.

Harris, R. J., & Joyce, M. A. (1980). What's fair? It all depends on how you phrase the question. *Journal of Personality and Social Psychology, 38,* 165–170.

Hochschild, J. L. (1981). *What's fair? American beliefs about distributive justice.* Cambridge, MA: Harvard University Press.

Homans, G. C. (1961). *Social behavior: Its elementary forms.* New York: Harcourt, Brace.

Kaufmann, W. A. (1973). *Without guilt and justice.* New York: Wyden.

Kelley, H. H., & Thibaut, J. W. (1978). *Interpersonal relations: A theory of interdependence.* New York: Wiley.

Lerner, M. J. (1977). The justice motive: Some hypotheses as to its origins and forms. *Journal of Personality, 45,* 1–52.

Lerner, M. J. (1980). *The belief in a just world: A fundamental delusion.* New York: Plenum Press.

Lerner, M. J., & Lerner, S. C. (1981). *The justice motive in social behavior.* New York: Plenum Press.

Lerner, M. J., Miller, D. T., & Holmes, J. G. (1976). Deserving and the emergence of forms of justice. In L. Berkowitz & E. Walster (Eds.), *Advances in experimental social psychology* (Vol. 9, pp. 133–162). New York: Academic Press.

Leventhal, G. S. (1980). What should be done with equity theory? New approaches to the study of fairness in social relationships. In K. J. Gergen, M. S. Greenberg, & R. H. Willis (Eds.), *Social exchange theory.* New York: Wiley.

Lind, E. A., Kurtz, S., Musante, L., Walker, L., & Thibaut, J. W. (1980). Procedure and outcome effects on reactions to adjudicated resolution of conflicts of interest. *Journal of Personality and Social Psychology, 39,* 643–653.

Major, B., & Deaux, K. (1982). Individual differences in justice behavior. In J. Greenberg & R. L. Cohen (Eds.), *Equity and justice in social behavior* (pp. 43–76). New York: Academic Press.

Major, B., McFarlin, D. B., & Gagnon, D. (1984). Overworked and underpaid: On the nature of gender differences in personal entitlement. *Journal of Personality and Social Psychology, 47,* 1399–1412.

Mikula, G. (1973). *"Gerechtigkeit" und "Zufriedenheit beider partner" als Zielsetzungen der Aufteilung eines von zwei Personen gemeinsam erzielten Gewinns* [Fairness and partner satisfaction as criteria for dividing a payment between two people]. Unpublished manuscript, Institut für Psychologie der Universität Graz, Graz, Austria.

Mikula, G. (1984). Justice and fairness in interpersonal relations: Thoughts and suggestions. In H. Tajfel (Ed.), *The social dimension: European developments in social psychology* (pp. 204–227). Cambridge: Cambridge University Press.

Nelson, S. A., & Dweck, C. S. (1977). Motivation, competence and reward allocation. *Developmental Psychology, 13,* 192–197.

Piaget, J. (1965). *The moral judgment of the child.* New York: Free Press.

Rawls, J. (1971). *A theory of justice.* Cambridge, MA: Harvard University Press.

Reis, H. T. (1979, August). Theories of interpersonal justice: From exploration through assimilation to accommodation. In J. Greenberg (Chair), *Recent developments in interpersonal justice theory and research.* Symposium presented at the meeting of the American Psychological Association, New York.

Reis, H. T. (1981). Self-presentation and distributive justice. In J. T. Tedeschi (Ed.), *Impression management theory and social psychological research* (pp. 269–291). New York: Academic Press.

Reis, H. T. (1984). The multidimensionality of justice. In R. Folger (Ed.), *The sense of injustice: Social psychological perspectives* (pp. 25–61). New York: Plenum Press.

Reis, H. T. (in press). The nature of the justice motive: Some thoughts on operation, internalization and justification. In J. Masters & W. Smith (Eds.), *Social comparison, social justice and relative deprivation: Theoretical, empirical and policy perspectives.* Hillsdale, NJ: Erlbaum.

Reis, H. T., & Burns, L. (1982). Self-awareness and reactions to overpay inequity. *Journal of Experimental Social Psychology, 18,* 464–475.

Reis, H. T., Haddad, Y., Levine, R. V., & Shanab, M. *Reward allocation in three cultures.* Unpublished manuscript, University of Rochester.

Ross, M., & Sicoly, F. (1979). Egocentric biases in availability and attribution. *Journal of Personality and Social Psychology, 37,* 322–336.

Sampson, E. E. (1969). Studies of status congruence. In L. Berkowitz (Ed.), *Advances in experimental social psychology* (Vol. 4, pp. 225–270). New York: Academic Press.

Shaver, K. (1970). *An introduction to attribution processes.* Cambridge: Winthrop.

Tedeschi, J. T., & Lindskold, S. (1976). *Social psychology: Interdependence, interaction, and influence.* New York: Wiley.

Thibaut, J., & Walker, L. A. (1975). *Procedural justice: A psychological analysis.* New York: Erlbaum/Halstead.

Thorngate, W. (1976). Possible limits on a science of social behaviour. In K. Gergen, F. Aboud, & G. Jahoda (Eds.), *Social psychology in transition.* New York: Plenum Press.

Tyler, T. R. (1984). The role of perceived injustice in defendants' evaluations of their courtroom experience. *Law and Society Review, 18,* 51–74.

Walster, E., & Walster, G. W. (1975). Equity and social justice. *Journal of Social Issues, 31,* 21–44.

Walster, E., Berscheid, E., & Walster, G. W. (1973). New directions in equity research. *Journal of Personality and Social Psychology, 25,* 151–176.

Walster, E., Walster, G. W., & Berscheid, E. (1978). *Equity: Theory and research.* Boston, MA: Allyn & Bacon.

Walster, G. W. (1975). The Walster et al. (1973) equity formula: A correction. *Representative Research in Social Psychology, 6*, 63–64.

Weber, M. (1904). *The Protestant ethic and the spirit of capitalism.* New York: Scribner.

Wexler, P. (1983). The social psychology of possessive individualism: A critique of equity theory. In K. Larson (Ed.), *Ideology and psychology.* Monmouth, NJ: Institute for Theoretical History.

Chapter 11

The Need Principle of Distributive Justice

THOMAS SCHWINGER

This chapter will present some theoretical deliberations and conclusions from empirical research about the *need principle* of distributive justice ("to each according to his or her needs"). In a review of theoretical and empirical research it is shown that the need principle has been conceptualized traditionally as a variant of the contribution principle. A theoretical approach of prototypic interpersonal relationships with their specific principles of resource transaction will be presented. In this approach the need principle is conceptualized as an independent form of distributive justice. Results of various questionnaire studies will be presented showing that subjects use such a concept.

TRADITIONAL THEORETICAL PERSPECTIVES

In social psychology empirical research on interpersonal justice started with a specific class of social situations: those of workers being under-, over-, or fairly paid by a company. These studies were based on the theoretical framework of equity theory (Adams, 1965), which was based partly on Homans's (1961) concept of distributive justice.

THOMAS SCHWINGER • Psychologisches Institut IV, Universität Münster, D-4400 Münster, West Germany.

In laboratory experiments, these situations were modeled by paying subjects for work they had done. The research question centered on subjects' reactions to inequitable payment. This inequity was experimentally induced by informing subjects that they were paid differently than others who had contributed a similar amount of work. *Equity* was defined as a state of equal relative gains for the participants of an exchange; *inequity* was defined as a state of unequal relative gains. A person's relative gain from an exchange is represented by the ratio of outcomes (i.e., wages and other benefits) to inputs (i.e., work and other task-relevant characteristics). The implicit conception of interpersonal justice followed the principle: "to each according to his merits." The experimental results, at least those of subjects who had been underpaid, were in accord with this conception of justice (see Greenberg, Chapter 18, this volume). These subjects behaved in such a way that they would receive a relative gain equal to that of their comparison persons. This conception of justice reflects the ideology of economic exchange (Willer, 1981), which is the dominant interpretive scheme within modern Western societies (Deutsch, 1975; Schwinger, 1980).

Soon, however, equity theory was tested by several researchers in experiments in which two persons had to do some cooperative work to attain a joint profit, which then was to be divided between the two dyad members by one of them (Leventhal, 1976; Mikula, 1980). Within this research new questions emerged about the allocation behavior of individuals and groups. This allocation behavior was seen by some theorists (e.g., Deutsch, 1975; Lerner, 1977; Leventhal, 1976; Mikula & Schwinger, 1978) as dependent on the type of interpersonal relationship existing in the experimental situation and on the personal goals of allocators. With respect to the allocation of joint rewards several principles of distributive justice were postulated by the previously mentioned authors. Three of these principles were seen as the most important ones: the *contribution* principle ("to each according to his merits"), the *equality* principle ("to each the same"), and the *need* principle ("to each according to his needs"). Note that the conceptions of the contribution and the equity principle are quite similar. In the equity theory approach this principle is assumed to be the standard for *all* interpersonal transactions, whereas in the multiprinciple approach several principles are conceived as norms for specific social situations. This last theoretical approach yielded various classifications of interpersonal relationships and justice principles. Based on Mikula and Schwinger (1978), Table 1 shows one example for such a theoretical assignment of principles to interpersonal relationships.

Some theorists (e.g., Deutsch, 1975, 1982; Schwinger, 1980, 1981) assumed that laypersons have a commonsensical, culturally embedded knowledge about the specific effects of the various principles on a group's social climate and productivity. Allocators were assumed to select certain

TABLE 1. Assignment of Justice Principles to
Interpersonal Relationships according to Mikula
& Schwinger (1978)

Affective relationship	Justice principle
Very positive	Need
Positive	Equality
Neutral	Contributions

principles depending on the given state of a group (see Table 1) and its members' orientations towards the social climate and the group's task. For example, the contribution principle is assumed to be used as an instrument for motivating group members to work hard, which simultaneously does not foster group members' socioemotional bonds (Greenberg & Leventhal, 1976). In addition, allocators were assumed to select principles according to the relationship of their own goals to the respective state of the group. For example, an allocator who wants to foster positive socioemotional bonds will tend to use the equality principle (Mikula, 1973).

Although in this theoretical approach three principles were assumed to be equally important forms of distributive justice, only a very few studies investigated the use of the need principle. The general assumptions about the situational determinants of an individual's choice among justice principles were tested almost always with respect to the alternative contribution and equality principles (Mikula, 1980).

There may be several reasons for this paucity of attention paid to the need principle. One of these is the way this principle has been conceptualized. There was a difficulty in linking the concept of the need principle to the assumptions about the contribution and the equality principle. Some authors formulated hypotheses about the situational determinants of the use of the need principle. The need principle was assumed to be typical for interpersonal relationships with intense positive feelings (Mikula & Schwinger, 1978), for groups whose members are inclined toward fostering all individual members' welfare (Deutsch, 1975), and for relationships in which at least one participant sees himself or herself as responsible for others (Leventhal, 1976). These hypotheses deal with a specific kind of interpersonal closeness that motivates and obligates people to concentrate on a specific other person's individual needs (cf. Greenberg & Cohen, 1982).

These assumptions, however, are not easily integrated with those about the two other principles and, more generally, with those of interpersonal justice. The contribution principle and the equality principle were integrated theoretically into a framework of assumptions about the orientation of problem-solving groups toward socioemotional goals as opposed to task-related goals. Decisions among the two allocation modes following from the contribution and the equality principle can be seen as referring simultaneously to the status structure, the social climate, and the division of labor with its implications for productivity (cf. Burnstein & Katz, 1972; Cohen, 1974; Sampson, 1969). These assumptions, however, do not provide a theoretical connection to the previously mentioned ideas about the need principle. In contrast, specific hypotheses about the use of the need principle in allocation situations were developed not by using a justice approach, but by referring to theory and research about helping behavior (e.g., Schwartz, 1975). A typical hypothesis is that "illegitimate" needs would not be considered in allocation situations (cf. Leventhal, 1976). This hypothesis was based on a result of several studies on helping behavior: If a victim is perceived as being behaviorally responsible for his or her need the victim will not receive help (cf. Lerner & Miller, 1978). The analogous hypothesis about need consideration stated that if a recipient's need is caused by that recipient, this need will be seen as illegitimate and will not be considered by an allocator.

As a consequence of such a conceptualization, the term *need* changed its meaning from a personal need (e.g., need for sex, self-realization, etc.) to a description of a *deficiency of material resources*. In typical experiments students were said to need money for buying books as a means of preparing for exams.

Finally, this way of conceptualizing the need principle led to the following problem. The principle has not yet been defined in a way comparable to the other two. Whereas the contribution principle and the equality principle can be operationalized as specific allocation modes, this is not true for the need principle. In contrast, it was simply assumed that in situations in which one of two or more recipients has some need deficiency, the allocator should grant him or her a greater share than others (cf. Leventhal, 1976). The same should be true if the need deficiency of one recipient was larger than those of others.

In summary, it can be said that the need principle has been vaguely defined and conceptualized as a principle of economic exchange.

CONSIDERATION OF NEEDS IN ALLOCATION SITUATIONS:
CONCLUSIONS FROM EXPERIMENTS

In equity theory (according to Walster, Walster, & Berscheid, 1978), individual needs are assumed to be seen as inputs entitling recipients to certain outcomes, which in turn will be added to other inputs. This makes it difficult to predict how needs will be considered in allocation situations. Because of the way the need principle was conceptualized in the multiprinciple approach (Deutsch, 1975; Lerner, 1977; Leventhal, 1976; Mikula & Schwinger, 1978), the same point of view was taken implicitly in the early empirical studies dealing with the need principle. In these early studies situations were created in which a material resource (money or goods) was to be divided between recipients. The effect of the need principle was hypothesized such that (a) the person with greater needs should receive more than an equal share; and/or (b) if there are differences in contributions among recipients, that person should get more than the contribution principle allows. To illustrate hypothesis (b) let us compare the following two situations of two recipients, A and B who have contributed differently to the attainment of a joint profit; A has contributed more than B. In the first case there is no given information about any differences in the two persons' needs. In this case, according to the contribution principle, A should receive a share, a, which is greater than B's share, b. In the second case, information is given that A has *greater needs* than B. Now A's share should be larger than in the first case ($a + x$). (If, however, B would have greater needs than A, B's share would be larger than in the first case, $b + y$.)

These hypotheses were confirmed by the results of various studies. Karuza and Leventhal (1976), for example, asked subjects to allocate units of food among hypothetical children who had either low or high need for food. Similarily, Leventhal and Weiss (1975) used the traditional allocation situation (two persons attain a joint profit by individual work, which is then summed up by the experimenter) and informed their subjects that their (fictitious) co-worker made a similar contribution but that he or she had either low or high need for money (because of higher or lower income). In both studies, subjects favored the needier recipient. Similar studies were conducted by Lamm and Schwinger (1980, 1983). Schwinger and Lamm (1981) investigated whether a recipient who had contributed less but who had greater need for money than his or her corecipient also would be favored. This was found to be the case.

A second research question referred to the causes of individual needs. Internally caused needs were hypothesized to be less frequently considered than externally caused ones. In the study by Lamm and Schwinger (1980), the causal locus of the recipients' needs was varied experimentally as being either external or internal. No differences in the shares allotted to the person with greater needs were found. In a later study by Kayser, Schwinger, and Kramer (1981), this hypothesis was tested again and here the causal locus of the need state was varied as either external, internal but not intentional, or internal and intentional. In this case a significant difference was found between externally versus intentionally caused needs: Intentionally caused needs were considered less than externally caused ones.

It could be argued, however, that allocators are taking needs into consideration independent of or even in contradiction to their own justice concepts. In allocation research a central hypothesis has been tested only in a few studies—namely, the assumption that allocation behavior will be influenced by the allocator's justice deliberations (Cohen, 1979). One way of testing this hypothesis would be to compare subjects' allocation behavior in the presence versus the absence of an explicit request to allocate justly. In a study by Lamm and Schwinger (1983) such a test was conducted. The standard situation of the previously mentioned experiments was compared with another one in which the subjects were requested to allocate justly. Because need consideration was found in both conditions the authors concluded that need consideration in allocation situations is compatible with norms of justice.

To summarize these results, it can be concluded that information about different amounts of resources needed by recipients will lead allocators to deviate from the equality and/or the contribution principle in favor of the needier recipient. This consideration of needs seems to be in line with the subjects' justice concepts.

Several authors have stated, in contrast to equity theorists, that the need principle is a specific *norm* for intense and positive relationships (e.g., Deutsch, 1975, 1982; Lerner, 1977, 1981; Mikula & Schwinger, 1978; Schwinger, 1980). This conception is much broader than that in the previously mentioned studies. There the need principle was conceived as an obligation to help a person by providing those resources needed by the person because of an actual deficiency. Here, in contrast, the need principle is seen as a norm ruling all transactions of resources in interpersonal relationships of identity, high interdependence, and intimacy (cf. Greenberg & Cohen, 1982).

First tests of this assumption were conducted in studies by Lamm and Schwinger (1980, 1983), Schwinger and Lamm (1981) and Kayser *et al.* (1981). In these studies experimental variations of the hypothetical recipients' interpersonal attraction were manipulated. Specifically, recipients were depicted as being either friends or casual acquaintances. The results of all four studies show that the share of the needier person was larger if he or she was friends with his or her co-recipient.

The assumption, however, of the need principle as a *general* rule of justice must still be considered unproven. This is especially true inasmuch as in these studies the individual needs were operationalized as some very specific deficiencies of resources. Furthermore, the assumption has been tested so far only with respect to two classes of interpersonal resources—money and goods (cf. Foa & Foa, 1980).

NEED SATISFACTION AS THE BASIS OF DISTRIBUTIVE JUSTICE

In the following section a theoretical scheme will be proposed that is based partly on the theory of intrapersonal contracts (Kayser, Koehler, Mikula, & Schwinger, 1980). This scheme can be used as a guideline for empirical research and as an interpretive framework for empirical results dealing with the need principle. Within this theoretical framework, the need principle is assumed to be valid for individual needs based on deficiencies and personal desires. That is, the principle deals with individual satisfaction. The assumption of such a general need principle is also inherent at least partly in the theoretical models of some other authors (cf. Deutsch, 1982; Lerner, 1981; Mikula & Schwinger, 1978).

One can conceive of the three principles of distributive justice (contribution, equality, and need) and their variants as rules that define an individual's entitlement to need satisfaction in different ways. The *contribution principle* states that the recipient of an allocation, or the participant of any exchange, is entitled to an amount of resources depending on the value of those resources he or she gives to the other parties (either directly, or in the case of a joint task, by his or her contributions). The contribution principle refers to economic exchange, which has to be differentiated from social exchange. In economic exchange transactions will result in costs for the person who transmits resources and benefits for the receiver. In social exchange, however, transactions will result in benefits—both for the receiver and for the transmitting person (Willer, 1981). The value of the resources is measured by the value definitions of units of interpersonal resources in the social marketplace and not with respect to the specific recipient of the resources and his or her use of the resources. The individual's entitlement to need satisfaction is therefore independent of specific needs and desires. In contrast, individuals are entitled to a certain amount of resources that may or may not satisfy their needs. The contribution principle is directed toward the distribution of resources and not toward the distribution of actual need satisfaction. Individual needs are thereby depersonalized. This is in line with the general assumption of several justice theorists (e.g., Deutsch, 1975; Lerner, 1977; Mikula & Schwinger, 1978) that inherent in the contribution principle is the emotional distance of the persons involved. The conception of the individual implied in this principle is that of a seller and buyer in the social marketplace and as an average person. (The values of resources are aggregated in the social market in such a way that if a specific person needs more of certain resources than others he or she has to pay the respective high price by transmitting an accordingly high amount of other resources.)

The *equality principle* states that an individual's entitlement to units of resources is the same for all persons involved. It cannot be, therefore, that one person is less entitled to resources than another. Because, however, individual needs and desires may differ between individuals, the actual amount of need satisfaction may differ again. On the other hand, this principle will be used in groups in which the common assumption is held that the members will engage in joint tasks with similar effort (cf. Lamm & Kayser, 1978). Furthermore, it can be assumed that actual, or at least, assumed similarity in many respects will be typical for positive relationships. The similarity of actors should also be true for personal needs. Extraordinary needs will be satisfied as an exception to set things back to the basic similarity (cf. Lerner's 1977 concept of the unit relationship). Here the conception of the individual is that of an equal member of a community consisting of similar persons.

The *need principle* states that entitlement to units of resources depends on an individual's needs and desires but is independent of his or her actions and of the size and nature of these needs and desires. The conception of the individual is quite different from those inherent in the two previously mentioned principles. The individual is seen as a very specific person with specific needs and desires. This means that economic exchange is replaced by social exchange and the mutual giving of satisfaction. Resource transactions do not necessarily mean costs for the transmitting persons. Transmissions also can be intrinsically rewarding in case of intimacy and empathy (cf. Blau, 1964).

In addition, with respect to the differentiation of economic and social exchange, one has to consider the type of resources exchanged. Foa and Foa (1980) proposed a classification of interpersonal resources and the following differentiation of resource classes: universalistic resources (e.g., money) and particularistic ones (e.g., love). Whereas the value of universalistic resources is independent of the involved persons, the opposite is true for particularistic resources. According to Foa and Foa (1980), giving particularistic resources to another person means no costs, or at least lower costs, for the transmitting person than giving universalistic ones. This differentiation of resources can be combined with the classification of the contribution, equality, and need principles as rules for neutral versus positive versus very positive relationships (see the preceding). Using this combination the following hypotheses can be advanced. Because in relationships with higher interpersonal attraction a greater amount of particularistic resources will be given, the principles refer to different numbers of resource classes. The contribution principle refers predominantly to universalistic resources whereas the two others refer to particularistic resources.

These three characterizations of the justice principles are ideal types of the principles and their assigned interpersonal processes. They refer to naive social psychological concepts of interpersonal processes that are assumed to be in accord with the scientific assumptions about the covariation of the degree of intimacy and interdependence between parties (cf. Greenberg & Cohen, 1982) with the three principles and their variants. Based on the theory of intrapersonal contracts (Kayser & Schwinger, 1982; Kayser et al., 1980; Kayser, Schwinger, & Cohen, 1984; Schwinger & Cohen, 1985), it is proposed that these ideal types of relationships and their regulations are used in everyday life as orientation points in interaction. An outline of this theoretical approach is given in the following section.

PROTOTYPES OF RELATIONSHIPS AND TRANSACTION PRINCIPLES

In contract theory (Kayser et al., 1980) it is assumed that individuals will orient themselves to their social environment by using a small number of prototype relationships. These prototypes, as they are described theoretically, are shown in Table 2.

The theoretical description of these prototypes has been developed on the basis of the empirical and theoretical work of various authors

TABLE 2. The Five Prototypes of Interpersonal Relationships according to the Theory of Intrapersonal Contracts (Kayser et al., 1980)

Characteristic	Type of relationship				
	Intimate	Friendship	Exchange	Competitive	Fighting
Cognitive-motivational orientations of the actors	Prosocial	Collective	Individualistic	Competitive	Aggressive
Affective relationship	Very positive	Positive	Neutral	Negative	Very negative
Typical resources	Particularistic	Universalistic, particularistic	Universalistic	Universalistic, particularistic	Particularistic
Typical direction of transaction	Giving	Giving	Giving and taking	Taking	Taking
Transaction principle	Need	Equality	Contribution	Maximum difference	Maximum harm

and tries to integrate different perspectives on the classification of relationships and principles. Note that the conception is somewhat similar to the classifications of interpersonal relationships presented by Lerner and Whitehead (1980) and Deutsch (1982). It has to be emphasized, however, that these prototypes are not to be seen as any objective descriptions of interpersonal relationships but as interpretive schemes within laypersons' naive social psychologies (Kayser & Schwinger, 1982; Kayser *et al.*, 1984).

Each of the five types is described as a configuration consisting of five characteristics: the actors' cognitive-motivational orientations, the affective nature of the relationship, the most important resource classes transacted in the relationship, the typical direction of the transactions, and the principle that governs those transactions.

Furthermore, it is assumed that upon perceiving a relationship a person will decide which category (see Table 2) the relationship belongs to. As a consequence, the person is able to make predictions about the interpersonal behavior within that relationship, especially about the regulation of transactions. Justice will appear on the stage if such predictions are falsified. In this case, the person will try to find a consensual definition of the given relationship. In this metacommunication the naive social psychology will be formulated in normative terms as an appeal to common interests in regulating interaction.

EMPIRICAL FINDINGS

Without going into detail here, some results of various questionnaire studies conducted by Kayser, Schwinger, and their co-workers will be summarized. In these studies subjects were asked to assign transaction principles to small groups. These groups were presented by using various methods and techniques. They were also presented by using various features of the previously mentioned scheme (see Table 2). Five principles (and in some cases additional variants of them) were presented that had to be rated for each group with respect to justice and typicality. In one study (Kayser, 1983), the opposite direction was used: groups were described by the principles that governed the group members' resource transactions and the subjects had to infer the remaining characteristics of the groups.

Also, these questions were asked separately for the six types of interpersonal resources as they are defined by Foa and Foa (1980): love, status, service, information, goods, and money. The reason for asking these questions was that the typical resource and the typical principle of transaction were assumed to vary with the type of interpersonal relationship.

The results bearing on the need principle will be presented here. In a study by Kayser, Feeley, and Lamm (1982) subjects had to answer questions about three-person groups that were said to have either positive or neutral characteristics (e.g., high or low interpersonal attraction, socioemotional or task orientation etc.). Furthermore, the subjects had to answer questions about either hypothetical groups or about groups of which they were themselves members. It was found in this study that for *money* the assumption about the covariation of distribution principles and relationship types was valid. Namely, the need principle was said to be the most just one for positive relationships, whereas this was not true for neutral relationships. The need principle was not said, however, to be the most frequently used one.

Different patterns of results were found for resource types other than money. Whereas for the hypothetical groups the need principle was said to be the just and typical one for the transaction of nearly all resources, this was different with real groups. In this case subjects indicated that the need principle was just and typical for information, love, services, and goods. This dominance of the need principle was stronger for positive groups than for neutral groups. For the remaining resource types, status and money, however, the contribution principle was preferred.

Similar results were found in some other studies that used other methods of group presentation (e.g., Kayser, 1983; Schwinger, 1983, 1984; Schwinger, Kayser, & Naehrer, 1982). Table 3 shows the overall results.

Table 3 shows that the preference for the need principle is related to the type of resource to be exchanged. The distribution of love, services,

TABLE 3. Transaction Principles Rated as Just for Different Relationship and Resource Types: Summarized Results of Various Studies by Kayser, Schwinger, and Co-workers

Resource type	Type of relationship (and corresponding interpersonal orientation)		
	Intimate (prosocial)	Friendship (collective)	Exchange (individualistic)
Love	Need	Need	Equality/Contribution
Status	Equality	Contribution	Contribution
Services	Need	Need/Equality	Contribution
Information	Need	Need	Contribution
Goods	Need	Equality	Contribution
Money	Need	Equality	Contribution

and information following the need principle was seen as just by our subjects for intimate relationships and friendships as well. For status, however, the need principle was not even accepted for intimate relationships. For goods and money a covariation of principles and relationship types was found that is in accord with respective traditional assumptions.

An additional result of these studies was that subjects tended to portray stimulus groups more positively than they had been presented experimentally. In two studies (Schwinger, 1983; Schwinger et al., 1982) the subjects changed the characteristics of the stimulus groups that were similar to groups of which they were members themselves. Groups presented as having an economic orientation and a neutral affective climate were portrayed by the subjects as groups of high interpersonal attraction. A quite clear result about this idealization of groups was found in a study by Schwinger and Cohen (1985). Here, subjects were asked to record the relative frequencies of the five group types (see Table 2) for their own interpersonal relationships and for the relationships of other people. It was found that subjects stated that "intimacy" and "friendship" were most frequent in their own relationships. For the relationships of others, however, subjects assigned highest frequencies to exchange relationships. Subjects reported their own relationships as being characterized by the prosocial and collective motives of the partners, whereas outside of their personal relationships they assumed individualistic motives and self-oriented exchanges to be predominant.

When we summarize these two patterns of results, a somewhat speculative conclusion will be drawn. The need principle and the assigned type of relationship are ideals and people prefer to think about their own relationships in an idealized way. This idealization also has to do with the resource types for which the need principle is evaluated very positively—namely love, services, and information. These resources are specifically transacted in very positive relationships, at least according to our subjects' answers. Nevertheless, such an idealization will have a great impact for very positive and intimate relationships: individuals will evaluate their partners' behavior at least partly against these ideals. More generally these ideals will influence the expectations that will be developed about the interaction flow in these types of relationships.

CONCLUSION

The reported studies show that in laypersons' conceptions of interpersonal relationships, the need principle as a general rule of social exchange is believed to exist in very positive and intense interpersonal relationships. This assignment is very similar to the respective theoretical elaborations of social psychologists. A possible conclusion is that social psychologists refer to everyday knowledge when they are constructing theoretical schemes. Furthermore, there are indications that the type of relationships with a joint orientation of the participants toward need satisfaction is more of an ideal state than an experience in everyday life.

Nevertheless, these results show that need considerations are more than a reaction to actual deficiencies of resources. The need principle can indeed by seen as a principle of distributive justice, one that is equivalent to other principles. This conclusion has important consequences for theories of interpersonal justice. The area of justice is much broader than the domain of economic exchange. Justice is relevant also for noneconomic social exchange in which only rewards are transacted. Therefore interpersonal justice is more than a moralistic rationalization of price-building systems in exchange. It can be seen as one form of everyday knowledge about the functioning of various interpersonal relationships. This knowledge can be formulated in descriptive terms as a naive social psychology (e.g., "principle x will probably be used") or in normative terms as naive ethics (e.g., "the transactions ought to follow principle x"). It has to be emphasized that in contrast to the culturally dominant contribution principle (Lerner, 1981; Schwinger, 1980) there is also an ideal being held up about quite another way of regulating interpersonal relationships.

Acknowledgments

For comments I am indebted to Ronald L. Cohen, Peter Dachler, and Jerald Greenberg.

REFERENCES

Adams, J. S. (1965). Inequity in social exchange. In L. Berkowitz (Ed.), *Advances in experimental social psychology* (Vol. 2, pp. 267–299). New York: Academic Press.

Blau, P. M. (1964). *Exchange and power in social life.* New York: Wiley.

Burnstein, E., & Katz, S. (1972). Group decisions involving equitable and optimal distribution of status. In C. G. McClintock (Ed.), *Experimental social psychology* (pp. 412–448). New York: Holt, Rinehart & Winston.

Cohen, R. L. (1974). Mastery and justice in laboratory dyads. *Journal of Personality and Social Psychology, 29,* 464–474.

Cohen, R. L. (1979). On the distinction between individual deserving and distributive justice. *Journal for the Theory of Social Behaviour, 9,* 167–185.

Deutsch, M. (1975). Equity, equality, and need: What determines which value will be used as the basis for distributive justice? *Journal of Social Issues, 31,* 137–150.

Deutsch, M. (1982). Interdependence and psychological orientation. In V. H. Derlega & J. Grzelak (Eds.), *Cooperation and helping behavior* (pp. 16–42). New York: Academic Press.

Foa, E. B., & Foa, U. G. (1980). Resource theory: Interpersonal behavior as exchange. In K. J. Gergen, M. S. Greenberg, & R. H. Willis (Eds.), *Social exchange* (pp. 77–94). New York: Plenum Press.

Greenberg, J., & Cohen, R. L. (1982). Why justice? Normative and instrumental interpretations. In J. Greenberg & R. L. Cohen (Eds.), *Equity and justice in social behavior* (pp. 437–469). New York: Academic Press.

Greenberg, J., & Leventhal, G. S. (1976). Equity and the use of overreward to motivate performance. *Journal of Personality and Social Psychology, 34,* 179–190.

Homans, G. C. (1961). *Social behavior: Its elementary forms.* New York: Harcourt Brace & World.

Karuza, J., & Leventhal, G. S. (1976, September). *Justice judgements: Role demands and perception of fairness.* Paper presented at the meeting of the American Psychological Association, Washington, DC.

Kayser, E. (1983). *Laymen's social psychologies: The inference from social behaviors to group type.* Universität Mannheim: Bericht aus dem SFB 24.

Kayser, E., & Schwinger, T. (1982). A theoretical analysis of the relationship among individual justice concepts, laymen's social psychology, and distribution decision. *Journal for the Theory of Social Behaviour, 12,* 47–51.

Kayser, E., Koehler, B., Mikula, G., & Schwinger, T. (1980). *Intrapersonale Kontrakte und Gerechtigkeit [Intrapersonal contracts and justice].* Universität Mannheim: Bericht aus dem SFB 24.

Kayser, E., Schwinger, T., & Kramer, V. (1981). *Distributive Gerechtigkeit, Attribution und moralische Reife [Distributive justice, causal attribution, and level of moral development].* Universität Mannheim: Bericht aus dem SFB 24.

Kayser, E., Feeley, W. M., & Lamm, H. (1982). *Laienpsychologie sozialer Beziehungen [Laypersons' social psychology of social relationships].* Universität Mannheim: Bericht aus dem SFB 24.

Kayser, E., Schwinger, T., & Cohen, R. L. (1984). Laypersons' conceptions of social relationships: A test of contract theory. *Journal of Social and Personal Relationships, 1,* 433–458.

Lamm, H., & Kayser, E. (1978). The allocation of monetary gain and loss following dyadic performance: The weight given to effort and ability under conditions of low and high intradyadic attraction. *European Journal of Social Psychology, 8,* 275–279.

Lamm, H., & Schwinger, T. (1980). Norms concerning distributive justice: Are needs taken into consideration in allocation decisions? *Social Psychology Quarterly, 43,* 425–429.

Lamm, H., & Schwinger, T. (1983). Need consideration in allocation situations: Is it just? *Journal of Social Psychology, 119,* 205–209.

Lerner, M. J. (1977). The justice motive: Some hypotheses as to its origins and forms. *Journal of Personality, 45,* 1–52.

Lerner, M. J. (1981). The justice motive in human relations: Some thoughts on what we know and need to know about justice. In M. J. Lerner & S. C. Lerner (Eds.), *The justice motive in social behavior* (pp. 23–51). New York: Plenum Press.

Lerner, M. J., & Miller, D. T. (1978). Just world research and the attribution process: Looking back and ahead. *Psychological Bulletin, 85,* 1030–1051.

Lerner, M. J., & Whitehead, L. A. (1980). Procedural justice viewed in the context of justice motive theory. In G. Mikula (Ed.), *Justice and social interaction* (pp. 219–256). New York: Springer-Verlag.

Leventhal, G. S. (1976). Fairness in social relationships. In J. Thibaut, J. Spence, & R. Carson (Eds.), *Contemporary topics in social psychology* (pp. 141–162). Morristown, NJ: General Learning Press.

Leventhal, G. S., & Weiss, T. (1975). *Perceived need and the response to inequitable distributions of rewards.* Unpublished manuscript, Wayne State University.

Mikula, G. (1973). *"Gerechtigkeit" und "Zufriedenheit beider Partner" als Zielsetzungen der Aufteilung eines von beiden Personen gemeinsam erzielten Gewinns* ["Justice" and "contentment of both partners" as an allocator's goals for the allocation of jointly attained profits.] Universität Graz: Bericht aus dem Institut für Psychologie.

Mikula, G. (1980). On the role of justice in allocation decisions. In G. Mikula (Ed.), *Justice and social interaction* (pp. 127–166). New York: Springer-Verlag.

Mikula, G., & Schwinger, T. (1978). Intermember relations and reward allocation. In H. Brandstaetter, J. H. Davis, & H. Schuler (Eds.), *Dynamics of group decisions* (pp. 229–250). Beverly Hills, CA: Sage.

Sampson, E. E. (1969). Studies of status congruence. In L. Berkowitz (Ed.), *Advances in experimental social psychology* (Vol. 4, pp. 225–270). New York: Academic Press.

Schwartz, S. (1975). The justice of need and the activation of humanitarian norms. *Journal of Social Issues, 31,* 111–136.

Schwinger, T. (1980). Just allocation of goods: Decisions among three principles. In G. Mikula (Ed.), *Justice and social interaction* (pp. 95–125). New York: Springer-Verlag.

Schwinger, T. (1981). Steuerung und Rechtfertigung sozialer Prozesse durch Gerechtigkeitsnormen [Regulation and legitimation of social processes by justice norms]. In W. Grunwald & H.-G. Lilge (Eds.), *Kooperation und Konkurrenz in Organisationen* (pp. 97–107). Bern: Haupt.

Schwinger, T. (1983). *Zwei Untersuchungen zur Gerechtigkeit der Vergabe von Geld und Zuneigung nach drei Transaktionsprinzipien* [Two studies of justice in transactions of money and affection]. Universität Mannheim: Bericht aus dem SFB 24.

Schwinger, T. (1984). Gerechtigkeit der Vergabe von Geld und Zuneigung nach drei Prinzipien in unterschiedlichen Sozialbeziehungen [Justice of transactions of money and affection following three principles in different types of social relationships.] *Psychologische Beiträge, 26,* 55–73.

Schwinger, T., & Cohen, R. L. (1985). *Frequency of different social relationships: Self and others.* Manuscript submitted for publication.

Schwinger, T., & Lamm, H. (1981). Justice norms in allocation decisions: Need consideration as a function of resource adequacy for complete need satisfaction, recipients' contributions, and recipients' interpersonal attraction. *Social Behavior and Personality, 9,* 235–241.

Schwinger, T., Kayser, E., & Naehrer, W. (1982, April). *Prinzipien der gerechten Vergabe von Geld und Zuneigung in verschiedenen Sozialsituationen* [Principles of just transactions for money and affection in various social situations]. Paper presented at the 24th Meeting of Experimental Psychologists, Trier.

Walster, E., Walster, G. W., & Berscheid, E. (1978). *Equity: Theory and research.* Boston, MA: Allyn & Bacon.

Willer, D. (1981). The basic concepts of the elementary theory. In D. Willer & B. Anderson (Eds.), *Networks, exchange, and coercion* (pp. 25–35). New York: Elsevier.

Chapter 12

Group Categorization and Distributive Justice Decisions

LAWRENCE A. MESSÉ, ROBERT W. HYMES, and ROBERT J. MacCOUN

This chapter explores how group categorization processes can mediate the perceived applicability of one's sense of justice to reward distribution decisions. Group categorization—that is, the tendency in people to categorize themselves and others into social aggregates, whereby the aggregates to which they belong are perceived as ingroups and those to which they do not belong are perceived as outgroups—has been shown to be relevant to a wide range of social psychological phenomena (Tajfel, 1978; Wilder, 1981). Empirical studies of group categorization, for the most part, have demonstrated *ingroup-favorability*; persons tend to react more positively to others whom they see as members of their ingroup than to those whom they see as belonging to outgroups (Brewer, 1979). Within this research tradition, there is a body of work (summarized in Tajfel, 1978; Tajfel & Turner, 1979; as well as elsewhere, e.g., Allen, 1982; Caddick, 1980) that has investigated the extent to which group categorization processes can affect reward allocation. Consistent with the notion of ingroup favorability bias, these studies have generated evidence that persons, when distributing rewards among persons in different group

LAWRENCE A. MESSÉ • Department of Psychology, Michigan State University, East Lansing, MI 48824. ROBERT W. HYMES • Department of Psychology, University of Michigan at Dearborn, Dearborn, MI 48128. ROBERT J. MacCOUN • Department of Psychology, Northwestern University, Evanston, IL 60201.

categories, will be more generous to ingroup members, even though such allocations violate accepted norms of fairness.

Rather than focus on ingroup favorability as a cause of injustice, as did much past work, in the present chapter we explored the possibility that group categorization can have a different, somewhat more subtle effect on reward allocation. More specifically, we examined the hypothesis that group categorization can mediate the extent to which a person perceives it to be appropriate to consider his or her own notions (or norms) of fairness when making decisions about how to distribute rewards to others. We reasoned that norms of distributive justice are specific instances of beliefs; and, as with any beliefs, their influence on particular actions—in this case, reward distribution behaviors—can be affected by a host of underlying factors. We speculated further that a potentially important mediator of the link between beliefs and actions for someone making reward distribution decisions is the perceived likelihood that the persons affected by the decisions (i.e., the recipients of the reward) share his or her ideas of distributive justice, and that such likelihood estimates are mediated by group categorization processes. Given this perspective, we felt that reasonable, specific predictions about the ways in which group categorization might mediate the impact of norms on allocations could be derived from general models that link beliefs and actions; for this purpose, we developed a perspective that incorporated principles from two somewhat disparate theoretical approaches: the theory of reasoned action of Martin Fishbein and Icek Ajzen (Ajzen & Fishbein, 1980; Fishbein, 1980), and role theory (Biddle & Thomas, 1966; Goffman, 1959).

REWARD DISTRIBUTION BEHAVIOR AS REASONED ACTION

In the theory of reasoned action, Fishbein and Ajzen seek to identify the processes that mediate the extent to which beliefs influence actions. The basic premise of their model is that a specific class of beliefs, behavioral intentions, has the strongest potential link to overt behaviors. According to the theory, the belief that a person has about the actions he or she intends to take (if measured appropriately) is the best cognition-based predictor of how that person will actually behave.[1] Thus, for a given situation, knowing the manner in which a person intends to distribute a reward among others gives us greater predictive powers than

[1]Whether or not behavioral intentions are, in fact, the best single predictor of actions, remains an open question (cf. Bentler & Speckart, 1981; Liska, 1984; Pagel & Davidson, 1984). However, there does exist reasonable evidence that this type of belief is strongly linked to subsequent behavior (e.g., Fishbein & Ajzen, 1975; Jaccard, Knox, & Brinberg, 1979).

does knowing that person's beliefs about what would constitute a fair allocation (i.e., his or her norms of distributive justice).

There are two major components to behavioral intentions: attitude toward the behavior and subjective norms. *Attitude toward the behavior* refers to the actor's evaluation of the expected consequences for his or he own welfare if a given behavior is performed (or not performed)— the more positive the evaluation, in both an absolute sense and relative to other response options, the stronger the behavioral intentions. Thus, this concept is similar to the exchange-theory notion of expected, or predicted, outcomes (cf. Blau, 1967, pp. 143–167; Crano & Messé, 1982, pp. 299–301; Kelley & Thibaut, 1978, pp. 209–239). The concept of *subjective norms* refers to the actor's beliefs about how significant others think he or she should act. In the model, *significant others* loosely refers to reference group members—persons whose approval and/or respect the actor is concerned about. Thus, subjective norms are composite beliefs about what psychologically important others perceive as good, correct, appropriate, or proper; and the greater the importance of the others, the more consistent the expectations are, and so forth, the stronger will be the actor's behavioral intentions.

Applied to a reward-distribution-to-others situation, the allocator's attitudes toward the behavior would refer to personal evaluations of the different affective feelings (e.g., guilt, anxiety, satisfaction, etc.) that he or she expects to experience as a result of the various possible distributions that could be imposed on the recipients. In contrast, subjective norms would refer to the allocator's sense of how important referents think the allocator should distribute the rewards. In this instance, possible referents could be anyone, such as the allocator's supervisor (i.e., the experimenter if the situation is a laboratory study), parents, persons who serve as religious/moral guides, and even other ingroup members. An actor's behavioral intention, then, would be to distribute rewards to the recipients in a way that is most consistent with the actor's attitudes toward the behavior and his or her relevant subjective norms.

As noted earlier, the theory of reasoned action has received compelling empirical support; intentions have been shown to be strong predictors of subsequent actions (e.g., Ajzen & Fishbein, 1980; Fishbein & Ajzen, 1975; Jaccard, Knox, & Brinberg, 1979). However, one can reasonably argue that the theory's focus on intentionality, which is its major strength, is also its major flaw. The model's reliance on concrete intentions—which, when measured most directly, are assessed by asking a person about his or her intentions regarding a specific set of response options in a particular setting—appears to optimize the predictive accuracy of isolated incidents at the expense of developing a more general, integrative understanding of the role that cognition plays in determining behavior. Ajzen and Fishbein recognize that other potentially influential factors, including other beliefs beside intentions, exist—these factors are termed *external variables* in their model—but systematic conceptual bases for understanding when (and why) these external variables affect reasoned actions have not as yet been incorporated into the theory. Thus, in its present form, the theory is difficult to disconfirm, because any embarrassing findings always can be attributed to the (generally, but not specifically, predicted) influence of external variables. What is needed, then, is the development of satellite models that state, *a priori*, the role that a given external variable (or set of interrelated external variables) plays in determining the cognitive antecedents of actions. In this chapter, we begin to develop one such model by exploring the potential impact of the external variable, target characteristics, on belief-based actions.

TARGET CHARACTERISTICS AS MEDIATORS OF NORM SALIENCE: A ROLE-THEORY ANALYSIS

Ajzen and Fishbein (1980, p. 34) note that the specific identity of a target of an actor's behavior can influence his or her evaluation of relevant response options, but they do not specify the operative dimensions of the target's characteristics or the psychological processes that are evoked by them. As noted, however, such a specification would help expand the predictive value of their theory. We felt that given its emphasis on the interpersonal nature of actions, role theory, as formulated by Thomas and Biddle (1966a,b,c,d), Goffman (1959), and others (e.g., Turner, 1962), would be a useful perspective in which to generate ideas about the manner in which target characteristics might mediate the link between beliefs and behaviors. The fundamental premise of role theory is that persons act in ways that they perceive as appropriate (expected of them, etc.) given their positions in a (formal or informal) social system. Through past (direct or indirect) experiences with similar situations, each participant has come to perceive certain behaviors (of self and other) as correct. These expected behaviors, or norms, combine to make up the roles that define the role relationship, which when enacted with facility helps manage the impression that the participants in the encounter are competent human beings (Goffman, 1952; Tedeschi, 1981).

For example, consider the behavior of a diner toward a waiter in a traditional restaurant context.[2] Within the framework of this rather impersonal role relationship, most persons have come to view giving the waiter a tip for his services—currently, in the amount of about 15% of the cost of the meal—as an integral part of the diner's role. Thus,

---

[2] We wish to thank Pam Folger for suggesting this example to us.

most diners, when paying for a meal, will usually conform to this tipping norm and act accordingly.[3] However, there can be characteristics of the waiter and/or the context that will alter the diner's sense of what is appropriate. For instance, the diner might learn that the waiter is the owner of the restaurant. In these circumstances, it is not so clear that a tip is called for. Or, it is the case in other societies—even those such as West Germany with which we share many social customs—that tipping, (especially in the magnitude of 15%) is not at all expected. Thus, knowing the local norm about tipping would cause American diners to alter their definition of the diner's role and cause them to diverge from their usual tipping behavior (perhaps, with some feelings of anxiety about generating the right impression).

Note that imbedded in this diner–waiter example are speculations about how role expectations and target characteristics, in general, can mediate the link between beliefs and behaviors. Within the framework of the theory of reasoned actions, it is likely that role expectations can affect behavioral intentions in two ways. First, they can affect intentions rather directly if the actor perceives that he or she shares these norms with important others—in other words, in this case, the role expectations are subjective norms. For example, within this theoretical framework, the belief that 15% is the usual tip for a waiter would affect a diner's actual behavior to the extent that the diner also believed that the waiter, respected peers, persons whose sense of etiquette the diner respected, and so forth, subscribed to this norm. Second, role expectations are also a type of attitude toward the action—that is, what is commonly meant in social psychology by the term *attitude*—and, as such, are external variables that can, if they are sufficiently salient, affect attitudes toward the behavior. For example, a diner who strongly believes that waiters are entitled to a 15% tip would, in turn, be likely to positively evaluate (in terms of guilt avoidance, making a good impression, etc.) possible actions that are consistent with this norm. Thus, Proposition 1: in general, the more well learned (and accepted) a role-related norm, the greater the influence it will have on intentions and subsequent overt behaviors.

However, relevant target characteristics—those aspects of the other person that warn the actor that he or she might not share the role expectations—can moderate the perception that the role-related norm is an appropriate guide for action. This idea is consistent with evidence

---

[3]This example is particularly compelling to one of us, for whom, for some reason, the tipping norm and accompanying concerns with impression management are highly salient. Thus, whenever his financial circumstances permit, he leaves a cash tip on the table, even though when he pays the bill at the cashier's station, he uses a credit card to charge the cost of the meal (and could have charged the tip, as well).

(e.g., Allen & Wilder, 1979; Williams, 1975) that group categorization mediates people's perceptions of general belief similarity; persons tend to perceive that they share beliefs with ingroup members to a greater extent than they do with outgroup members. Given this link between group categorization and perceived belief similarity, it follows that target characteristics that mediate ingroup/outgroup perceptions will affect perceived norm salience. Thus, Proposition 2: the perception that the target of a behavior is an outgroup member will weaken the intention to behave in the usual, norm-consistent manner. Moreover, the type of behavior that is expressed toward the outgroup member, to some extent, is dependent on what the actor knows about the beliefs held by such people—that is, the extent to which a relevant stereotype (Hamilton, 1979) exists for the outgroup. Thus, Proposition 2a: when the norms of the outgroup regarding the behavior in question are relatively unknown, the actor will act in a less extreme manner than usual, in other words, the actor might still use role-based norms as guides for reasoned actions, but the overt behaviors that are expressed will be tempered by uncertainty (and the heightened concerns with impression management that uncertainty tends to evoke). And, Proposition 2b: when the actor holds beliefs about the norms of the outgroup, his or her overt behaviors will, to some extent, reflect these assumed expectations.

These propositions have implications for understanding group categorization effects on the links between beliefs and behaviors in a wide variety of social settings, but they seem especially relevant to situations in which well-accepted norms are known to have a substantial impact on reasoned actions. Because research indicates that reward allocation behaviors are strongly influenced by norms (e.g., equity, equality, social welfare), we thought that it would be reasonable to begin examining the validity of our approach to group categorization, beliefs, and actions within the context of distributive justice decisions.

GROUP CATEGORIZATION AS A MEDIATOR OF THE INFLUENCE OF THE NORM OF EQUITY ON REWARD DISTRIBUTIONS TO WORKERS

A vast array of empirical work has demonstrated that norms—in this case, standards about appropriate, or just, reward allocations—have a major impact on how persons act and react with regard to reward distribution decisions (cf. Berkowitz & Walster, 1976; Greenberg & Cohen, 1982). These studies have shown that such distributive justice norms influence both the manner in which persons allocate rewards to themselves and/or others and persons' evaluations of externally imposed distributions. Moreover, consistent with the tenets of role theory, research also has shown that features of the context in which rewards are being distributed can affect the relative weights accorded to a (small) number of potentially relevant norms. Findings from a variety of studies, for example, have been consistent with Deutsch's (1975) speculation that the norm of equity—which prescribes that persons should be rewarded in a manner that takes into account their relative and absolute achievements—is perceived as most applicable to situations that promote concerns with individual accomplishments, whereas the norms of social welfare (i.e., a need-based standard) and equality are seen as most applicable in other contexts (e.g., Clark, 1984; Leventhal & Whiteside, 1973; Leventhal, Weiss, & Buttrick, 1973; Watts & Messé, 1982). Thus, as Deutsch discusses in Chapter 1 of this volume, people accept the idea that equity-based distributions of rewards are very appropriate in task-oriented settings where worker productivity is a primary concern. Therefore, consistent with Proposition 1 (and much past work), we would expect that persons enacting the role of supervisor, in general, would pay their workers in a reasonably equitable manner—that is, they would give the more productive worker a bigger share of the reward.

The reasoned action–role theory approach to belief–behavior consistency that we presented earlier, however, suggests that there are external variables that can mediate the salience of the norm of equity in task-oriented, work situations. Consistent with Proposition 2, we would expect that the influence of the norm of equity on supervisors' reward distributions to workers would be moderated by group categorization processes. When workers are outgroup members whose beliefs about distributive justice are unknown, supervisors should temper their inclinations to base pay allocations on differences in worker productivity (Proposition 2a); and, when workers are members of social aggregates whose beliefs about reward distribution are known, supervisors (irrespective of their own group category) should take these beliefs into consideration when allocating pay (Proposition 2b). In the two sections that follow, we review research findings that bear on the validity of these predictions—especially those of two studies that we had conducted to explicitly explore group categorization effects on distributive justice decisions (Messé, Hymes, & MacCoun, 1984a,b).

SUPERVISORS' PAY ALLOCATIONS WHEN OUTGROUP NORMS ARE UNKNOWN

In a recent study, (Messé, Hymes, & MacCoun, 1984a), we attempted to invoke group categorization processes in a sample of subjects in a way that precluded them from having *a priori* beliefs about outgroup members' norms of distributive justice. To do so, we used the minimal groups procedure, in which subjects are distinguished on some trivial characteristic, to establish ingroup/outgroup perceptions. Past work using a number of different trivial characteristics—for example, preferences for types of abstract art; the tendency to overestimate or underestimate the correct number of dots on a guessing task—has demonstrated that this technique can induce people to have remarkably strong "we-they" feelings, which are, however, unaccompanied by any established stereotypic beliefs about the outgroup (cf. Brewer, 1979; Tajfel, 1978). In our study, subjects had to allocate pay to two workers whose group categorizations were systematically varied; each worker was identified as being either an ingroup member (who shared a trivial, but distinguishing characteristic with the supervisor) or an outgroup member (who differed from the supervisor on that characteristic). Based on the reasoned action–role theory approach that was developed previously—and consistent with the results of many earlier studies—we predicted that in general, reward distributions would be congruent with the norm of equity (i.e., they would reflect differences in work performance); however, we also expected that the influence of the norm would be attenuated when subjects had to decide the pay of workers who were outgroup members. Finally, based on the results of past work on group categorization and reward allocation, summarized previously, we also expected that subjects' pay to the two workers, to some extent, would reflect an ingroup-favorability bias.

To tests these hypotheses—and to explore the possibility of sex of allocator effects—we recruited male and female undergraduates to participate in behavioral research for pay. A session always involved two actual subjects and four confederates, who pretended to be subjects. The subjects were led to believe that for reasons of efficiency, they would be participating in two separate studies during the session.

The first study involved a perceptual estimation task in which arrays of dots were briefly projected on a screen. The experimenter explained that past research had demonstrated that people rarely respond very accurately to stimuli of this type; instead, they tend to be underestimators or overestimators. (Moreover, it was hinted—but never specified in any detail—that being an underestimator or overestimator had implications for the type of personality a person possessed.) By varying performance feedback, a subject was induced to believe that he or she was either an overestimator or an underestimator and that two other participants in the session shared this attribute (whereas the three remaining participants were the other type).

The second study was an industrial stimulation in which the six participants were divided into two 3-person units to work on an envelope addressing task. In each unit, a supervisor (always a subject) evaluated the individual work output of two subordinates (always confederates). Both workers supposedly addressed and stuffed envelopes for about 20 minutes, but one worker always appeared to substantially outperform the other (by just over a 2-to-1 ratio). Supervisors looked over this work and then allocated pay (up to $9 total) to each subordinate.[4] In addition, they completed a brief questionnaire in which they evaluated their workers' performances.

Analyses of these evaluations indicated that as intended, subjects perceived significant differences in the productivity of the two workers, perceptions that could have been the bases for unequal, but equitable, pay allocations to the two workers. As predicted, actual pay allocations, in fact, did reflect concerns with equity; but, also as predicted, the extent to which this was true was mediated by the workers' group categories (ingroup or outgroup). Subjects were more equitable in their reward distribution when the worker (whether the better or worse performer) was an ingroup member than when the worker was an outgroup member. Moreover, Table 1, which presents percentage differences in relative pay as a function of the group categories of each worker, indicates that it was in the condition in which both workers were outgroup members that the impact of the equity norm was moderated to a substantial degree. Finally, it is important to note that the pattern of pay distribution to ingroup and outgroup members did not match the evaluations of work performance, which primarily reflected output differences irrespective of the workers' group categories.

In contrast, the study yielded no systematic evidence of ingroup favorability. For example, subjects did not evaluate the output of ingroup

TABLE 1. Difference in Pay Allocation (in Percent of Total Available) as a Function of Workers' Group Categorizations

Group categorization of more productive worker	Group categorization of less productive worker	
	Ingroup	Outgroup
Ingroup	26$_a$	23$_a$
Outgroup	24$_a$	14$_b$

Note. Values identified with different subscripts differed significantly from each other ($p < .05$).

[4]It is important to note that care was taken to insure that subjects knew that their pay allocation decisions would not affect their own pay in any way. Thus, at this point in a session, subjects knew that their pay had been predetermined (but, of course, they would not learn the specific amount of their own pay until after they had distributed pay to their workers).

members any more favorably than they did that of outgroup workers—
if anything, such judgments tended to favor outgroup members. Perhaps
of more importance, pay allocations did not reflect ingroup bias either.
Supervisors of mixed-group dyads divided the reward in the same manner, irrespective of the group categorizations of the better and worse
workers. Furthermore, a parallel analysis of total amount of money allocated to both workers yielded no significant effects for worker's group
category—results that reflect the fact that supervisors did not give any
more money, in total, to dyads that contained one (or two) ingroup
member(s) than they did to dyads with two (or one) outgroup mem-
ber(s). Thus, the present results failed to replicate past work (e.g., Caddick, 1980; Ng, 1984; Tajfel, 1970) that has demonstrated an ingroup-
favorability bias in reward distribution decisions.

In summary, the results of this study supported the hypotheses
derived from the reasoned action–role theory perspective outlined earlier. Specifically, these findings indicate that reward distributions in a
work context reflect the influence of the norm of equity (thereby repli-
cating the findings of many past studies), but that group categorization
moderates compliance to the norm when the allocation target is a member of a social aggregate whose relevant beliefs are unknown. In a second
study (Messé, Hymes, & MacCoun, 1984b), we attempted to extend
these results by examining reward distributions in a different group
categorization situation, one in which the allocators had established
ideas about the outgroup members' relevant norms. To do so, we explored
supervisors' pay distributions to male and female workers.

SUPERVISORS' PAY ALLOCATIONS WHEN BELIEFS EXIST ABOUT WORKERS' RELEVANT NORMS

There is substantial evidence to support the conclusion that in
many social contexts, including work settings, sex acts as a group category identifier (e.g., Broverman, Vogel, Broverman, Clarkson, &
Rosenkrantz, 1972; Dipboye, Fromkin, & Wilback, 1975; Eagly & Wood,
1982; Kirkpatrick, 1963; Taylor, Fiske, Etcoff, & Ruderman, 1978; Towson, Lerner, & de Carufel, 1981). Moreover, there also is evidence that
suggests that persons believe—with some justification (cf. Major & Deaux,
1982, pp. 46–51)—that males and females differ somewhat in their ideas
about appropriate reward distribution; in general, the norm of equity is
seen as more salient in males, whereas norms that reflect more interpersonal concerns (e.g., kindness, egalitarianism) are seen as more salient in females. Two studies bear most directly on this last point. In an
investigation of race and sex effects on estimates of general belief similarity, Williams (1975) found that both females and males felt they held

more similar beliefs, and had more in common, with another person of their own sex than one who was of the other sex. And, results of a study of evaluative impressions of reward allocators (Watts & Messé, 1982) indicate that evaluators of both sexes believed it was more appropriate for a male to distribute rewards equitably, but it was more appropriate for a female to be egalitarian and generous. Thus, we thought that the sex of a worker would be a reasonable target characteristic to use in an initial test of the hypothesis that allocators take into account the assumed beliefs of their workers when distributing pay to them.

More specifically, for this second study, we conducted a questionnaire-based simulation in which female and male undergraduates were asked to play the role of supervisors in three different industrial/business contexts. In each case, subjects had to make a decision about some management problem and then report their thoughts about, and reactions to, the situation. In the crucial scenario (which was always presented second), these respondents were asked to allocate pay to two temporary workers who had been employed for a morning; information supplied on the questionnaire indicated that for the same time spent at the job, one worker had substantially outperformed the other.[5] Furthermore, by systematically varying the workers' names (e.g., Alice versus Allen), we were able to manipulate the sexes of the better and worse performers. As in Messé et al. (1984a), we examined the relative and total pay that supervisors gave to the workers, as well as their evaluations of the workers' output. Based on the propositions derived from the reasoned action–role theory perspective that we have outlined in this chapter, we predicted that pay distributions would, to some extent, reflect differences in performance (Proposition 1); but, given that females, as a social category, are believed to be somewhat less concerned with equity (and somewhat more concerned with interpersonal issues) than are males, we also expected that supervisors—regardless of their own sex—would be more egalitarian when allocating pay to female workers (Proposition 2b).

Paralleling the results of Messé et al. (1984a), we also found in this second study that subjects based their evaluations of the workers on relative productivity. The composite evaluation scores indicated that respondents judged the more productive worker to have worked substantially harder and better, and to have accomplished more, than did

[5]Actually, to insure that subjects' reactions were not specific to the particular work context that was examined, two forms of this scenario were constructed. Both forms were the same with regard to their essential features, but they differed in minor details (e.g., job setting, type of work, exact time worked, etc.). Results indicated, however, that these differences did not systematically affect the group categorization effects that were the focus of the study.

his or her less productive co-worker. And, it was also the case that these differential evaluations were remarkably stable across the various conditions of worker sex.

Perhaps of more importance, analyses of the pay allocation data from this study yielded reasonable support for the hypotheses that were derived from Propositions 1 and 2b. First, consistent with Proposition 1, payment scores reflected performance differences. On the average, respondents paid the better worker over 10% more than they paid the less productive counterpart, a value that is significantly greater than equality.[6] Second, the pattern of pay allocations supported the hypothesis derived from Proposition 2b. Table 2 presents the mean differences in pay to the better and worse workers (in terms of percentage of total allocated) as a function of their sex. As evidenced by these data, the difference in pay allotted to the two workers was smaller when one of them (especially the better worker) was a female. It is especially noteworthy that the biggest difference in means occurred between the conditions in which both workers were males and both were females. Given that the worker's actual output, as well as supervisors' perceptions of that output, were constant across conditions, these findings indicate that systematic differences in pay allocations were due solely to the sex composition of the work dyad. Overall, then, the pattern of these results supports the inference that supervisors, when paying their workers, took into account their stereotypic belief about how females and males differ with regard to their relative concerns for equity.

TABLE 2. Difference in Pay Allocation (in Percent of Total Available) as a Function of Workers' Sexes

Sex of more productive worker	Sex of less productive worker	
	Male	Female
Male	12.1_a	10.5_{ab}
Female	9.2_{ab}	8.2_b

Note. Values that do not share a common subscript differed significantly from each other ($p < .05$).

[6]Note that this pay differential appears substantially less than the equivalent value obtained in our first study (which, as Table 1 indicates, approached 22%). In both research contexts, the two workers had spent the same amount of time on the job. However, in the minimal groups study (Messé et al., 1984a), subjects paid and evaluated persons who had worked for a relatively short period of time, whereas the time duration in the second study (Messé et al., 1984b) was considerably longer. Thus, this difference in a potentially relevant work input (cf. Lane & Messé, 1972) is likely to have contributed to the observed difference between the two studies with regard to relative payment to the two workers.

Congruent with past results (summarized in Major & Deaux, 1982), the data from both the sex-of-worker study and the minimal groups study indicated that the sex of the supervisor/subjects had little systematic effect on pay allocation decisions. These findings, although only suggestive, are congruent with the role theory approach summarized previously. Certainly, there is ample evidence that females often prefer a different reward distribution norm to equity (e.g., Major & Adams, 1983; Watts, Messé, & Vallacher, 1982); but, it also appears to be the case that females are most inclined to act in a manner that reflects these preferences when other persons are not likely to react negatively to their inequitable actions (Callahan-Levy & Messé, 1979; Leventhal & Lane, 1970; Major, McFarlin, & Gagnon, 1984; Watts et al., 1982). For example, in one of the earliest studies of sex differences in reward distributions to self and other, Leventhal and Lane (1970) found that females were egalitarian when they had outperformed their co-worker, but were equitable (i.e., gave themselves less of the reward) when the co-worker had done better. In contrast, when females (and males) occupy roles for which the appropriate norms are reasonably well defined, they are likely to make decisions and act in ways that are consistent with the role expectations. And, as noted above, in task-oriented work situations, persons in supervisory positions are expected to try to promote individual achievement by allocating pay according to differential work inputs. Thus, it is reasonable that both men and women supervisors did so in the two studies summarized here, as well as in past work (e.g., Leventhal & Whiteside, 1973).

This argument is not meant to convey the idea that people are slaves to the role expectations that are evoked by a social context. Rather, we are proposing a somewhat more complex perspective: that situation-based role expectations can, and often do, have substantial effects on reasoned actions; but, at the same time, a person's intentions and behaviors frequently reflect other concerns as well, including the motives and other personal characteristics that one typically brings to the situation (cf. Aronoff & Wilson, 1985). Both the minimal groups study and the sex-of-worker study, in fact, yielded data that are consistent with this more complex approach. Certainly, the difference in the pay that subjects in both research contexts allocated to their better and worse workers reflected compliance with a norm (equity) that was congruent with their role (work supervisors). However, the pay decisions of females also reflected an additional, more personal concern—altruism. Results indicated that both sets of female allocators allotted significantly more of the total reward to their worker dyads than did their male counterparts, findings that conceptually replicate past work (e.g., Lane & Messé, 1971; Leventhal & Lane, 1970; Major & Adams, 1983; Watts et al., 1982) which has demonstrated that females tend to be more concerned about the welfare of others than are males.

Other potential effects of the sex of a supervisor are relevant to the issue of ingroup favorability biases. It was possible that supervisors would have acted more kindly to workers of their own sex. However, in this study, the analyses produced no evidence to support this speculation. The supervisor's sex did not interact significantly with the sex of either worker to affect evaluations, nor did the pattern of means show any indication that respondents evaluated same-sex workers more positively. Similarly, neither relative pay nor total amount allocated reflected an ingroup bias. For example, if anything, female supervisors tended to allocate the most pay, total, to male–male work dyads, whereas males were the most generous to mixed-sex dyads.

In summary, the results of our second study (Messé et al., 1984b) were consistent with both the reasoned action–role theory perspective, in general, and specific hypotheses that were derived from it. On the other hand, neither this research nor the minimal groups study (Messé et al., 1984a) summarized earlier yielded any evidence of ingroup favorability, a point that we discuss in some detail in the next section.

IMPLICATIONS OF REASONED-ACTION–ROLE-THEORY APPROACH FOR PAST AND FUTURE WORK

Perhaps, the major contribution that the reasoned-action–role-theory approach can make toward helping to understand distributive justice decisions is the perspective it provides on the many studies that have shown that persons—even those in task-oriented settings—do not always allocate rewards in strict accordance with the norm of equity (or any other norm, for that matter). A number of past reviewers (most notably, Leventhal, 1976, 1980; Mikula, 1980; Schwinger, 1980) have commented on this discrepancy between norm-based predictions and actual behavior, and have used this "lack of fit" as a basis for developing multidimensional models of justice. Although these models provide a more realistic picture of the complex cognitive bases for reward allocation, they really do not specify the underlying psychological mechanisms that mediate the relative weights that various norms and other factors are accorded in the process of making a distributive justice decision. We felt that viewing justice norms as a type of attitude would be helpful in this regard, because it would allow us to apply the extensive literature on the link between attitudes, in general, and behavior (cf. Petty & Cacioppo, 1981, pp. 22–29; 193–204) to the problem of identifying mediators of the impact of justice norms on reward allocations.

Specifically, in this chapter we have used a well-established and comprehensive approach to understanding how and when attitudes can affect behavior (the theory of reasoned action) to provide insight into how certain target characteristics might affect intentions to act on the norm of equity. However, the same theoretical framework can also be used to interpret past findings on reward allocation. For example, implicit in Ajzen and Fishbein's construct of attitude toward the behavior is the notion of *hedonic relevance*—persons' intentions to act in part are a function of the perceived implications of the behavior for their welfare. Past research on attitudes (Sivacek & Crano, 1982), in fact, has demonstrated that hedonic relevance mediates the link between beliefs and overt behavior, a result that is consistent with the well-replicated finding that persons (especially American males) are likely to distribute rewards equitably when it is in their economic advantage to do so. Similarly, it seems reasonable to assume that direct experience mediates the perceived connection between a behavior and its consequence (a component of attitude toward the behavior). Studies of direct experience with attitude-relevant events (cf. Fazio & Zanna, 1981) have consistently shown that this variable mediates the link between beliefs and actions, a relationship that helps to explain the findings (e.g., Austin, McGinn, & Susmilch, 1980; Messé & Watts, 1982) that direct past experience with a given level of pay affects evaluations of reward allocations.

Moreover, we felt that integrating principles of role theory with the theory of reasoned action serves to enhance the predictive and explanatory power of Ajzen and Fishbein's model, especially as it applies to distributive justice decisions. For example, as noted above, the idea that persons can be constrained by role relationships helps explain why they sometimes will allocate rewards in ways that are not completely consistent with their personal preferences. Similarly, there is evidence (e.g., Mikula, 1974; Morgan & Sawyer, 1967) that an established role relationship that is somewhat antithetical to concerns with individual achievement (friends) will attenuate the salience of the norm of equity for reward allocation decisions. From a reasoned action perspective, it is likely that a friend's coparticipation in a work-oriented encounter generates a subjective norm that weakens one's intention to act on the belief that in such settings, persons should get what they deserve.

We specifically applied this reasoned-action–role-theory perspective to group categorization effects on supervisors' pay allocation to workers. Initially, we viewed this framework as a complement to the work of Henri Tajfel, and others, who repeatedly have demonstrated an ingroup-favorability bias in reward distributions to others. Thus, for example, in the minimal groups study we expected our results to reflect a similar bias, as well as show a more general attenuation of equity when the worker was an outgroup member. As noted, however, we found no evidence of ingroup favorability in any of our results. Of course, there are major differences (as well as some similarities) in the methods that we and these other investigators have employed. For instance, unlike the present approach, many past studies did not examine allocation to same-group sets of targets (i.e., all ingroup or all outgroup members), and some researchers (e.g., Commins & Lockwood, 1979, p. 285) have explicitly denied that data from such conditions are relevant to understanding group categorization effects on reward distribution decisions. We disagree.

Consider, for example, the study by Towson et al. (1981), which used sex as the group categorizer. In this research, fifth- and sixth-grade children allocated a monetary reward between two workers (always a male and a female) who individually performed a box-stacking task. In one condition (low competition), allocators were led to believe that the workers simply were co-acting, whereas in a second condition (high competition), they were told that the workers were members of same-sex teams engaged in an ongoing contest. In addition, the sexes of the better and worse worker were systematically varied (female better versus male better). Results indicated that with one exception—when the workers were competing and the female did better—the pay allocations of male and female subjects did not differ, with both giving the better worker about 60% of the reward.

Compared to this pattern, in the deviant condition male allocators distributed pay in a more egalitarian fashion, whereas females paid the better worker even more (67%). These findings can be interpreted as showing that a confluence of factors (a contest between the sexes in which the female triumphs) can trigger ingroup favorability. However, given that we do not know what would have happened if allocators had also paid two competitors of the same sex, it is also possible that Towson et al.'s results reflect a difference in the beliefs that females and males have about how female "winners" want themselves and the "loser" to be treated. Thus, including same-group worker pairs in a research design helps to clarify the extent to which outcomes really reflect cognitive biases.

Of more theoretical interest, past studies have tended to examine reward allocation in contexts in which the salience of the norm of equity would be greatly attenuated—nonwork settings (e.g., Tajfel, 1970) or situations in which task performance was obviously a consequence of luck (e.g., Ng, 1984). In these circumstances, reward allocation seems to be much more an exercise in gift giving than behavior that reflects distributive justice norms. And, it might be the case that the gift-giving context is particularly susceptible to biases generated by group categorization processes. In contrast, the present research had, as an explicit intention, the goal of inducing subjects to see themselves as participating in a situation in which meaningful work was being performed, and, as such, it was appropriate to be concerned with individual achievements. In this setting, the norm of equity was found to have had a substantial effect on pay allocations, and the ways in which group categorization processes moderated this effect were somewhat more complex than past work on ingroup bias would have led us to expect.

Moreover, the few past studies that have examined group categorization effects on pay allocations for work (e.g., Caddick, 1980; Commins & Lockwood, 1979; Ng, 1984) tended to have used a procedure that was likely to generate defensive attributional processes (Shaver, 1970) as the basis for apparent ingroup favorability. In a typical example of this work, Commins and Lockwood (1970) used the same task feedback as the basis for group categorization and as the data on workers' relative performances. Thus, in this study, the ingroup favorability in reward allocation that was observed very well might have been a consequence of defensive attributions about task performance—whereby allocators paid workers whose performance matched their own what they thought they, themselves, deserved. If this interpretation is valid, it suggests that ingroup favorability in pay allocations of the sort that Tajfel speculated about (e.g., Tajfel, 1978) is limited to those situations in which the basis for group categorization is also seen as a work input.

There is another possible reason for the differences in findings that were obtained in our work and in past studies. Research by Ng (1981) has produced evidence that directly challenges the straightforward ingroup favorability bias explanation of group categorization effects on reward allocation. Ng (1981) demonstrated that the multiple-allocator procedure typically employed in past work—in which subjects know that other allocators (both ingroup and outgroup members) are providing rewards to the same targets—is a necessary condition for generating biased distributions. Thus, it appears that past results do not reflect allocators' inclinations to favor fellow ingroup members at the expense of the outgroup as much as they do allocators' concerns that their outgroup counterparts were biased in their decisions (cf. Kelley & Stahelski, 1970; Miller & Holmes, 1975). Ng's results are relevant to Messé et al. (1984a,b), because in these studies we used a single-allocator procedure, and, thus, supervisors did not have to worry about anyone else controlling the pay of their workers. As such, an allocator in our research did not have to overpay ingroup workers as a "preemptive strike" against the possibility that another (outgroup allocator) would mistreat them.

Based on a review of the range of studies that now have been conducted on group categorization effects on reward allocation, it appears reasonable to conclude that the impact of ingroup favorability is more limited and/or subtle than originally thought. It is probable that such biases, if they operate at all, are most likely to occur in contexts (a) that promote a sense of integroup competition (as in Towson *et al.*, 1981); (b) that provide allocators with few other bases for their decisions (e.g., Tajfel, 1970); and/or (c) that generate defensive reactions—defensive attributions, outgroup distrust, and so forth (e.g., Commins & Lockwood, 1979; Ng, 1981, 1984). In other contexts, such as the work settings examined by Messé *et al.* (1984a,b), group categorization appears to mediate a different psychological process—the perceived applicability of distributive justice norms to pay distributions.

Turning to needed future work, we feel that three extensions of the present research would be especially appropriate next steps in exploring the utility of the reasoned-action–role-theory approach that we are advocating. First, whereas it is true that a large number of studies (including Messé *et al.*, 1984a,b) have yielded results that are consistent with the idea that the more accepted a role-related norm is, the more it will influence reasoned actions (Proposition 1), there exist few studies that have examined this relationship directly. One investigation of the connection between norm salience and behavior (Fullerton, 1978), in fact, was a reward distribution study, and its results strongly supported Proposition 1. This research asked subjects (before and/or after they had received performance feedback) how important equity was to them as a reward distribution norm. Results indicated that subjects' pay distributions to self and a (better or worse) co-worker were strongly related to the degree of importance ascribed to the norm. These findings suggest that comprehensive exploration of the relationships between norm salience, intentions, and overt behaviors in work, as well as other contexts would be worthwhile.

Second, it is clear that we did not measure behavioral intentions directly in either of the studies discussed above. Rather, we assumed (with some justification) that actions—in this case pay allocations—would reflect intentions. Still, it would be very useful to explore more directly the hypothesized links between distributive justice norms and intentions *per se*, as well as how group categorization processes mediate these links. Third, it also is clear that the impact of other external variables (including other target characteristics), in addition to group categorization, needs to be systematically explored with regard to their effects on the link between norms, intentions, and overt behaviors. As noted earlier, such explorations have the potential to substantially expand the general relevance of Fishbein and Ajzen's model.

In conclusion, we would like to reiterate our sense that viewing distributive justice norms, in general, as particular examples of beliefs is a perspective that potentially has great utility, especially for generating a more precise and comprehensive understanding of how, when, and why such norms influence behavior. Even if, ultimately, Fishbein and Ajzen's specific model proves to be less useful than some other approaches, we think that it still would be the case that norms, and their impact on actions, will be found to be mediated by the same processes that affect attitudes and other, similar types of social cognitions.

REFERENCES

Ajzen, I., & Fishbein, M. (1980). *Understanding attitudes and predicting social behavior.* Englewood Cliffs, NJ: Prentice-Hall.

Allen, V. L. (1982). Effects of conformity pressure on justice behavior. In J. Greenberg & R. L. Cohen (Eds.), *Equity and justice in social behavior* (pp. 187–215). New York: Academic Press.

Allen, V. L., & Wilder, D. A. (1979). Group categorization and attribution of belief similarity. *Small Group Behavior, 10,* 73–80.

Aronoff, J., & Wilson, J. P. (1985). *Personality in the social process.* Hillsdale, NJ: Erlbaum.

Austin, W., McGinn, N. C., & Susmilch, C. (1980). Internal standards revisited: Effects of social comparisons and expectancies on judgments of fairness and satisfaction. *Journal of Experimental Social Psychology, 16,* 426–441.

Bentler, P. M., & Speckart, G. (1979). Models of attitude-behavior relations. *Psychological Review, 86,* 452–464.

Berkowitz, L., & Walster, E. (Eds.). (1976). *Advances in experimental social psychology* (Vol. 9). New York: Academic Press.

Biddle, B. J., & Thomas, E. J. (Eds.). (1966). *Role theory: Concepts and research.* New York: Wiley.

Blau, P. M. (1967). *Exchange and power in social life.* New York: Wiley.

Brewer, M. B. (1979). In-group bias in the minimal intergroup situation: A cognitive motivational analysis. *Psychological Bulletin, 86,* 307–324.

Broverman, I. K., Vogel, S. R., Broverman, D. M., Clarkson, F. E., & Rosenkrantz, P. S. (1972). Sex-role stereotypes: A current appraisal. *Journal of Social Issues, 28,* 59–78.

Caddick, B. (1980). Equity theory, social identity, and intergroup relations. In L. Wheeler (Ed.), *Review of personality and social psychology* (Vol. 1, pp. 219–245). Beverly Hills, CA: Sage.

Callahan-Levy, C. M., & Messé, L. A. (1979). Sex differences in the allocation of pay. *Journal of Personality and Social Psychology, 37,* 433–446.

Clark, M. S. (1984). Record keeping in two types of relationships. *Journal of Personality and Social Psychology, 47,* 549–557.

Commins, B., & Lockwood, J. (1979). The effects of status differences, favoured treatment and equity on intergroup comparisons. *European Journal of Social Psychology, 9,* 281–289.

Crano, W. D., & Messé, L. A. (1982). *Social psychology: Principles and themes of interpersonal behavior.* Homewood, IL: Dorsey Press.

Deutsch, M. (1975). Equity, equality, and need: What determines which issues will be used as the basis of distributive justice? *Journal of Social Issues, 31,* 137–149.

Dipboye, R. L., Fromkin, H. L., & Wilback, K. (1975). Relative importance of applicant sex, attractiveness, and scholastic standing in evaluations of job applicant resumes. *Journal of Applied Psychology, 60,* 39–45.

Eagly, A. H., & Wood, W. (1982). Inferred sex differences in status as a determinant of gender stereotypes about social influence. *Journal of Personality and Social Psychology*, 43, 915–928.

Fazio, R. H., & Zanna, M. P. (1981). Direct experience and attitude-behavior consistency. In L. Berkowitz (Ed.), *Advances in experimental social psychology* (Vol. 14, pp. 162–202). New York: Academic Press.

Fishbein, M. (1980). A theory of reasoned action: Some applications and implications. In H. Howe & M. Page (Eds.), *Nebraska symposium on motivation* (Vol. 27). Lincoln, NE: University of Nebraska Press.

Fishbein, M., & Ajzen, I. (1975). *Belief, attitude, intention, and behavior: An introduction to theory and research*. Reading, MA: Addison-Wesley.

Fullerton, T. D. (1978). *Equity or equality: A question of relevant input and norms*. Unpublished master's thesis, Department of Psychology, Michigan State University, East Lansing, MI.

Goffman, E. (1952). On cooling the mark out: Some aspects of adaptation to failure. *Psychiatry*, 18, 213–231.

Goffman, E. (1959). *The presentation of self in everyday life*. New York: Doubleday.

Greenberg, J., & Cohen, R. L. (Eds.). (1982). *Equity and justice in social behavior*. New York: Academic Press.

Hamilton, D. L. (1979). A cognitive-attributional analysis of stereotyping. In L. Berkowitz (Ed.), *Advances in experimental social psychology* (Vol. 12, pp. 53–84). New York: Academic Press.

Jaccard, J. J., Knox, R., & Brinberg, D. (1979). Predictions of behavior from beliefs: An extension and test of a subjective probability model. *Journal of Personality and Social Psychology*, 37, 1239–1248.

Kelley, H. H., & Stahelski, A. J. (1970). The social interaction basis of cooperators' and competitors' beliefs about others. *Journal of Personality and Social Psychology*, 16, 66–91.

Kelley, H. H., & Thibaut, J. W. (1978). *Interpersonal relations: A theory of interdependence*. New York: Wiley.

Kirkpatrick, C. (1963). *The family as process and institution* (2nd ed.). New York: Roland Press.

Lane, I. M., & Messé, L. A. (1971). Equity and the distribution of rewards. *Journal of Personality and Social Psychology*, 20, 1–17.

Lane, I. M., & Messé, L. A. (1972). The distribution of insufficient, sufficient, and over-sufficient rewards: A clarification of equity theory. *Journal of Personality and Social Psychology*, 21, 228–233.

Leventhal, G. S. (1976). The distribution of rewards and resources in groups and organizations. In L. Berkowitz & E. Walster (Eds.), *Advances in experimental social psychology* (Vol. 9, pp. 91–131). New York: Academic Press.

Leventhal, G. S. (1980). What should be done with equity theory? New approaches to the study of fairness in social relationships. In K. G. Gergen, M. S. Greenberg, & R. H. Willis (Eds.), *Social exchange: Advances in theory and research* (pp. 27–55). New York: Plenum Press.

Leventhal, G. S., & Lane, D. W. (1970). Sex, age, and equity behavior. *Journal of Personality and Social Psychology*, 15, 312–316.

Leventhal, G. S., & Whiteside, H. D. (1973). Equity and the use of reward to elicit high performance. *Journal of Personality and Social Psychology*, 25, 75–83.

Leventhal, G. S., Weiss, T., & Buttrick, R. (1973). Attribution of value, equity, and the prevention of waste in reward allocation. *Journal of Personality and Social Psychology*, 27, 276–286.

Liska, A. E. (1984). A critical examination of the causal structure of the Fishbein/Ajzen attitude-behavior model. *Social Psychology Quarterly*, 47, 61–74.

Major, B., & Adams, J. B. (1983). Role of gender, interpersonal orientation, and self-presentation in distributive-justice behavior. *Journal of Personality and Social Psychology, 45,* 598–608.

Major, B., & Deaux, K. (1982). Individual differences in justice behavior. In J. Greenberg & R. L. Cohen (Eds.), *Equity and justice in social behavior* (pp. 43–76). New York: Academic Press.

Major, B., McFarlin, D. B., & Gagnon, D. (1984). Overworked and underpaid: On the nature of gender differences in personal entitlement. *Journal of Personality and Social Psychology, 47,* 1399–1412.

Messé, L. A., & Watts, B. L. (1982). The complex nature of the sense of fairness: Internal standards and social comparison as bases for reward allocation. *Journal of Personality and Social Psychology, 45,* 84–93.

Messé, L. A., Hymes, R. W., & MacCoun, R. J. (1984a, August). *Minimal group membership and reward distribution behavior.* Paper presented at the Meeting of the American Psychological Association, Toronto.

Messé, L. A. Hymes, R. W., & MacCoun, R. J. (1984b, May). *The impact of gender distinctions on distributive justice judgments.* Paper presented at the Invitational Conference on Gender and Sex Roles, Nags Head, NC.

Mikula, G. (1974). Nationality, performance, and sex as determinants of reward allocation. *Journal of Personality and Social Psychology, 29,* 435–440.

Mikula, G. (1980). On the role of justice in allocation decisions. In G. Mikula (Ed.), *Justice and social interaction* (pp.127–166). New York: Springer-Verlag.

Miller, D. T., & Holmes, J. G. (1975). The role of situational restrictiveness and self-fulfilling prophesies: A theoretical and empirical extension of Kelley and Stahelski's Triangle Hypothesis. *Journal of Personality and Social Psychology, 31,* 661–673.

Morgan, R. W., Sawyer, J. (1967). Bargaining, expectations and the preference for equality over equity. *Journal of Personality and Social Psychology, 6,* 139–149.

Ng, S. H. (1981). Equity theory and the allocation of rewards between groups. *European Journal of Social Psychology, 11,* 439–443.

Ng, S. H. (1984). Equity and social categorization effects on intergroup allocation of rewards. *British Journal of Social Psychology, 23,* 165–172.

Pagel, M. D., & Davidson, A. R. (1984). A comparison of three social-psychological models of attitude and behavior plan: Prediction of contraceptive behavior. *Journal of Personality and Social Psychology, 47,* 516–533.

Petty, R. E., & Cacioppo, J. T. (1981). *Attitudes and persuasion: Classic and contemporary approaches.* Dubuque, IA: Wm. C. Brown.

Schwinger, T. (1980). Just allocations of goods: Decisions among three principles. In G. Mikula (Ed.), *Justice and social interaction* (pp. 95–125). New York: Springer-Verlag.

Shaver, K. G. (1970). Defensive attribution: Effects of severity and relevance on the responsibility assigned for an accident. *Journal of Personality and Social Psychology, 14,* 101–113.

Sivacek, J., & Crano, W. D. (1982). Vested interest as a moderator of attitude–behavior consistency. *Journal of Personality and Social Psychology, 43,* 210–221.

Tajfel, H. (1970). Experiments in intergroup discrimination. *Scientific American,* pp. 96–102.

Tajfel, H. (1978). *Differentiation between social groups: Studies in the social psychology of intergroup relations.* London: Academic Press.

Tajfel, H., & Turner, J. (1979). An integrative theory of intergroup conflict. In W. G. Austin & S. Worchel (Eds.), *The social psychology of intergroup relations* (pp. 33–47). Monterey, CA: Brooks/Cole.

Taylor, S. E., Fiske, S. T., Etcoff, N. L., & Ruderman, A. J. (1978). The categorical and contextual bases of person memory and stereotyping. *Journal of Personality and Social Psychology, 36,* 778–793.

Tedeschi, J. T. (Ed.). (1981). *Impression management theory and social psychological research.* New York: Academic Press.

Thomas, E. J., & Biddle, B. J. (1966a). The nature and history of role theory. In B. J. Biddle & E. J. Thomas (Eds.), *Role theory: Concepts and research* (pp. 3–19). New York: Wiley.

Thomas, E. J., & Biddle, B. J. (1966b). Basic concepts for classifying the phenomena of role. In B. J. Biddle & E. J. Thomas (Eds.), *Role theory: Concepts and research* (pp. 23–45). New York: Wiley.

Thomas, E. J., & Biddle, B. J. (1966c). Basic concepts for the properties of role phenomena. In B. J. Biddle & E. J. Thomas (Eds.), *Role theory: Concepts and research* (pp. 46–51). New York: Wiley.

Thomas, E. J., & Biddle, B. J. (1966d). Basic concepts for the variables of role phenomena. In B. J. Biddle & E. J. Thomas (Eds.), *Role theory: Concepts and research* (pp. 51–63). New York: Wiley.

Towson, S. M. J., Lerner, M. J., & de Carufel, A. (1981). Justice rules or ingroup loyalties: The effects of competition on children's allocation behavior. *Personality and Social Psychology Bulletin, 7,* 696–700.

Turner, R. H. (1962). Role taking: Process versus conformity. In A. M. Rose (Ed.), *Human behavior and social processes* (pp. 20–40). Boston, MA: Houghton Mifflin.

Watts, B. L., & Messé, L. A. (1982). The impact of task inputs, situational context, and sex on evaluations of reward allocators. *Social Psychology Quarterly, 45,* 254–262.

Watts, B. L., Messé, L. A., & Vallacher, R. R. (1982). Towards understanding sex differences in pay allocation: Agency, communion, and reward distribution behavior. *Sex Roles, 8,* 1175–1188.

Wilder, D. A. (1981). Perceiving persons as a group: Categorization and intergroup relations. In D. L. Hamilton (Ed.), *Cognitive processes in stereotyping and intergroup behavior* (pp. 213–257). Hillsdale, NJ: Erlbaum.

Williams, D. C. (1975). *Race and sex as determinants of perceived belief similarity.* Unpublished doctoral dissertation, Department of Psychology, Michigan State University, East Lansing, MI.

Chapter 13

Children's Use of Justice Principles in Allocation Situations

FOCUS ON THE NEED PRINCIPLE

INGEBORG WENDER

INTRODUCTION

This chapter is primarily concerned with the development of distributive justice in children. It will concentrate on the knowledge the child can activate in hypothetical situations and will discuss the child's organization of this knowledge in the course of his or her development. Discussion will focus on the cognitive developmental model and will draw primarily on the work of Piaget (1932/1973) and Damon (1977). A comparison of Piaget's and Damon's models will provide the context for a discussion of allocation research done with children. Research conducted over the past several years at the Technical University at Braunschweig, as well as research on prosocial behavior, suggests that children develop social understanding very early in their lives, and that this development affects their ideas of justice.

INGEBORG WENDER • Seminar für Psychologie, Fachbereich 9 der Technischen Universität Braunschweig, 3300 Braunschweig, West Germany.

COGNITIVE DEVELOPMENTAL MODELS OF DISTRIBUTIVE JUSTICE

According to Kohlberg (1981), justice is the first virtue of morality. It gives all human beings equal and universal rights. Each individual is under an obligation to respect another person's rights and claims, as he would his own. Thus, justice aims toward a basic pattern of balance and harmony within a group or society. These ideas about justice are not held as opinions or beliefs, but rather are represented as knowledge that relates to others without sacrificing the self (as opposed to altruism, which demands self-sacrifice). This knowledge is manifest as spiritual strength, which, in a philosophical or intuitionist context, takes on a form of ideal virtue. This ideal form does not change, regardless of the differences among cultures or social communities.

Some notion of justice or reciprocity seems present from the very beginning of life; this might have a biological basis that constitutes a necessary, but not yet sufficient, condition for the development of justice. As early as infancy, Piaget (1932/1973) sees the first signs of jealousy and imitation, and the resulting sympathy, as indicating very early reactions of altruism and sharing. Jealousy prevents one from being used by others and the need for company prevents the self from using others. There is a balance between the two. The primitive forms are not to be seen as a kind of instinct or as a product of an individual predisposition; rather they are a cornerstone for the active construction of a concept of justice.

Piaget (1932/1973) attempted to devise a stage model of the child's understanding of distributive justice. He constructed various short stories and then asked children questions about them. In the first of the three stages Piaget distinguished (up to 7–8 years old), the child has no concept of distributive justice. Justice is attributed to the authority of adults. Accordingly, in distribution situations the adult or the older child is entitled to the larger share.

Reciprocal relations are, however, present from the very beginning. The seeds of equality can be found in a child's earliest relationships, for example, in the need for mutual affection. However, this equality is only expressed by small children as long as they are not suppressed by authority (e.g., instructions from parents), or when there is no possibility of a conflict with authority. Even in relationshps among children, the authority of the older children wins over equality.

In the second stage (from approximately 8–11 years old), equality predominates against all other elements. The need for equality does not develop in a rigid form, but rather makes way for a more finely shaded understanding of moral conflicts. The development of the notion of equality moves in the direction of relativity. Instead of looking for equality in identity, the child understands the equal right of individuals only by considering the particular situation of each individual. Piaget (1932/1973) does not think that this leads to a preference for one particular person, but that equality between individuals is more effectively established than previously. The cases pointed out by Piaget illustrate that judgments of justice appear to refer to personal infirmities. This point becomes evident with regard to criteria such as need or lack of ability or talent (owing to the fact, for example, that children are comparatively small or young). When children reach Piaget's third stage (at the age of 11–12 years), they are thought to arrive at a higher form of equality, where equity in the form of need is taken into account.

Damon (1977) likewise considers distributive justice to be one of the first social concepts developed by the child. Knowledge of justice regulates the transactions that organize, maintain, and transform relationships between persons. According to Damon, two of the main transactions where children are concerned are sharing (you possess something and give it away) and allocation of various goods (you are given something such as sweets, money, toys, play possibilities, etc. to distribute).

Damon (1977) distinguishes three principles of distributive justice: equality, equity, and need. These three principles form the focus of interest for a child in each of the various stages of development. In Damon's view, the criterion of strict equality appears first and is then followed by the criterion of merit. Finally, the need criterion differentiates itself in the child's thinking. At the highest developmental stages of distributive justice, the child coordinates them systematically and regulates the individual claims corresponding to the situation. This makes it possible to find a solution to the conflict of sharing, one which leads to a relatively harmonious arrangement.

Basing his findings on epistemological and empirical analyses, Damon (1977) formulated a six-level model of distributive justice. His studies began with intensive interviewing based on hypothetical dilemmas, which were more complicated and standardized than those of Piaget. Damon describes these levels as a series of conflict resolutions taking place in the child's thoughts. Each cognitive change in the level sequence brings about a better and more comprehensive understanding of distributive justice.

During the first level (0-A, age 4), the child does not consider it necessary to explain his judgment of justice to anyone else. He reacts by describing his own wishes. The possibility of conflicting with the wishes of others is simply not considered. In the next level (0-B, age 5), the child has already introduced an element of objectivity, by relating his judgment to external, observable characteristics of the other person, for example, age or size. However, the judgment is still based on his own viewpoint. At this level the child prefers an unequal distribution of goods that favors age or size.

At the next level (1-A, age 6), the child does recognize the claims of others, but he expects the same self-interest from everyone, that is, he believes that everyone operates on the same basis. In order to avoid conflicts and disagreements, everyone is accorded the same claim; everyone is entitled to an equal share of what is to be distributed. At this level there is preference for the equality principle. During the 1-B level (age 7), the child sees claims in a more differentiated way. He now accepts that a person who has achieved something, who has benefitted the group in some way, should be rewarded accordingly. Different accomplishments are attributed to different people, and these are to be taken into account when distribution takes place. At this level there is a preference for the equity principle.

During the 2-A level (age 8), the child accepts the existence of conflicting claims of various people. He also tries to find a compromise among the various claims, but he is not yet capable of a systematic coordination among the various points of view. Special emphasis is given to the need of one of the persons involved. The child perceives that a situation of deficiency means that the needy person is operating on a different basis than the others. At this level there is a preference for the need principle. By the time the last level (2-B, ages 8–9) is reached, the child is able to accept all claims and weigh them systematically; mutual positions are acknowledged and integrated into the situation in question. At this level there is no special preference for a principle.

The main difference between Piaget's (1932/1973) and Damon's (1977) models concerns the need principle. Piaget suggested that the use of the need principle marked the highest development of distributive justice. In Damon's model the use of the need principle is greatest at level 2-A, followed by level 2-B, where the child weighs and integrates all principles systematically.

INVESTIGATIONS INTO CONCRETE ALLOCATION BEHAVIOR

Little of the vast social psychological literature on allocation behavior concentrates on analyzing children's knowledge. However, it is still possible to identify an age-related trend in distribution preferences, from self-preference through preference for equality to special emphasis on the principle of equity (Hook & Cook, 1979; Major & Deaux, 1982; Mikula, 1972; Streater & Chertkoff, 1976). Equity distributions need to be distinguished on the basis of ordinal or proportional correspondence between performance and reward. Hook (1978) demonstrated that children only gradually develop the ability for proportional thinking required to perform the mental calculations necessary for a precisely equitable distribution. Proportional equity distributions are first used by teenagers and adults (Hook & Cook, 1979). In very few of these investigations has the need principle been systematically examined. In one of these studies (employing a bargaining task), only the 10- and 11-year-old children chose the need principle (Simons & Klaassen, 1979).

These investigations of allocation behavior not only suggest a trend toward a stage series; they also seem to reflect the relationship between children's selection of fairness principles and different contexts, for example, task, aims, and group structures (see Anderson & Butzin, 1978; Berndt, 1982; Lerner, 1977).

Piaget (1932/1973) argued that the stages of moral development cannot be as easily limited with respect to age as can, for example, the development of logical thought. Damon prefers the word *level* instead of stage, to make it plain that the stages that can be so clearly differentiated in theory, cannot be distinguished as easily during empirical investigations with children.

STUDIES OF DISTRIBUTIVE JUSTICE

The studies on allocation conducted at the Technical University at Braunschweig and summarized here were all carried out with the specific aim of understanding children's conceptions of justice. Hypothetical distribution stories were employed, but in order to increase the level of reality in the stories, whenever possible children were shown video tapes and were then invited to distribute whatever was to be allocated (e.g., pieces of chewing gum, money). The design involved asking the children to help the experimenter divide goods between two other children, and the analyses focused on the children's distributive behavior and the reasons they offered for it (Gerling & Wender, 1981, 1982; Wender & Gerling, 1985). The investigations focused on the following questions:

1. Do preschool children differentiate between just and unjust aims in hypothetical distributive situations where performance is varied?

2. To what extent do preschool children take the principles of equity or need into account in their just distributions: (a) when only the performance or the need of the stimulus figures is varied? or (b) when both the performance and the need of the stimulus figures are simultaneously varied?

3. To what extent do primary school children in their second year make use of the principles of equity and need: (a) when only the need

variable of the stimulus figures is varied? (no study with primary school children varied only the performance), or (b) when both the performance and the need of the stimulus figures are simultaneously varied?

4. Can preschool and primary school children be influenced to give more priority to the need principle in their distributions by procedures designed to affect empathy and attribution of responsibility?

DIFFERENTIATION BETWEEN JUST AND UNJUST AIMS

When directly asked what they understood by "justice," most 5- and 6-year-old children could give no direct answer. However, given certain distribution situations, they were able to apply the concepts of justice and injustice. For example, one child responded: "If somebody has got something, and somebody else has got nothing, and he is still very little and he starts to cry, then the one who's got something has to give something to the other one."

After observing these types of reactions, which show a high social sensitivity in some of the very young children, we attempted to gain further insight from more systematic examinations. For this purpose, we studied the extent to which preschool children were able to distinguish among "just," "unjust," and "unrestricted" ways of allocation. The experimental situation was made as simple as possible for the children: two puppets contributed different levels of performance by carrying different numbers of books from one room to another, and were rewarded with chewing gum (four pieces in all), which the subject had to distribute between them. We found a significant difference between the subjects' just and unjust distributions. Told to be "unjust," almost all the boys and the girls distributed unequally. Told to be "just," however, the girls distributed equally, whereas some of the boys took the number of books into account. Told that there was no restriction, all the boys and most of the girls preferred an equal allocation. When giving their reasons, the children showed that they were aware of why they decided to distribute as they did, and that their reasons were plausible. The justifications for the unjust distribution often referred to a deviation from the just distribution (Gerling & Wender, 1981).

These results suggest that preschool children already possess ideas of distributive justice and can apply them. We should not overemphasize differences between the sexes (the boys attached distributive justice more strongly to performance than did girls), as the results in other, similar, studies are not consistent. Damon (1977) found no differences between the sexes, and our own subsequent studies showed no significant difference. Given this, it seems reasonable to adopt Underwood and Moore's (1982) interpretation of sex differences in children's prosocial behavior:

All differences observed seem to point in the same direction, but the size of the difference appears to be quite small.

PRESCHOOL CHILDREN'S PREFERENCES FOR JUSTICE PRINCIPLES

To answer the question of whether and to what extent preschool children take performance into account when allocating justly, consider first the data from the investigation described above. When only the performance of the stimulus figures is varied, two thirds of the children prefer the equality principle, one third the equity principle (Gerling & Wender, 1981).

Varying only the puppets' needs led to a preference for the need principle (Gerling & Wender, 1982). Two thirds of the children chose the need principle, one third the equality principle. The experimental procedure here was as simple as in the preceding experiment. Need was operationalized in the following way. Both puppets felt the desire for chewing gum while reading. Puppet A found chewing gum in its closet, whereas puppet B found none. The subject's task was to allocate four pieces of chewing gum between the puppets. In our later investigations using human twins rather than puppets as stimulus figures, we were not able to replicate the strong priority given to need in the distributive behavior of the preschool children when need alone was varied.[1] Instead about two thirds of the children preferred equal distribution, and one third chose need as a criterion for fair distribution.

When both the need and performance of the stimulus figures (two puppets) were varied simultaneously, we found that more than two thirds of the preschool children preferred equal distribution; the remaining children produced distributions based on need or performance, with need given greater priority than performance (Gerling & Wender, 1981).

In summary, although the results are not entirely consistent, on the whole we may postulate a preference for the principle of equality. However, this preference seems to be rather unstable. Some of the subjects chose the need principle, whereas others chose the equity principle, though need receives by far more emphasis than equity.

PRIMARY SCHOOL CHILDREN'S PREFERENCES FOR JUSTICE PRINCIPLES

In studies with primary school children (second graders about 8 years of age), the roles of the stimulus figures on the videotapes were played by twins. In the first investigation (Wender & Gerling, 1985),

---

[1]The data come from the unpublished *Diplomarbeit*, "Encouraging the Consideration of Need in Allocation Situations," studies for which were conducted and evaluated by A. Kühling and I. Lienemann.

which varied only the figures' needs, children preferred the equal distribution. Need was taken into account only rarely. In a second investigation that employed children from schools in a more middle-class setting, almost all the subjects chose need as the criterion for their distribution.[2]

When the performance and the need variables were varied simultaneously, almost all the children chose the principle of equality in a first, spontaneous distribution.[3] During a subsequent set of paired comparisons in which the children had to choose between two possible principles of fairness, they most often preferred the equality principle, followed by the principle of need. The equity principle was chosen very infrequently.

Thus, the results of the investigations with primary school children are similar to those with preschool children. We find a preference for the principle of equality, followed by that of need. The equity principle is very rarely preferred. There seems to be the same instability between the preference for equality and need as there was in the preschool investigations.

ENCOURAGING THE CONSIDERATION OF NEED

In accordance with investigations of prosocial behavior we have tried to locate systematic influences that would stabilize children's preference for need in justice distributions. The relevant literature (e.g., Bierhoff, 1980; Mussen & Eisenberg-Berg, 1977) identifies empathy and social responsibility in particular as motivational components of helping behavior. The possible impact of empathy for the consideration of need in distributive situations was supported by children's spontaneous utterances in our first investigations. In justifying their distributions, they accented the socioemotional consequences for the stimulus figures (e.g., "otherwise her heart will bleed," "so that one isn't crying and the other happy").

Hoffman (1982) identifies a series of stimuli that can trigger off substitute affective reactions, such as facial expressions, which indicate that a person is in need. In one of the first of the present studies (Gerling & Wender, 1981), puppet A, who already had some chewing gum, was represented as happy and laughing, whereas puppet B, the puppet in

---

[2]These data come from the unpublished *Diplomarbeit*, "Empirical Studies of Preferences for the Need Principle," studies for which were conducted and evaluated by E. Gietz and B. Jünke.

[3]These data come from the unpublished *Diplomarbeit*, "The Influence of Empathy, Attributions of Responsibility, and Sex on Allocation Behavior," studies for which were conducted and evaluated by H. Nübel.

need, was shown as unhappy and crying. Verbal hints were also added. Preschool children did not react to these stimuli in the expected manner. They responded verbally in their comments and justifications to these signs of sadness and trouble, but the impact of need on distributions did not increase. It is possible that children recognize the cues designed to increase empathy, but this is not sufficient to bring about a change in their behavior.

In the next study, we tried to increase the empathy of the preschool children by means of a short role play.[4] The subjects were asked to act out what they had seen in the film about the two puppets, with the experimenter acting one of the parts. A first distribution showed no effect, but a second distribution showed a significant difference in the priority given to need.

In subsequent investigations (Wender & Gerling, 1985), we tried to boost children's empathy reaction by a modeling procedure. The children watched a film with twins as stimulus figures, but in the presence of an older child who was introduced as a friend of the twins. This older child (the model) expressed empathy both verbally and by means of facial expressions. We could not, however, produce a significant change in the subjects' distribution patterns, either with the preschool groups or with the primary school groups.

An additional important factor in the motivation of prosocial behavior is the attribution of responsibility. Its influence lies mainly in the field of self-regulating and controlling processes (Waller, 1980, p. 145). It is important that children recognize that the welfare of other people depends on their own future willingness to act. In other words, the child must perceive himself or herself as the cause (or causal agent) of the welfare and happiness of other people. Hoffman (1977) found that the sort of reasoning which correlated most consistently with measures of children's moral internalization was "other oriented induction," or "reasoning in which the parent points out to the child the causal relationship between the child's behavior and positive or negative consequences for other people (e.g., 'You can see Paul is sad. You can make him feel better.')" (Perry & Perry, 1983, p. 115).

We tried (Wender & Gerling, 1985) to increase such an awareness of responsibility and causality in children in much the same way. The attribution of responsibility was especially emphasized in the film by the commentary of a somewhat older child, a friend of the twins, who represented a model for the children. The model told the children: "We

---

[4]These data come from the unpublished *Diplomarbeit*, "Encouraging the Consideration of Need in Allocation Situations," studies for which were conducted and evaluated by A. Kühling and I. Linemann.

can do something in order to make [the puppet] not feel sad, but happy." By itself, such an induction of responsibility did not lead to a significant change in the patterns of children's distributions.

When both attribution of responsibility and empathy boosting were introduced together, however, preschool and primary school children took need more into account in their distribution than children in a control group. For preschool children, there was only a trend for need-based distributions to increase, whereas for primary school children, the priority given to need-based distributions increased significantly.

In summary, empathy induction, at least in the form operationalized in this research, is insufficient in itself to bring about a significant increase in the choice of distribution principles based on need. The same is true for attribution of responsibility. However, the combination of both variables significantly increases the weight given to need, at least for primary school children.

SUMMARY AND CONCLUDING REMARKS

DISTINGUISHING JUST FROM UNJUST

It is apparent that even pre-school children are able to distinguish between the just and the unjust. Most of the preschool children who participated in the Braunschweig research program described unequal distributions as unjust. In the justifications they offered for their behavior, we found elements of obligation and generalizability. This confirms earlier work by Damon (1977) and is consistent with the description of the 5- and 6-year-old child as an intuitive moralist who identifies moral prescriptions as obligatory, unalterable, and general (Shweder, Turiel, & Much, 1981).

PREFERENCE FOR EQUALITY

Preschool children and children of the early primary grades first identify the equal distribution as the just one. It seems reasonable to suggest that these children tend towards equal distribution primarily in complex situations that they cannot fully understand. For them, this is the simplest solution, cognitively and socially. They do not have to concern themselves with the claims of various people, and complaints and dissatisfaction within the group can be avoided; that is, equal distribution is seen as a means towards harmony in the group (see Mikula, 1980; Schwinger, 1980).

This last point is illustrated very clearly by the explanation some of the children gave for distributing rewards as they did. They chose equal distribution to avoid producing sadness and jealousy. Piaget's (1932/1973) participants answered in a similar way: "She [the mother] should give them both [both children] the same . . . because she would otherwise be angry and would take revenge upon her sister" (Dis, an 11-year-old girl; p. 301).

INSTABILITY IN THE PREFERENCE FOR EQUALITY

In both age groups investigated, the preference for equal distribution seems to be rather unstable. From the current studies it seems reasonable to conclude that the distribution pattern of the children can be influenced by several different factors.

Complexity

The degree of complexity of the task and the experimental material is one such factor. Though we did not vary this systematically, Donaldson (1982) has demonstrated convincingly that children can take on the perspective of others much earlier than described by Piaget and Inhelder (1975). This happens when the task in question is based on the child's sphere of experience and has a simple structure. Kohlberg (1981) and Damon (1977) see social perspective taking as a basic premise for the development of the concept of justice.

Motivational Components

Increasing emphasis on the motivational components of empathy and the attribution of responsibility tends to increase the impact of need, especially in older children. The modeling technique would be effective in modifying these variables. To what extent acting out the needy situations in a role-playing format would further the awareness of need in preschool children is unclear; this possibility requires further investigation.

Class

The social class of the children seems to be another factor which may influence the distribution patterns, though we did not vary this factor systematically. Enright, Enright, Manheim, and Harris (1980) found that lower-class children lag behind their middle-class peers in distributive justice reasoning. This lag was found in both black and white samples. The authors conclude that distributive justice is one moral component that clearly separates the social classes. In the Simons and Klaassen study (1979), each level of distributive justice reasoning generally was employed by children somewhat older than the children employing that level in Damon's work. Simons and Klassen attribute this to the lower social class of the Dutch children.

CHILDREN'S SOCIAL KNOWLEDGE

These empirical results are not easily integrated into Damon's (1977) theoretical model, which suggests that equality is predominant in the 5 to 6 year age range. In addition, several other pieces of research (e.g., Crott, Oldigs, Reihl, & Wender, 1976; Piaget, 1932/1973; Simons & Klaassen, 1979) find that children as old as 8, or even 11, prefer equal distributions. In order to integrate these kinds of findings into Damon's model, it would seem necessary to make two assumptions: (a) that both preschool and early primary school children are in a kind of transitional state, and (b) that children in such a state may be able to move on to later stages if they are exposed to certain kinds of influences.

The work conducted at Braunschweig (and elsewhere; for example, Anderson & Butzin, 1978; Hook, 1978) suggests that small children are aware of various principles, such as equality, equity, and need. However, it seems likely that these principles are reflected upon more consciously, and more systematically applied, later in the course of the development process (Berndt, 1982, p. 262, 263).

Damon (1977) criticizes the interpretation that children integrate cognitive, social, and sociocognitive skills into their activities much earlier than has usually been assumed by cognitive developmental psychologists. Even if Lewis's (1975) studies suggest that organizing principles, such as reciprocity, already play a part in controlling the social interaction of babies, Damon mocks efforts to demonstrate in young children abilities such as compensation, moral intention, or perspective taking by means of a sophisticated experimental paradigm. Damon doubts that the actions of very young children demonstrate the same organization of social knowledge as that present in older children. Certain similarities between the reactions of very young and somewhat older children should provide information about certain invariants of the process of human development, but, as Damon argues, should not confuse us as to the qualitative differences between activities of children of different age groups.

One should not exclude the possibility that qualitatively different forms of knowledge of justice express themselves in identical distribution choices and in similar justifications. In the Braunschweig experiments, need and performance are experimentally induced by easily observable criteria. In their justifications of just distributions, it is mostly the older children who assimilate the verbal example of the model, that is, to turn an unhappy person into a happy one. One might conclude from this that 7- and 8-year-olds link the idea of fairness with equally distributed well-being. If certain conditions stimulate such thoughts, these children may link fairness with an inner psychological meaning and with possibilities of restoring this well-being. This activation of diverse inner psychological components apparently poses greater difficulties for younger children.

THE NEED PRINCIPLE

In the current investigations there was a clear preference for the principle of need as opposed to the principle of equity in both age groups. Damon (1977) and Piaget (1932/1973) both argue that the comprehension of reciprocity of action and merit develops first. A strong emphasis on need and the experience of deficiency situations follow in the next, qualitatively higher, stages.

If one traces a parallel between consideration of the person in need in distribution situations, on the one hand, and altruistic, prosocial behavior toward the needs and wants of others, on the other, then it should be possible to draw on the studies of altruism as a comparison. In Eisenberg's (1982) stage model of prosocial moral judgment, stage 2 (5–6 years) is formulated as the "needs of other's orientation: The individual expresses concern for the physical, material and psychological needs of others, even though the other's needs conflict with one's needs" (p. 234).

In their review of the development of altruism, Zahn-Waxler and Radke-Yarrow (1982) point out that the first signs of reaction to need in another person appear as early as the first year of life and in an astonishingly unified form. This points toward a universal biological or maturing mechanism in the development of the concepts of altruism and justice (see Piaget, 1932/1973). Perhaps there is a social preadaptation in the very young child, as Schaffer (1977) postulates for the mother–child interaction; this preadaptation may be responsible for the development of the prosocial and justice concept in the first years of life. From the age of two and a half onwards, the emotional reaction responses and motivation concerning need in others undergo differentiation (Zahn-Waxler & Radke-Yarrow, 1982).

It might be easier to integrate the data on distributive justice if individually differing lines of development were taken into account.

Differences in dispositional components of empathic reactions, differences in upbringing, and differences in experience with peers may influence the course of development of social knowledge and social behavior, and thereby children's understanding of justice (Gilligan, 1982; Hoffman, 1977; Piaget, 1932/1973). In time, this could lead to varying preferences for distribution principles among adults (Schmitt & Montada, 1982; Winterhoff & Herrmann, 1979).

The findings accumulated in the Braunschweig program of research and discussed in the current chapter suggest that Damon's (1977) model requires modification. Most specifically, Damon's suggestion that the equity principle appears earlier in development than the need principle must be questioned. Even more basically, given the divergence in the research literature, it may be important to ask whether it still makes sense to attempt to construct a developmental stage model of moral judgment. Such a question was in fact raised by Piaget:

> It is, however, natural, that the development of moral judgment . . . in view of the numerous possible influences, is less regular than that of a simple cognitive judgment. In moral psychology we cannot, therefore, speak of clearly delimitated stages. (1973, p. 302)

Whether or not clearly delimited stages exist, future research should continue to examine the factors that stimulate children to give priority to the justice principles of equity and need.

Acknowledgments

Thanks are due to Tracy Colsh and Ann MacGlashan for their help in translating the text from German into English. Further, the author wishes to express her appreciation to Ronald Cohen for his many suggestions regarding the content and the fluency of this chapter.

REFERENCES

Anderson, N. H., & Butzin, C. A. (1978). Integration theory applied to children's judgments of equity. *Developmental Psychology, 14,* 593–606.
Berndt, T. J. (1982). Fairness and friendship. In K. H. Rubin & H. S. Ross (Eds.), *Peer relationships and social skills in childhood* (pp. 253–278). New York: Springer-Verlag.
Bierhoff, H. W. (1980). *Hilfreiches Verhalten* [Prosocial behavior]. Darmstadt: Steinkopff.
Crott, H., Oldigs, J., Reihl, D., & Wender, I. (1976). *Eine Untersuchung zum Gewinnaufteilungsverhalten verschiedener Altersstufen* [A study of allocation behavior of various agestages]. Bericht aus dem SFB 24 der Universität Mannheim.
Damon, W. (1977). *The social world of the child.* San Francisco: Jossey-Bass Publishers.
Donaldson, M. (1982). *Wie Kinder denken* [Children's minds]. Bern: Huber.

Eisenberg, N. (1982). The development of reasoning regarding prosocial behavior. In N. Eisenberg (Ed.), *The development of prosocial behavior* (pp. 219–249). New York: Academic Press.

Enright, R. D., Enright, W. F., Manheim, L. A., & Harris, B. E. (1980). Distributive justice development and social class. *Developmental Psychology, 16,* 555–563.

Gerling, M., & Wender, I. (1981). Gerechtigkeitskonzepte und Aufteilungsverhalten von Vorschulkindern [Justice concepts and allocation behavior of preschool children]. *Zeitschrift für Entwicklungspsychologie und Pädagogische Psychologie, 13,* 236–250.

Gerling, M., & Wender, I. (1982). Gerechtigkeitsvorstellungen von Kindern in Aufteilungssituationen: Die Bedürfnisberücksichtigung als Prinzip distributiver Gerechtigkeit [Justice concepts of children in allocation situations: Need as a principle of distributive justice]. *Psychologische Beiträge, 24,* 242–252.

Gilligan, C. (1982). *In a different voice.* Cambridge, MA: Harvard University Press.

Hoffman, M. L. (1977). Moral internalization: Current theory and research. In L. Berkowitz (Ed.), *Advances in experimental social psychology* (Vol. 10, pp. 86–135). New York: Academic Press.

Hoffman, M. L. (1982). Development of prosocial motivation: Empathy and guilt. In N. Eisenberg (Ed.), *The development of prosocial behavior* (pp. 281–313). New York: Academic Press.

Hook, J. G. (1978). The development of equity and logico-mathematical thinking. *Child Development, 49,* 1035–1044.

Hook, J. G., & Cook, T. D. (1979). Equity theory and the cognitive ability of children. *Psychological Bulletin, 86,* 429–445.

Kohlberg, L. (1981). *Essays on moral development: Vol. 1 The philosophy of moral development.* San Francisco: Harper & Row.

Lerner, M. J. (1977). The justice motive: Some hypotheses as to its origins and forms. *Journal of Personality, 45,* 1–52.

Lewis, M. (1975). *Friendship and peer relations.* Cambridge, MA: Harvard University Press.

Major, B., & Deaux, K. (1982). Individual differences in justice behavior. In J. Greenberg & R. L. Cohen (Eds.), *Equity and justice in social behavior* (pp. 43–76). New York: Academic Press.

Mikula, G. (1972). Die Entwicklung des Gewinnaufteilungsverhaltens bei Kindern und Jugendlichen [The development of allocation behavior of children and juveniles]. *Zeitschrift für Entwicklungspsychologie und Pädagogische Psychologie, 4,* 151–164.

Mikula, G. (1980). Zur Rolle der Gerechtigkeit in Aufteilungsentscheidungen [On the role of justice in allocation decisions]. In G. Mikula (Ed.), *Gerechtigkeit und soziale Interaktion* (pp. 141–183) [Justice and social interaction]. Bern: Huber.

Mussen, P., & Eisenberg-Berg, N. (1977). *The roots of caring, sharing, and helping.* San Francisco: Freeman.

Perry, D. G., & Perry, L. C. (1983). Social learning, causal attribution, and moral internalization. In J. Bisanz, G. L. Bisanz, & R. Kail (Eds.), *Learning in children* (pp. 105–136). New York: Springer-Verlag.

Piaget, J. (1973). *Das moralische Urteil beim Kinde* [The moral judgment of the child]. Frankfurt: Suhrkamp. (Original work published 1932)

Piaget, J., & Inhelder, B. (1956). *The child's conception of space.* London: Routledge & Kegan Paul.

Schaffer, R. (1977). *Mothering.* London: Fontana.

Schmitt, M., & Montada, L. (1982). Determinanten erlebter Gerechtigkeit [Determinants of perceived justice]. *Zeitschrift für Sozialpsychologie, 13,* 32–44.

Schwinger, T. (1980). Gerechte Güter-Verteilungen: Entscheidungen zwischen drei Prinzipien [Just allocations of goods: Decisions among three principles]. In G. Mikula

(Ed.), *Gerechtigkeit und soziale Interaktion* (pp. 107–140) [Justice and social interaction]. Bern: Huber.

Shweder, R. A., Turiel, E., & Much, N. C. (1981). The moral intuitions of the child. In J. H. Flavell & L. Ross (Eds.), *Social cognitive development* (pp. 288–305). Cambridge: Cambridge University Press.

Simons, R., & Klaassen, M. (1979). Children's conceptions and use of rules of distributive justice. *International Journal of Behavioral Development, 2*, 253–267.

Streater, A. L., & Chertkoff, J. M. (1976). Distribution of rewards in a triad: A developmental test of equity theory. *Child Development, 47*, 800–805.

Underwood, B., & Moore, B. S. (1982). The generality of altruism in children. In N. Eisenberg (Ed.), *The development of prosocial behavior* (pp. 25–52). New York: Academic Press.

Waller, M. (1980). Die Entwicklung prosozialen Verhaltens [The development of prosocial behavior]. In M. Waller (Ed.), *Jahrbuch für Entwicklungspsychologie* [Yearbook of developmental psychology] 2/1980 (pp. 127–165). Stuttgart: Klett-Cotta.

Wender, I., & Gerling, M. (1985). Empathie und Verursachungszuschreibung als Entwicklungsbedingungen der aufteilenden Gerechtigkeit [Empathy and responsibility attribution: Determinants of development of distributive justice]. *Zeitschrift für Entwicklungspsychologie und Pädagogische Psychologie, 17*, 341–350.

Winterhoff, P., & Herrmann, T. (1979). Verteilungsgerechtigkeit als Persönlichkeitsmerkmal [Distributive justice as a personal disposition]. Arbeiten der Forschungsgruppe Sprache und Kognition am Lehrstuhl Psychologie III, Universität Mannheim.

Zahn-Waxler, C. & Radke-Yarrow, M. (1982). The development of altruism: Alternative research strategies. In N. Eisenberg (Ed.), *The development of prosocial behavior* (pp. 109–137). New York: Academic Press.

Part IV

APPLICATIONS OF JUSTICE RESEARCH

Chapter 14

Two Rotten Apples Spoil the Justice Barrel

FAYE CROSBY, LAURA BURRIS, CATHERINE
CENSOR, and E. R. MacKETHAN

INTRODUCTION

Trying to contain sex discrimination is like catching fireflies. You look outside the window on a dark summer evening and see the entire lawn brightened by an airborne Morse code. You grab a jar; you rush outdoors; and the illumination level drops instantly. What had—at a distance—appeared as a thick clump of night beetles now disperses. The jar remains near empty.

Systematic research can help us to understand the mercurial image of sex discrimination. The most important clue to the now-you-see-it-now-you-don't aspect of sex discrimination is the differentiation between aggregate and individual levels of analysis. What can be clearly and plainly seen at the aggregate level eludes perception when one focuses on individual cases. Look at the lawn from a distance, and you know there are fireflies. But focus on this one or that one, and you are left empty handed.

The distinction between discrimination at the individual and aggregate levels proved crucial in one study of worker satisfaction. It was, in

FAYE CROSBY • Department of Psychology, Smith College, Northampton, MA 01060. LAURA BARRIS • Department of Psychology, Georgetown University, Washington, DC 20007. CATHERINE CENSOR • The Dalton School, 450 West End Avenue, New York, NY 10024. E. R. MacKETHAN • Department of Psychology, Yale University, New Haven, CT 06520.

part, to explicate the theory of relative deprivation that the survey study was conducted. The theory of relative deprivation states that deprivations are experienced relative to a social standard rather than simply as a function of a person's objective conditions. Employed women, employed men, and housewives in a Boston suburb were interviewed during 1978 and 1979 (Crosby, 1982, 1984b). The survey produced a surprising concatenation of three findings. One finding (not surprising in itself) was that the employed women in the study earned significantly less money than the employed men, even though the two groups were exactly matched in terms of all the job-related attributes we measured. The two groups had exactly the same NORC job prestige scores, the same years of education and training, the same ages, the same levels of motivation, and they worked the same number of hours per week. Yet, the 163 employed women in the study earned, on average, only 60 cents of every male dollar.

Only slightly more surprising was the second finding: the employed women in the survey expressed as much satisfaction (on eight different scales) with their jobs as did the employed men. This finding replicated other studies (e.g., Deaux, 1979; Miller, Labovitz, & Fry, 1975; Schreiber, 1979; Weaver, 1978). Nor did the vast majority of the employed women in the survey mention sex discrimination as a particular problem in their own work lives. Again, other researchers have also documented the unwillingness or inability among women to admit that one has suffered from discrimination (e.g., deLamater & Fidell, 1971; Linn, 1971; Walsh & Stewart, 1976).

Given the first two findings, one might expect to find that the employed women in the Boston suburb denigrated women, thought women less deserving than men, or somehow failed to acknowledge the existence of gender bias in our society. On the contrary, the employed women recognized the extent of sex discrimination in general and felt upset about it. On a number of measures of awareness and dissatisfaction, the employed women in the survey differed significantly from the employed men and the housewives. More specifically, the employed women were most likely to: (a) express resentment and dissatisfaction about the situation of working women in America, (b) see that women are not receiving what they want from work, (c) see a discrepancy between what women want and what women have, (d) feel disappointed about gender equality, and (e) feel pessimistic about the future for women.

Taken as a whole, the findings of the relative deprivation study suggest that women, who were themselves the victims of discrimination, denied their own plight while remaining quite alive to the plight of working women generally. Other researchers have shown similar patterns to exist among other disadvantaged groups—American blacks in the late 1960s (Abeles, 1972) and Canadian Francophones (Guimond & Dube-Simard, 1983), for example. Apparently, people can perceive situations at a general level without thinking about what occurs at the level of the individual.

What accounts for the lack of parallel between the sensitivity to injustice at a general level and the blindness to injustice at the individual level? Surely, part of the discrepancy comes from defensiveness. Melvin Lerner (1981) has demonstrated in a quite compelling way that people feel upset when they see another individual suffer an injustice. Indeed, so upsetting is a threat to one's belief in the just world that when people cannot adequately compensate the victim of injustice, they tend to denigrate the victim. If a person is motivated to avoid the perception that any individual suffers injustice, how much more threatened must she be to consider that the suffering individual in question is herself! It seems quite a natural (albeit illogical) wish to envision oneself as exempt from the unpleasant realities that one sees all around (Stevens & Jones, 1976).

Defensive attributions do not present the only means of accounting for the discrepancy between people's awareness of unfairness at a group level and their blindness to unfairness at the individual level. Cognitive factors are also important. As Crosby (1984a) argues, it is extremely difficult to demonstrate sex discrimination when one focuses on the individual case. Idiosyncrasies exist; and unless the standard for evaluation is strict and rigid (e.g., promotion goes to the one who can type n number of words per minute), idiosyncrasies leave room for explanations about why someone did or did not receive a certain outcome. In other words, when one compares the outcome of an individual woman and an individual man, one can usually find a "good reason" why the man receives the better outcome. But when one looks at a series of individual cases, in which the idiosyncrasies are averaged away, one can readily perceive systematic biases.

The importance of averaging away idiosyncrasies has been shown in an experiment by Crosby, Clayton, Hemker, and Alksnis (in press). Thirty male undergraduates at a prestigious Eastern school reviewed materials about a fictitious company consisting of 10 separate departments. The subjects received information about the salaries of males and females in each of the departments and information about the four input characteristics relevant to salary (level within the organization, education, years of experience, and performance ratings). The subjects were asked to assess the likelihood of gender bias in salaries.

All of the subjects in the experiment by Crosby et al. (in press) received the information in two different formats. The total-picture format presented all of the relevant information for all 10 departments on a single sheet of paper. When assessing the information in the total picture format, subjects rated the probable sexism in Company X as a whole. In the second format, dubbed the dribble format, the subjects were presented with the information for each department separately and singly. They made separate judgments about each department. Order was, of course, counterbalanced, so that half of the subjects encountered the total picture format first and half encountered the dribble format first.

Subjects were specifically instructed, when making their evaluation of the company as a whole, to count each department equally. If the formatting of the information had no effect on judgments, then the assessments of discrimination in the company as a whole should not have differed from the average of the 10 assessments of the individual departments. In other words, if a subject perceived that there was an 80% probability that sex discrimination influenced salaries at Company X overall, then the average of the probability ratings for the 10 departments ought to have been somewhere around 80%.

In fact, subjects in the experiment said that there was significantly more discrimination when the information was presented all at once than when it dribbled in. To the question "Would you say that there is sex discrimination in terms of pay?" subjects' answers averaged 6.47 (on a 10-point scale where 1 meant no and 10 meant yes) when they rated the company as a whole; but the average of their individual ratings was 5.58. When asked to "pick a percentage between 0% and 100% likelihood that sex discrimination exists," subjects averaged 62.3% for their ratings in the total-picture format, but the average of the 10 departmental ratings was only 52.5%. The average rating of the seriousness of the discrimination was 5.66 on an 11-point scale (where 0 meant none), whereas the average of the 10 departments was 4.97. In all three instances, the differences due to formatting were statistically significant. Order was not consistently important.

The role of information formatting in the perception of injustice raises an interesting question: when people look at an array of data, will they be better able to perceive discrimination in a system when there are some flagrant cases of injustice than when there are none? Oftentimes, serious discrimination results from the accretion of slight injuries, few of which are serious in themselves. Occasionally, there are one, two, or three obvious cases of discrimination. Will people perceive gender bias more easily when they can identify one particular case of discrimination than when the same inequality is spread out over a number of cases?

Given cognitive biases in the perception of injustice, it seems reasonable to expect that people will be more likely to perceive discrimination when there is some clear-cut case of injustice than when there is an equivalent accumulation of minor unfairness. The purpose of the present experiment is to test this expectation. A secondary purpose is to corroborate the finding that discrimination is more easily perceived when the relevant information is presented in aggregate form than when it is a question of individual comparisons.

Subjects in our experiment read information about a mythical organization that had recently hired or promoted eight employees. Subjects were told that a man and a woman competed in each selection; that, all told, two of the people selected were female and six male; and that the organization had hired outside consultants to determine if the selection reflected discriminatory practices. Subjects were further informed that the selection outcomes were supposed to be decided on the basis of four input characteristics that ought to have been given equal weight. For each of the four characteristics with each of the eight selections, the subjects were given the allegedly impartial conclusion of the outside consultants about whether the male was superior; the female was superior; or the two candidates were equal. Subjects knew the selection (male or female) in each instance.

In all conditions, we arranged the materials so that the number of times (out of a total of 32 times) a male was supposedly judged superior on input characteristics equaled the number of times a female was judged superior. What varied, across the conditions, was the distribution of superiority ratings. In one condition, the instances of female superiority were spread across candidates so that one could not identify a clear-cut case in which a very superior woman lost out to a man. In other conditions, one could see one, two, or three blatant cases of sex discrimination. A fifth, control condition presented only the aggregate ratings and results and did not present the results for the eight individual cases.

We hypothesized that the students in our experiment—themselves rather unconcerned about sex discrimination—would readily see the discrimination when the data were presented in aggregate form. When the information was presented in terms of individual comparisons, we expect little perception of sex discrimination in the absence of a flagrant case. We wondered: how many flagrant cases does it take for people to see discrimination?

METHODS

SUBJECTS

The subjects were 80 students who volunteered to participate in the experiment during the summer of 1984. They attended Yale College Summer School or Georgetown University.

PROCEDURES

After obtaining verbal consent, one of the three experimenters gave the subject(S) a booklet. On the first page was the cover story concerning the hiring system or promotion system of a company or university. The second page presented the materials in one of five formats. Subjects then assessed the amount of sex discrimination at the hypothetical institution.

When the materials concerned promotion [or hiring] in a university, the introductory page read:

> Sex discrimination is hot news in today's world. It is a fact that people sometimes overlook discrimination. The opposite is also true. In today's climate, people sometimes see sex discrimination where none exists. Last year the University of Z became concerned that it might be acting in a sex-discriminatory manner with respect to the promotion [hiring] of its faculty. If any injustices somehow existed, the University wanted to rectify them.
>
> The statistics show that only two women are promoted [hired] for every six men. The issue is: is this a reflection of discriminatory promotional [hiring] practices on the part of the University of Z? To decide the question, the president of the University ordered a study conducted by the American Association of University Professors. Each of the eight major departments in the University was asked to provide information concerning its candidates for promotion [for employment] when a man and a woman were competing for the promotion [a position]. Only data from the most recent promotions were considered [Only the most recent data were considered].
>
> Four factors are considered in determining promotions [in hiring new faculty] at the University. Each factor is weighted equally in arriving at a final decision. The consultants looked at all information pertinent to each factor and decided, by unanimous vote, which candidate (the man or the woman) was superior in each category.
>
> Your task is not to question the validity of each factor, but simply to decide, based on the committee's evaluations, whether or not the actions of the University were discriminatory.

Half of the subjects received the story about the University. An analogous story about Company Z was given to the other half of the subjects.

On the second page of the experimental booklet appeared one of five sets of information. Sixteen subjects received the information in summary form, learning that the experts determined that out of 32 instances (8 cases times 4 characteristics), the man was deemed superior 12 times, the woman was deemed superior 12 times, and the man and woman were deemed equal 8 times. Another sixteen subjects saw a table such as Table 1. This format was considered to present no blatant case of discrimination; the distributions of the 12 Ms (denoting male superiority), the 12 Ws (denoting female superiority), and the 8 equal signs occurred in such a way that no one case stuck out as unfair. Tables 2A, 2B, and 2C show how the materials were presented to the subjects in

TABLE 1. Stimulus Materials when There is
No Blatant Case of Sex Discrimination

Case	Evaluation criteria				Who was promoted
	A	B	C	D	
1	W	M	=	M	M
2	M	=	W	=	M
3	W	=	W	M	W
4	M	W	M	=	M
5	W	W	W	W	W
6	M	M	W	=	M
7	=	W	M	M	M
8	M	=	W	M	M

Note: In these materials, as in the control condition, the
female candidate is judged superior in 12 instances (the
12 Ws) and the male candidate is judged superior in 12
instances (the 12 Ms). In 8 instances they are judged of
equal merit. Six males and two females were selected.

the conditions representing one blatant case, two blatant cases, or three
blatant cases of sex discrimination.

After seeing the material, the subject was asked four questions about
the extent of discrimination at the institution. The first read: "Would
you say that there is sex discrimination in the University of Z's [Company
Z's] promotional [hiring] practices?" Subjects were instructed to circle a
number on a scale from 1 (no) to 10 (yes). The second question asked
the subject to estimate the likelihood of sex discrimination in the institution, from 0% to 100%. The third question asked "How serious is the
existing discrimination?" Subjects could circle a number from 0 (none)
to 10 (very serious). An open-ended question came next, asking the
subject "Why do you think there is or is not discrimination?" The first
four questions reproduced the questions asked by Crosby et al. (in press).

To determine whether the reported perception of bias is, itself,
influenced by the words used to ask about the perception, we included
a question that tapped perceived injustice without using the word "discrimination." Question five appeared in two forms. For half of the subjects, we asked "Do the promotional [hiring] practices of the University
of Z [Company Z] seem fair?" The other half of the subjects were asked:
"Does the University of Z [Company Z] seem less likely to promote
[hire] women than men?"

The experimental materials concluded by asking subjects if they
would describe themselves as feminist. We timed how long the subjects
spent examining the experimental materials and reaching a conclusion.

TABLE 2A. Stimulus Materials in One
Blatant Case of Sex Discrimination

| Case | Evaluation criteria | | | | Who was promoted |
	A	B	C	D	
1	M	W	M	=	M
2	M	W	M	M	M
3	M	=	W	=	W
4	W	=	W	W	M
5	W	M	W	W	W
6	=	M	M	W	M
7	W	=	=	M	M
8	M	W	=	M	M

TABLE 2B. Stimulus Materials in Two
Blatant Cases of Sex Discrimination

| Case | Evaluation criteria | | | | Who was promoted |
	A	B	C	D	
1	M	=	W	=	M
2	W	W	=	W	M
3	W	=	M	W	W
4	M	M	=	M	M
5	M	W	W	M	W
6	=	M	M	M	M
7	W	=	W	W	M
8	M	W	M	=	M

TABLE 2C. Stimulus Materials in Three
Blatant Cases of Sex Discrimination

| Case | Evaluation criteria | | | | Who was promoted |
	A	B	C	D	
1	M	M	M	M	M
2	W	=	W	W	M
3	W	W	M	=	W
4	W	W	W	=	M
5	=	W	=	=	W
6	M	M	M	M	M
7	=	W	W	W	M
8	M	M	M	M	M

RESULTS

PRELIMINARY ANALYSES

There were no effects due to the experimenters or the version of the materials used. Three experimenters, including two females and one male, administered the sessions, but three separate one-way analyses of variance (ANOVAs) for the three major dependent variables (perception of discrimination overall; perceived likelihood; and perceived seriousness) revealed no statistically significant effects. We also verified that subjects were no more or less likely to see discrimination overall when they read about the university than when they read about a company. Nor did the version (University of Z or Company Z) affect the perceived likelihood ratings or the seriousness ratings.

TESTING THE HYPOTHESES

To test the hypothesis that the format of the information affects the perception of discrimination, we conducted a series of 2 × 4 ANOVAs that crossed the gender of the subjects (male, female) with the manner of presenting the information (no clear case, one clear case, two clear cases, three clear cases). Significant main effects for the manner of presentation emerged on all three dependent measures of perceived discrimination. There was no main effect for gender on any of the variables and no interaction effects. Table 3 summarizes the statistical findings.

For the perception of discrimination overall (Figure 1), for perceived likelihood (Figure 2), and for perceived seriousness (Figure 3), both male and female subjects do not rate the situation as discriminatory when

TABLE 3. Summary of Statistical Findings

Dependent variables	Main effects and interaction effects in the 2 × 4 ANOVAs		
	Main effect for the manner of presentation	Main effect for gender of subject	Interaction effect
Perception of discrimination	$F = 8.66\ (3,41)$ $p = .0001$	$F = 0.49\ (1,41)$ n.s.	$F = 0.58\ (3,41)$ n.s.
Perceived likelihood	$F = 8.23\ (3,41)$ $p = .0001$	$F = 0.02\ (1,41)$ n.s.	$F = 1.69\ (3,41)$ n.s.
Perceived seriousness	$F = 4.31\ (3,41)$ $p = .01$	$F = 0.00\ (1,41)$ n.s.	$F = 0.88\ (3,41)$ n.s.

Note: The numbers in parentheses are the degrees of freedom; n.s. denotes not significant.

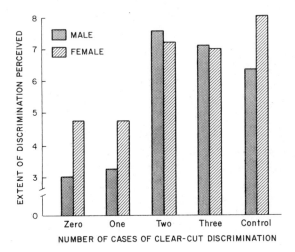

FIGURE 1.   Perceived discrimination as a function of the manner of presentation.

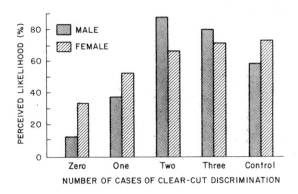

FIGURE 2.   Perceived likelihood of discrimination as a function of the manner of presentation.

there are no obvious imbalances or only one obvious case. In contrast, subjects do perceive discrimination when there are two or three clear cut cases. Figures 1, 2, and 3 illustrate the data.

Planned comparisons substantiate the impression that the discontinuity occurs between one clear-cut case and two clear-cut cases. For the perception of discrimination overall, a 2 × 2 ANOVA (gender times the manner of presentation) shows no main effect for manner of presentation ($F = .122$; $df = 1,13$; $p = .73$) when the two levels of manner of presentation are (a) two clear-cut cases, and (b) the control group.

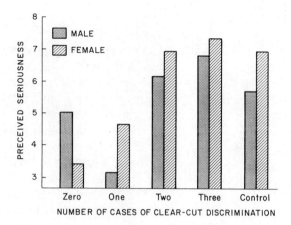

FIGURE 3.   Perceived seriousness as a function of the manner of presentation.

If the same analysis is repeated with one clear-cut case (rather than two) and the control group, manner of presentation emerges as significant ($F = 10.831$; $df = 1,14$; $p = .006$). In other words, for the perception of discrimination overall, there is no difference between the control condition, in which the data are presented in summary form, and the condition in which the distribution of male and female scores results in two clear-cut cases of injustice, but there is a difference between the control condition and the condition in which one clear-cut case emerges.

The same findings hold for the perceived likelihood and seriousness of discrimination. For likelihood the 2×2 ANOVA (gender and manner) shows no significant main effect for manner ($F = .099$; $df = 1,14$; $p = .75$) when the two levels of the variable are (a) two clear-cut cases, and (b) the control group. The main effect is significant, however, when the two levels of manner are (a) one clear-cut case, and (b) the control group ($F = 5.121$; $df = 1,14$; $p = .03$). For perceived seriousness, the figures show that there is no difference between the control condition and the condition of two clear-cut cases ($F = .189$; $df = 1,14$; $p = .67$), but one clear-cut case is rated significantly less serious than the same data in summary form ($F = 8.929$; $df = 1,14$; $p = .01$).

In sum, individual comparisons do, as hypothesized, make sex discrimination less visible than do group or aggregate comparisons. When the data are presented in the form of individual comparisons, however, two cases of blatant unfairness suffice to allow one to perceive sex discrimination.

Additional Analyses

Wording

The word *discrimination* may arouse images of malicious intent. It is therefore possible that subjects are unwilling to claim that they perceive discrimination unless the evidence of unequal treatment seems extremely strong. To check the effect of wording, half of the subjects were asked a question on fairness and the other half were asked whether the institution seemed less likely to select women than men. Two separate 5 × 2 ANOVAs crossed the manner of presentation (including the control condition) with the wording of the questions. In neither analysis was there a main effect for wording. Among the subjects who received the unfairness version of the questionnaire, the scores were essentially the same when the subjects rated discrimination as when they rated unfairness ($F = 0.160; df = 1,31; p = .69$). Similarly, among the subjects who received the more neutrally worded question about the likelihood of promotion, the scores were essentially the same when the subjects responded to the question: "Would you say there is sex discrimination . . .?" as when they responded to the question "Does the University of Z [Company Z] seem less likely to promote [hire] women than men?" ($F = 1.01; df = 1,32; p = .323$).

Both of the ANOVAs showed a main effect for the manner of presentation, as would be expected from the main analyses. In both analyses, furthermore, there was a significant interaction effect; but *ad hoc* comparisons failed to indicate any particular comparison that accounted for the significant findings. On the whole, therefore, it seems very improbable that our major findings concerning the importance of information formatting are limited only to instances in which one uses the word *discrimination*.

Feminist Orientation

In the experiment by Crosby *et al.* (in press), the feminist attitudes of the subjects made no difference in their ability to perceive discrimination. Feminist attitudes were also unimportant in the present experiment. Scores extended over the full range of our 5-point item measuring self-reported feminism with a mean score of 3.09. Feminism did not correlate with the perception of discrimination overall ($r = 0.06$), the perceived likelihood of discrimination ($r = -0.08$), or the perceived seriousness of discrimination ($r = 0.10$). Nor did self-rated feminism correlate with how long the subject spent analyzing the materials ($r = -0.08$). The perception of discrimination was, in other words, quite uninfluenced by the attitudes of the subjects.

Time Spent

No limit was set on the amount of time subjects could study the materials, and the time they actually spent in coming to a determination about sex discrimination was recorded. Time spent on the materials ranged between 3 and 30 minutes; the mean was 12 minutes. The amount of time spent studying the materials did not vary as a function of the manner of presentation, as a function of gender, or as a function of the interaction of manner and gender (all Fs less than one in a 4×2 ANOVA). Nor did the ratings correlate with the amount of time spent studying the materials. The correlations between minutes spent studying the materials and (a) the perception of discrimination overall, (b) perceived likelihood of discrimination, and (c) perceived seriousness of discrimination were $r = 0.05$, $r = 0.00$, and $r = -0.02$, respectively.

DISCUSSION

To perceive sex discrimination is no simple matter. Gender inequalities that appear obvious in the aggregate seem to evaporate when one scrutinizes the relevant information in detail. With sex discrimination, as with an impressionist painting, the further you stand from the canvas, the better.

Given the difficulty of perceiving discrimination in its atomized, as opposed to aggregate form, the question arises: do some patterns of events make discrimination easier to perceive than do others? The arrangement of information was manipulated by creating a plausible scenario in which an institution made eight choices between a male and a female candidate. For each of the eight choices, there were four input characteristics on which the male could be judged superior, the female could be judged superior, or the two could be judged equal. In all versions of the story, the male was superior 12 times, the female was superior 12 times, and the two were equal 8 times. The versions differed in how the scores were distributed—spreading them out so that a subject could not discover a clear-cut case of sex discrimination or lumping them up so that a subject could see one, two, or three clear-cut cases of discrimination. We found that people can perceive the existence of sex discrimination when the materials are arranged so that there are at least two cases in which the female candidate ought to have been, but was not, chosen. Otherwise, the atomized view fails to lead to a perception of discrimination. The conclusion holds whether one asks people directly about discrimination or phrases the question otherwise.

In our experiment, as in the experiment by Crosby *et al.* (in press) that preceded this experiment, the characteristics of the subjects did not at all influence their ability to perceive discrimination. Males and females did not differ in their reactions. Nor did the subjects' self-reported feminism affect their perceptions of the materials. In the present experiment, perceptions of discrimination were entirely determined by the stimulus materials and not by attitudes and personalities. The implication for social activists is clear: if you wish to make people more aware of the sex discrimination around us, do not work on their attitudes; worry instead about how to present the materials.

The difficulty that people experience in perceiving sex discrimination at the individual level and in the absence of clear-cut examples may help to explain a paradox that has puzzled some researchers. Kahn and Crosby (1985) have documented an enormous shift during the last few decades in the average citizen's attitudes toward women in the work place and toward related issues, such as child care. Despite attitudinal change, behavioral realities have remained unchanged: along a number of dimensions, the position of women in the paid labor force today differs little from the position of women in the paid labor force at the end of World War II. As Kahn and Crosby point out, behavioral change will only come through the accumulation of individual instances in which one person or group remedies the imbalances that exist in individual organizations. But here we have a catch-22: an individual imbalance can be rectified only when one notices it; but as long as one focuses on individual instances, imbalances are virtually impossible to perceive. What is the lesson here for the social activist? We counsel patience but not resignation: as soon as the barrel contains two rotten apples, others besides yourself may also notice the smell.

REFERENCES

Abeles, R. P. (1972). *Subjective deprivation and Black militancy.* Unpublished doctoral dissertation, Harvard University.
Crosby, F. J. (1982). *Relative deprivation and working women.* New York: Oxford University Press.
Crosby, F. J. (1984a). The denial of personal discrimination. *American Behavioral Scientist,* 27, 371–386.
Crosby, F. J. (1984b). Relative deprivation in organizational settings. In B. Staw & L. L. Cummings (Eds.), *Research in organizational behavior* (Vol. 6, pp. 51–93). Greenwich, CT: JAI Press.
Crosby, F. J., Clayton, S. D., Hemker, K., & Alksnis, O. (in press). Cognitive biases of the failure to perceive discrimination. *Sex Roles.*
Deaux, K. (1979). Self evaluations of male and female managers. *Sex Roles,* 5, 571–580.

deLamater, J., & Fidell, L. S. (1971). On the status of women: An assessment and introduction. *American Behavioral Scientist, 15,* 163–171.

Guimond, S., & Dube-Simard, L. (1983). Relative deprivation theory and the Quebec Nationalist Movement. *Journal of Personality and Social Psychology, 44,* 526–535.

Kahn, W., & Crosby, F. J. (1985). Change and stasis: Discriminating between attitudes and discriminatory behavior. In L. Larwood, B. A. Gutek, & A. H. Stromberg (Eds.), *Women and work: An annual review* (Vol. 1, pp. 215–238). Beverly Hills, CA: Sage.

Lerner, M. J. (1980). *The belief in a just world.* New York: Plenum Press.

Linn, E. L. (1971). Women dentists: Career and family. *Social Problems, 18,* 393–404.

Miller, J., Labovitz, S., & Fry, L. (1975). Inequities in the organizational experiences of women and men. *Social Forces, 54,* 365–381.

Schreiber, C. T. (1979). *Changing places.* Cambridge, MA: MIT Press.

Stevens, L., & Jones, E. E. (1976). Defensive attributions and the Kelley cube. *Journal of Personality and Social Psychology, 34,* 809–820.

Walsh, M. R., & Stewart, A. (1976, March). *The professional women.* Paper presented at the Conference on Women and Mid-Life Crisis. Cornell University, Ithaca, NY.

Weaver, C. R. (1978). Sex differences in the determinants of job satisfaction. *Academy of Management Journal, 21,* 265–274.

Chapter 15

Justice as Fair and Equal Treatment before the Law

THE ROLE OF INDIVIDUAL VERSUS GROUP DECISION MAKING

SIEGFRIED LUDWIG SPORER

Previous research on the psychology of justice has taught us a great deal about various aspects of justice in interpersonal relationships; it has elaborated the guiding principles of justice considerations for small social units, such as dyads and small groups, and for the system as a whole (Brickman, Folger, Goode, & Schul, 1981). It has been concerned primarily with perceptions of fairness, both of participants and outside observers, in a great variety of conditions under which resources may be distributed (i.e., distributive justice; Homans, 1961). Although most researchers have restricted themselves to the study of positive outcomes, some others have brought the allocation of negative outcomes (e.g., in the form of punishment reactions; Miller & Vidmar, 1981) to our attention (see also Hogan & Emler, 1981, on retributive justice).

Despite these broadening conceptualizations, however, virtually all of these approaches are restricted to the intrapsychological aspects of justice. In the present paper, I will adopt a different vantage point— namely, the societal level of justice. Specifically, I would like to start with the argument that our historically evolved body of laws may be conceived as a distillation of justice considerations, many of which are based upon implicit psychological assumptions.

SIEGFRIED LUDWIG SPORER •• Erziehungswissenschaftliche Fakultät der Universität, 8500 Nürnberg 30, West Germany.

Second, I will narrow my focus on specific procedural aspects of justice to the area of legal decision making. Particularly, I will use examples from a cross-national legal perspective to advance the argument that in order to safeguard just and equal treatment before the law, the power to make important legal decisions has been bestowed upon groups rather than individual decision makers. Hence, I will examine some of the empirical evidence relevant to the inherent psychological assumption that group decision making will lead to more egalitarian treatment than individual decisions. Data from two experiments on the sentencing decisions of judges will be presented to support this point. In concluding, the fruitfulness of law-related procedural justice research for the broadening of our conceptions of justice will be argued.

IMPLICIT PSYCHOLOGICAL ASSUMPTIONS IN THE LAW

Social psychological justice researchers have focused primarily on individuals' perceptions and cognitions about what they consider to be fair or just. In contrast, I would like to start from a societal level, making the fundamental observation that society as a whole has also determined for certain domains of human conduct what it considers to be appropriate treatment of its individual members. Whether our area of concern is family law, the law of torts, tax law, or criminal law, there exists an institutionalized body of rules and regulations that reflect what our lawgivers have deemed to be just and fair solutions to the respective legal situations.

Although we do not believe that most legal systems are to be equated with justice we would also not want to go as far as to assume that they do not have anything to do with each other. One way to conceptualize their relationship is to conceive our body of laws as the distillation of justice considerations that historically have developed in the settlement of conflicting legal interests.

We are not willing to accept the fairness of the solutions the law provides for these conflicting interests at face value. But, the important point for us to note here is that many of our laws, rules, and regulations that provide these solutions themselves rest on implicit psychological assumptions that are subject to empirical investigation. Much of the recent psycholegal research has attempted to make these inherent psychological assumptions explicit, to reformulate them into testable hypotheses in light of psychological theory, and to subject them to empirical testing (Sporer, 1985). Examples in point are developmental psychological studies as a prerequisite for the determination of age norms of civil and criminal responsibility, or psycholinguistic research into the appropriate wording of judicial instructions to a jury that are supposed to guarantee an adequate understanding of the "beyond a reasonable doubt" standard by jurors.

The empirical nature of these psychological underpinnings, as well as their relativity over time and space, becomes especially transparent when we employ either a historical or a transnationally comparative perspective in our analysis of the body of legal writings (e.g., civil and criminal codes, laws of procedure, and their respective commentaries). In this perspective, the concepts of fairness of outcome and fairness of procedure that have proven useful in studies conducted at the individual level of analysis (e.g., Thibaut & Walker, 1975; Tyler, 1984) will also prove useful when employed in the present framework. Here, the contribution of psychology lies in the investigation of procedures that are perceived to be fair by both the participants in the legal process, and by society at large. Psychology also can contribute to the creation and evaluation of alternative new procedures that will produce outcomes perceived to be most fair.

EQUALITY BEFORE THE LAW AS A MINIMUM STANDARD

EQUALITY BEFORE THE LAW AS A GENERAL DESIDERATUM

The public image that a legal system has created in citizens' minds is an indirect indicator of the perceived fairness of that system. Sarat (1977) has reviewed numerous survey studies that have attempted to assess public attitudes toward the American legal system (e.g., the police, lawyers, or the courts). One of Sarat's major conclusions was that popular dissatisfaction with the legal system may be traced to unequal treatment as the single most important factor: "Americans believe that the idea of equal protections, which epitomizes what they find most valuable in their legal system, is betrayed by police, lawyers, judges and other legal officials" (Sarat, 1977, p. 434).

Moreover, this dissatisfaction appears to be greater with persons who have had contact with legal authorities than those who have not. Although the explanation for this observation is open to debate (e.g., contact with the law is often experienced in a period of personal crisis), it also lends empirical support to a sarcastic adage prevalent in German legal culture—namely, that "having to do with the courts" is to be considered as something intrinsically negative. A field experiment by Schwartz and Skolnick (1962) on the stigmatizing effects of mere involvement with legal authorities dramatically illustrates this point.

Thus, it comes as no surprise that despite their general willingness to participate in the legal system, people will do so only in a reluctant and defensive way (Sarat, 1977). If we combine these different notions, we may conclude that in general people prefer not to be bothered by the law but if they must be involved, they want to be treated fairly by being treated equally with others.

PROCEDURES TO ENSURE EQUALITY BEFORE THE LAW IN LEGAL DECISION MAKING

To make the scope of this discussion more manageable, I will restrict myself to only one aspect of the legal system—legal decision making. Past studies on citizens' satisfaction with the legal system have been conducted under the assumption that satisfaction would be determined by the absolute level of outcome (e.g., severity of sentence or magnitude of fine) received (Tyler, 1984). Tyler has criticized such a restrictive economic model by showing that outcome satisfaction is not sufficient to account for the available evidence. It needs to be replaced with a more encompassing psychological model that also takes into account the prior expectations and the fairness of both the outcomes (distributive fairness) and the procedures by which those outcomes are distributed (procedural fairness).

For example, the program of research by Thibaut and Walker (1975) and their co-workers has shown that satisfaction with verdicts is determined, in part, by the perceived fairness of the procedures by which they are determined. Tyler (1984), in his interview study of defendants in traffic and misdemeanor courts, demonstrated that the perceived fairness of the procedure—which in turn was strongly related to trial characteristics such as "Did the judge take enough time to consider your case?"—was of critical importance in explaining subjects' attitudes toward the courts over and above outcome level and outcome fairness. However, as Tyler also noted, this finding may be limited to the absolute level of the outcome at stake in this type of court. When more severe sentences are expected, outcome level may become more prevalent (e.g., Casper, 1978).

The importance placed on the principle of equality before the law is not at all a recent discovery by sociologists of law. Practically as long as we have had written histories of political constitutions and their respective legal systems (e.g., in Aristotle's writings) we find evidence that lawmakers have attempted to constitute courts in such a way as to ensure fair treatment to their citizens. And, as there also has always been the potential for abuse, procedural safeguards have been adopted to counteract aberrant decisions and to reduce the possibility for bias.

The safeguards may be of a *personal* nature. For example, only honorable citizens may qualify as lay judges, or jurors are supposed to be peers, or judges are only elected for a limited term. Safeguards may also be of a *structural* nature. Here, I am referring to the type of information made available to a judge (Schünemann, 1983), or of the importance of environmental psychological variables (e.g., the shape of a jury table, cf. Saks & Hastie, 1978). Currently, there are a variety of ongoing feasibility experiments in the Federal Republic of Germany that investigate the consequences of bifurcating the trial into two stages similar to the Anglo-American system in which the determination of guilt and the sentencing decisions are arrived at independently, or the influence of "round table discussions" on the flow of communication between trial participants in juvenile courts (Schöch, 1983). Unfortunately, these studies have not assessed the perceptions of fairness by the defendant, so we can only speculate as to the effects of these structural changes on a defendant's evaluations of outcome or acceptance of verdict and sanction.

These personal or structural safeguards may also be subsumed under the more general heading of *procedural* safeguards whose effects on the guarantee of equal treatment before the law needs to be empirically determined. Other such procedural safeguards include, among many others, the right to a public trial (by a judge or a jury), the right to counsel, and the right to appeal a decision.

One such safeguard that also may contribute to more egalitarian treatment before the law is to defer important legal decisions to more than one individual. Let us examine in more detail the evidence in support of this claim.

INDIVIDUAL VERSUS GROUP DECISION MAKING IN THE LEGAL PROCESS

EXAMPLES FROM A COMPARATIVE LEGAL ANALYSIS

The history of law has provided us with numerous examples of procedural safeguards through which the power of individual decision makers has been curtailed. Inherent in these safeguards seems to be the assumption that many individuals, when bestowed with far-reaching discretionary power, will abuse such power. Already two millennia ago, Aristotle (in *The Politics*, 1962) described how the courts had to change their members periodically either by selection or by lot—by random assignment. On the surface, this constitutional provision expressed the belief that any citizen would be considered capable of rendering judicial decisions. This belief is still shared today by any legal system that employs a jury of "peers" for the finding of truth.

Alternatively, we also may interpret this practice as an inherent distrust in the cognitive (or moral) capabilities of the individual. In such cases, the individual decision makers have to be periodically removed from office, as Aristotle had described, or they have to share their responsibilities with other court officials. This general argument is further supported from a comparative legal analysis showing that in many legal systems the most important legal decisions are ones rendered by group decision-making bodies rather than by individuals.

For example, the United States Supreme Court is composed of nine judges, but decisions at lower state courts reside in the hands of individual judges. In Austria, criminal juries are composed of eight members, and in English common law, 12 members. In the United States, there used to be 12 members but since a series of Supreme Court decisions in the 1970s (see Saks, 1977), reduction in jury size to 6 members has become possible (and is common for juries in civil cases). In fact, there have been heated debates among the courts, legal scholars, and social scientists on the effects of reducing jury size and/or changing the unanimity rule (see Saks, 1977, 1982).

In the Federal Republic of Germany, major felonies (those with an expected sentence of more than 3 years) are to be judged by three professional judges and two lay judges, whereas for lesser offenses one professional judge and two lay judges make up the bench. The German Supreme Court consists of nine members, the highest state court of five members.

The principle of deferring responsibility for a judicial decision to more than one person is not restricted to the criminal justice system. For example, in labor courts in the Federal Republic of Germany (*Arbeitsgerichte*), decisions are reached by majority rule in a tribunal of three judges, constituted by a presiding professional judge and two lay judges, one appointed by the employers' association and one by the labor union (see Brandstätter, Bleckwenn, & Kette, 1984, for an interesting empirical study of their functioning). Despite the asymmetric structure of this decision-making body (the law-trained professional judge is likely to exert more influence by virtue of his "expert power") the participation and voting right of the two lay judges from two opposite political camps supposedly guarantees that the respective divergent interests are being voiced in the discussion and enter into the final decision. Many more such examples—with some exceptions, of course—can be found in other democratically oriented countries.

The universal procedure of getting a second opinion, or even the opinion of a whole group of decision makers, is not only found in judicial and political decisions, but can be found virtually any place where no perfectly clear-cut standards for decisions exist, or where the prevailing standards cannot be employed without recourse to discretion. In any judgment of a piece of art, in judging performance in sports competitions, in evaluating the accomplishments of scientists, or even in the selection of Miss World or Mister Universe—that is, whenever the critical stimulus dimensions are ill-defined—the ultimate decision is not rendered by a lone individual, but by a decision-making group ("jury") usually composed of three or more members. Of course, the larger the decision-making body, the easier it is also to ensure representativeness of its members. This is another principle of procedural fairness (although it is not addressed here any further).

Decision Making by Jurors, Juries, and Judges: Social Psychological Evidence

As we have seen, group decision making is widely used in the legal process. However, the reasons why groups are preferred over individuals are seldom spelled out. Also, the evidence for our presumption that group decision making may further equal treatment has been at best of an indirect nature. Therefore, let us examine what social psychology suggests about this proposition.

Social psychologists have long been involved in discourse about the functions of a jury. Gustave LeBon (1895/1960) was probably one of the first to comment on the decision-making processes of the jury. Although LeBon did not think too highly of the intellectual functioning of a jury—as of any "crowd," including a gathering of scientists or even of Parliaments—he still preferred them over the individual power of the magistrates.

LeBon's astute observations were largely grounded in speculation. Since the beginning of the 1970s, however, we have witnessed a tremendous upsurge in empirical studies at the psychology–law interface, particularly in the area of juridical decision making (for recent reviews, see Horowitz & Willging, 1984; Kerr & Bray, 1982; Sales, 1981). These studies have been guided by a variety of theoretical views (e.g., information integration models, scripts, attribution, social exchange, and equity theories). They have taught us a great deal about the composition, structure, process, and outcome of juries.

However, most of these studies have been conducted with individual "jurors," rather than deliberating juries, and there are relatively few studies that have compared the effects of jury deliberation and/or group decisions with individual decision making. And of those that do, practically all are concerned with the main effects of the manipulated variables and whether or not the differences between means observed for individual decision makers are also obtained after group discussion. For example, Hans & Doob (1976) found that information about a defendant's prior criminal record—a typical extralegal factor (Sporer, 1978)—dramatically increased the likelihood of a guilty verdict by juries, but not of individuals. Other studies also have found an enhancement effect as a function of group deliberation, normally however in the direction of a more lenient decision (see Sporer, 1982, for a review). Penalty shifts of this kind—both severity and leniency shifts—usually have been discussed as special cases of the group polarization hypothesis (cf. Lamm & Myers, 1978; Sporer, 1982).

Together, these studies indicate that group discussion may lead to more extreme decisions—generally in the direction of leniency. Yet, none of the studies have been explicitly concerned with the thesis advanced here—that group decision making would lead to more egalitarian treatment. In the following sections, two experiments are reported that have specifically addressed this issue. Rather than dealing with the decision making of jurors/juries (whose primary task is the "finding of truth" in the trial), they are concerned with the sentencing behavior of judges.

SENTENCING COUNCILS AND THEIR EFFECTS ON EQUAL TREATMENT BEFORE THE LAW

Judges hold a most central and powerful position in the legal system, and probably the most significant of their activities is sentencing behavior. Sentencing behavior, as well as other decision-making processes in the criminal justice system, is most aptly characterized by the principle of *discretion* (Shaver, Gilbert, & Williams, 1975). Discretion is considered essential to guarantee flexibility in a legal system that attempts to make punishment not only fit the crime but also the criminal. However, in the sentencing process discretion has led to a frequently criticized violation of the principle of equal treatment before the law: the problem of sentencing disparity (e.g., Diamond & Zeisel, 1975; Frankel, 1972; Lovegrove, 1984; Sporer, 1982). Of course, according to equity considerations, differences in sentences are to be expected in proportion to the seriousness of the offense and/or the offender's past criminal behavior. Sentencing disparity becomes disturbing, however, when it is observed in the variability between (and within) judges' sentencing decisions for similarly situated defendants convicted of highly similar offenses (for a detailed discussion of the various types of disparities, see Sporer, 1982).

Various legal procedures have been proposed to curtail the disparity problem, that is, to heed the equality principle. There is little empirical research as to the efficacy of these reform proposals, although the available evidence does not point to a single "good" solution to the disparity problem (see Lovegrove, 1984, on appellate review; Saks, 1982, on sentencing guidelines). One possible way of reducing sentencing disparities is to employ sentencing councils in which several judges, after studying the pre-sentence report of a particular defendant, discuss what each one of them would consider as an appropriate sentence (Diamond & Zeisel, 1975; Frankel, 1972; Sporer, 1982; Zimmerman, 1976). In contrast to sentencing tribunals or jury sentencing, in which the group as a unit determines the final sentence, the council's function is purely advisory. The judge presiding over the particular case remains in charge.

From a social psychological analysis (Sporer, 1982), we would expect that the distribution of sentences after group decisions would converge toward the mean (cf. Hofstätter, 1971; Sherif, 1936)—more precisely, that there would be less variance among the sentences (i.e., less disparity) than before (Hypothesis 1). Along with the studies on jury decision making (cited above) that frequently employed sentencing as an additional dependent variable (for a review, see Kerr & Bray, 1982, pp. 290–292), we might also expect a leniency shift as a function of group discussion (Hypothesis 2). Figure 1 shows hypotheses 1 and 2 combined. In the following sections two experiments are summarized that test these hypotheses with two-member and three-member councils, respectively.

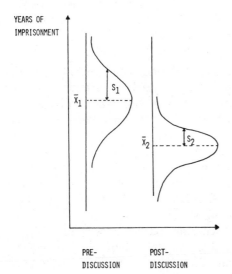

YEARS OF
IMPRISONMENT

PRE-
DISCUSSION

POST-
DISCUSSION

FIGURE 1 Hypotheses 1 and 2 combined: hypothesized reduction of variability, and leniency shift as a function of group decision.

METHOD

Subjects

Participants were 96 law students from the Franklin Peirce Law Center in Concord, New Hampshire (32 females and 64 males), who were paid for participating in the experiment. The experiment was carried out in two sessions (Experiment 1 and Experiment 2). In Experiment 1 participants were grouped randomly into 24 three-member councils ($n_1 = 72$; 48 males, 24 females). In Experiment 2 they were randomly grouped into two-member councils ($n_2 = 24$; 16 males, 8 females).

Material

Participants were presented with a detailed summary of a fictitious rape case (see Sporer, 1978, for a complete description). The case description was styled after the case summaries found in pre-sentence reports prepared by a probation officer (cf. Poulos, 1976), which frequently serve as the major information available to a judge when deliberating on his or her sentencing decision. In the case, a 35-year-old man forced an attractive woman into his car and drove off to rape her. Later on, the man was apprehended and charged with rape, to which he pleaded guilty.

Participants were asked to assume the role of judges and to decide both on a minimum sentence (after which the defendant would be eligible for parole) and a maximum sentence.

Procedure

Two experimenters (one female and one male) introduced the experiment as a study in "legal psychology," dealing with judicial sentencing. Participants were assured that no deception was involved, and they were asked to cooperate fully by judging the case after considering all its details. Each participant received a booklet containing the case description and scales for the minimum and maximum sentence. After the participants filled out the questionnaire individually, they were asked to form sentencing councils—either in groups of three members (in Experiment 1) or two members (in Experiment 2). In the councils they were instructed to discuss the sentences they had given and the reasons for it. After about 15 minutes of discussion, participants were asked to dissolve the council and again judge the defendant by themselves, "carrying the ultimate responsibility and enjoying the constitutionally guaranteed independence of judgment." Participants were then told the nature of the study and paid for participating.

Dependent Variables

Participants were asked to decide on the maximum prison sentence the defendant should receive by circling a number from 1 year to 50 years (life), and to decide on a minimum sentence by indicating after how many years the defendant should be eligible for parole, again by circling a number of years from 1 to 50. These sentencing options correspond to the maximum/minimum sentence scheme employed in many jurisdictions in the United States (cf. Sporer, 1982).

Analyses

Data were analyzed separately for Experiment 1 and Experiment 2. The reduction of disparity hypothesis was examined as a one-tailed significance test for the difference between correlated samples (Ferguson, 1976, p. 180)—which is analogous to a homogeneity of variance test—for the minimum and maximum sentences before and after group discussion. The leniency shift hypothesis was tested as two-tailed repeated measures t tests for the pre- and postdiscussion minimum and maximum sentences.

RESULTS

Reduction in Sentencing Disparity

Data for both three-member councils (Experiment 1) and two-member councils (Experiment 2) strongly suggest that sentences given after discussion in sentencing councils show considerably less overall variation (expressed as s^2) than before (see Table 1).

This was especially true for the reduction of variances for the minimum sentences; three-member councils: $t(70) = 5.145$, $p < .000015$; two-member councils: $t(22) = 3.819$, $p < .005$. For the maximum sentences, these differences in variances were also apparent but less pronounced; three-member councils: $t(70) = 1.381$, $p < .084$; two-member councils: $t(22) = 1.825$, $p < .039$.

Leniency Shifts

The leniency shift hypothesis was supported in both experiments (three-member and two-member councils) for the decision on the minimum sentence but not for the maximum sentence (see Table 2). After

TABLE 1. Reduction of Sentencing Disparity (Variance) as a Function of
Discussion in Sentencing Councils

Dependent variable	Experiment 1	Experiment 2
	Three-member council $(n = 72)$ s^2	Two-member council $(n = 24)$ s^2
Minimum sentence[a]		
Prediscussion	169.3***	130.5***
Postdiscussion	70.5	61.3
Maximum sentence[b]		
Prediscussion	246.8*	192.3**
Postdiscussion	201.3	118.3

[a]Number of years after which parole eligibility could be granted, from 0 to 50 years.
[b]Number of years of imprisonment, from 0 to 50 years (life).
*$p < .10$; **$p < .05$; ***$p < .001$ (All tests are one-tailed).

TABLE 2. Leniency Shift in Sentencing as a Function of Group
Discussion in Sentencing Councils

Dependent variable	Experiment 1	Experiment 2
	Three-member council $(n = 72)$ M	Two-member council $(n = 24)$ M
Minimum sentence[a]		
Prediscussion	13.5**	10.9*
Postdiscussion	10.3	8.5
Maximum sentence[b]		
Prediscussion	21.9	19.2
Postdiscussion	20.7	18.5

[a]Number of years after which parole eligibility could be granted, from 0 to 50 years.
[b]Number of years of imprisonment, from 0 to 50 years.
*$p < .055$; **$p < .005$ (All tests are two-tailed).

group discussion in the councils, the mock judges were willing to mitigate the minimum sentence; three-member councils: $t(71) = 2.88$, $p <$
.005; two-member councils: $t(23) = 2.02$, $p < .055$. The differences for
the maximum sentences were in the expected direction but were not
significant (both $ts < 1$).

DISCUSSION

The results of both experiments confirmed the hypotheses derived
from psychological theory on group decision making. They are also in

accord with the intuitive observations of legal scholars. As expected, sentencing disparity was significantly reduced after the council discussions than before. The fact that this finding was obtained both for three-member councils and two-member councils increases our confidence in the possibility of reducing sentencing disparity through sentencing councils. The reduction in variability was not only statistically significant, but also substantively significant: 58.3% and 53% reduction of variance of the minimum sentences, and 18.4% and 38.5% of the variance of the maximum sentences, for three-member councils and two-member councils, respectively.

It should also be noted that the reduction was more substantial for the minimum sentence (i.e., the sentence the defendant would have to spend in prison before he would be eligible for parole), than the maximum sentence. Although we have no data to explain this difference in reduction of disparity, it should be pointed out that the decision as to when to release the defendant into the community is of crucial importance. To be able to reduce this disparity, and thereby to make sentencing more egalitarian and predictable is a most desirable feature of sentencing reform (cf. Frankel, 1972; Saks, 1982).

The leniency shift observed for the minimum sentence is also of some practical importance. After discussion in the council, mock judges reduced the minimum sentence on the average by 2 to 3 years (although there were also some increases in minimum sentences that might also suggest occasional severity shifts as a function of group discussion if the evidence is perceived to be very incriminating (see Myers & Kaplan, 1976). The leniency shift here seems partially a function of the reduction of extremely harsh sentences, which implies that sentencing councils also should be considered by sentencing reformers who advocate substantial reduction in criminal sanctions (e.g., Hirsch, 1976).

We should caution the reader against overgeneralizing these findings. The present study employed a repeated measures design that is more sensitive both to the reduction of variablity and the leniency shift hypotheses. For example, the leniency shift was not obtained by Sporer (1982), who employed an extension of the Solomon-four-group design that provides a stricter test of this hypothesis. On the other hand, in that study there was strong evidence that reduction of variability could be substantially reduced within three-member councils, but not necessarily across councils as in the present study.

Discussion in sentencing councils is a very global intervention, and therefore warrants, at best, only speculative conclusions about the factors responsible for its effects. Future research will be needed to reveal the specific variables operating in sentencing councils and to establish their effectiveness for different types of cases. For example, Sporer (1982), using a case of armed robbery, showed that variability within councils after discussion was further reduced when the mock judges had not recorded their initial sentence recommendations than when they had done so (which presumably committed them more to that prejudgment).

It should also be stressed that the experimental paradigm employed here—first individual decision, then group discussion, and again independent individual decisions—presents the weakest manipulation to show the moderating effect of group discussion on the final outcome. Other, more powerful procedural interventions, such as "discussion until consensus, followed by individual judgments" (Zimmerman, 1976), majority rule vote (as in German courts), or even a unanimous group decision are conceivable, but were not employed here (to preserve the constitutionally guaranteed independence of the sentencing judge). For those forms of judicial decision making, where these more powerful forms of group discussion/decision may be legally appropriate, even stronger conformity and/or polarization effects would be expected on the basis of widely accepted social psychological theory.

Of course, the operation of many of the principles advocated here still would have to be demonstrated in naturalistic settings. Appropriately designed evaluation studies of sentencing councils (e.g., Diamond & Zeisel, 1975) or other forms of group decision making are needed before we can think of launching such far-reaching procedural reforms in the criminal justice system. But the experimental studies presented here can serve as a demonstration that such a procedural-interventionist approach (Sporer, 1982) may be a fruitful first step in studying the effects of alternative legal procedures.

CONCLUSIONS

We have started with the fundamental assumption that our historically developed body of laws incorporates basic considerations about the nature of justice that are largely subject to empirical test. A cursory comparative legal analysis reveals that, at the macrolevel of justice, the principle of equal treatment before the law seems to be of paramount importance. Drawing on a distinction from justice research on fairness of outcome and fairness of procedure, we have reviewed evidence that shows the latter to be a crucial determinant for satisfaction with the legal system.

When we focus on procedures in the criminal justice system, particularly on the area of criminal sentencing, we note that there exists a variety of procedural safeguards that may or may not help to ensure equal treatment before the law. Of the various procedures reviewed, the principle of deferring important legal decisions to groups has been analyzed both from a legal and a social psychological perspective. Two experiments are reported that show some potential benefits of group procedures for more egalitarian treatment.

Future research should elaborate additional procedural safeguards and empirically test their validity in furthering the ideal of equal treatment before the law. Other research efforts might also benefit from the approach advocated here. Justice researchers should analyze other legal principles, recouch them into (social) psychological hypotheses and test their validity empirically both *in vitro* and *in situ*.

Acknowledgments

The author gratefully acknowledges the support and advice of E. Allan Lind, Daniel C. Williams, and R. Michael Latta for the two experiments reported here. He would also like to acknowledge the thoughtful suggestions by Tom R. Tyler on the procedural justice aspects, and to Jerry Greenberg and Hans Werner Bierhoff for their constructive editorial comments on a preliminary version of this chapter.

REFERENCES

Aristotle. (1962). *The politics.* Harmondsworth: Penguin Books.
Brandstätter, H., Bleckwenn, M., & Kette, G. (1984). Decision making of industrial tribunals as described by professional and lay judges. *International Review of Applied Psychology, 33*, 137–159.
Brickman, P., Folger, R., Goode, E., & Schul, Y. (1981). Microjustice and macrojustice. In M. J. Lerner & S. C. Lerner (Eds.), *The justice motive in social behavior* (pp. 173–202). New York: Plenum Press.
Casper, J. D. (1978). Having their day in court: Defendant evaluations of the fairness of their treatment. *Law and Society Review, 12,* 237.
Diamond, S. S., & Zeisel, H. (1975). Sentencing councils: A study of sentence disparity and its reduction. *University of Chicago Law Review, 43,* 109–149.
Ferguson, G. A. (1976). *Statistical analysis in psychology and education* (4th ed.). New York: McGraw-Hill.
Frankel, M. E. (1972). *Criminal sentences.* New York: Hill & Wang.
Hans, V. P., & Doob, A. N. (1976). S.12 of the Canada Evidence Act and the deliberations of simulated juries. *Criminal Law Quarterly, 18,* 235–253.
Hirsch, A. v. (1976). *Doing justice.* New York: Hill & Wang.
Hofstätter, P. R. (1971). *Gruppendynamik [Group dynamics].* Hamburg: Rowohlt.
Hogan, R., & Emler, N. P. (1981). Retributive justice. In M. J. Lerner & S. C. Lerner (Eds.), *The justice motive in social behavior* (pp. 125–143). New York: Plenum Press.
Homans, G. C. (1961). *Social behavior: Its elementary forms.* New York: Harcourt.
Horowitz, I. A., & Willging, T. E. (1984). *The Psychology of law: Integrations and applications.* Boston, MA: Little, Brown & Company.

Kerr, N. L., & Bray, R. M. (1982). *The Psychology of the courtroom*. New York: Academic Press.

Lamm, H., & Myers, D. G. (1978). Group-induced polarization of attitudes and behavior. In L. Berkowitz (Ed.), *Advances in experimental social psychology* (Vol. 11, pp. 145–195). New York: Academic Press.

LeBon, G. (1960). *The crowd*. New York: Viking Compass Edition. (Original work published 1895)

Lovegrove, A. (1984). An empirical study of sentencing disparity among judges in an Australian criminal court. *International Review of Applied Psychology, 33,* 160–175.

Miller, D. T., & Vidmar, N. (1981). The social psychology of punishment reactions. In M. J. Lerner & S. C. Lerner (Eds.), *The justice motive in social behavior* (pp. 145–170). New York: Plenum Press.

Myers, D. G., & Kaplan, M. F. (1976). Group-induced polarization in simulated juries. *Personality and Social Psychology Bulletin, 2,* 63–66.

Poulos, J. W. (1976). *The anatomy of criminal justice*. New York: Foundation Press.

Sales, B. D. (1981). *The trial process*. New York: Plenum Press.

Saks, M. J. (1977). *Jury verdicts: The role of group size and social decision rule*. Lexington, MA: D.C. Heath.

Saks, M. J. (1982). Innovation and change in the courtroom. In N. L. Kerr & R. M. Bray (Eds.), *The psychology of the courtroom* (pp. 325–352). New York: Academic Press.

Saks, M. J., & Hastie, R. (1978). *Social psychology in court*. New York: Van Nostrand-Reinhold.

Sarat, A. (1977). Studying legal culture: An assessment of survey evidence. *Law and Society Review, 11,* 427–488.

Schöch, H. (1983). Experimente in Strafverfahren und ihre Auswirkungen auf strafrechtliche Sanktionen [Experiments in criminal proceedings and their effects on criminal sanctions]. In H. J. Kerner, H. Kury, & K. Sessar (Eds.), *Deutsche Forschungen zur Kriminalitätsentstehung und Kriminalitätskontrolle* (Vol. 6, pp. 1083–1108). Köln: Heymanns.

Schünemann, B. (1983). Experimentelle Untersuchungen zur Reform der Hauptverhandlung in Strafsachen [Experiments on the reform of the trial in penal matters]. In H. J. Kerner, H. Kury, & K. Sessar (Eds.), *Deutsche Forschungen zur Kriminalitätsentstehung und Kriminalitätskontrolle* (Vol. 6, pp. 1109–1151). Köln: Heymanns.

Schwartz, R., & Skolnick, J. (1962). A study of legal stigma. *Social Problems, 10,* 133–138.

Shaver, K. G., Gilbert, M. A., & Williams, M. C. (1975). Social psychology, criminal justice, and the principle of discretion: A selective review. *Personality and Social Psychology Bulletin, 1,* 471–484.

Sherif, M. (1936). *The psychology of social norms*. New York: Harper & Row.

Sporer, S. L. (1978). *Legal and extra-legal factors in judicial sentencing*. Unpublished master's thesis, University of New Hampshire.

Sporer, S. L. (1982). *Reducing disparity in judicial sentencing: A social-psychological approach*. Frankfurt am Main: Peter Lang Verlag.

Sporer, S. L. (1985). Rechtspsychologie vs. Forensische Psychologie [Legal psychology vs. forensic psychology]. In F. J. Hehl, V. Ebel, W. Ruch (Eds.), *Bericht über den Kongress der angewandten Psychologie*. Bonn: Deutscher Psychologenverlag.

Thibaut, J., & Walker, L. (1975). *Procedural justice: A psychological analysis*. New Jersey: Erlbaum.

Tyler, T. R. (1984). The role of perceived injustice in defendants' evaluations of their courtroom experience. *Law and Society Review, 18,* 52–74.

Zimmerman, S. E. (1976). Sentencing councils: A study by simulation. *Dissertation Abstracts International, 37,* 1819A (University Microfilms No. 76–19, 290).

Chapter 16

The Psychology of Leadership Evaluation

TOM R. TYLER

Social psychologists have a long history of interest in understanding the factors that group members consider when evaluating the leaders of organized groups (Cartwright & Zander, 1953; Gibb, 1954, 1969). This concern has been motivated by an intrinsic interest in the basis of people's satisfaction in group settings and by an instrumental concern with the effective functioning of groups. The latter concern has motivated the study of leadership evaluation because of the belief that the endorsement of group leaders by group members enhances their ability to lead effectively by conferring legitimacy on them (French & Raven, 1959).[1]

Concern over the factors used in the evaluation of leaders has not been confined to social psychologists. A similar set of concerns is also found in the writings of organizational theorists. Irrespective of whether

---

This chapter, originally presented at the conference on Justice and Intergroup Relations, Marburg, West Germany, July 19, 1984, was written while the author was a Visiting Scholar at the American Bar Foundation.

[1]Efforts by social psychologists to define leadership in interpersonal settings have focused on the ability to influence or control group tasks and outcomes (Bass, 1981; Gibb, 1968; Hollander, 1978). In the context of formal groups leaders can be defined as those who occupy formal positions of leadership. The role of those occupying such positions is to exercise authority over the nature of the tasks the group performs and the allocation of benefits and burdens controlled by the group.

TOM R. TYLER • Department of Psychology, Northwestern University, Evanston, IL 60201.

they have been considering political, legal, or industrial leadership, organizational theorists have been concerned with the basis of the evaluations of formal leaders made by the members of their groups. As among social psychologists, this concern is in part motivated by the view that the effective functioning of organizations requires the existence of a "reservoir" of good will and support on which leaders can draw. Within theoretical writings directed toward understanding political and legal organizations it has been argued that democratic governments need willing compliance with leaders on the part of followers if they are to function effectively (Easton, 1965, 1968, 1975; Engstrom & Giles, 1972; Gamson, 1968; Tyler, 1986). This willing compliance is hypothesized to grow out of positive citizen evaluations of political authorities. Similar arguments for the substantive importance of positive leadership evaluations also have been made in the context of industrial organizations (Barnard, 1938; Hollander 1978; Katz & Kahn, 1966). Industrial leaders, whether executives, managers, or union leaders, require discretionary power to be able to manage effectively. Such discretionary power depends in part on the support of those about whom management decisions are being made (see Greenberg, Chapter 18, this volume).

This chapter will focus on one of many potentially important aspects of leadership evaluation: the factors that influence group members' leadership evaluations. In other words, it will be concerned with why group members support or fail to support their leaders and/or the institutional frameworks within which those leaders operate. This question is an important one both because psychological theories differ in their predictions concerning important inputs into leadership evaluation and because those theories differ greatly in their substantive implications.

FACTORS INFLUENCING LEADERSHIP EVALUATIONS

A general typology of potential factors utilized in evaluating leaders requires distinguishing such potential inputs along two dimensions. The first is whether evaluations do or do not involve issues of fairness; the second is whether they involve judgments about outcomes or about procedures.

Traditional psychological treatments of leadership evaluation have viewed group members' evaluations of their leaders as developing from the performance of those leaders; that is, from their skill in providing benefits for group members or in solving group problems (Hollander & Julian, 1970). Such concern does not involve issues of fairness and is outcome oriented. A focus on outcomes fits well into a similar focus in the economic-theory-based public choice models that have recently dominated political and organizational theory (see Tyler, 1986).

One alternative to absolute outcome-based perspectives on leadership evaluation is to view evaluations as resulting from outcomes received relative to expectations, as in adaptation level theories (Helson, 1964). An example of such a theory is Davies' J-curve model of relative deprivation (Davies, 1962, 1969), which suggests that societal dissatisfaction results from violated expectations. This perspective utilizes the psychological concept of expectancies, but does not involve judgments of fairness, because no claim is made that reactions to violations in expectancies involve reference to concepts of fairness or deservedness (Lawler, 1977).

In addition to the previously outlined theories there is a group of psychological theories that suggests that concerns of justice or fairness are an important factor in leadership evaluation. Two bodies of psychological theory might potentially be important in a justice-based conception of leadership evaluation: theories of distributive justice and theories of procedural justice. Distributive justice is concerned with the comparison of outcomes received to some standard of fairness or deservedness (Walster, Walster, & Berscheid, 1978); procedural justice involves a judgment about the fairness of the manner in which allocation decisions are made (Thibaut & Walker, 1975).

Several recent studies in the literature on leadership evaluation have suggested that distributive fairness judgments might be an important factor in the evaluation of leaders. For example, Michener and Lawler (1975) identified two key inputs into leadership: competence, inferred from group success, and fairness, inferred from within-group reward distribution. Michener and Lawler do not explicitly label their fairness factor to be a concern with distributive fairness, but that interpretation is suggested by their discussion of fairness. It is also consistent with the general approach taken in past studies of leadership endorsement in industrial, legal, and political settings (Hollander & Julian, 1970; Sarat, 1977). The traditional emphasis on distributive fairness has been recently supplemented by an interest in the justice of the procedures by which decisions are made. This additional concern with procedural fairness has developed as a result of the important work of Thibaut and Walker (1975), work that has examined the influence of judgments about procedural fairness on outcome satisfaction. Thibaut and Walker have shown that the procedures used to settle disputes independently influence outcome satisfaction. They have done so in the context of legal trials by contrasting the inquisitorial and the adversary methods of dispute resolution (see Lind, 1982; and Walker & Lind, 1984, for reviews).

Procedural justice also has been found to be important in a wide variety of settings less formal than the courtrooms studied by Thibaut and Walker (1975). It has been found to matter in interpersonal allocations (Barrett-Howard & Tyler, 1986), in the allocation of grades by teachers (Tyler & Caine, 1981), in management decisions (Greenberg, Chapter 18, this volume; Sheppard & Lewicki, 1984), and in the resolution of conflict in managerial settings (Lissak & Sheppard, 1983). There is also some evidence that procedural justice is important in legal and political settings (Edelman, 1964; Murphy & Tanenhaus, 1969; Saphire, 1978).[2]

As this review suggests, there are several theories that identify factors thought to influence leadership evaluation. The key distinction between such theories is whether they do or do not involve attention to issues of fairness. The existence of alternative theories raises two empirical issues concerning inputs into leadership evaluation. The first is the general role of fairness—distributive and procedural—in leadership evaluations. The second is the degree to which such a fairness influence, if it is found, is linked to procedural, rather than distributive, concerns.

RESEARCH

Several recent studies on leadership evaluation have attempted to explore the role of each of the potential inputs into leadership evaluation that have been identified. Those inputs are absolute outcomes, outcomes relative to expectations, judgments of distributive justice, and judgments of procedural justice. In this chapter the influence of those factors on leadership evaluation will be examined using two recent studies. In examining these studies two issues will be addressed: (a) the relationship between overall judgments of outcome level (relative and absolute) and overall judgments of fairness (distributive and procedural), and (b) the influence of each judgment on leadership evaluation.

The first issue to be considered is whether justice judgments are distinct from outcome-level judgments. Although it is possible to distinguish between judgments about the level of outcomes received, judgments about the fairness of those outcomes, and judgments about the

[2] Anecdotal evidence from writers in a variety of fields has recognized the importance of procedural concerns in evaluating leaders. In fact, such concerns can be found as early as the classic study of democratic, autocratic and laissez-faire leadership styles conducted by Lewin, Lippitt, and White (1939). That study found that democratic leaders, whose election to office could be seen as more procedurally just, were more effective in securing voluntary group compliance. In this early work, however, such concerns were not explicitly linked to a theory of procedural justice because, prior to the work of Thibaut and Walker (1975), no theory of procedural justice existed.

fairness of the procedures by which they were determined, it is only important to do so if in natural settings individuals actually make this distinction. It is equally possible, and often suggested, that judgments about the justice or injustice of a decision or outcome are post-hoc justifications for reactions to allocations or decisions that are actually based on whether those allocations or decisions are personally beneficial (see Reis, Chapter 10, this volume). If so, such judgments should not be distinct from the outcomes a person receives and would contribute nothing to the understanding of leadership evaluation beyond what could be known from information about outcome favorability.

The second issue of concern is the influence of each judgment on leadership evaluation. Of particular interest is the relative influence of fairness judgments in relationship to judgments about the level of outcomes the leader is producing for the individual. At issue here is the basis of leadership evaluation. In other words, when group members evaluate their leaders, to what extent do they do so based on the performance of those leaders and to what extent do they do so based on the fairness of the leader's distribution of outcomes and of the procedures through which the leader makes decisions and allocates resources.

This chapter focuses on only two studies of leadership evaluation. Although many studies have considered factors influencing leadership evaluations, the two studies to be reported have two features that make them ideally suited for consideration here. First, both consider all of the potential inputs into leadership evaluation that have been outlined. Inclusion of all possible inputs is important because only such an inclusion will yield a fully specified model. Without such a model it is possible for the relative influence of a factor to be incorrectly represented. Second, both are surveys. As a result, both of the issues outlined can be explored in each study. The first study explores legal authority, the second explores political authority.

THE EVALUATION OF LEGAL AUTHORITY

In the first study (Tyler, 1984a) the influence of citizen experiences in court on citizen views about the judge and the legal system was explored. The respondents in the study were 121 citizens who had been to traffic or misdemeanor court as defendants.

Respondents were interviewed by telephone following appearances in court. In the interviews they were asked about the disposition of their case, that is, their absolute outcomes, about their outcomes relative to their prior expectations and to the outcomes of others, and about the fairness of their outcome. They were also asked about the fairness of the trial procedure. The impact of these judgments on outcome satisfaction, evaluations of the judge, and evaluations of the overall court system was then examined. From the perspective of this discussion the most important dependant variables were evaluations of the judge, the formal leader in the courtroom, and evaluations of the overall court system, which represent respondents' generalization from their personal experience to broader evaluations of the rules of the court system itself.

When the relationship between outcomes received and fairness judgments was considered, it was found that the two types of judgment were distinguishable, but not totally independent (mean $r = .39$). This suggests that respondents distinguished between the favorability of outcomes and distributive/procedural fairness, but that those who received favorable outcomes regarded their experience as fairer.

The second issue explored was the influence of outcome favorability and distributive and procedural fairness on views about the legal system. Regression analysis was used to assess this relationship (see Table 1). That analysis found that judgments about the justice or injustice of the respondent's experience had an independent impact on views

TABLE 1. Justice and the Endorsement of Legal Authorities

	Outcome satisfaction		Evaluation of the judge		Evaluation of the court	
	Beta	R^2	Beta	R^2	Beta	R^2
Outcome level						
Absolute	.02	.13***	.03	.12**	.02	.03
Relative						
To prior expectations	.16	—	.02	—	−.01	—
To others in general	.21*	—	.10	—	.17	—
To specific others	.08	—	.09	—	.16	—
Total	—	.42***	—	.27***	—	.09*
Total	—	.44***	—	.30***	—	.09*
Fairness						
Distributional	.48***	.62***	.45***	.64***	.12	.19***
Procedural	.18	.47***	.41***	.61***	.38*	.24***
Total	—	.63***	—	.70***	—	.24***
Total	—	.67***	—	.70***	—	.24***
Usefulness analysis						
Outcome level beyond fairness	—	.04***	—	.00	—	.00
Fairness beyond outcome level	—	.23***	—	.40***	—	.15***

Note. Entries in the columns marked beta are standardized regression coefficients. Entries in the columns marked R^2 are the adjusted square of the multiple correlation coefficient. From Tyler (1984a).
*$p < .05$; **$p < .01$; ***$p < .001$.

about the judge and on overall views about the court system, explaining 40% and 15% of the variance in such views, respectively, beyond what could be explained by outcome judgments. Although case dispositions (i.e., favorability of absolute outcome) and relative outcome judgments jointly influenced outcome satisfaction (R-squared = 4%), they did not independently influence the impact of the courtroom experience on evaluations of the judge or views about the court system (explaining 0% of the variance beyond fairness judgments). In other words, although case dispositions influenced outcome satisfaction, only judgments of fairness uniquely influenced views about the judge and the court.

If we look within the overall construct of fairness, the results suggest that both distributive and procedural justice were independent influences on evaluations of the judge (beta for distributive justice = .45, $p < .001$; for procedural justice beta = .41, $p < .001$). In contrast, views about the court system resulted only from judgments about the justice of the procedures used to handle the case (beta = .38, $p < .05$), not from judgments of distributive justice (beta = .12, n.s.) or from absolute outcome judgments (beta = .02, n.s.).

Although a direct influence of outcomes on attitudes toward judges and the court system was not found, it is possible that a full causal model would show assessments of justice to be partially dependent on outcomes. To examine this possibility a path analysis was conducted. The key addition of a path model is its ability to test for indirect influences of outcomes on evaluations through their influence on judgments about fairness. The results of the path analysis support the view that indirect outcome influences occur. Both case dispositions and expectancy violations influence distributive and procedural justice judgments. In other words, case outcomes and expectancy violations influence outcome satisfaction and evaluations of the judge and court system indirectly, through their influence on views about the justice of the courtroom experience. As a result, outcomes received are clearly not totally unimportant in evaluations of the judge and court. They are, however, not the major input into such evaluations. The major input is a fairness assessment.

THE EVALUATION OF POLITICAL AUTHORITY

The second study (Tyler, Rasinski, & McGraw, 1985) explored political views among a random sample of 300 Chicago-area residents interviewed by telephone during the spring of 1983. The study examined perceived inputs into evaluations of President Reagan and the political system itself. These two dependent variables were similar to those utilized in Tyler (1984a): evaluation of the formal leader and of the overall system. The difference is that in the second study evaluations were not necessarily based on a specific experience. In addition, inputs into political evaluations were more complex; people were asked about their satisfaction with government benefits, the level of taxes they paid, and with government policies.

The first inputs examined in the second study were respondents' judgments about the level of benefits they received from the federal government and the level of federal taxes they paid. For each issue respondents were asked to indicate the absolute and relative level of benefits they received and taxes they paid, as well as the fairness of the benefits they received and taxes they paid. They were also asked to judge the fairness of the procedures used to allocate benefits and to determine tax rates.

The second type of input considered concerned respondents' public policy evaluations in the economic and social arenas. Respondents were asked to indicate whether Reagan administration policies in each arena had helped or hurt them and about the distributive fairness of those policies. They were also asked about the procedural justice of the Reagan administration's policy-making process.

As in Tyler (1984a), the first empirical issue addressed in this study was the relationship between outcome based judgments not involving fairness and judgments of fairness. In the case of benefits and taxes the relationship was low, with a mean correlation of $r = .17$. With policy issues it was similar in magnitude to Tyler (1984a), with the mean $r = .36$. In other words, as in Tyler (1984a), the fairness-based and non-fairness-based judgments were distinct, but not independent. As before, those advantaged in an outcome sense were more likely to view administration policies as fair.

When the relative influence of fairness-based and non-fairness-based judgments on evaluations of the president and the government more generally was considered, it was found that the primary influence on evaluations was fairness-based judgments. This was true when the judgments considered were judgments about government policies and when they were judgments about benefits received and taxes paid (see Table 2). Judgments about personal gain and loss from the Reagan administration's economic or social policies or of personal gain or loss from the Reagan administration's allocation of benefits and taxes explained virtually no independent variance in support for Reagan or for the government itself (average R-squared under 1%). In contrast, judgments of the fairness or unfairness of policies and benefits/taxes explained a substantial amount of independent variance (average R-squared = 24%). In the case of benefit/tax satisfaction and policy agreement outcomes were slightly more important (average R-squared = 3%), but were still less important than were fairness judgments (average R-squared = 13%).

TABLE 2. Justice and the Endorsement of Political Authorities

	Benefit/tax satisfaction		Policy agreement		Evaluation of President Reagan		Trust in the national government	
	Beta	R^2	Beta	R^2	Beta	R^2	Beta	R^2
Outcome level								
Absolute	.17**	.11***	.23***	.16***	.09	.08***	.11	.08***
Relative	−.07	.00	−.01	.00	−.04	.00	−.04	.00
Total	—	.11***	—	.16***		.08***	—	.07***
Fairness								
Distributional	.11	.09***	.25***	.29***	.11*	.18***	−.01	.03**
Procedural	.38***	.24***	.27***	.30***	.47***	.41***	.61***	.34***
Total	—	.25***	—	.43***	—	.45***	—	.34***
Demographics								
Party	.08	—	.11**	—	.20***	—	−.10	—
Liberalism	−.17**	—	.16***	—	.16***	—	−.03	—
Age	−.14	—	−.01	—	−.07	—	.00	—
Education	−.02	—	−.01	—	.00	—	−.02	—
Race	.03	—	.19***	—	.06	—	.00	—
Sex	.03	—	.10*	—	.13	—	−.05	—
Total	—	.11***	—	.30***	—	.30***	—	.00
Total	—	.32***	—	.55***	—	.54***	—	.34***
Usefulness analysis								
Outcome level beyond fairness and demographics	—	.02***	—	.04***	—	.00	—	.01***
Fairness beyond level and demographics	—	.13***	—	.13***	—	.19***	—	.28***
Demographics beyond level and fairness	—	.04***	—	.09***	—	.09***	—	.00

Note. Entries in the columns marked beta are standardized regression coefficients. Entries in the columns marked R^2 are the adjusted multiple correlation coefficient. Data are from Tyler, Rasinski, and McGraw (1985).
*p < .05; **p < .01; ***p < .001.

If we distinguish between the influence of distributive and procedural fairness, it was procedural justice that was found to be the key to evaluations of President Reagan and of the government more generally (average beta = .54). In addition, in the case of evaluations of President Reagan a smaller influence of distributive justice judgments was also found (beta = .11).

As in Tyler (1984a) path analysis was utilized to examine the direct and indirect influences of outcome-based judgments on benefit/tax

satisfaction, policy agreement, evaluations of the incumbent administration, and evaluations of the government system itself. The purpose
of this analysis was to test the possibility that outcomes exert an indirect
influence on those dependent variables through their influence on fairness judgments. The results of such an analysis indicate evidence of
indirect outcome effects on justice judgments and of major direct justice
effects on satisfaction, policy agreement, and incumbent/government
evaluations. As in Study 1, outcomes do exercise some influence on
evaluations through their influence upon fairness judgments.

OTHER RESEARCH

This review has focused on only two studies. If other studies were
reviewed, however, they would suggest conclusions similar to those
reached here (see Tyler, 1986, for such a review). Similar results have
been found in other survey studies of legal and political evaluations
(Tyler, 1984b; Tyler & Caine, 1981; Tyler & Folger, 1980), in surveys
conducted in industrial settings (Alexander & Ruderman, 1984), and in
experiments in many settings (see Greenberg, Chapter 18, this volume;
and Tyler & Caine, 1981).

Particularly relevant to the questions addressed here is the study
by Alexander and Ruderman (1984). That study compared job-related
judgments of distributive and procedural fairness among 2,822 federal
employees and found the two types of judgment to be distinct, but not
independent, with a mean correlation between judgments of $r = .17$.
They also found that procedural justice judgments generally predominated over distributive justice judgments in their impact on leadership
evaluations. Similarly, Reis (Chapter 10, this volume) found evidence
for a distinct procedural fairness dimension in his examination of the
criteria used by subjects to separate various allocation methods. Unfortunately, neither of these studies includes nonfairness factors, so neither
examines the relationship between fairness and nonfairness factors.

IMPLICATIONS

The studies reviewed suggest two key conclusions about inputs
into leadership endorsement in political, legal, and industrial settings.
The first is that justice-based judgments are distinct from judgments of
personal benefit or harm. In other words, people do distinguish between
personally good or bad outcomes and fair or unfair distributions and
procedures. As a result, justice judgments are a potentially important
independent influence on leadership endorsement.

The common suggestion that justice judgments are wholly or largely *post hoc* justifications for reactions to allocations or decisions that are not actually based on fairness is not supported by either of the studies examined. Instead, fairness judgments are substantially independent of outcome-based judgments. At the same time that justice judgments are distinct from judgments about gain or loss, however, the two types of judgment are not totally independent. Those who receive positive outcomes have a self-serving tendency to view those outcomes and the procedures used to arrive at them as fairer.

The second conclusion of the studies reviewed is that justice-based judgments do have an important independent direct impact on leadership evaluations and system evaluations in natural legal, political, and industrial settings. In fact, the studies reviewed suggest that justice judgments are the major input into such evaluations. Distributive and procedural concerns influence the evaluation of formal leaders, whereas procedural concerns are the key to systemic level evaluation. Overall, the results reviewed suggest that, in formal settings, group members' leadership and systemic evaluations are heavily justice based in character, with group members acting as naive moral philosophers, judging the actions of leaders against abstract criteria of fairness.

The heavily justice-based character of leadership and system evaluations suggests that the use of economic models in organizational settings ignores important justice-based influences on evaluations. Because such models, collectively labeled theories of public choice, have dominated recent writing by organizational theorists in legal, political, and organizational settings, these results suggest a need for substantial expansion of the theoretical framework in which such evaluations are viewed (Tyler, 1986).

The principal new finding of the studies outlined is that there is a major role played by procedural fairness in leadership endorsement. In fact, the results reviewed suggest not only that procedural fairness is important, they point to procedural concerns as key factors in leadership evaluations. This finding is important because past studies of leadership endorsement have basically ignored procedural inputs and focused on outcomes. These findings suggest a need for an expanded model of potential inputs into such evaluations that includes procedural factors.[3]

---

[3]It is important to note several potential limits on the conclusions about leadership reached here. First, it is important to recognize that both of the studies reviewed in this chapter are correlational in nature. As a result, causal assertions must be made with caution. Fortunately, the correlational findings reported are supported by a number of experiments. Second, there are clear indirect effects of outcomes on leadership endorsement through the self-serving effects of outcomes on views about fairness. This suggests that outcomes have some importance in evaluations, even if only indirectly.

The studies reviewed suggest that procedural factors are important in a wide variety of allocation and dispute resolution settings. As a result, they suggest that the procedural justice hypothesis originally advanced by Thibaut and Walker (1975) may have a much broader range of applicability than the formal trial settings initially studied by those authors. This broad range of procedural influences is also illustrated by recent studies finding procedural justice effects in industrial organizations (see Greenberg, Chapter 18, this volume), and in interpersonal settings (Barrett-Howard & Tyler, 1986).

Because of the past neglect of procedural questions two important issues have not been explored: (a) understanding what people mean by procedural justice, that is, the criteria people use to establish whether or not the procedures used by leaders are fair; and (b) considering factors that mediate the degree to which procedural justice is an important issue in evaluations, that is, assessing when procedural justice matters.

THE MEANING OF PROCEDURAL JUSTICE

Given that feeling fairly treated influences leader and system evaluations, it is important to consider what it is that gives people the feeling that they have experienced a procedure that is fair. Tyler (1984a) explored that issue in the context of encounters with legal authorities and found that people place great weight on the time taken by the judge to listen to and consider their case. The idea that people value having their side of the case listened to and carefully considered is not a new one. In a manual written for judges during the 6th Dynasty (2300–2150 B.C.), the Pharoah Ptahhotep advised leaders:

> If you are a man who leads
> Listen calmly to the speech of one who pleads;
> Don't stop him from purging his body
> Of that which he planned to tell.
> A man in distress wants to pour out his heart
> More than that his case be won.
> About him who stops a plea
> One asks: "Why does he reject it?"
> Not all one pleads for can be granted,
> But a good hearing soothes the heart.
> (from Mashaw, 1981, p. 885)

Although these comments reflect the view of an authority, not of those appearing before a leader, they suggest the same sensitivity to the opportunity to speak and to have one's views considered that is found in studying defendents in court (Tyler, 1984a). Both argue that providing the opportunity for those involved to be listened to and taking the views they express seriously are important components to build into a procedure if it is desired that those subjected to it emerge feeling justly treated. Tyler and Folger (1980) reached similar conclusions in a study of police–citizen contacts. They suggested that satisfaction in such encounters is linked to citizens' views about whether their rights are taken seriously by those police officers with whom they deal.

Unfortunately, the previous discussion does not distinguish between having an opportunity to speak, or process control, and actually influencing decisions, or decision control (Thibaut & Walker, 1975). When these two factors have been considered separately, it has been found that the degree to which a procedure is seen to afford an opportunity to speak is much more important in terms of its perceived justice as a procedure than is whether decisions are actually seen as influenceable under the procedure. In fact, the opportunity to speak heightens perceived procedural justice equally under conditions of high and low decision control. In other words, people do not seem sensitive to whether or not their increased process control actually influences the decisions made when judging the justice of a procedure (Lind, Lissak, & Conlon, 1983; Tyler, Rasinski, & Spodick, 1985).

The failure of individuals to be sensitive to the issue of decision control suggests that leaders could use the important role of procedural justice concerns in evaluation as a means of social control, drawing followers' attention away from whether a procedure leads to tangible benefits and toward the opportunities it provides to state grievances. Radical critiques of American society suggest that such efforts at beguilement actually do occur, with leaders presenting citizens with the myth that their needs are an important input into decisions, when in fact they are not.

In his chapter in this volume, Cohen points out that political scientists have expressed puzzlement about why the poor, who outnumber the rich, do not use their electoral power as a means of redistributing wealth (Hochschild, 1981). Such puzzlement reflects the traditional assumption that citizen evaluations of social allocation mechanisms are focused on their outcomes; that is, that people see that they or others like themselves do not receive a fair outcome in life and reject the rules by which social status is determined. It is possible that, instead of focusing on outcomes, people are focusing on the procedures by which such outcomes are determined.

In the United States the idealized conception of the mechanism of social status allocation is an open contest in which everyone has an equal chance. As a result of equal opportunity, differences in achievement reflect differences in effort and ability rather than structural barriers to success (Schlozman & Verba, 1979; Turner, 1960). If the poor or disadvantaged focus on this procedural "myth," and view it as a just allocation procedure, without considering whether that procedure has, in fact, led them to have equal opportunity or has actually led to opportunities for social mobility, this would explain why the poor accept their status.

Of course it would be wrong to assume that procedural justice is always judged in terms of process control or voice instead of in terms of decision control. It may be that this is true in some settings, but not others. One possibility is that voice effects will occur when the decision maker is believed to be neutral—as is the case with the judges and teachers studied by Lind *et al.* (1983) and Tyler *et al.* (1985), and in systems, like the American contest mobility system, which are generally regarded as fair. In the context of industrial organizations, where workers and managers may sometimes have an adversarial relationship, decision control may be a more important means used to assess procedural justice than is process control (see Cohen, Chapter 4; and Greenberg, Chapter 18, this volume).

A more general question underlying the issue considered here is whether people always want the same things from procedures, that is, whether the justice of a procedure is always linked to the same issues. It might be, for example, that in some settings the consistency of a procedure would be the key issue in determining its fairness, whereas the ability to suppress bias would be most important in other settings. If this is the case it is unlikely that there could be universally fair procedures, because no single procedure typically maximizes all potential criteria of a just procedure. If people want different things from procedures in different settings, a typology of procedures will ultimately be required.

WHEN IS PROCEDURAL JUSTICE IMPORTANT?

Although procedural justice is clearly an important influence on leadership evaluation, it does not always have an equally important influence. An example of such varying importance is found in the previously reported research on the differing importance of outcome and procedures in influencing personal outcome satisfaction and leadership evaluation. In the case of personal outcome satisfaction, outcomes received are more important vis-à-vis procedures than is true with leadership evaluation.

One hypothesis concerning the relative influence of procedural concerns is that the degree of procedural influence depends on the goals being pursued in the relationship underlying the allocation. This argument has been made by several justice writers concerned with determining which distributive justice rules, that is, equity, equality, or need, will be utilized in an allocation (Deutsch, 1975, Chapter 1, this volume; Lamm, Chapter 3, this volume; Lamm, Kayser, & Schwinger, 1982; Mikula & Schwinger, 1978; Schwinger, Chapter 11, this volume). In that research tradition a number of studies have demonstrated that concerns about social solidarity and welfare lead to the use of equality and need as distribution rules, whereas concerns about productivity lead to the use of equity.

A goal-based approach can also be used to examine when justice will be an important issue in allocations. Barrett-Howard and Tyler (1986) did so by constructing scenarios representing possible social relationships underlying allocations (following Deutsch, 1982). Individuals were then asked to imagine themselves making allocations within that relationship, to indicate the goals they would pursue, and to estimate the importance they would place on fairness and nonfairness factors in their allocation behavior. It was found that concerns about social solidarity and welfare maximization increased the general importance attached to distributive and procedural justice in allocation decisions to a greater degree than did concerns about maximizing productivity. Maximizing productivity heightened concern with nonfairness criteria, such as implementability. In other words, the attention given to fairness depended on the goals being pursued in the interaction.

Although the results of Barrett-Howard and Tyler do not deal directly with the issue of leadership evaluation, they suggest that procedural justice will be important in a given situation when concerns about social solidarity and welfare maximization are high. Because concerns of social solidarity and welfare maximization are important to people within organizational settings, especially those involving legal and political organizations, leadership evaluations in such settings should be heavily fairness based.

The goal-based analysis presented here is similar to Folger's suggestion that people are thinking about different issues when making leadership evaluations than they are when reacting on a personal level (see Folger, Chapter 8, this volume). In addition to focusing more on issues of social solidarity and welfare, judgments about leaders may involve a longer time frame. This longer time perspective explanation is supported by Reis's finding that a focus on procedures was related to delay of gratification, that is, to a longer time perspective on rewards (Reis, Chapter 10, this volume).

The idea that procedural concerns are related to a longer time perspective is quite consistent with Easton's distinction between incumbent and system evaluations (specific vs. diffuse system support). Easton (1965, 1975) argued that support for the rules of government was based on the belief that, in the long run, one would benefit from participating in a particular political system, even if immediate decisions/ outcomes were not favorable. It seems appropriate, given that view, that the studies discussed find the strongest procedural inputs into system evaluations. Because individuals cannot judge whether to support a system based on one outcome, they must instead focus on the procedures used to reach that outcome. If those procedures are fair, they can infer that, irrespective of the outcome they have received, they will ultimately be well off if they participate in the system. In making such judgments, citizens or employees are focusing on different issues that are important in judgments of personal satisfaction.

Acknowledgments

The research described was conducted in collaboration with four graduate students in the Northwestern University Psychology Department: Edith Barrett-Howard, Eugene Griffin, Kathleen McGraw, and Kenneth Rasinski.

REFERENCES

Alexander, S., & Ruderman, M. (1983, August). *The influence of procedural and distributive justice on organizational behavior.* Paper presented at the 91st annual convention of the American Psychological Association, Anaheim, CA.

Barnard, C. I. (1938). *The functions of the executive.* Cambridge, MA: Harvard University Press.

Barrett-Howard, E., & Tyler, T. R. (1986). Procedural justice as a criterion in allocation decisions. *Journal of Personality and Social Psychology, 50,* 296–304.

Bass, B. M. (1981). *Stogdill's handbook of leadership.* New York: Free Press.

Cartwright, D., & Zander, A. (1953). *Group dynamics.* New York: Harper & Row.

Davies, J. C. (1962). Toward a theory of revolution. *American Sociological Review, 27,* 5–19.

Davies, J. C. (1969). The J-curve of rising and declining satisfactions as a cause of some great revolutions and a contained rebellion. In H. D. Graham & T. R. Gurr (Eds.), *The history of violence in America* (pp. 690–730). New York: Bantam.

Deutsch, M. (1975). Equity, equality, and need: What determines which value will be used as the basis of distributive justice? *Journal of Social Issues, 31,* 137–149.

Deutsch, M. (1982). Interdependence and psychological orientation. In V. J. Gerlega & J. Grzelak (Eds.), *Cooperation and helping behavior: Theories and research* (pp. 15–42). New York: Academic Press.

Easton, D. (1965). *A systems analysis of political life.* Chicago, IL: University of Chicago Press.

Easton, D. (1968). Political science. In D. L. Sills (Ed.), *International encyclopedia of the social sciences* (Vol. 12, pp. 282–298). New York: Macmillan.

Easton, D. (1975). A reassessment of the concept of political support. *British Journal of Political Science, 5*, 435–457.

Edelman, M. (1964). *The symbolic uses of politics.* Urbana, IL: University of Illinois Press.

Engstrom, R. L., & Giles, M. W. (1972). Expectations and images: A note on diffuse system support for legal authority. *Law and Society Review, 6*, 631–636.

Folger, R., & Greenberg, J. (1985). Procedural justice: An interpretive analysis of personnel systems. In K. Rowland & G. Ferris (Eds.), *Research in personnel and human resources management* (Vol. 3, pp. 141–183). Greenwich, CT: JAI Press.

French, J. R. P., Jr., & Raven, B. (1959). The bases of social power. In D. Cartwright (Ed.), *Studies in social power* (pp. 150–167). Ann Arbor, MI: Institute for Social Research, University of Michigan.

Gamson, W. A. (1968). *Power and discontent.* Homewood, IL: Dorsey.

Gibb, C. A. (1954). Leadership. In G. Lindzey (Ed.), *Handbook of social psychology* (Vol. 2, pp. 877–920). Cambridge, MA: Addison-Wesley.

Gibb, C. A. (1969). Leadership. In G. Lindzey and E. Aronson (Eds.), *Handbook of social psychology* (Vol. 4, pp. 205–282). Reading, MA: Addison-Wesley.

Helson, H. (1964). *Adaptation-level theory.* New York: Harper.

Hochschild, J. (1981). *What's fair.* Cambridge, MA: Harvard University Press.

Hollander, E. P. (1978). *Leadership dynamics.* New York: Free Press.

Hollander, E. P., & Julian, J. W. (1970). Studies in legitimacy, influence, and innovation. In L. Berkowitz (Ed.), *Advances in experimental social psychology* (Vol. 5, pp. 33–69). New York: Academic Press.

Katz, D., & Kahn, R. L. (1966). *The social psychology of organizations.* New York: Wiley.

Lamm, H., Kayser, E., & Schwinger, T. (1982). Justice norms and other determinants of allocation and negotiation behavior. In M. Irle (Ed.), *Studies in decision making* (pp. 359–410). New York: Walter de Gruyter.

Lawler, E., III. (1977). Satisfaction and behavior. In B. M. Staw (Ed.), *Psychological foundations of organizational behavior* (pp. 45–57). Santa Monica, CA: Goodyear.

Lewin, K., Lippitt, R., & White, R. K. (1939). Patterns of aggressive behavior in experimentally induced "social climates." *Journal of Social Psychology, 10*, 271–299.

Lind, E. A. (1982). The psychology of courtroom procedure. In N. L. Kerr & R. M. Bray (Eds.), *The psychology of the courtroom* (pp. 13–37). New York: Academic Press.

Lind, E. A., Lissak, R. I., & Conlon, D. E. (1983). Decision control and process control effects on procedural fairness judgments. *Journal of Applied Social Psychology, 13*, 338–350.

Lissak, R. I., & Sheppard, B. H. (1983). Beyond fairness: The criterion problem in research on dispute intervention. *Journal of Applied Social Psychology, 13*, 45–65.

Mashaw, J. L. (1981). Administrative due process: The quest for a dignitary theory. *Boston University Law Review, 61*, 885–931.

Michener, H. A., & Lawler, E. J. (1975). The endorsement of formal leaders: An integrative model. *Journal of Personality and Social Psychology, 31*, 216–223.

Mikula, G., & Schwinger, T. (1978). Intermember relations and reward allocations: Theoretical considerations of affects. In J. Brandstätter, J. H. Davis, & H. Schuler (Eds.), *Dynamics of group decisions* (pp. 229–250). Beverly Hills, CA: Sage.

Murphy, W. F., & Tanenhaus, J. (1969). Public opinion and the United States Supreme Court. In J. B. Grossman & J. Tanenhaus (Eds.), *Frontiers in judicial research* (pp. 273–306). New York: Wiley.

Saphire, R. B. (1978). Specifying due process values. *University of Pennsylvania Law Review, 127*, 111–195.

Sarat, A. (1977). Studying American legal culture: An assessment of survey evidence. *Law and Society Review, 11*, 427–488.

Schlozman, K. L., & Verba, S. (1979). *Injury to insult: Unemployment, class, and political response.* Cambridge, MA: Harvard University Press.

Sheppard, B. H., & Lewicki, R. J. (1984, August). *Toward dimensions of justice in supervision.* Paper presented at the 92nd annual convention of the American Psychology Association, Toronto.

Thibaut, J., & Walker, L. (1975). *Procedural justice.* Hillsdale, NJ: Erlbaum.

Turner, R. H. (1960). Sponsored and contest mobility and the school system. *American Sociological Review, 25,* 855–867.

Tyler, T. R. (1984a). The role of perceived injustice in defendants' evaluations of their courtroom experience. *Law and Society Review, 18,* 51–74.

Tyler, T. R. (1984b). Justice in the political arena. In R. Folger (Ed.), *The sense of injustice: Social psychological perspectives* (pp. 189–225). New York: Plenum Press.

Tyler, T. R. (1986). Justice and leadership endorsement. In R. R. Lau & D. O. Seals (Eds.), *Political cognition.* Hillsdale, NJ: Erlbaum.

Tyler, T. R., & Caine, A. (1981). The influence of outcomes and procedures on satisfaction with formal leaders. *Journal of Personality and Social Psychology, 41,* 642–655.

Tyler, T. R., & Folger, R. (1980). Distributional and procedural aspects of satisfaction with citizen–police encounters. *Basic and Applied Social Psychology, 1,* 281–292.

Tyler, T. R., Rasinski, K., & McGraw, K. (1985). The influence of perceived injustice on the endorsement of political leaders. *Journal of Applied Social Psychology, 15,* 700–725.

Tyler, T. R., Rasinski, K., & Spodick, N. (1985). The influence of voice upon satisfaction with leaders: Exploring the meaning of process control. *Journal of Personality and Social Psychology, 48,* 72–81.

Walker, L., & Lind, E. A. (1984). Psychological studies of procedural models. In G. M. Stephenson & J. H. Davis (Eds.), *Progress in applied social psychology* (Vol. 2, pp. 293–313). New York: Wiley.

Walster, E., Walster, G. W., & Berscheid, E. (1978). *Equity: Theory and research.* Boston: Allyn & Bacon.

Chapter 17

When Expectations and Justice Do Not Coincide

BLUE-COLLAR VISIONS OF A JUST WORLD

JOANNE MARTIN

INTRODUCTION

Psychological theories of distributive justice, such as equity, exchange, and relative deprivation, offer a picture of an economic world that is, in its broad outlines, perceived as just. For example, drawing on an extensive and persuasive body of experimental research, Lerner (1980) found that people usually expect the world to be a just place and will go to great lengths to rectify perceived injustice. If behavioral rectification is not possible, people will generally use psychological means of maintaining a "just world" view, such as blaming rape victims for their misfortune.

In accord with this just world perspective, distributive justice research has generally found that people direct their discontent only at relatively minor perturbations in the overall distribution of wealth. Thus, people usually compare what they earn to what others in comparable positions earn, expressing contentment when similar inputs, such as education, yield similar outcomes (e.g., Adams, 1965; Berkowitz & Walster, 1976; Homans, 1974). Larger inequalities in wealth, for example

JOANNE MARTIN • Graduate School of Business, Stanford University, Stanford, CA 94305.

between the rich and the poor, are not usually a source of discontent (e.g., Patchen, 1961; Runciman, 1966).

QUESTIONING THE CONTENTMENT OF THE DISADVANTAGED

It seems logical that relatively advantaged people, who are the beneficiaries of current economic distributions, would be content with expected income distributions, equating what is expected with what they consider just. But why should members of chronically disadvantaged groups feel content, as long as others are equally disadvantaged? Why do they not abandon Lerner's just world assumption and conclude that they can expect the world to be an unjust place that underrewards all members of their disadvantaged group?

There is considerable evidence that even the disadvantaged are unwilling to perceive the world as unjust. Some disadvantaged groups consistently earn less than potentially relevant comparison groups. Nevertheless, members of these disadvantaged groups often do not find their expected economic reward levels to be unjust, as indicated by research on blacks (e.g., Pettigrew, 1967), women (e.g., Crosby, 1982; Northcraft & Martin, 1982), and blue-collar workers (e.g., Patchen, 1961; Runciman, 1966).

The accuracy of this portrait of the contentment of the disadvantaged has been challenged, theoretically (e.g., Martin & Murray, 1983; Wexler, 1983) and empirically (e.g., Gurr, 1970; Martin, 1981; Skocpol, 1979; Smelser, 1980; Wedderburn, 1974). This criticism has not disturbed most distributive justice researchers, in part because they can cite congruent findings from political science and sociological research (for example, on working class conservatism, see Rainwater, 1974). In effect, distributive justice researchers have responded with Homans (1974), who declared that "It is not to say that this is some wonderful moral standard. It is simply what many men [sic] find fair" (p. 249).

But do the disadvantaged accept the existing distribution of wealth and find it just? Much of the data, cited as supporting evidence by distributive justice researchers, is misleading. What people expect has been confused with what they would consider perfectly just. Current distributions of economic or other valued outcomes—what is—are not necessarily the same as what, ideally, ought to be. Nevertheless, distributive justice research has often failed, empirically and sometimes even conceptually, to maintain this distinction. When a given distribution fails to arouse discontent or dissatisfaction, researchers conclude that the distribution is considered just. In fact, such statements may simply mean that the distribution fits expectations, perhaps expectations of injustice. Thus, theories of distributive "justice" reflect economic expectations, rather than judgments about what would be perfectly just.

The objectives of this chapter are to substantiate this claim of shortcomings in previous research, present some data that do not suffer from these shortcomings, and then, in light of those results, reconsider the claim that, for the relatively disadvantaged, expectations and justice coincide. The next section of this chapter examines how previous distributive justice research has dealt with the relationship between what is expected and what is considered just.

EQUITY AND EXCHANGE

The distinction between expectations and justice is explicitly blurred in much equity and exchange research. For example, Homans does not deny the conceptual distinction between what is expected and what is considered just, but he argues that empirically, over time, the distinction disappears:

> Any distribution of reward, however unjust it may have appeared at one time, that does in fact persist long enough—but how long is that—to become the expected thing will also become the just thing and cease to arouse resentment. (Homans, 1974, p. 263)

Homans argues that chronic discontent with an expected situation is unlikely because people do not like to feel badly about a problem that is unlikely to be ameliorated: "A man [sic] does not go on forever making comparisons that show him to be unjustly treated, if he can do nothing about it" (Homans, 1974, p. 253).

Other equity and exchange researchers are less explicit than Homans, but they, too, blur the distinction. For example, Blau (1964) acknowledges that some standards of expectations are "merely anticipations," but argues that other, more normative expectations are equivalent to moral standards of justice:

> The going rate of exchange in a group gives rise to expectations that certain returns will be received for certain services. Whereas these standards of expectation are not moral norms but merely anticipations that influence conduct, the normative expectations that a service that required a certain investment deserves a certain return are moral standards, the violation of which evokes social disapproval. (pp. 155–156)

The blurring of the conceptual distinction between expectations and perceptions of justice is often reinforced on the empirical level by the use of measures that are ambiguous. Subjects in equity and exchange research are usually asked if a reward distribution is dissatisfying, unfair, or if it causes discontent or resentment. When subjects answer, it is not clear, even with questions about fairness, whether the subjects are assessing their contentment in relation to pay levels they could reasonably expect to receive or in comparison to pay levels they would find perfectly just.

A reanalysis (Martin & Murray, 1983) of Homans's (1974) and Patchen's (1961) data suggests that expressions of contentment or fairness did not reflect belief in the justice of a given reward distribution. Instead, people were satisfied because their pay was as high as could be reasonably expected, given current industrial norms. Often, contentment with low pay was contingent on the expectation of future improvement.

A few equity and exchange researchers have drawn a careful distinction between expectations and justice. For example, Cook (1975) found support for Homans's contention, that "what is" comes to be perceived as just. However, these results occurred only when subjects' initial expectations were not clearly defined. When initial expectations were clear, violation of these expectations was perceived as unjust and, given the opportunity, subjects usually rectified the injustice. It is noteworthy, however, that both patterns of Cook's results suggest a congruence between expectations and justice—only the unexpected was considered unjust.

Austin and Walster (1974) led their subjects to expect either justice or injustice. When subjects in both conditions actually experienced injustice, distress was greater when the injustice was unexpected. Thus, even when equity and exchange researchers have been careful to maintain a conceptual and empirical distinction between expectations and justice, they have found that injustice that was a surprise caused greater distress than injustice that was expected.

This research leaves open an intriguing question: If a person expects to be unjustly treated, why does this not cause more distress than an unexpected injustice? This question is particularly germane outside the laboratory, where expected injustices, for example those experienced by racial minorities, can be expected to occur time and time again. Unexpected injustice, in contrast, is by definition a rare event.

RELATIVE DEPRIVATION

Researchers working outside the confines of equity and exchange theories have generally been careful to acknowledge the distinction between justice and expectations. This awareness, however, has not produced agreement. Relative deprivation theorists have a long-standing debate on this issue. In accord with the equity and exchange research discussed earlier, some relative deprivation researchers have argued that feelings of deprivation are generally caused by unexpected injustices (e.g., Crosby, 1976; Runciman, 1966). Others have taken the opposite point of view, insisting that feelings of deprivation are stronger when injustice is expected to persist indefinitely (e.g., Gurr, 1970; Martin & Murray, 1984). Resolution of these differences of opinion has been difficult because, as in equity and exchange research, relative deprivation studies have generally relied on ambiguous measures that blur judgments of what is considered just, what is satisfying, and what is expected (cf., Martin, 1981; Messick & Sentis, 1983).

Recently, relative deprivation researchers have made considerable progress on this issue. Cook, Crosby, and Hennigan (1977) drew a conceptual distinction between people's past and future expectations, suggesting that feelings of deprivation would be more intense when people's past estimates of the probability of improvement had been high, and when their estimates of future improvement were low. Bernstein and Crosby (1980) found evidence supporting this contention.

Folger, Rosenfield, and Rheaume (1983) clarified this argument by broadening the definition of past expectations, which they labeled feasibility, to include any "reasonable" conceptualization of a desired outcome state, whether imagined or experienced. Using this broader definition, they found that resentment was more intense when feasibility was high and the likelihood of attaining that desired state in the future was low. To restate this finding in the terms used previously, perceptions of injustice were greater when a feasible distribution of outcomes—one that could "reasonably" be expected—was unlikely to occur, that is, when expectations were violated. Once again, the possibility of chronic, expected injustice remains unexplored.

In subsequent work, Folger (Chapter 8, this volume) has further expanded this argument, arguing that perceptions of injustice stem from "referent cognitions." In addition to the usual social comparisons and reference groups that lie at the heart of equity and relative deprivation theories, these referent cognitions might include internal, nonsocial standards of comparison, such as previously held expectations, past experience, and even (and this is a new emphasis) vividly imagined alternative outcomes. Folger suggests that these imagined outcomes might be a source of comparative judgment even when no one has had experience with them. For example, ideological statements that describe the way rewards ought to be distributed could be a source of comparative discontent, even though this ideally just distribution is never realistically expected to occur. Thus, referent cognitions might include some alternative reward distributions that could reasonably be expected to exist, and other distributions that are considered perfectly just, but unlikely ever to occur.

Once this conceptual distinction is made, several interesting empirical questions emerge. The research cited above demonstrates that people can and do make comparisons to individuals, to groups, and to internal standards of what might "reasonably" be expected. However, can people—particularly disadvantaged people—envision radically different reward distributions that have never existed, do not now exist, and may never come to be? If disadvantaged people can construct visions of perfect justice, to what extent do these visions coincide with what can "reasonably" be expected?

Self-Blame and the Disadvantaged

Research on the legitimation of structural inequality is relevant to these questions. This research argues that the disadvantaged are accepting of current norms of economic distribution because they have accepted an ideological or cultural rationale that legitimizes the status quo. Wexler puts the argument succinctly:

> Social emancipation is inhibited by the internalized self-restraint and self-deformation of the powerless and the oppressed. Domination is self-limitation and it is in the accomplishment of this voluntary servitude that the operationalization of culture is important. (1983, p. 26)

Why should disadvantaged people enter this "voluntary servitude"? Psychologists and some sociologists usually offer a self-esteem or self-blame explanation. For example, Stolte (1983) argued that low reward levels produce lowered self-evaluations, so the disadvantaged come to blame themselves, concluding that they deserve no more. Locus of control research, however, suggests that this argument may be incompletely specified. Initial research on locus of control and the disadvantaged produced inconsistent results (cf., Crosby, 1976; Rotter, 1966). Subsequently, the concept and its measurement have been refined, particularly in relationship to the disadvantaged (Cohen, 1982; Gurin & Epps, 1975; Gurin & Gurin, 1976). Those refinements suggest the propositions outlined below.

When people have an internal locus of control, they tend to take personal responsibility for whatever shortcomings occur. If they receive less income than another, it is because they personally are to blame. The greater the discrepancy between one's own income and the income of a comparative referent, the greater the potential threat to an internal person's self-esteem. Thus, when members of an economically disadvantaged group have an internal locus of control, they should blame themselves for their lack of prosperity.

In contrast, people with an external locus of control tend to blame the system, rather than themselves personally, when they receive less than others. Large, as well as small, discrepancies in income levels should not threaten the self-esteem of external individuals, because whatever shortcomings occur are the fault of the system. Thus, when members of disadvantaged groups have an external locus of control, they should not blame themselves for being in a disadvantaged position.

Furthermore, the source and magnitude of discrepancies, between what is expected and what is considered just, may differ, depending on whether members of a disadvantaged group have an internal or an external locus of control. This idea is elaborated in the following, focusing on members of a particular disadvantaged group: blue-collar workers.

HYPOTHESES

To avoid threats to their self-esteem, blue-collar workers with an internal locus of control should restrict their attention to unexpected injustices that they personally can hope to rectify. Because most organizations severely limit mobility from blue-collar into management ranks, most blue-collar workers cannot reasonably expect to reach managerial pay levels. However, the highest pay level within a blue-collar job classification is usually achievable by all who remain within a given job classification, because most organizations allocate blue-collar pay primarily on the basis of seniority rather than merit. In order to avoid threats to their self-esteem, blue-collar workers with an internal locus of control should imagine perfectly just pay plans that raise the ceiling on pay levels within their own blue-collar group, rather than questioning the larger pay inequalities between labor and management. Therefore the following hypotheses were made.

1. For blue-collar workers with an internal locus of control, the magnitude of inequality among blue-collar workers that is considered just will be significantly larger than that which is expected, primarily because of a desire for a higher ceiling on blue-collar pay levels.

2. For blue-collar workers with an internal locus of control, the magnitude of inequality between blue-collar and managerial pay levels that is expected will coincide with that considered just.

Blue-collar workers with an external locus of control are expected to share, with internals, a concern with pay inequalities within blue-collar ranks. However, in contrast to internals, externals should not find consideration of large economic inequalities, for example between labor and management, threatening to their self-esteem. Although external blue-collar workers may have no realistic hope of attaining managerial pay levels, they should believe their disadvantaged position is not their own fault. Thus, externals' visions of economic justice should be freer than those of internal blue-collar workers to consider radical, broad-ranging changes in the system of reward distribution, including reduction of expected inequalities between labor and management. Therefore the following hypothesis was made.

3. For blue-collar workers with an external locus of control, the magnitude of labor–management pay inequality considered perfectly just will be significantly smaller than that which is expected.

In summary, blue-collar visions of economic distributions that are expected should differ significantly from those that are considered just. However, the specific source of that discrepancy between expectations and justice should differ, depending on the locus of control. These hypotheses were tested in the study described in the following.

METHOD

SUBJECT SAMPLE

The subjects were 83 skilled blue-collar employees, recruited from the day, evening, and night (graveyard) shifts at seven plants of a large industrial corporation. The volunteers were paid by the company, at their usual rate, for one hour's work at their plant site. The study description was brief: it was to gather "opinions about pay levels at another company."

The demographic characteristics of the subject sample were representative of the population from which they were drawn. The subjects ranged in age from 22 to 60 years, with a mean age of 41. Two percent had college degrees, 47% had quit after 1 or 2 years of college, and 51% had a high school diploma or less. Nine percent were women and 8% were black.[1] Most of these subjects were providing family support. Seventy-nine percent were currently married and 86% had children.

Some information about the subjects' wage rates is relevant as a context for understanding their visions of ideal and expected pay systems. At the time the study was conducted, these subjects were receiving wages slightly in excess of current industrial norms for highly skilled blue-collar jobs. The average weekly pay of these subjects was $299 before taxes and without overtime, an annual rate of $15,548. With overtime, the weekly rate before taxes was $360, an annual rate of $18,720.

---

[1]These small percentages precluded analysis of sex and race differences. Indeed, white males were so demographically dominant that consistent use of the female pronoun in questionnaire items, or inclusion of blacks and/or females in the stimulus materials was upsetting to pretest subjects, who erroneously concluded that the present study was a test of racial and sexual prejudice.

At this corporation, as at most corporations in the area, promotion from blue-collar into managerial ranks was an exceedingly rare event.

Locus of Control

Upon entering a conference room adjacent to their working area, the subjects were asked to complete an attitude questionnaire that contained two items measuring locus of control: (a) for people who grew up when you did, how much would you say a person's chances for getting ahead in life depended on himself/herself and how much on things beyond his/her control? and (b) thinking about your current job, how much would you say advancement depends on how well a person can do a job and how much on other things?

Subjects responded to these items on 5-point scales. The wording of these items is drawn from that used by Patchen (1961), thus facilitating comparison with his results. More importantly, locus of control has been shown to vary sharply by situation (e.g., Gurin & Epps, 1975; Gurin & Gurin, 1976). These items are the only preexisting measures that focus explicitly on job- and pay-related locus of control in a manner appropriate for use with adult subjects who hold full-time jobs.

Political Ideology

Research on the legitimation of structural inequality (e.g., Stolte, 1983) suggests that subjects with liberal or radical political viewpoints might have a more egalitarian approach to labor–management pay differentials than subjects whose political ideology is conservative. For this reason, the attitude questionnaire also contained seven items measuring aspects of political ideology. These items were answered on 7-point scales, with the endpoints (unless otherwise noted) labeled "strongly agree" and "strongly disagree":

1. Labor does not get its fair share of what it produces.
2. There will always be poverty, so people might just as well get used to the idea.
3. Every person should have a good house, even if the government has to build it for him.
4. I think the government should give a person work if he can't find another job.
5. The government ought to make sure that everyone has a good standard of living.

6. On issues like patriotism and religion, my beliefs are generally: . . .(The endpoints of this item were labeled "liberal and untraditional" and "conservative and traditional," with the midpoint being "middle-of-the-road.")
7. Considering only economic issues, my views are usually closest to those of: . . . (The endpoints of this item were labeled "Democrats" and "Republicans," with the midpoint being "middle-of-the-road.")

VIDEOTAPE

The subjects then watched an unstaged documentary videotape, filmed at a large utility corporation (not the subjects' organization). Occupants of two jobs were portrayed performing their normal tasks and, as usual, taking breaks and joking. The first job was a highly skilled blue-collar position, referred to as the technician's job. This job was technically complex, requiring manual skill and detailed knowledge of electrical equipment, much like the subjects' own job requirements.

The second job was a first level managerial position, referred to as the supervisor's job. Supervisors in the videotape were clearly older and better dressed (in a jacket and a tie) than the technicians. The supervisor's job required considerable paperwork, as well as the responsibility for handling pressure from customers and higher levels of management.

EXPECTED, SATISFYING, AND PERFECTLY JUST PAY-PLAN DESIGNS

After watching the videotape, the subjects were asked to complete a second questionnaire. They were asked to design three pay plans for the jobs portrayed in the videotape. Each pay plan consisted of six weekly pay levels (before taxes and without overtime): the highest, average, and lowest pay for technicians and the highest, average, and lowest pay for supervisors. The specifications for each pay plan were as follows.

> The Expected Pay Plan: The people in the videotape really are technicians and supervisors at a local company. Based on what you EXPECT most companies to pay people for jobs like these, how much do you think these people actually earn?
>
> The Satisfying Pay Plan: Design a pay plan that would make the average technician SATISFIED with his pay.
>
> The Pay Plan of Perfect Justice: Pretend that the government of a foreign country has hired you to design an experimental pay plan in a new kind of factory. They want you to design a pay plan that is PERFECTLY JUST AND FAIR. You can pay everyone exactly the same amount. Or you could pay the supervisors a lot more than the technicians. Or you could pay the technicians a lot more than the supervisors. Use your imagination to design an ideal pay plan that would be perfectly just and fair.

The wording of the latter pay plan, particularly the specification of a foreign country and several radically different distribution alternatives, was designed to help the subjects imagine a situation substantially different from what they had personally experienced.

RESULTS

POLITICAL PROFILE

As in previous studies of working class political attitudes, factor analysis of the seven political measures revealed a minimum of three orthogonal factors, with no single factor tapping liberalism or conservatism. The instability of these factors, depending on the type of factor analysis procedure used, was in part due to low variance. Responses to each of these items were highly skewed.

Although these attributes of the political data preclude some types of analyses, (such as contrasting the pay plans of liberal and conservative subjects), the mean scores on each item provide an informative profile of the subject sample's political attitudes. These data are presented in Table 1.

Most responses were slightly left of the middle-of-the-road midpoint of the 7-point scales, with the most liberal responses ($\bar{x} = 2.98$) reserved for the item "labor does not get its fair share of what it produces." Other items concerning more generalized redistribution of economic goals (alleviation of poverty, jobs programs, standard of living) also received left of center responses, with the exception of more conservative reactions to the item assessing attitudes about the provision

TABLE 1. Mean Scores on
Political Ideology Items

Item	Mean
Labor	2.98
Poverty	3.41
Housing	4.96
Jobs	3.45
Standard of living	3.59
Patriotism and religion	4.11
Economic views	3.08

Note. $N = 83$.

of public housing. The subjects described their economic views as closer to those of the Democrats ($\bar{x} = 3.08$) than the Republicans. This generally liberal, but certainly not radically leftist, political profile was supplemented by conservative and traditional views on the subjects of partriotism and religion. Marxist or socialist views of labor–management pay inequalities should therefore be rare among these blue-collar workers.

VISIONS OF A PERFECTLY JUST WORLD

The two locus of control items were summed, separately for each subject, then split at the median to create two groups: internals and externals. Table 2 presents the mean pay levels for each of the three pay plans, broken down by locus of control.

Before analysing these data in detail, a general overview may be helpful. The mean pay for the average paid technician in all three pay plans, for both internal and external subjects, ranged from $246 to $317 a week, figures quite close to the subjects' own mean weekly wage, $299. The mean pay levels for supervisors and technicians tended to be highest in the just pay plan, intermediate in the satisfying pay plan,

TABLE 2. Mean Expected, Satisfying, and Just Pay Levels by Locus of Control

Job level	Pay plan		
	Expected	Satisfying	Just
Lowest technician			
Internal	229	232	253
External	208	236	274
Average technician			
Internal	263	269	304
External	246	275	317
Highest technician			
Internal	309	314	361
External	288	318	385
Lowest supervisor			
Internal	302	300	326
External	306	291	308
Average supervisor			
Internal	351	353	390
External	346	333	349
Highest supervisor			
Internal	411	411	464
External	397	382	403

Note. Pay levels reported in dollars per week, before taxes, not including overtime. $N = 83$.

and lower in the expected pay plan. In all three pay plans, for both internals and externals, there was inequality within each job classification and between the two job classifications. In all three pay plans, supervisors generally earned more than technicians, although there was some overlap between the higher technician and lower supervisory pay levels. Thus, in spite of encouragement in the wording of the "perfectly just" pay plan description, none of these pay plans departed radically from current labor–management pay differentials.

One way to clarify the meaning of the pay-plan designs is to use these data to create two variables, measuring the magnitude of inequality within technician pay levels and the magnitude of inequality between the pay levels of the technicians and the supervisors.

In accord with Hypothesis 1, for internal subjects the magnitude of the inequality between the lowest and the highest pay levels for technicians was $80.24 in the expected pay plan, $81.76 in the satisfying pay plan, and $108.60 in the perfectly just pay plan. This difference between the expected and the just pay plans of the internal subjects was significant ($t = -1.69$, 77 df, $p < .05$), as was the difference between the satisfying and the just pay plans ($t = -1.89$, 77 df, $p < .05$).

As indicated by the means in Table 2, these differences were primarily due to an increase in the highest pay level for technicians in the just pay plan. Because blue-collar pay differentials are predominantly earned by seniority, a high ceiling on blue-collar pay should represent an achievable aspiration for all workers, presuming they accumulate sufficient seniority. Thus, this type of expected injustice should provide no threat to the self-esteem of blue-collar workers with an internal locus of control. A similar trend in the magnitudes of inequality within technician pay levels was found for external subjects, but differences between the expected, satisfying, and just pay plans (means = $79.51, $82.50, and $110.95, respectively) were not significant, due to large variances.

The data concerning the magnitude of inequality between blue-collar and managerial pay levels also conformed to predictions. In accord with Hypothesis 2, internal subjects found a moderately large between-group inequality in pay to be expected, satisfying, and just, as indicated by mean differences between the average pay level for technicians and the average pay level for supervisors of $88.68, $83.85, and $85.63. None of these differences among these three pay plans were significant. Thus, in accord with Hypothesis 2, for internal subjects, expected labor–management inequalities were considered just.

External subjects, in contrast, drew a sharp distinction between what they expected and what they would consider perfectly just. The external subjects expected a relatively large mean difference between the average pay for technicians and the average pay for supervisors:

$100.24. A somewhat smaller mean difference was considered satisfying, $58.33, and an even smaller mean difference, $31.46, was considered just. In accord with Hypothesis 3, the magnitude of labor–management inequality that external subjects considered just was significantly smaller than the magnitude they expected to find ($t = 2.48$, 79 df, $p < .025$). The difference between internal and external subjects, in the magnitude of the labor–management inequality considered just, was significant ($t = 2.22$, 79 df, $p < .03$).

DISCUSSION

For these blue-collar subjects, expectations and perceptions of justice did not coincide. Both internals and externals expected patterns of pay inequality they considered unjust. These results clearly indicate that it is important to maintain a conceptual and empirical distinction between what is expected and what is considered just. Use of ambiguous measures, such as dissatisfaction, discontent, resentment, or unfairness blur these distinctions. In the present study, satisfaction measures seemed to tap feelings intermediate between expectations and judgments of perfect justice, results that are consistent with previous research on the relationship between satisfaction and perceptions of justice (Messick & Sentis, 1983).

Although expectations and perceptions of justice did not coincide in the present study, the source of the discrepancy varied, as predicted, with locus of control. Blue-collar workers with an internal locus of control tended to expect injustice in the magnitude of pay inequality within the blue-collar ranks, and desired a higher ceiling on blue-collar wages; these internals generally considered expected labor–management differentials to be just. In contrast, blue-collar workers with an external locus of control tended to expect injustice in the magnitude of labor–management pay differentials, and desired a more egalitarian economic distribution than they expected to find.

LIMITED VISIONS OF PERFECT JUSTICE: WHY?

It is important to note, however, that even the external subjects' visions of perfect economic justice did not depart radically from current industrial pay norms. The questionnaire description of the perfectly just pay plan encouraged consideration of radically different imaginary alternatives. Nevertheless, even the external blue-collar subjects' just pay plans generally included considerable pay inequality in the labor and the management classifications; with minor overlap at the edges, managers consistently earned more than blue-collar workers. Thus, although expectations and perceptions of justice did differ significantly, internal and external subjects envisioned perfectly just worlds that were relatively minor variations within familiar parameters.

The results of the present study raise the problem encountered by Marxists in the late 1920s and 1930s, when the objective economic conditions in Western capitalist countries seemed generally appropriate for a revolution by the proletariat. When that revolution failed to occur, critical Marxists were puzzled: "The problem is not that the ruling class disseminates and defends its ideology; the problem is why the masses accept it." (Reich, 1972, p. 56, quoted in Wexler, 1983, p. 56).

To restate this problem in terms of the results of the present study: Why were these blue-collar employees so accepting of current norms of economic distribution? The conservatism of their visions of perfect economic justice might reflect a deep and abiding contentment with the rules that currently govern the distribution of economic goods. In accord with the legitimation of the structural inequality argument, these subjects could be classic working class conservatives who have adopted an ideology that, in Wexler's (1983) terms, facilitated their domination and "voluntary servitude."

The political ideology data in the present study makes this explanation seem unlikely. These blue-collar subjects were generally liberal on most issues, with the exceptions of public housing, religion, and patriotism. On the issue most germane to the subject of the present study, concerning labor's proper share of the goods they produce, these subjects clearly did not endorse a conservative viewpoint.

The self-esteem or self-blame explanation for acceptance of the economic status quo, favored by psychologists and some sociologists, was a somewhat more successful explanation. Blue-collar subjects with an internal locus of control were more likely than externals to focus on minor perturbations in labor and management pay differentials. However, even externals did not consider radically different changes in the magnitude of pay inequality between labor and management. Thus, locus of control offers an incomplete explanation for these blue-collar employees' acceptance of the economic status quo. These results suggest that a focus on attitudes, such as political ideology, self-esteem, or self-blame may have only limited explanatory value. In what follows, a different type of explanation is offered.

COGNITIVE LIMITS OF IMAGINATION

The acquiescence of the disadvantaged may occur for predominantly cognitive reasons. Perhaps people have a cognitively limited ability to envision radically different worlds. Cognitive research has found that, even when asked to imagine an idealized world, people generally do not stray far from what they already know. Kahneman and Tversky offer two somewhat different explanations for these findings. The first draws on prospect theory, the second, on the notion of availability. Both are outlined below, with reference to ideal states of economic justice.

Prospect theory (e.g., Tversky & Kahneman, 1981) suggests that the inherent conservativism of perfectly just world views may stem from cognitive limitations. Prospect theory describes cognitive biases that are predictable departures from the assumptions of rationality that underlie utility theory (and, not incidentally, equity and exchange theories as well). Examples of departures relevant to visions of economic justice include overvaluing small amounts of money, being overly concerned about the costs of losing (as opposed to the value of winning), and overweighting a sure small gain (in contrast to a reasonable probability of a much larger gain). Each of these departures would contribute to the construction of perfectly just world views that focus on minor perturbations in current economic distributions, not too different from current realities.

A different cognitive explanation for the conservativism of views of economic justice was suggested by Folger, Rosenfield, and Rheaume (1983). They justify their emphasis on feasibility, and what can "reasonably" be expected, with an availability argument (Tversky & Kahneman, 1973). According to this point of view, it is more difficult to conceive of things that are cognitively not readily available, so that relevant instances of a phenomenon do not easily come to mind.

Most availability research has focused on the retrieval of instances from memory. Folger and his colleagues note the relevance of a recent extension of the availability argument to include the construction of possible instances that have not yet occurred. Kahneman and Tversky (1982) refer to this process as a simulation heuristic. Results of their research indicate that subjects' imagined simulations are more likely to include "downhill" changes that remove surprising or unexpected aspects of an instance, rather than "uphill" changes (adding unlikely occurrences) or "horizontal" changes (substituting equally arbitrary or likely occurrences). These results suggest that, in accord with the findings of the present study, visions of perfectly just worlds should not deviate strongly from what has been experienced and is expected to recur.

The Generation of Radically Different Just World Views

Prospect theory and availability research offer little hope for the creation of visions of perfect justice that differ substantially from what is expected. The cognitive biases uncovered in this research are not easily changed. Even experts, such as scientists and statisticians, show similar biases in their inference processes (e.g., Nisbett & Ross, 1980).

Sewell's (1974) study of working class politics in 19th century Marseille offers an extension to the availability argument that has slightly less conservative implications for social change. Sewell argues that Marxist thought gained considerable acceptance, reflected in political activism, among the artisans of Marseille. These were relatively prosperous members of the working class, who had experienced aspects of the idealized economic world described by Marx. As craftsmen, these artisans had owned the means of production, experienced elimination of the middleman, and had directly received the profits of their labor.

In contrast to the artisans, factory workers of this period had no such first-hand experience of the alternative Marx described. Although they were objectively more destitute than the artisans, the factory workers were less active in Marxist political movements. Sewell concludes that, having enacted aspects of the Marxist alternative, the artisans were more able than the factory workers to accept and work towards this vision of economic justice.

To restate Sewell's (1974) argument in availability terms, the Marxist vision of justice was more available to the artisans, who had lived through aspects of this vision, than to the factory workers, who had only heard about or observed these alternatives. Sewell's research suggests that disadvantaged people may be able to generate visions of perfect justice that differ substantially from what is expected only if they have enacted central aspects of those visions. Observation or *post hoc*, second-hand accounts can not substitute for participation.

If this explanation is correct, then it may be possible to enlarge visions of justice through participation in small experiments that demonstrate alternative ways of distributing economic outcomes. In this context, small scale innovations (such as communes, employee ownership plans, and charitable drives) seem less quixotic in their often short-lived isolation. Perhaps people must live through an alternative before they can envision it on a larger scale.

REFERENCES

Adams, J. S. (1965). Inequity in social exchange. In L. Berkowitz (Ed.), *Advances in experimental social psychology* (Vol. 2, pp. 267–299). New York: Academic Press.

Austin, W., & Walster, E. (1974). Reactions to confirmations and disconfirmations of expectancies of equity and inequity. *Journal of Personality and Social Psychology, 30,* 208–216.

Berkowitz, L., & Walster, E. (Eds.). (1976). *Advances in experimental social psychology* (Vol. 9). New York: Academic Press.

Bernstein, M., & Crosby, F. (1980). An empirical examination of relative deprivation theory. *Journal of Experimental Social Psychology, 16,* 442–456.

Blau, P. M. (1964). *Exchange and power in social life.* New York: Wiley.

Cohen, R. L. (1982). Perceiving justice: An attributional perspective. In J. Greenberg & R. L. Cohen (Eds.), *Equity and justice in social behavior* (pp. 119–160). New York: Academic Press.

Cook, K. (1975). Expectations, evaluations, and equity. *American Sociological Review, 40,* 372–388.

Cook, T. D., Crosby, F., & Hennigan, K. M. (1977). The construct validity of relative deprivation. In J. M. Suls & R. L. Miller (Eds.), *Social comparison process: Theoretical and empirical perspectives* (pp. 307–333). New York: Hemisphere Press.

Crosby, F. (1976). A model of egoistical relative deprivation. *Psychological Review, 83,* 85–113.

Crosby, F. (1982). *Relative deprivation and working women.* New York: Oxford University Press.

Folger, R., Rosenfield, D., & Rheaume, K. (1983). Roleplaying effects of likelihood and referent outcomes on relative deprivation. *Representative Research in Social Psychology, 13,* 2–10.

Gurin, P., & Epps, E. (1975). *Black consciousness, identity and achievement: A study of students in historically black colleges.* New York: Wiley.

Gurin, G., & Gurin, P. (1976). Personal efficacy and the ideology of personal responsibility. In B. Strumpel (Ed.), *Economic means for human needs: Social indicators of well-being and discontent* (pp. 131–157). Ann Arbor, MI: Institute for Social Research.

Gurr, T. R. (1970). *Why men rebel.* Princeton, NJ: Princeton University Press.

Homans, G. C. (1974). *Social behavior: Its elementary forms.* New York: Harcourt Brace Jovanovich.

Kahneman, D., & Tversky, A. (1982). The simulation heuristic. In D. Kahneman, P. Slovik, & A. Tversky (Eds.), *Judgment under uncertainty: Heuristics and biases* (pp. 200–208). New York: Cambridge University Press.

Lerner, M. J. (1980). *The belief in a just world: A fundamental delusion.* New York: Plenum Press.

Martin, J. (1981). Relative deprivation: A theory of distributive injustice for an era of shrinking resources. In L. L. Cummings & B. M. Staw (Eds.), *Research in Organizational Behavior* (Vol. 3, pp. 53–107). Greenwich, CT: JAI Press.

Martin, J., & Murray, A. (1983). Distributive injustice and unfair exchange. In D. M. Messick & K. S. Cook (Eds.), *Theories of equity: Psychological and sociological perspectives* (pp. 169–205). New York: Praeger.

Martin, J., & Murray, A. (1984). Catalysts for collective violence: The importance of a psychological approach. In R. Folger (Ed.), *The sense of injustice: Social psychological perspectives* (pp. 95–139). New York: Plenum Press.

Messick, D. M., & Sentis, K. (1983). Fairness, preference, and fairness biases. In D. M. Messick & K. S. Cook (Eds.), *Equity theory: Psychological and sociological perspectives* (pp. 61–94). New York: Praeger.

Nisbett, R., & Ross, L. (1980). *Human inference: Strategies and shortcomings of social judgment.* Englewood Cliffs, NJ: Prentice-Hall.

Northcraft, G., & Martin, J. (1982). Double jeopardy: Why some women and minorities object to affirmative action programs. In B. Gutek (Ed.), *Sex-role stereotyping and affirmative action policy: Problems, processes, and solutions* (pp. 81–130). Los Angeles, CA: Institute for Industrial Relations, University of California at Los Angeles.

Patchen, M. (1961). *The choice of wage comparisons.* Englewood Cliffs, NJ: Prentice-Hall.

Pettigrew, T. (1967). Social evaluation theory: Convergences and applications. In D. Levine (Ed.), *Nebraska symposium on motivation* (Vol. 3, pp. 241–318). Lincoln, NE: University of Nebraska Press.

Rainwater, L. (1974). *What money buys: Inequality and the social meaning of income*. New York: Basic Books.

Reich, W. (1972). *Character analysis* (Revised edition translated from the German by V. R. Carfagno). New York: Farrar, Straus, & Giroux, Inc.

Rotter, J. B. (1966). Generalized expectancies for internal versus external control of reinforcement. *Psychological Monographs: General and Applied, 80*(1), 1–28.

Rubin, Z., & Peplau, L. A. (1975). Who believes in a just world? *Journal of Social Issues, 31*(3), 65–89.

Runciman, W. G. (1966). *Relative deprivation and social justice: A study of attitudes to social inequality in twentieth century England*. London: Routledge & Kegan Paul.

Sewell, W. H., Jr. (1974, November). Social change and the rise of working-class politics in 19th century Marseille. *Past and Present*, pp. 75–109.

Skocpol, T. (1979). *States and social revolutions*. Cambridge: Cambridge University Press.

Smelser, N. (1980). Theoretical issues of scope and problems. In M. D. Pugh (Ed.), *Collective behavior: A source book* (pp. 7–11). St. Paul, MN: West. (Reprinted from the *Sociological Quarterly*, 1964, 5, 116–122.)

Stolte, J. F. (1983). The legitimation of structural inequality: Reformulation and test of the self-evaluation argument. *American Sociological Review, 48*, 331–342.

Tversky, A., & Kahneman, D. (1973). Availability: A heuristic for judging frequency and probability. *Cognitive Psychology, 4*, 207–232.

Tversky, A., & Kahneman, D. (1981). The framing of decisions and the psychology of choice. *Science, 221*, 453–458.

Wedderburn, D. (Ed.). (1974). *Poverty, inequality, and class structure*. London: Cambridge University Press.

Wexler, P. (1983). *Critical social psychology*. Boston, MA: Routledge & Kegan Paul.

Chapter 18

The Distributive Justice of Organizational Performance Evaluations

JERALD GREENBERG

Traditionally, concern about matters of justice and fairness among scientists interested in organizational behavior has focused on ways of determining equitable payment and assessing behavioral and attitudinal reactions to inequitable payment (Greenberg, 1982). This orientation toward money as the primary medium through which justice is studied is reflected not only in some of the other contributions to this volume on justice, but also in much of the organizational literature (e.g., Vecchio, 1982). At the same time, however, there also appears to be a growing recognition that matters of justice are involved in several nonfinancial exchanges taking place within organizations (see Nord, 1980). The chapter by Martin (Chapter 17, this volume) and the recent chapter by Crosby (1984) in an organizationally oriented serial represent excellent examples of this trend. Much of the present author's recent work on procedural justice (e.g., Folger & Greenberg, 1985, Greenberg, in press-a) also reflects an appreciation for the idea that considerations of justice are involved in many forms of nonmonetary social exchange in organizations.

JERALD GREENBERG • Faculty of Management and Human Resources, Ohio State University, Columbus, OH 43210-1399. Preparation of this chapter was supported in part by grant INT-8304375 from the National Science Foundation.

The present chapter is in keeping with this orientation. It represents an outgrowth of the author's recent conceptual statements (Folger & Greenberg, 1985; Greenberg & Folger, 1983; Greenberg & Tyler, 1986) and empirical reports (Greenberg, 1986, in press-a,b) demonstrating how concerns about justice manifest themselves in one particular aspect of organizational life—performance appraisal. Specifically, the present chapter will present some new conceptualizations of distributive justice that are relevant to performance appraisal situations and some data that bear on them. The focus will be on *distributive justice*—the fairness of evaluations received—as opposed to *procedural justice*—the fairness of the procedures on which those evaluations are based, a topic treated in detail elsewhere (Greenberg, in press-a). After presenting these ideas, their implications, both for conceptualizations of justice and for organizational theory and practice, will be discussed.

DISTRIBUTIVE JUSTICE IN THE CONTEXT OF PERFORMANCE APPRAISAL

One day not long ago one of the author's students, in an obviously distressed state, came to his office. She found a grade of "D" on her university grade report despite the fact that she had received positive performance feedback all term long. On further investigating this situation, the author found that he actually had given the student a grade of "A," but that a clerical error in another office was responsible for the much lower grade she received. After arranging for an official correction of the student's grade, the author began thinking about how typical the problem faced by this student probably was—at least as it may exist in the minds of offended parties.

Although the young woman in this story was actually the innocent victim of a clerical error, anyone who has ever taught probably has encountered students who believed the final grade they received was not representative of the quality of work they performed. In many ways, this claim is similar to that voiced by workers who complain that the pay raises they receive are not commensurate with their positive performance evaluations. Their distress, of course, can be readily understood in terms of equity theory's claim that persons receiving outcomes (a final grade in the case of the student and a pay raise in the case of the worker) lower than merited by their inputs (their academic performance or job performance, respectively) will feel angry (Adams, 1965; Walster, Walster, & Berscheid, 1978).

CHANNELS OF INFLUENCE IN APPRAISAL SYSTEMS

As appealing as this reasoning may be, it overlooks an important aspect of the situation (one that came up in discussion with the distressed student)—namely, whether the performance evaluation is viewed as an outcome in itself, or an input that demands certain other associated outcomes for equity to be established. An illustration summarizing the structural elements of justice in a performance evaluation situation is shown in Figure 1. The diagram shows two distinct channels of influence operating in a performance appraisal system: a direct one and an indirect one. That is, evaluations can either operate as outcomes themselves or serve as intermediate steps through which administrative decisions, operating as outcome, are made.

Let us consider how these processes may have been operating in the case of the author's distressed student. It will be recalled that the student thought the professor believed her to be performing at a high level of proficiency. If this evaluation is taken as a direct outcome—an intrinsic reward (Deci, 1975)—the student would be positively influenced. She would feel proud and happy that she performed well and pleased the evaluating authority figure. However, as it was (and often is the case), the positive evaluation was not responded to as an end in itself. Instead, it operated indirectly, as a secondary reinforcer that should have led to a positive administrative decision that accurately reflected the positive evaluation. In this sense, the evaluation operated more as an input than as an outcome. By defining her inputs as positive, an expectation was created for receipt of an administrative reward that reflected that evaluation.

The author has encountered the same phenomenon in some of his organizational consulting experiences. Workers are often distressed at not being paid in a manner consistent with their evaluations. Knowing

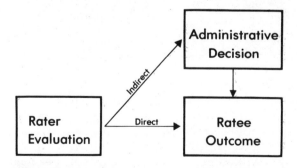

FIGURE 1.   Channels of influence in organizational performance appraisal systems.

that this happens (sometimes because of economic difficulties within their organizations), supervisors sometimes give low performance ratings merely to justify the low pay raises they know will be forthcoming. The cost of doing this, of course, is borne in terms of the worker's job development. "Why," a worker might ask, "if I am doing everything correctly, am I receiving a poor evaluation?" Using the evaluation to justify the outcome may bring about an immediate reward–performance congruity, but because the performance feedback is inaccurate, it might also be very detrimental to employee training and development (Wexley & Latham, 1981).

These illustrations highlight some very fundamental, yet often overlooked, points about justice in work organizations, especially the role of performance evaluations in assessing the justice of organizational outcomes. By focusing on the relationship between performance evaluations and distributive justice it is the intent of the present chapter to shed some new light on both the study of justice and the study and practice of organizational phenomena.

PERFORMANCE APPRAISAL AND ORGANIZATIONAL JUSTICE

By *performance appraisal*, we are referring to "the process by which an organization measures and evaluates an individual employee's behavior and accomplishments for a finite time period" (DeVries, Morrison, Shullman, & Gerlach, 1981, p. 2). It is a process that occurs in one form or another in most contemporary business and government organizations (Bernardin & Beatty, 1984). Although performance evaluations are used to help develop employees' skills and to facilitate the making of personnel decisions, it is safe to say that much of industry's concern about performance appraisals comes as a reaction to attempts to comply with recent legislation and court rulings demanding the use of *fair* appraisal procedures. Although it is beyond the scope of the present chapter to detail the performance appraisal process and the legal rulings bearing on it (the interested reader is referred to Latham & Wexley, 1981), Table 1 summarizes this information vis-à-vis their corresponding organizational justice concerns.

As this table shows, the appraisal phases in which job information is collected (steps 1 and 2) and performance ratings are made (steps 3 through 5) are conceptualized as bearing more on matters of procedural justice than distributive justice (and are analyzed by Greenberg, in press-a). It is those phases of the performance appraisal process in which evaluations are communicated and appropriate administrative actions are taken (steps 6 through 8) that relate most clearly to distributive justice—the focus of the present chapter. Indeed, laws such as the 1978

TABLE 1. Performance Appraisal: Steps, Legal Considerations, and Organizational Justice Issues

Performance appraisal steps[a]	Legal considerations[b]	Organizational justice issues
1. Conduct job analysis 2. Develop appraisal instruments	Evaluations must be based on the work actually done. Instruments must tap job-relevant criteria.	
3. Select raters 4. Train raters 5. Measure performance	Raters must be familiar with the work, the rating scales, and must have an opportunity to observe and measure the ratees' performances.	Procedural justice: appraisal procedures should be free from biasing influences.
6. Share appraisal with ratee 7. Set new performance goals 8. Reward or punish performance	Qualifications for pay raises, promotions and transfers must be publicized. Personnel decisions must be justified by a valid performance appraisal procedure.	Distributive justice: administrative decisions should be commensurate with appraisal outcomes.

[a]Adapted from Latham & Wexley (1981).
[b]Adapted from Klasson, Thompson, & Luben (1980).

Civil Service Reform Act clearly require personnel actions to be based on employees' (validly assessed) job skills and qualifications (see Klasson, Thompson, & Luben, 1980). Using the terminology of justice researchers, we would say that distributive justice requires administrative decisions to be commensurate with appraisal outcomes. In the following sections of this chapter we will analyze the conceptual complexities involved in implementing these requirements.

A TAXONOMY OF ORGANIZATIONAL PERFORMANCE EVALUATIONS AS OUTCOMES

In many ways the performance evaluations received in work settings can be understood as being outcomes in the sense of the term suggested by equity theory. They are received in recognition of workers' accomplishments. A positive evaluation is, after all, rewarding and a negative one is punishing, regardless of whether or not it is followed up by appropriate administrative actions. In fact, the high status that workers are accorded from positive evaluations are specifically identified by Adams (1965, p. 278) as an outcome. As we have already noted, however, a performance evaluation may not always function as an outcome directly (recall Figure 1). It may be direct in that the positive evaluation can function as an end in itself. Alternatively, it can function indirectly by leading to the administration of other rewards. Table 2 will help us examine more closely the implications of these direct and indirect avenues of influence by presenting a classification system of evaluations as outcomes.

This simple taxonomy is composed of two dimensions: terminality of evaluation and level of analysis. The *terminality* dimension is used to distinguish between how final, or terminal, the evaluations are as outcomes. A distinction is made between penultimate outcomes and ultimate outcomes. An evaluation operating as a *penultimate outcome* is one that leads to other outcome judgments. An *ultimate outcome* is one that functions as an end state in itself. A distinction is also made with respect to the level of analysis by which outcomes can operate. A distinction is made between outcomes that influence employees' organizational standing and those that influence their psychological state.

For example, a positive evaluation would be considered a penultimate outcome if it serves as the basis of a subsequent organizational decision to give the good worker a high pay raise or a promotion. At a more psychological level we also may consider attributions of performance causality to be penultimate outcome evaluations. These are judgments about what causes a person's behavior, judgments that lead to subsequent judgments about what the person is like as a worker. These

TABLE 2. A Classification System of Evaluations as Outcomes

Level of analysis	Terminality of Evaluation	
	Penultimate (Evaluations leading to other outcome judgments)	Ultimate (Evaluations as end-state judgments)
Psychological	Attributional mediation of performance	Communication of self-worth and value
Organizational	Administrative decisions (e.g., salary, promotion, entry into training programs)	Communication of career potential

correspondent inferences (Jones & Davis, 1965) are penultimate relative to more general performance judgments. (For example, the evaluations that someone produced twice as many units as the average employee may lead to the judgment that he or she is a good worker.)

Evaluations can also operate as ultimate outcomes. As such, they operate as end-state judgments in themselves. A positive evaluation of a worker's performance can function at a psychological level of impact by communicating the rater's beliefs about the worker's worth to the organization. A positive evaluation may mean a good feeling for the worker (Leskovec, 1967). From an organizational perspective, a positive evaluation can have a related positive impact by communicating something encouraging about the employee's future with the organization.

In the case of evaluations as ultimate outcomes, we may expect them to operate like any other outcome in the equity equation. This expectation stands regardless of the fact that performance evaluations have not previously been studied as outcomes from an equity theory perspective. Even more interesting situations emerge if we consider how performance evaluations may function indirectly, as penultimate outcomes. Before proceeding further with this analysis, it is necessary to engage in a slight digression to clarify an important underlying assumption.

THE INPUT-DEFINING FUNCTION OF ORGANIZATIONAL PERFORMANCE EVALUATIONS

It is important to note that the ambiguity of performance standards on many jobs may make it difficult, if not impossible, for workers to know exactly how well or poorly they are working. (This is contrasted with laboratory studies, in which explicit input feedback is provided.) In this sense, it can be said that the *evaluation serves an input-defining function*. Cognitive theories of motivation, such as expectancy theory (e.g., Vroom, 1964) suggest that *expectancy* (the perceived link between effort and performance) and *instrumentality* (the perceived link between performance and reward) contribute to motivation. As illustrated in Figure 2, performance appraisal may be seen as playing an important role in defining the quality of one's inputs. Not knowing how good a "good job" is, performance appraisals may help workers to define the quality of their inputs, which may, in turn, create outcome expectations.

It is precisely in this connection that concerns about distributive justice arise. An organizational authority agent who appraises performance can lead workers to accept as legitimate their assessment of the

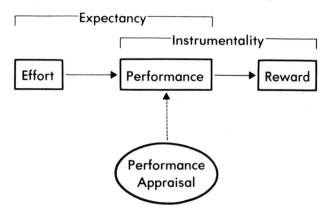

FIGURE 2.   Performance appraisal in the context of expectancy theory.

worker's performance. The appraiser who does this, in effect, creates expectations for outcomes. If these ultimate outcomes (pay) match the appraisals, then the reward received will be seen as fair. If they do not match, they will likely be seen as unfair. This is precisely what equity theory predicts.

PERFORMANCE EVALUATIONS AS ULTIMATE AND PENULTIMATE OUTCOMES: RESEARCH EVIDENCE

Several of the author's recent studies address these predictions. These investigations simultaneously demonstrate how evaluations may operate as ultimate and penultimate outcomes.

USING PERFORMANCE EVALUATIONS TO QUALIFY REACTIONS TO MONETARY OUTCOMES

In one study, Greenberg (1984) had 176 college students perform a clerical task that had an ambiguous performance referent—one that made it difficult for them to be able to tell how well or poorly they were doing until they were told. Specifically, the task consisted of copying numbers from a printed list onto a computer coding form, a task found to be highly susceptible to acceptance of false performance feedback in several earlier studies (e.g., Greenberg, 1977). Twice during their work periods subjects were given either very positive or very negative performance evaluations. Specifically, they were told either that they had been performing "much better than" or "much worse than" most others.

Also manipulated was the terminality of the evaluation. This was accomplished by either paying subjects for their work or by not paying them at all. It was reasoned that a monetary payment would make the evaluations operate as penultimate outcomes—ones whose satisfaction would be gauged relative to the ultimate outcomes, the monetary payment. As equity theory suggests, payment outcomes congruent with evaluations (acting, in this case, as inputs) would lead to more positive reactions than incongruent states. By contrast, no monetary payments would make the evaluations operate as outcomes themselves. As a hedonic comparison (Brickman & Bulman, 1977), workers would be expected to be more satisfied with positive evaluations than with negative ones. With this in mind, an outcome manipulation was designed in which subjects received either higher pay than expected, lower pay than expected, or no pay, with none expected.

The dependent variable of interest was a satisfaction index. It consisted of a cluster of highly intercorrelated questionnaire measures assessing overall satisfaction with the experiment, satisfaction with the experimenter, and fairness of treatment in the experiment. The pattern of mean satisfaction-index scores as a function of payment (outcome terminality) and performance evaluation is shown in Figure 3.

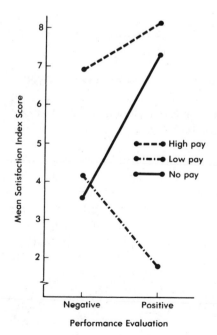

FIGURE 3.   Mean levels of reported satisfaction as a function of performance evaluation and payment level in the study by Greenberg (1984).

These results support the above outlined hypotheses. Specifically, it was found that subjects were more satisfied with high pay than low pay overall, but this was qualified by the evaluation they received. Subjects were more satisfied with their low pay when they believe it followed from poor performance evaluations than from good ones. In fact, no workers were more upset than poorly paid good workers. Although the effect was not as great for highly paid workers, the high payment following from a poor evaluation lowered satisfaction relative to highly paid workers who were positively evaluated, although not to a statistically significant degree. These findings are perfectly in keeping with equity theory's predictions regarding the balance of outcomes and inputs as a determinant of satisfaction (see Walster *et al.*, 1978).

The more interesting aspect of these findings resides in the case in which evaluations served as ultimate outcomes (i.e., the no pay condition). In this case, satisfaction was found to be as high or as low as it was when pay and performance evaluations were congruent. High evaluations seemed to serve as positive outcomes in themselves, making workers feel highly satisfied. Low evaluations seemed to serve as negative outcomes in themselves, making workers feel dissatisfied.

These data, then, show how evaluations of performance can serve as ultimate outcomes themselves, or as penultimate outcomes (acting as inputs, creating expectations for monetary rewards).

USING PERFORMANCE EVALUATIONS TO QUALIFY REACTIONS TO JOB TITLES AS OUTCOMES

Another illustration of this phenomenon can be seen in two studies by Greenberg and Ornstein (1983). These investigations, only a small portion of which will be reported here, were designed to demonstrate a related idea about the ambiguity of high status job titles—whether they operated as outcomes or as inputs.

The subjects in these investigations were college students who performed a proofreading task in exchange for pay. In the earned title condition, subjects were told that they had performed very well. This good performance, they were told, earned them the title of "senior proofreader" and the added responsibility of checking others' work during an additional hour for which they would not be paid. In the unearned title condition the title and the extra work were given, but without any performance evaluation serving as the basis of the decision. In two experiments it was found that by the end of the final work period, subjects in the unearned title condition were performing at a significantly lower level than their counterparts in the earned title condition. It will be recalled that the difference between the two conditions was that a positive performance evaluation preceded the decision to grant the high status job title and the associated responsibilities in the earned title condition. In other words, subjects performed at a higher level when they were given a high status job title and a positive evaluation than when they were just given the high status job title without any performance evaluation.

The positive performance evaluation justified the higher status and added responsibilities, leading workers to feel their treatment was equitable, and to maintain a consistently high level of performance. The performance evaluation made the high status appear real and accepted as genuine. However, without any evaluation, subjects ultimately believed that the experimenter was being manipulative—giving them a meaningless title in an attempt to justify the increased inputs expected of them. This illustrates another sense in which evaluations may serve as indirect influences on outcomes. The evaluation justified the bestowal of high status as legitimate and warranted, thereby legitimizing the expected increase in inputs. The granting of the identical status without an appraisal led subjects to challenge the subsequent rewards. Simply put, the evaluation information qualified the effects of other outcomes.

To summarize, these studies show that performance evaluations can alter perceptions of inputs and outcomes, therefore altering perceptions of distributive justice.

IMPLICATIONS

If the foregoing analyses have any value, it is to be found in their implications—both for conceptualizations of distributive justice and for organizational theory and practice. We will turn our attention to these implications in this closing section.

IMPLICATIONS FOR CONCEPTUALIZATIONS OF DISTRIBUTIVE JUSTICE

One of the primary implications of studying distributive justice in the context of performance appraisals is that doing so highlights the importance of several previously neglected aspects of distributive justice. Most basic in this regard is the suggestion that performance evaluations can function as outcomes in affecting people's perceptions of distributive justice. This is not only a contribution in that it redirects our attention from more traditionally studied monetary outcomes, but also in that it qualifies our understanding of monetary outcomes. The research summarized in this chapter clearly demonstrates that the perceived meaning of pay and reactions to pay may be qualified by beliefs about the performance evaluations through which that pay appears to have been determined. As a result, caution needs to be exercised in: (a) interpreting the results of field studies in which there are different payment outcomes, and (b) generalizing from simple laboratory studies in which payment outcomes are manipulated in the absence of performance evaluations. The present conceptualization may be viewed as a call for further investigation into the interrelationships among different forms of distributive outcomes in general, and between performance evaluations and pay in particular.

One of the most perplexing problems in studying equity and distributive justice in complex organizational settings is the inherent ambiguities involved in distinguishing between outcomes and inputs (Tornow, 1971). The present chapter suggests that performance evaluations can operate either as outcomes (directly or indirectly), as inputs (i.e., information justifying employees' claims to future outcomes), or both. This state of affairs raises serious questions about the validity of attempts to study complex organizational exchanges from the same structural model used for studying simple dyadic interaction. If outcomes and inputs, as our basic building blocks, are rendered uninterpretable, what orientation to studying distributive justice can supplant it? Although it may be premature to answer this question definitively at the present time, a promising approach is suggested by the work of Mikula (Chapter 6, this volume). His unstructured approach to assessing the perceived determinants of distributive justice in social situations may be useful to offering insight into complex distributive questions, just as Sheppard's (1984) unstructured interviewing approach to organizational bargaining has proven useful in explaining complex procedural questions.

Another implication of the present conceptualization for future work on distributive justice is that a wider level of analysis—perhaps an organizational level—may be useful. Although Reis notes the importance of the level of analysis issue in his chapter in the present volume, it is Brickman, Folger, Goode, and Schul (1981) whose arguments about levels of analysis are most relevant here. Their suggestion that justice at the individual level does not ensure justice at a broader societal level applies well to the present application of distributive justice. A macro perspective on justice at an organizational level would force our attention away from concerns of individual evaluation decisions to overall evaluation-decision histories and policies. Such an orientation, it may be claimed, would be more sensitive to the complexities of distributive justice in organizational settings suggested in the present chapter than more traditional micro level approaches.

Implications for Organizational Theory and Practice

Performance appraisal practitioners have emphasized the importance of basing evaluations on observable incidents of work behavior (Carroll & Schneier, 1982). If we consider a performance evaluation as an outcome, and the work behavior as relevant inputs, then it follows from equity theory that the recommended evaluation–behavior linkage would promote distributive justice. Another common recommendation— and legal requirement (Klasson et al., 1980)—is to make administrative decisions commensurate with evaluations (DeVries et al., 1981). In the present terminology, the evaluation is a secondary, or penultimate outcome. It serves to define expectations of forthcoming personnel decisions. Functionally, then, it serves as an input, requiring a match with ultimate outcomes to be distributively just. Combining these points, it would be correct to suggest that distributive justice requires congruence between perceptions of performance excellence, resulting performance evaluations, and personnel actions made on the basis of those evaluations.

Using the terminology shown in Figure 2, one of the most effective things a supervisor could do during a performance appraisal interview would be to strengthen employees' instrumentality beliefs. That is, supervisors should attempt to make sure that employees have well-defined beliefs about what outcomes they may expect to receive for the work they do. Although these contingencies are formally spelled out in some pay plans (such as the piece rate system), it is incumbent on supervisors working under less formal reward contingency systems to promote beliefs in reliable reward–performance contingencies. In an attempt to foster instrumentality beliefs managers may be required to stipulate clearly what the relevant job behaviors and rewards are—a key component of any performance evaluation interview (Carroll & Tosi, 1973). Just as importantly, it would be critical for managers to make it possible for those instrumentalities to materialize. Instrumentality beliefs about receiving a certain raise in response to a certain production increase communicated during a performance appraisal interview may only be effective insofar as they can be expected to be met. If an organization has a history of not meeting its promises, then not only might immediate dissatisfaction result, but it also may be difficult to establish believable instrumentality perceptions in the future. This point also further illustrates the potential value of studying the justice of performance appraisal from an organization-wide perspective.

It may be expected that many of the adverse reactions to organizational inequities noted as reactions to monetary-based inequities (such as withdrawal, dissatisfaction, and impaired performance; see Greenberg, 1982) would also result from evaluation-based inequities.

Moreover, it may be speculated that some portion of the global dissatisfaction expressed as inequity in some studies (e.g., Finn & Lee, 1972) may be the result of reactions to unfair performance evaluations. Given the highly sensitive nature of the performance evaluation process, it is quite likely to be a substantial part of expressions of organizational dissatisfaction based on claims of injustice.

Acknowledgments

The author gratefully acknowledges the helpful comments of Ronald Cohen on an earlier draft of this chapter.

REFERENCES

Adams, J. S. (1965). Inequity in social exchange. In L. Berkowitz (Ed.), *Advances in experimental social psychology* (Vol. 2, pp. 267–299). New York: Academic Press.

Bernardin, H. J., & Beatty, R. W. (1984). *Performance appraisal: Assessing human behavior at work*. Boston, MA: Kent.

Brickman, P., & Bulman, R. J. (1977). Pleasure and pain in social comparison. In J. M. Suls & R. L. Miller (Eds.), *Social comparison processes* (pp. 149–186). Washington, DC: Hemisphere.

Brickman, P., Folger, R., Goode, E., & Schul, Y. (1981). Microjustice and macrojustice. In M. Lerner & S. C. Lerner (Eds.), *The justice motive in social behavior* (pp. 173–204). New York: Plenum Press.

Carroll, S. J., & Schneier, C. E. (1982). *Performance appraisal and review systems*. Glenview, IL: Scott, Foresman.

Carroll, S. J., Jr., & Tosi, H. L. (1973). *Management by objectives: Applications and research*. New York: Macmillan.

Crosby, F. (1984). Relative deprivation in organizational settings. In B. M. Staw & L. L. Cummings, (Eds.) *Research in organizational behavior* (Vol. 6, pp. 51–94). Greenwich, CT: JAI Press.

Deci, E. L. (1975). *Intrinsic motivation*. New York: Plenum Press.

DeVries, D. L., Morrison, A. M., Shullman, S. L., & Gerlach, M. L. (1981). *Performance appraisal on the line*. New York: Wiley.

Finn, R. H., & Lee, S. M. (1972). Salary equity: Its determination, analysis, and correlates. *Journal of Applied Psychology, 56*, 283–292.

Folger, R., & Greenberg, J. (1985). Procedural justice: An interpretive analysis of personnel systems. In K. Rowland & G. Ferris (Eds.), *Research in personnel and human resources management* (Vol. 3, pp. 141–183). Greenwich, CT: JAI Press.

Greenberg, J. (1977). The Protestant work ethic and reactions to negative performance evaluations on a laboratory task. *Journal of Applied Psychology, 62*, 682–690.

Greenberg, J. (1982). Approaching equity and avoiding inequity in groups and organizations. In J. Greenberg & R. L. Cohen (Eds.), *Equity and justice in social behavior* (pp. 389–435). New York: Academic Press.

Greenberg, J. (1984). *Performance evaluations as penultimate outcomes: A preliminary study*. Unpublished manuscript, The Ohio State University, Columbus, OH.

Greenberg, J. (1986). Determinants of perceived fairness of performance evaluations. *Journal of Applied Psychology, 71*.

Greenberg, J. (in press-a). Organizational performance appraisal procedures: What makes them fair? In M. Bazerman, R. Lewicki, & B. Sheppard (Eds.), *Research on negotiating in organizations*. Greenwich, CT: JAI Press.

Greenberg, J. (in press-b). Using diaries to promote procedural justice in performance appraisals. *Social Justice Review*.

Greenberg, J., & Folger, R. (1983). Procedural justice, participation, and the fair process effect in groups and organizations. In P. B. Paulus (Ed.), *Basic group processes* (pp. 235–256). New York: Springer-Verlag.

Greenberg, J., & Ornstein, S. (1983). High status job title as compensation for underpayment: A test of equity theory. *Journal of Applied Psychology, 68*, 285–297.

Greenberg, J., & Tyler, T. (in press). Why procedural justice in organizations? *Social Justice Review*.

Jones, E. E., & Davis, K. E. (1965). From acts to dispositions: The attribution process in social perception. In L. Berkowitz, (Ed.), *Advances in experimental social psychology* (Vol. 2, pp. 118–156). New York: Academic Press.

Klasson, C. R., Thompson, D. E., & Luben, G. L. (1980). How defensible is your performance appraisal system? *Personnel Administrator, 25*, 77–83.

Latham, G. P., & Wexley, K. N. (1981). *Increasing productivity through performance appraisal*. Reading, MA: Addison-Wesley.

Leskovec, E. (1967). A guide for discussing the performance appraisal. *Personnel Journal, 46*, 150–152.

Nord, W. R. (1980). The study of organizations through a resource-exchange paradigm. In K. J. Gergen, M. S. Greenberg, & R. H. Willis (Eds.), *Social exchange: Advances in theory and research* (pp. 119–139). New York: Plenum Press.

Sheppard, B. H. (1984). Third party conflict intervention: A procedural framework. In B. M. Staw & L. L. Cummings, (Eds.) *Research in organizational behavior* (Vol. 6, pp. 141–190). Greenwich, CT: JAI Press.

Tornow, W. W. (1971). The development and application of an inout-outcome moderator test on the perception and reduction of inequity. *Organizational Behavior and Human Performance, 6*, 614–638.

Vecchio, R. P. (1982). Predicting worker performance in inequitable settings. *Academy of Management Review, 7*, 103–110.

Vroom, V. H. (1964). *Work and motivation*. New York: Wiley.

Walster, E., Walster, G. W., & Berscheid, E. (1978). *Equity: Theory and research*. Boston, MA: Allyn & Bacon.

Wexley, K. N., & Latham, G. P. (1981). *Developing and training human resources in organizations*. Glenview, IL: Scott, Foresman.

Author Index

Subject Index